THE IMMORTALS

DIARY OF THE MOST IMPROBABLE SEASON IN THE HISTORY OF THE PREMIER LEAGUE

THE PEOPLE'S CHAMPIONS

G2 entertainment

Published by G2 Entertainment Ltd

© G2 Entertainment 2016

ISBN: 978-1-78281-597-6

AUTHOR: Harry Harris

EDITOR: Sean Willis

DESIGNER: Paul Briggs

PUBLISHERS: Edward Adams and Jules Gammond

PICTURES: Action Images

PRINTED IN EUROPE

DEDICATED TO:

Claudio Ranieri, who conducted himself in such an exemplary manner, and to the fans who have loved every minute of it.

SPECIAL THANKS TO:

Christian Smith, former General Manager at Leicester City FC,
Gordon Taylor, OBE, Chief Executive of the Professional Footballers' Association,
Richard Bevan, Chief Executive of the League Managers Association
and ⁣ e.

CONTENTS

"A fabulous football fairy tale and a perfect example to any team of what can be achieved with team spirit, resilience and self-belief.

From the bottom of the Premier League to the top in twelve months as 5,000 to 1 outsiders speaks volumes. Every player from Kasper Schmeichel, Wes Morgan, Andy King, Ngolo Kante, Riyad Mahrez and Jamie Vardy et al is a story in itself under a Manager, Claudio Ranieri who bounced back from the nadir of his career in Greece to the zenith of his career with Leicester City.

An "Everest like" climb that has thrilled the nation and inspired sportsmen and women everywhere and rightly received recognition of the highest awards the game has to offer."

GORDON TAYLOR, OBE
CHIEF EXECUTIVE OF THE PROFESSIONAL FOOTBALLERS' ASSOCIATION

"The LMA members voted Claudio Ranieri as the clear winner of the LMA Manager of the Year for the 2015-16 season. LMA President, Roy Hodgson, presented Claudio with the association's most prestigious award at the end of season LMA Annual Awards Dinner, in front of a 1000-strong audience of fellow managers, football stakeholders and LMA sponsors and friends.

Claudio guided Leicester City to their first Barclays Premier League title in their 132-year history. He has achieved what almost everyone in the game thought was an impossible dream.

His calm, open and positive leadership style, combined with his significant experience gained from over 40 years managing top sides in Europe, guided his team to the ultimate achievement, all the while allowing his players to stay relaxed and focussed. His squad clearly has a remarkable togetherness blending application, hard work and team spirit.

His often self-deprecating press conferences and optimistic approach throughout the season not only alleviated the pressure from his players but also made the nation and the football world want Leicester to win.

Such remarkable achievements are once in a lifetime occurrences. We applaud Claudio and know that he will inspire a future generation of coaches and managers to pursue a career in the game and set out to realise their dreams."

RICHARD BEVAN
CHIEF EXECUTIVE OF THE LEAGUE MANAGERS ASSOCIATION

DIARY OF THE MOST IMPROBABLE SEASON IN THE HISTORY OF THE PREMIER LEAGUE

Gary Lineker ✓
@GaryLineker

☼   ⚲ Follow

YES! If Leicester win the @premierleague I'll do the first MOTD of next season in just my undies.

PANTS

Gary Lineker, former Everton, Barcelona, Tottenham Hotspur, England and Leicester City striker, promises via his highly active 4.6 million, and rising, twitter account that he would perform the first *Match of the Day* of the 2016-17 season in "just my undies" if his old club won the Premier League.

He made that jokey pledge on 14 December 2015, still convinced it couldn't possibly happen, and with every game the Foxes won, he would get another round of ribbing on *MOTD* from pundit Alan Shearer who wore a smirky grin every time he reminded his *MOTD* 'host' of the undies promise.

It really didn't conjure up great images, but you were willing Leicester on just to see Gary's undies, hopefully a shade of red to match his face, or perhaps a nice shade of Leicester City blue, to contrast with that red face and greying goatee beard.

Gary Lineker enjoys a laugh and a joke, a raised eyebrow on *MOTD*, but he took to the front page of *The Guardian* on 14 March 2016 for an in depth analysis of his beloved Leicester City's season and his personal emotions.

5,000 - 1

In that 'piece' he used the phrase "sporting immortality" that awaited his home town team should they fulfil the seemingly impossible task of winning the Premier League on such a modest budget when at the outset of the season they were declared a laughable chance for such lofty ambitions, with the bookies labelling them a 5,000-1 shot.

Yes, 5,000-1! Now let's just put that into some sort of context. According to the bookies, the following events were **MORE** likely to occur:

500/1 - The Loch Ness monster to be discovered.

1,000/1 - Sir Alex Ferguson to win *Strictly Come Dancing*, the Queen to have the Christmas number one, or Dean Gaffney to win a best actor Oscar.

2,000/1 - Elvis being found alive, Kim Kardashian for US president, or Claudio Ranieri to be next England manager.

2,500/1 - Piers Morgan as Arsenal manager, David Moyes to become an *X Factor* judge, or David Cameron (who, of course, supports Aston Villa…or is it West Ham) to replace Tim Sherwood as Aston Villa manager.

And, at the same odds of 5,000-1, bookmakers William Hill had Radio 1 DJ Nick Grimshaw to win an Olympic gold in Rio.

Would you have backed any of those?

Despite the seemingly outrageous odds and quite ridiculous outcome a few speculative punters grabbed the opportunity. And, as the football season approached its climax desperate bookmakers began to offer buyouts to those who got in on the 5,000-1 odds. William Hill spokesman Graeme Sharpe estimated that the Foxes winning the title would cost the English sportsbooks more than £10 million in payouts. "The fairytale is definitely alive for punters, and the bookies' nightmare is becoming a reality," Sharpe said with just weeks of the season to go. They, alone, had 25 bettors who plunked down money on Leicester when the team was 5000/1. William Hill offered £2,800 for each £1.00 bet, trying to lure those who had bet on the Foxes at 5000/1 to make a deal. A day later the offer rose, and then became £3,200 per each £1.00 bet after Leicester's next win. William Hill were able to make abbreviated deals with some gamblers.

Some punters did start cashing-out while others, like their team, held their nerve. James Weller, for one, rejected a cash-out offer of £25,000, backing his team to complete the job as he stood to win a £50,000 from his original £10 bet.

The beginning-of-the-season 5000/1 odds were considered historic. "These types of odds are not offered in any other sport," said John Avello, director of the sportsbook at *The Wynn* in Las Vegas. "Teams in other sports are thought to have much better chances to win than the teams at the bottom of the Premier League. David Williams, of British betting shop Ladbrokes, said the payout for the company will be the most expensive single payout in football history.

Club legend Alan Birchenall said: "It is crazy isn't it - 5,000-1 at the start of the season? The few people who bet on us had probably had a few glasses of happy water. Good luck to them but I would be very surprised if they hadn't have had a drink."

THE IMMORTALS

The very first Football League season kicked-off in 1888. It was contested between the 12 historic founder members, and by early 1889 Preston North End were crowned as the first ever champions of England, having gone the entire season unbeaten. Not only that, they also clinched the FA Cup too, and so were declared "The Invincibles".

Leicester City were formed in 1884 and joined the Football League, Division Two, in 1894. In 132 years the Foxes' highest ever finish in the top flight of English football was as runners-up in 1928-29 and, let's be honest, even top 10 finishes had been a rarity.

Arsenal then gave us the modern version of "The Invincibles" going through 2003-04 season unbeaten, But now Leicester City have spawned "The Immortals" as the 'Fox in the box', that was a hallmark of Gary Lineker's playing career, had hoped and prayed might happen.

The Immortals have trumped The Invincibles in many ways, not least because the mighty Gunners always had the firepower within their budgets, while Leicester City were far more likely to have been relegated than end up top of the pile.

As Graeme Souness extoled the virtues of 'Mission Impossible', describing the possibilities of Claudio Ranieri's team being champions as the greatest story in Premier League history (which began in the 1992-93 season), Jamie Carragher seated beside him in the Sky Sports studio wanted to go one better and said it would be the greatest feat in football history.

THE PEOPLE'S CHOICE

However, let's not forget how Liverpool last won the Champions League, or that Nottingham Forest performed a similar feat in the League and then went on to win the European Cup under Brian Clough twice. 'Cloughie' was the 'People's Choice' to become England manager but he was never an FA 'blazer', and, similarly, Leicester City became the 'People's Choice' as champions even amongst those elite clubs who all slipped by the wayside at one stage or another.

I bumped into one of the Clough stars, England striker Tony Woodcock, on a train bound for Waterloo not long before the season end and, with time on our hands, he told me how he felt for some time that Leicester's penchant for work rate and scaring defences by being prepared for the hard work to run into the channels and exploit weaknesses with the blistering pace of Jamie Vardy would bring great success. Woodcock, though, felt they had some way to go to emulate the feats of Clough at Forest. But Leicester City will now have their chance in the Champions League. Yes, that's right, the Champions League! This - Leicester City reaching the summit of the English game in this 'modern age' - is arguably harder to believe than the surprises of Nottingham Forest and, to a lesser extent, Derby County back in the 1970s.

The 'People's Choice' is reflected in this book in the way that the fans' views, both followers of Leicester City as well as 'neutrals', are given great emphasis in amongst the thoughts of the manager, universally loved for his feel good factor style, and the team of unsung heroes, journeymen and bit-part players who formed a bond like no other before it to produce some amazing football results.

As the Leicester City story unfolded, such were their incredible exploits that they gained ever increasing global recognition and amazement in equal quantities. The fact is that all the superlatives have been used up to describe the indescribable.

The entire nation, in fact many new fans emerging around the world, were willing the improbable to happen, living every kick and dramatic twists and turns along the way.

Now you can re-live these incredible twists and turns in the story of "The Immortals", which is a comprehensive scrapbook of the entire season, from a blow-by-blow account of every game, to the views from the dressing room led by Claudio Ranieri's dissection of every game, to the way the media covered the enthralling story, and how fans reacted from the local support base through to the new fans growing rapidly across the globe.

Through the machinations of 'The Tinkerman' turned Superman the teams' exploits on the field are of paramount importance, but what goes on behind the scenes can be just as vital; from the owners to the administration. This book looks at all aspects of the club.

Most importantly is the 12th man. The fans. And this book, for the first time in any such diaries, looks at the rollercoaster emotions of the fans, through their social media postings. From the biggest fan, the Foxes most famous barrow boy himself Gary Lineker, with his near 5 million Twitter followers, and his obsessive social media ramblings, to the ordinary supporters (not punters, we do not use that term here). Social media empowers ordinary fans to have their say, and this diary encapsulates their fears, hopes and excitement as well as their anger when ticket prices are beyond their reach for the final home game of the season when normal tickets are sold out within half an hour of going on sale and the profiteers are then taking over.

Of course, there are the actual punters, dozens of real punters holding their breath ready to claim the biggest-priced single winner in sporting history, those who had wagered on the 'joke' bet of Leicester winning the title at 5,000-1.

Besides the pay-out for those who put their small change on the no hopers, Lineker put his smalls on the line. This book will make you laugh as well as cry along with Claudio.

ODDS SHORTEN

The entire season can be encapsulated in the way the betting odds fluctuated so wildly with every win, every three points that took the team closer to the finishing line. Having started the season as football's biggest ever outsiders, Leicester began the season with a flourish, victories in their opening two games against Sunderland and West Ham which saw their odds drop from 5,000/1 to 3,000/1. Their only loss, a 5-2 defeat by Arsenal, in their opening 10 games saw their odds shorten to 1,000/1. Clearly, hardly favourites though.

Wins against West Brom, Watford and Newcastle and suddenly it was cut to 100/1; still no ringing endorsement that they really had much of a chance.

Significant movement followed a draw against Manchester United and consecutive victories over Swansea, Chelsea and Everton that brought the odds down to a very respectable 16/1, but, in reality, the pundits were still predicting that the team would explode, that it was all a lovely story that would fizzle out any minute now.

The forecasts were that their time was up, they would run out of steam despite heading into a clash with Liverpool - the 18th game of the season - still having lost just once.

The blip everyone was expecting came. They lost to Liverpool before home draws against Manchester City and Bournemouth saw their odds creep up to 28/1. They had failed to score a single goal in those three games and the football sages were nodding their heads in that familiar 'told you so' way.

The fans were living a rollercoaster ride every bit as up and down as the odds. A victory against title rivals Spurs at the Lane and Leicester were back to 14s. A minor slip against bottom club Aston Villa aside, Leicester were on another impressive run beating Stoke, Liverpool and Manchester City. With 13 games left they were as short as 11/5.

Then came the result that was supposed to, finally, signal the beginning of the end; a last-second defeat by Arsenal at the Emirates after going down to 10 men. Surely now the jokers at the top of the Premier League pack had finally had their last laugh.

But six wins and a draw, coupled with their rivals' inconsistencies and slip-ups of their own, saw Leicester's odds shorten again week after week.

The dramatic shortening of the odds over the course of the season were recorded as follows: 1 August: 5,000-1; 1 September: 1,500-1; 1 October: 1,500-1; 1 November: 500-1; 1 December: 66-1; 1 January: 16-1; 1 February: 7-1; 1 March: 3-1; 1 April: 4-7. 25 April: 1-16.

So what were the motivations behind this phenomenal, probably once in a life time season?

This book delves behind the scenes and looks carefully at many of the stories and comments to paint a picture of players and manager having fun. Fun appeared to be a word that had been wiped out of the so called 'beautiful game' tainted by too much money, far too much power from the Premier League clubs, and the disillusionment with the ethos of the game from the very top of a discredited and corrupt FIFA.

It took humble little Leicester with a manager who still occasionally struggled to articulate his thoughts in English to put the fun back into the bloated Premier League - a league which was over-stuffed with the Fat Cats predictably, perpetually hogging the top four places, and gorging on a new £8billion worth of new TV rights both domestically and overseas coming their way in the next three year cycle.

RANIERI

No one epitomised the new smiling face of football more than Claudio Ranieri himself.

He enjoys Andrew Lloyd Webber musicals and Lincolnshire sausages. "My wife used to come up to antique fairs in Lincolnshire when we were in London and I shopped for sausages in Newark in the marketplace - they're delicious," he says. As a butcher's son he knows a thing or two about sausages. His love of show tunes has seen him break in to song in interviews in the past, but this is not always popular in the Leicester dressing room. However, after his abysmal treatment at Chelsea when he was mocked as The Tinkerman, and suffering the knife in the back as 'The Dead Man Walking' having already been effectively replaced by José Mourinho while still in the job, there was an outpouring of affection for him when he was finally pushed out of the door.

Claudio felt like everyone's favourite uncle and now, at the age of 64, he'd been round the block and back again and certainly knew how to organise a team with Italian defensive steel and a love of flair players. After being unceremoniously and contentiously kicked out by Chelsea with the arrival of Roman Abramovich, it was another twist to the season that the second coming of the self-proclaimed 'Special One' should end in tears with an incomprehensibly farcical defence of the Premier League crown. Instead 'The Tinkerman" had become the 'Special One'. How ironic that Mourinho's last match before being sacked for a second time was defeat by Ranieri's Leicester City.

Former Chelsea captain Marcel Desailly claimed that Ranieri's exploits were fuelled by revenge after his sacking in 2004. Desailly, who played under the Italian at Chelsea from 2000-2004, believed his former boss was bursting to show everyone in England what he can do. "Remember, Ranieri should have won the Premier League with Chelsea in 2004, but lost out to Arsenal's Invincibles," Desailly told BeIN Sport. "That was actually Chelsea's year, too, but because Arsenal went unbeaten he got sacked for Mourinho. Now, he has got his revenge. Mourinho got sacked after losing to him and he's going to go on and win the league." Desailly made his comments with eight games to go, and he didn't believe then that any of the sides chasing Leicester were capable of putting a run together to catch up with them.

While it was fun for the fans, football was given its smile back. The antics of the players were more about the enjoyment of the sport, than the money. Ranieri slated his players' choice in dressing room music, joking that he switches it off as soon as they leave so he can enjoy peace and quiet. The Grease Megamix and Abba could be heard coming from Leicester's inner sanctum after victory at Watford and Ranieri has revealed it is not a one-off. He said laughing in his broken English: "It is bad music. Who is this? Abba, Mamma Mia! It is never my choice. When they go out I switch it off. Finally!" Team spirit was the reason behind their success and a questionable play list of ironic pop tunes further aided their unity.

The Italian was producing more than mere revenge on Abramovich and Mourinho, he was setting the League alight in a way no one thought possible, by breaking the domination of the mega wealthy elite, and creating such a feel good factor that Leicester City become everyone's second favourite team and if their club couldn't win it, they wanted Leicester to walk off with Mission Impossible.

Little wonder the club feared a defection of their top players and loveable manager. But Ranieri professed his desire to stay as the season reached an incredibly exciting climax. He declared his unflinching love affair with the club, how much he was happy with life there, and hoped to retire at the end of his time there, spending the final "six or seven years" at the King Power Stadium.

After spells with a host of Europe's top clubs, he got his unexpected chance back in the Premier League when least expected, and was hardly universally welcomed when pundits such as Gary Lineker felt it was a huge mistake.

But, instead of the expected battle to avoid the drop, Ranieri still had something quite special to offer English football in his debut season at the club, creating what the commentators declared would be one of the greatest achievements in English footballing history. Months, even weeks earlier they were saying exactly the opposite; the bubble would burst, it wasn't possible to sustain it on such a flimsy squad of no-hopers.

At one stage he was even linked with a return to Stamford Bridge. A most unlikely tale indeed. Even so, it sparked rumours about his future. Then, in an interview with Spanish sports paper *Marca* the 64-year-old insisted "I am fine in Leicester and do not think about moving. I think this will be my last club. I hope they give me a long contract, six or seven years, and then I can retire here. I've always had a lot of opportunities. I'm a lucky man to work in what I love most - for almost 30 years I have enjoyed my greatest passion. When I came to Leicester the chairman asked me in the first two years of my contract to stay in the Premier League. This was paramount. He is an ambitious but quiet man, who knows only building a project from the base can qualify for higher levels. However, this season everything has changed. But we know that we have not done anything. Everyone expects us to win the Premier League. It's amazing that in the era of money a small team is performing this feat. If we were Chelsea, Arsenal, City or United we would think about the title. We do not. Leicester is a small club. We have achieved the most important goal. We have already won, we will play next season in the Premier League. Now let's fight for Europe. And if we go up, we will try to enter Champions League and then be champions. But we must go slowly."

A few days later, it was clear that Antonio Conte was quitting the Italian national team at the end of the Euros to head to the Bridge, but Ranieri was not keen to follow him to the national job. Conte announced he will leave the national side after Euro 2016, but Ranieri said he had no intention of leaving the King Power Stadium. "No team can change my mind. I am very proud if they are thinking about me in Italy and everywhere but this is my club. I want to stay here, if my owner is happy I stay here. There is nothing to change my mind. There are a lot of things to do here. We are just starting to build. If the owner is happy with me, I am happy with him. If it's possible I would like to stay (for) a long time."

OUT OF DARKNESS

Ranieri brought sunshine to a club to replace the storm clouds of its recent past.

Leicester were screened just eight times live by Sky Sports and BT Sport combined the previous season but that had more than doubled. The previous season they earned £71.6m from Premier League central funds for finishing 13th; that would now exceed £100m from TV alone.

It's difficult to imagine the hardships that might have brought closure not so long ago, making this all the more a remarkable story.

Matt Elliott captained the League Cup-winning side in 2000, their second League Cup success in three years, and only two years later long-serving members of staff were sacked to cut costs and the club went into administration, on the verge of extinction. Chelsea and Manchester City broke the mould of the established clubs, but only with the help of billionaire owners. "People don't look at Leicester like that," said Elliott, "In most people's eyes, Leicester are viewed as relative underdogs. Even going back to Blackburn Rovers, when Jack Walker came in and bought top players in 1995. Nothing wrong with that, but it was deemed as buying the title. At Leicester, it's been little by little. The spending hasn't been frivolous or over extensive. It's been done in a structured way."

Their very existence was in doubt until a consortium, led by Gary Lineker, helped save them. "It was quite a harrowing time and it followed very soon after we'd had our successful days." said Elliott. "Only a year-and-a-half after winning the League Cup we were staring relegation in the face and facing financial ruin. It was a dire time. Players' wages were deferred, but my most vivid emotion was disappointment at seeing people lose their jobs, quite long-standing employees. And they never came back. But it helped us focus even more and gave us extra determination to get the club back where it should be."

Though there was a swift return to the Premier League, the club were quickly relegated again and eventually struggled in the Championship.

Matt Oakley, former club captain, suffered relegation to League One in 2008. Oakley arrived in January 2008, with the club on the verge of slipping into League One. "When I went there they were in a real mess, bottom of the Championship and really struggling," recalls Oakley. "There was a lot going on behind the scenes. It was the time when Milan Mandarić had taken over (in 2007). We then got relegated and that was the real bottom point. But that was when Nigel Pearson came in and we won League One the next year by quite a way."

Pearson was sacked in the wake of the post-season tour to Thailand. In two spells at the club (2008-10 and then 2011-15), he hauled Leicester out of League One under Mandarić, then returned under new owner, Vichai Srivaddhanaprabha, to take them into the Premier League and last season keep them there in remarkable fashion. He laid the foundations. Pearson came across as a prickly character, but players say otherwise. "When we got relegated to League One and they were talking about him coming in I thought: 'Oh, no'," says Oakley. "The only time I'd seen him was on TV. He seemed to have a kind of arrogance about him. He doesn't like doing the Press or being asked certain questions. When he did his first team meeting in front of everyone he had a real presence but I thought: 'I'm not going to like this'. Then when I walked out on the training field, he caught up with me, put an arm round me and said: 'Right, so you going to stay then?' I said: 'What do you mean?' And he said: 'Well, you need to help me get this team out of this league.' And that was it. We hit it off. He's a brilliant manager. He's close to people, not stand-offish, and he's comfortable in and around the team."

Leicester had gone back to Pearson in 2011, after trying supposedly more fashionable managers in Paulo Sousa and Sven-Göran Eriksson. "I think if Nigel had just been left in place we would have gone on again," said Oakley. "He gets a very good team together, Steve Walsh is head of recruitment and Shaky (Craig Shakespeare) does the coaching. He built a nice core group. Steve had contacts at Manchester United and clubs like that to pull in loans. We had (Tom) Cleverley and people like that to add that little bit of quality. It was only a matter of time before we got out of the Championship. But unfortunately they made the change, brought in Paulo and it didn't work out for him. Sven did his thing with signing everyone under the sun. It sort of became a little bit of a mess. Then they went back to Nigel, who brought structure and stability."

#FEARLESS

A key moment for the second spell with Pearson was losing in the Championship play-off semi-final to Watford. Remarkably that day, Drinkwater, Vardy and Kane - on loan from Spurs - (each one a future England player), all started on the Leicester bench. It was a heartbreaking season for the club. They were top until a run of one win in 14 games. They clawed their way back into the play-offs and were beating Watford when Anthony Knockaert had a last-minute penalty to take them to Wembley. He missed, Watford broke and Troy Deeney scored to put them through. The dream died in 60 seconds. Yet Andy King believes it was a turning point. "We have always had a good team spirit here, especially with moments like that, the way we bounced back from it," said King, "We stuck together as a group and rectified it the season after. We've got big personalities, as we've shown time and again; dealing with the Watford loss, getting promoted, then being bottom for a long time last season and getting out of it." The core of that team in Andy King, Jamie Vardy, Danny Drinkwater, Kasper Schmeichel, Wes Morgan and Jeff Schlupp all remain. They came back and won the Championship with 102 points, nine clear of second-placed Burnley.

Of course, it is well documented that only a year before topping the Premier League they embarked on their Great Escape, winning seven of their last nine games to avoid relegation. "When push came to shove they dug in together and turned the season around," said Elliott. "On the back of that, players certainly developed confidence and realised they could achieve results at this level. For a lot of them it was a new experience. When it came to a do-or-die situation they showed they could cope as individuals and collectively, which gave them confidence for this season. That's when things really turned around, though no one expected what they have achieved."

They were used to tense end-of-season finales and, even if the prize a year earlier was different, it was still as huge.

But there was this indefinable team spirt driving them on from the manager's office to the training ground, manifesting itself on the pitch.

"We're going to take it game by game," said Drinkwater during the latter stages of the drive toward the title. "We have a week to train and work on the opposition to see if we can sniff out the three points. I don't think we would ever fear anyone as a Leicester team. We have a fearless attitude."

'Fearless' became their unofficial motto forged over long hard years of adversity. Not only that, good karma abounded around the place as they were regularly being blessed by Buddhist monk Phra Prommangkalachan. For the last three years the Thai Buddhist and fellow monks visited the Thai-owned club to bless the King Power Stadium pitch and hand out lucky talismans to the players. But it wasn't just in the owner's homeland where the message was spreading.

GLOBAL AUDIENCE

Globally, Leicester were vying to be the sixth-most watched Premier League team on TV and could make the top 10 in the world. A couple of papers compiled a summary of the global reach. The *Daily Mail* and the *Sunday Times* illustrated that it wasn't just on Sky and BT Sport that they will whetting the appetite of TV audiences and fans:

Brazil:
Nicknamed by locals as the Premier League's 'Prince Charming'.

Argentina:
They call them 'Cinderella' as they follow Argentina rugby hero Marcos Ayerza at Leicester Tigers as well as Leonardo Ulloa.

Africa:
Figures supplied by Premier broadcaster SuperSport show audiences for games up by 78 per cent with interest in Ghana stars Jeff Schlupp and Daniel Amartey.

Algeria:
Riyad Mahrez made Leicester a household name. Sports writer Samir Lamari says: "Before Mahrez, Leicester were unknown in Algeria where Liverpool was the most popular club. Now Leicester are more popular, with more viewers than the local league." Big crowds gather at cafes to watch games and replica shirts are selling despite a £45 price tag, close to half of what a low-paid worker makes in a month.

United States:
Leicester City matches shown live on American TV now doubled the previous season of 13 times.

Even the game against Aston Villa attracted more than a million viewers, a top-10 draw of the season. Ten of the club's first 13 games were picked to go 'network', and all the final 15 games were given main stream coverage. The club will be playing in the International Champions Cup in the summer, earning millions from fixtures against Barcelona, PSG and Celtic. Dan Masonson, vice-president of communications for NBC Sports was quoted in the *Sunday Times*: "This is the story of an undersold team winning, American Premier League audiences are growing strongly and Leicester help. Having compelling games and great stories is what draws people in. That's what Leicester provide." The club have been on the cover of *Newsweek* and the *Wall Street Journal* and it is being described as "the greatest Cinderella story in sports." Ranieri was commissioned for a column in *The Players' Tribune*: "I am 64 years old, so I do not go out much, but lately, I have indeed been hearing the noise from all over the world. It is impossible to ignore. I have heard we even have some new supporters in America."

Europe:

Often the 'main feature' match in the 3pm slot on Saturdays in France, for whom N'Golo Kanté has won his first cap this season. In Denmark media focused on a second Schmeichel becoming a Premier League-winning goalkeeper. They were the most featured team on Viasat Baltic in Estonia, Latvia and Lithuania. In Spain interest was described as "gigantic". In Italy it was just huge. A Serb philosopher even wrote an article about Leiceter City FC, novelist fan Julian Barnes, and the meaning of life and belonging.

Thailand:

Thai-owned Leicester were the fifth-most popular Premier League team last season with 10.5m watching their games live. Only the Manchester clubs, Liverpool and Chelsea had more. King Power stores sold out of replica shirts.

Israel:

Newspaper articles on Leicester City tripled and the team became the focus in a battle of broadcasters. Premier League rights-holding channels Sport1 and Sport2 promoted Leicester's story as indicative of a balanced, competitive, exciting league, in contrast to the 'predictable' La Liga, shown by rivals One TV. 'Miracle of Leicester' was a cover story in the *Maariv*, Israel's second biggest selling newspaper.

Japan:

Shinji Okazaki's presence made Leicester City a huge story, every game shown live, drawing hundreds of thousands in the early hours; a typical 3pm GMT UK Saturday game ends at 2am locally. "People are paying attention, watching on TV." says Okazaki. "It's become a big thing back home, a lot of people are supporting me and I'm very happy for that." He outstripped Shinji Kagawa and Keisuke Honda (currently Borussia Dortmund and AC Milan respectively) as the nation's most followed oversees player.

China:

"Everyone wants to buy Leicester shirts" reported a journalist who now covers every game.

THE POWERBROKERS AND KEY PERSONNEL
BEHIND THE FAIRY TALE

Claudio Ranieri and the squad of players are the instantly recognisable face of Leicester City Football Club. However, it takes a huge 'team' effort in order to maximize sporting potential, and here's a look at some key individuals (not an exhaustive list) behind this amazing football story:

Khun Vichai Srivaddhanaprabha (Chairman)

The owner is valued at around £2bn by *Forbes*, and has invested a small fortune in the club since he bought Leicester City for £39 million in August 2010. After securing promotion in 2014, he pledged that the Foxes would be a top-five club within three years, and has so far spent £77m on transfers to achieve that. He tends to travel to and from the stadium by private helicopter.

Khun Aiyawatt Srivaddhanaprabha (Vice Chairman)

He is the son of Vichai and widely known as 'Top'. He is in charge of the daily running of the club, and also has a column in the matchday programme.

Supornthip 'Tippy' Choungrangsee (Executive Director)

One of a few women serving on the board of a Premier League club, the Thai businesswoman is also a jewellery designer, CEO of Branded the Agency Co. Ltd, Tippy Co Ltd, and Working Diamond Co. Ltd. Thailand *Tatler* says her "projects and parties are a draw for other celebrities, which given her contacts and experience, should come as no surprise."

Apichet Srivaddhanaprabha (Executive Director)

Also a son of Vichai, he has a Bachelor of Science in Marketing with Psychology and forms part of King Power's Human Resources Management Department.

Susan Whelan (Chief Executive Officer)

Dublin-born Susan was appointed CEO in July 2011 and has executive responsibility for all aspects of the Club's day-to-day management.

Jon Rudkin (Director of Football & Academy Director)

Rudkin's association stretches back over two decades; schoolboy in the club's youth academy, he became coach in 1998, took position at the then Centre of Excellence, helping develop players such as Emile Heskey. He replaced Terry Robinson as director of football in December 2014.

Andrew Neville (Football Operations Director)

Neville has a long association at the club, joining in December 1998. He was formerly the club's head of football administration and also worked at Norwich City.

Craig Shakespeare (Assistant Manager)

Shakespeare originally joined Leicester City as Assistant Manager to Nigel Pearson in July 2008. After following Pearson to Hull City in 2010, Shakespeare returned to take up his role as assistant once again in November 2011.

Steve Walsh (Assistant Manager)

Walsh also returned to Leicester City in November 2011 to begin a second spell at the club and continue the work he started in July 2008. Walsh is the man most heralded for the club's superb recruitment over the past few years. Signing the likes of N'Golo Kanté, Jamie Vardy and Riyad Mahrez, for comparatively tiny fees, is a feather in his cap - particularly the Algerian, who Walsh spotted playing for Le Havre when he had been sent to watch another player.

Paolo Benetti (Assistant Manager)

Benetti is a former professional footballer for a total of eight Italian teams throughout his playing career. His introduction into the world of football coaching started as manager of Lazio's youth team, spending two years there before linking up with Ranieri for the first time at Italian giants Juventus in 2007. Since then the pair have been in partnership at Juventus, Roma, Inter, Monaco and Greece - with mixed results - before this year's achievements with Leicester.

Dave Rennie (Head Physiotherapist)

After initially obtaining a degree in Sports Science from the University of Surrey, Dave re-trained in Physiotherapy and graduated from the University of Nottingham with first class honours in 1994. Dave is responsible for the physiotherapy treatment of all of the professional players. His main duties include prevention, assessment, treatment and rehabilitation of all professional players at the club. One of his great successes has been the use of a state-of-the-art cryotherapy chamber - in which temperatures can get as low as -135C - to help players' recovery after games. It has meant that Leicester's key players have missed almost no football this season.

Paul Balsom (Head of Sports Science and Performance Analysis)

Having re-joined the club in December 2011 Paul is responsible for the development and enhancement of the sports science and performance analysis support offered to the first team professional players and coaching staff at the club. Using an integrated proactive approach to the scientific management of player development, the aim is to improve individual and team performance. Paul graduated with a PhD in Exercise Physiology from the Karolinska Institute, Stockholm, in 1995.

Matt Reeves (Head of Fitness and Conditioning)

Matt is responsible for ensuring the implementation of effective sports science services at the football club. His main objectives surround reducing injury occurrence, whilst improving physical preparation, athletic development and overall performance. In order to achieve this, he works closely with the coaches to ensure that players can successfully meet the demands of the game.

Mitch Willis (Strength & Power Coach)

A former Leicester Tigers Strength and Conditioning Coach, Mitch made the switch from rugby to football at the start of the 2012-2013 campaign. His main objective is to optimise gym based preparation for the first team squad, with a dual focus on performance enhancement and injury prevention. Mitch places a large emphasis on the development of player strength which he delivers as part of a tailored programme, specific to each individual. He also focuses on improving power, speed and overall robustness whilst hoping to reduce the frequency of soft tissue injuries.

Ken Way (Performance Psychologist)

Ken focuses on the 'mental game' for all first team and U21 players - working on aspects such as confidence, focus, belief, concentration, mental toughness and resilience. He has also worked with Nigel Pearson at Southampton and Hull City. His experience includes working with three international teams as well as UK, Commonwealth and World Champions in different sports.

Andy Blake (Senior First Team Performance Analyst)

Andy is responsible for utilising various modes of technology to provide information to the manager, coaching staff, and players. Primarily focusing on upcoming opponents, Andy produces detailed reports for the coaching staff, and also pre-match presentations to be delivered to the players, along with other information to assist with match preparation. On match days, Andy is involved in the live analysis, communicating with the manager and coaching staff to review key events, and preparing footage to be relayed at half-time and full-time.

HAPPY FAMILIES

Thai owner Vichai Srivaddhanaprabha, Khun Vichai as he is known in Thailand, stated, following Leicester's promotion to the Premier League in 2014, that he would spend £180m to break into the top five within three years. That kind of delusional prophecy has been the domain of many a mad owner who has lost his marbles believing it would be an easy ride in football. Yet, his team achieved his seemingly ludicrous target in two years with less than a third of his planned budget.

Reputedly worth £2bn, Khun Vichai made his fortune through his King Power duty-free stores which have a monopoly in the country's three major airports.

Since he bought the club from Milan Mandarić for £39m in 2010, Leicester have spent £77m on transfers and amassed a net spend of a mere £62.8m.

Khun Vichai converted £103m of Leicester's debt into shares in 2013, wiping out the club's liabilities and forfeiting his ability to call in the money in one swoop.

Leicester's wage bill had increased to £36.3m in their promotion-winning season two years ago. Such an outlay left the club's accounts consistently in the red. Leicester posted a loss of £20.4m during that promotion-winning campaign, more than any Premier League club except Fulham and Manchester City that same season, and apparently well in excess of the maximum £8m loss as determined by the Football League's financial fair play rules. The club insists they were "in compliance" with the regulations as much of the loss came from exempt expenditure. But that the Football League has not yet accepted the accounts, and Leicester could yet face a hefty fine if found guilty of breaching the rules.

The extremely wealthy and somewhat reclusive Khun Vichai has not been out of touch with the fan base though. Coach travel to away games is capped at £10 no matter Leicester's opposition, clappers are attached to seats for every home game at a reported cost of £12,000 and fans have been offered a free beer and doughnut on occasions. Scarves and shirts have also been given to travelling fans.

Foxes Trust chairman, Ian Bason, was pleased even before this startling season. "Because of what happened elsewhere fans were wary initially." Bason told *Sportsmail*. "Most people worry that owners will change the culture and the shirt colour but they made clear from day one they won't do that at all. They very much respect the heritage of the club. Ticket prices have risen only minimally since we were playing Championship football and I just don't see a huge rise even if we qualify for Europe. For the owners it seems to be more about prestige and the name being worldwide than making money from fans."

Top, a popular presence at the training ground, is tasked with overseeing the running of the club in England, assisted by Chief Executive Susan Whelan, who is also on the board of King Power. His affection for Leicester is rooted in the first game he saw live in this country, the 1997 League Cup final at Wembley, when Emile Heskey scored a late equaliser to force a replay. Leicester then beat Middlesbrough in extra time at Hillsborough.

An Agusta helicopter aside, that lands on the pitch at the King Power stadium to take them home to Berkshire about half an hour after games, the Srivaddhanaprabha family are not owners who make a great show of their wealth. Unlike other foreign contemporaries, the eccentricities have not been disrespectful to the club's history nor obtrusive on the team.

Khun Vichai travels to and from his homeland in style. In October 2013, he bought a Gulfstream G650 business jet, capable of flying non-stop from the Far East to Britain, for £43m from Bernie Ecclestone's wife, Fabiana Flosi. When Leicester won promotion he invited the squad for a meal of caviar and fine wine in an up-market west London restaurant and picked up the bill. He then gave each player and staff member a £1,000 chip to gamble at a private members' club nearby. Any time the players travel abroad they want for nothing. Flights are in the incredibly luxurious 'royal class', where each passenger gets an individual cabin, seven-foot reclining bed, and personal attendant. Accommodation is six-star and bags are carried by assistants.

The owners bring a touch of nobility to the Premier League, having played polo in the same team as Prince Charles and Prince William, while they have also been bestowed a regal surname by the world's longest-reigning monarch. The family's surname used to be Raksriaksorn but by December

2012 King Bhumibol Adulyadej, on the throne for 70 years this June, had granted a new title in recognition of their success and extensive charity work. It was a highly prestigious honour. Khun Vichai's connection to the British monarchy comes through his love of polo. He has almost single-handedly promoted the sport in Thailand and in June 2005 played a charity match in Richmond, the Chakravarty Cup.

He was made president of Ham Polo Club in London for four years from 2008 and in 2014 started a King Power team who, in their first summer, stunned seasoned observers by reaching the final of the Gold Cup, the UK's premier competition. Top played in the side and was highest scorer. He is a very useful footballer, too. In a Leicester staff game at the training ground a few years ago he impressed participants by claiming a hat-trick. Ham chairman Nicholas Colquhoun-Denvers, a friend of the family, explained to *Sportsmail*: "They are very pleasant to be with. Some people in our sport get very wound-up and over-excited, whereas they are the sort who, win or lose, will say, 'Wasn't that fun?' They seem much more philosophical than others. Whether that comes from their religion I don't know."

The Srivaddhanaprabhas did not initially arrive in English football with the same impact as Abramovich or Sheikh Mansour, but they have certainly done so now, and in their own way.

The family are devout Buddhists and have invited monks to bless the squad on more than one occasion. While celebrating their Championship title victory in 2014 the squad visited the Phra Maha Mondop Buddhist temple in Bangkok. Another passion of Khun Vichai's is collecting Buddha statues.

DIARY OF A SEASON
JULY 2015

WEDNESDAY, 1 JULY

LIFE AFTER PEARSON

The owners, the board and advisors assembled a short list following the sacking of Nigel Pearson yesterday.

Nigel Pearson had guided Leicester to a miraculous Premier League survival the previous season and was named Manager of the Month for April. His side spent 140 days at the bottom of the table but won seven of their last nine matches to comfortably stay up and finish 14th.

He also flirted with controversy and in February was fired, then reinstated, following a bizarre incident in which he throttled James McArthur around the neck during defeat to Crystal Palace. He was told he was sacked by Chairman Vichai Srivaddhanaprabha, only for his son Aiyawatt, the co-chairman, to counsel for patience and ensure Pearson continued in the role. But he does bring focus for his off-field actions too. In December he had an altercation with a fan following abuse, and has had two fiery run-ins with journalists. During the part of last season when Leicester's results showed little signs of life, Director of Football, Terry Robinson was sacked instead of Pearson.

There was no such U-turn this time, with players reporting back for pre-season training in a state of shock at the developments.

Gary Lineker, an honorary vice-president of the club, called the decision "stupid".

Lineker tweeted: "Leicester City have sacked Nigel Pearson! Really? WTF! Could you kindly reinstate him like the last time you fired him?"

The Foxes favourite son added: "So, after not only getting LCFC promoted but also pulling off the most miraculous escape in PL history, Pearson is sacked. Those who run football never cease to amaze with their stupidity."

A Leicester City statement read on the day of the sacking: "The board of directors recognises the success Nigel has helped to bring to Leicester City during his two spells in charge of the club, particularly during the last three and a half years. However, it has become clear to the club that fundamental differences in perspective exist between us. Regrettably, the club believes that the working relationship between Nigel and the board is no longer viable. Leicester City's owners, Vichai and Aiyawatt Srivaddhanaprabha, and the board of directors would like to place on record their thanks to Nigel for the considerable contribution he has made during his time with the club and wish him well in the future. Khun Vichai and Khun Top remain wholly committed to the club's long-term development and to on-going investment in a squad that will continue to be competitive in the Premier League. We trust that the club's supporters will recognise that the owners have always acted with the best interests of the club at heart and with the club's long-term future as their greatest priority. Craig Shakespeare and Steve Walsh will take charge of first team duties while the club begins its recruitment of a new manager. There will be no further comment until this process has concluded."

Pearson was apparently astonished when told his contract would be terminated by Vice-chairman Aiyawatt Srivaddhanaprabha.

The key issue centred on the dismissal of his son James for his part in an "orgy" in Bangkok while on a goodwill tour of Thailand, the owners' home country. The Srivaddhanaprabha family were infuriated when a video of the distasteful incident emerged, involving James, captain of the Under 21 side, striker Tom Hopper, goalkeeper Adam Smith and three local women. The leaked video infuriated the Srivaddhanaprabha family, who are Buddhists and place great value on decency and manners.

Returning to Leicester, Hopper was immediately issued with a letter terminating his contract, while Adam Smith and James Pearson had separate disciplinary meetings to determine their fate. James had two hearings with Chief Executive Susan Whelan with a Professional Footballers' Association (PFA) representative for support, and was sacked afterwards. Nigel Pearson was not involved in the disciplinary process but disagreed with his son's treatment given he did not abuse the women.

James was deciding whether to appeal, with assistance from the PFA. Hopper and Smith last week found employment with Scunthorpe and Northampton respectively but Pearson had not, making the situation more acute.

The club had had no specific candidate in mind when they dismissed Pearson on Tuesday even though the season started in five weeks and some players reported back to training yesterday, with the majority returning next week.

Bolton boss Neil Lennon was the bookies' favourite. He would have liked the job as he still held Leicester close to his heart but had, as yet, had no contact about the vacancy. The former Celtic manager spent four years as a player at the club, winning two League Cups, and wanted to manage in the Premier League.

Sam Allardyce ruled himself out as he wanted to relax with his family before returning to the game after leaving West Ham, but Sean Dyche, relegated with Burnley, was interested in a return to the top flight.

Shinji Okazaki arrived from Mainz for £7.2million last week, adding to the £3m capture of Stoke defender Robert Huth and free transfer of Christian Fuchs from Schalke. Leicester agreed a new four-year contract with versatile Jeffrey Schlupp, ending speculation over the 22-year-old's future, who was linked with moves to Aston Villa, Arsenal and Swansea. The Ghana international played a key role in Pearson's side, helping them stay up. His form from left wing-back was a key factor in pulling off a miraculous escape and was critical to ensure Pearson's 3-4-1-2 system worked. His new deal expired at the end of the 2018-19 season.

Director of football John Rudkin, who oversaw Schlupp's development in his previous academy post, played an influential role in the player's decision. Rudkin, who lead the hunt for a new manager, has a close working relationship with Top and an appointment to galvanise fans, who were still in disbelief that Pearson has gone, was his priority. Rudkin was expected to be inundated with applications. The club did not have a successor lined up, but Sam Allardyce and Harry Redknapp lead the bookmakers' odds.

Leicester offered their condolences after learning that the mother of Marc Albrighton's partner Chloe was killed during the attacks on a beach in Tunisia. Chloe's mother Sue was a victim in an attack by a gunman that killed 38 people, as was Sue's partner Scott.

The club released a short statement on their website offering their support to the devastated family. The statement read: "Leicester City Football Club offers its sincerest condolences to Marc Albrighton, his partner Chloe and their family, after learning of the deaths of Chloe's mother, Sue, and her partner, Scott, during Friday's attacks in Tunisia. They are all in our thoughts and prayers. We continue to offer our support to Marc and Chloe's family at this time of great personal tragedy."

THURSDAY, 2 JULY

Guus Hiddink emerged as a contender. The former Chelsea manager left his role coaching the Dutch national team on Monday and would appeal to Leicester given his Premier League experience. He also possesses a pull in the Far East after his huge success coaching South Korea to fourth place at the 2002 World Cup. Hiddink, 68, left his Dutch role following an unsuccessful period. But he did well when interim boss of Chelsea in 2009, rejuvenating an underperforming side and winning the FA Cup. He could be offered an advisory role by Leicester with a younger coach taking charge of day-to-day business.

Bolton Wanderers boss Neil Lennon was an option but had yet to be approached. He was said to be interested. Steve Cotterill, who guided Bristol City into the Championship, was an outside contender for the vacancy.

MONDAY, 6 JULY

The players reported for the first day of pre-season training as the club's owners continued their search for a big-name manager.

Having sacked Pearson merely a week earlier, assistant manager Craig Shakespeare was left to welcome the players back after their summer holidays.

Not all of the squad were present as captain Wes Morgan, Jamie Vardy and new signings Christian Fuchs and Shinji Okazaki were granted extra time off following their international exertions.

Last season's player of the year Esteban Cambiasso was also missing as he had not signed his new contract offer from City.

Lennon remained as the favourite to succeed Pearson, but the club's Thai owners were keen to appoint a big-name manager with an international profile. Hiddink fitted the bill. Ex-boss Martin O'Neill was also linked with the vacancy.

TUESDAY, 7 JULY

Peter Schmeichel emerged as a shock candidate. The goalkeeping legend, whose son Kasper plays for the Foxes, hurled his hat into the ring, resulting in Sky Bet pricing the 51-year-old at just 11/2 to venture into the management arena for the first time. Schmeichel applied for the vacancy. The Danish icon has no managerial experience, but the appointment would represent an interesting move by Leicester, who are currently preparing for their second successive season in the top-flight.

Claudio Ranieri narrowly led the way at the top of the market, ahead of former Foxes manager Martin O'Neill, who was at this stage still believed to be the club's preferred candidate to return to the East Midlands dugout. In the 1990s O'Neill led Leicester into the Premier League, before winning a brace of League Cups with the club. The 63-year-old remains a popular figure at the King Power Stadium, but it may take some persuasion to lure the Ulsterman away from his post at the Republic of Ireland.

WEDNESDAY, 8 JULY

Claudio Ranieri would be "thrilled" to manage in the Premier League once again after being linked with a move to Leicester. Ranieri, nicknamed 'The Tinkerman' during his time at Chelsea for constantly changing his starting line-up, was now one of the frontrunners to take over the reins at the King Power Stadium following Pearson's shock dismissal. The Italian was keen on filling the void left by Pearson due to his love for managing in England.

Speaking to Scotland's *Sunday Post*, he said of returning to England: "Greece is behind me now and I am waiting for the next good project to come along. So far I have not had any contact from Leicester but if they were to call me then I would be ready to listen to what they had to say. I say this because I would be thrilled to return to coach in the English Premier League. For me it truly is the best league in Europe. It is well above La Liga because in Spain there is the constant focus on possession. This can be valued almost above all other aspects of the game which is not the way it should be. I am very happy to have had the opportunity to coach in the Premier League because there they have the values I learned as a child."

The 63-year-old Ranieri had been out of management since being sacked from his role as the Greece national team boss in November 2014.

FRIDAY, 10 JULY

The odds on Ranieri becoming manager plummeted in the latest twist in the managerial saga. Ranieri became the new odds-on favourite in Sky Bet's next Leicester City manager market, replacing Martin O'Neill, who had been heavily backed. O'Neill dropped back to second in the betting at 6/4, but Ranieri was supported to as short as 10/11. Predrag Radosavljević (8/1), Neil Lennon (10/1), Roberto Di Matteo (12/1) and Bob Bradley (12/1) were other names towards the front of the market.

MONDAY, 13 JULY

RANIERI APPOINTED!

Claudio Ranieri was the shock appointment on a three-year contract.

The 63-year-old Italian had not worked in England since leaving Stamford Bridge in 2004, and was sacked as a hugely disappointing Greece manager.

"Since I left Chelsea I have dreamt of another chance to work in the best league in the world again," he said. "I wish to thank the owner, his son and all the executives of the club for the opportunity they are giving me. Now I've only one way for returning their trust: squeeze all my energies to getting the best results for the team."

Ranieri left as manager of Atletico Madrid to join Chelsea in September 2000 and during his four-year spell, finished runners-up in the Premier League, reached the Champions League semi-final and were FA Cup finalists. He was replaced by José Mourinho. He went on to manage Valencia, Parma, Juventus, Roma, Inter Milan and Monaco.

He took over as Greece coach after the 2014 World Cup in Brazil but was sacked four months later after a home defeat by the Faroe Islands.

BBC Sport's Gary Lineker said: "Claudio Ranieri is clearly experienced, but this is an uninspired choice by Leicester. It's amazing how the same old names keep getting a go on the managerial merry-go-round."

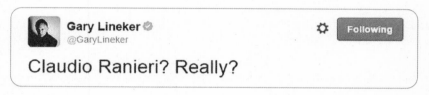

Gary Lineker ☑
@GaryLineker
☼ Following

Claudio Ranieri? Really?

TUESDAY, 14 JULY

Ranieri arrived at Leicester off the back of an ignominious exit from his last job. So bad in fact that his employer came out to apologise and take "full responsibility" for "the most unfortunate choice of coach."

Greece had lost at home 1-0 to the Faroe Islands. Wow! That was one of the all-time lows for Greek football, over which Ranieri had presided. The Hellenic Football Federation's president, Giorgos Sarris, sacked Ranieri and confessed his decision to appoint him had "resulted in such a poor image of the national team being put before the fans". The Greek FA sacked Ranieri, four months into his €1.6m, two-year contract.

Ranieri was paid off with €800,000 and had not worked since. Yet, to be fair, apart from the blip with Greece, his CV was not too shabby but not that impressive either. That made the Leicester decision baffling unless it is taken in the context that Ranieri is genial, in direct contrast to Pearson's abrasive image in front of the media, and arguably one of the nicest men in football.

RIGHT MAN FOR THE JOB?

As one journalist put it: "If they wanted someone to keep them in the Premier League, then they may have gone for the wrong guy."

The fallout from the Ranieri appointment was greeted with a mixture of disbelief and much amusement; mostly it was not at all complimentary.

Naturally the newspapers and the online media had a field day resurrecting some of the more colourful comments from his days in west London:

On being called "The Tinkerman": "If it is the case that you need just a first 11 and three or four more players, then why did Christopher Columbus sail to India to discover America?"

On his selection dilemmas: "When I don't put Damien Duff in the squad, my mother, who is 84 years old, asks why? She kills me about it, it is true."

On his imminent departure from Chelsea: "Before you kill me, you call me the 'Dead Man Walking'. I must buy you an espresso. But only a little one - I am Scottish."

At a press conference before Chelsea were knocked out of the Champions League by Monaco in 2004: "Hello my sharks, welcome to the funeral."

WEDNESDAY, 15 JULY

Ranieri's return to English football, 11 years after he became the first managerial casualty of the ruthless Roman Abramovich regime at Chelsea, was understandably such a shock to many. In fact, it was difficult to find much praise at all.

Gary Lineker had led the way in condemning the appointment of Ranieri but, of course, he wasn't alone in having egg on his face. Great looking back on their words of wisdom:

Phil Thompson thought he was being funny on Sky Sports: "They should really have signed his agent. He got all those jobs for him! I may be quite wrong, but I don't think he's ever won anything. He's been there, seen it, not done it, at all those places. Nigel Pearson did ever so well, and for Ranieri to get this job was quite incredible. I hope he does well, because he is a nice guy, but he's fortunate."

Matt Le Tissier would drop his shoulder and send defenders the wrong way, but on Sky Sports he sold himself a dummy: "With Leicester I think it could be a massive struggle this season. I think he might struggle with the spirit there."

Dietmar Hamann, a master of midfield in his prime, was arguably the most pessimistic of them all. On Twitter, he wrote: "Can't believe Leicester appointed Ranieri...Great club, great fanbase but I'm afraid MK rather than Old Trafford season after next."

Harry Redknapp is always on the ball. "Ranieri is a nice guy, but he's done well to get the Leicester job. After what happened with Greece, I'm surprised he can walk back into the Premier League."

The former Leicester City striker Tony Cottee was none too better at the predictions lark. On Sky Sports he remarked: "I'm astonished. I just didn't see this one coming. Obviously there have been many people linked to the job but as far as I'm aware, Ranieri wasn't one and for me, it is a strange appointment. They made a massive risk getting rid of Nigel Pearson who did such a good job football-wise towards the end of last season. To appoint Ranieri now, bearing in mind where he has been the last 10 years, is a huge gamble."

Robbie Savage said on the BBC: "Ranieri, good manager but for me not Leicester. If you play for the Foxes you need someone you can relate to as a manager. O'Neill, Pearson are managers the players can relate to. I'd have gone back to O'Neill or Lennon. It will be a relegation battle whoever was manager. Big name, bad choice in my opinion. Time will tell. Hopefully I am wrong."

Stan Collymore commented in the *Daily Mirror*: "Last season's Great Escape will have instilled incredible belief at the King Power. Having met Nigel Pearson on a number of occasions last season, he was in no doubt that the Foxes would claw themselves to safety. Unfortunately, the script has changed. I'm not convinced about 'Tinkerman' Claudio Ranieri. Pearson had the dressing room. The players believed in him. Ranieri has a job on his hands earning the same respect. Don't underestimate the loss of Esteban Cambiasso, either. But I think the players believe. That could be enough. It may be just as messy as it was last time, though."

Alan Smith was highly sceptical at first as he commented in the *Daily Telegraph*: "Replacing Nigel Pearson with Claudio Ranieri can only be described as a huge punt. The risk is that City now lose some of the energy, aggression and spirit that pulled them to safety."

Michael Owen remarked on Twitter: "Right then here we go again #Top6Bottom3: Top 6: Chelsea, Man Utd, Arsenal, Man City, Liverpool, Spurs. Bottom 3: Bournemouth, Leicester, Watford. Let's see yours!"

BBC Sport managed to find a few more rounded, open-minded opinions:

Mark Bosnich, ex-Aston Villa and Manchester United goalkeeper, signed for Chelsea by Ranieri: "He was a bit of father figure. In general he was very thorough and at the time he was little bit of a novelty in English football. There weren't as many foreign coaches in the Premier League and I think some of his ways gave him a little bit of an advantage. His communication skills weren't great because he couldn't speak the language. That was understandable but didn't help and everybody was basically living a little bit on edge whether they played well or not. That contributed to a lot of the players feeling a little bit insecure under him. A lot of people will say that is good and it keeps people on their toes but if players play well they should know they will be in the team. That type of tinkering was not really conducive to continuity and sometimes it came across that he had a few problems with the bigger players in the team if they didn't swim in the right direction. He relied a lot on his coaches, who were very good. He let them do their stuff and would always oversee everything until it came down to the tactics when he really took on a hands-on role. A lot of the time he relied on the translator so it was very tricky to give a Churchillian speech at half-time. He had his way of getting his point across. I remember a time at Derby when we weren't playing well and he came in and waited for three or four minutes before he said anything. He didn't like to get overly emotional because he believed that would be detrimental to the side. Claudio suffered a bit because he was new to English football and maybe didn't quite understand the culture. He was different and a decent manager but I didn't really think he had it in him to get a side to win trophies. But that may suit him. His remit will be to keep Leicester up, so I do think being here before and having the experience he has had will give him a good perspective on how to approach this job. I don't think he is the right manager in terms of getting the side to battle but I think you will see a profound change in the way Leicester play. The owners seem to want them to play in a different way that is much more attractive on the eye."

Frank Sinclair, former Chelsea and Leicester City defender: "I was very surprised he was appointed. There was lots of talk about Martin O'Neill and Neil Lennon going back to the club where they are truly loved. But Claudio's experience and some of the clubs he has managed is phenomenal. From what I know of his time at Chelsea, from speaking to the likes of John Terry, he is a very strict manager and very much a disciplinarian, who knows the game inside out. He had a very successful period at Chelsea and some people have forgotten that. He was a bit unlucky. It was part and parcel of the way Roman Abramovich was running Chelsea. If I was a player at Leicester still I would be excited given the players he has worked with in the past - very excited. But for the next manager at Leicester, the job in hand is stabilising the club. I don't think they are looking to win things yet. If they can be a mid-table team then he will be doing a fantastic job. He will have funds but won't have ridiculous money. But Leicester finished the season as good as anybody last season and the squad is quite strong so they only need to strengthen in two or three positions."

Gabriele Marcotti, England-based Italian sports journalist, author and presenter: "He's very experienced, and has been in lots of different situations. Above all he is someone who is generally unfazed and unflustered by some of the challenges ahead. If it's a big personality, he approaches it like he's seen it before and he knows what to do and how to get through it. We often make a mistake when we compare people to their past and things that happened 11 years ago. He is a different manager to the guy he was in 2004 when he had that unique job with Roman Abramovich just coming in at Chelsea with limitless funds. Along the way he has been in different situations. He is more difficult to rattle than before, having dealt with some very tricky high-profile, high-pressure situations at Juventus, Roma and Monaco. That will stand him in very good stead. He is not the sort of manager who gets involved in transfers. He generally describes the profile of the player he wants and leaves it up to the club to deliver. My understanding was that Nigel Pearson was more of a top-down manager but with Ranieri that will not happen. He would not deal with agents or other clubs with signings. He would approve them but would not be driving negotiations. If you define success as Leicester staying up then I think Ranieri can deliver that. If you are looking at long-term growth and rebuilding then maybe that is not it. What you are getting above all is a very good pragmatist who can handle difficult situations."

Matt Spiro, France-based football writer and broadcaster: "I saw him work at Monaco for a couple of very successful seasons and I was impressed. He joined in the second division and got them promoted, winning the league title and in their first season in the top flight they were competing with Paris St. Germain up until the last month of the season. Generally he was very well perceived in France and it was very surprising and no one really understood why he was sacked at the end of his second season when Monaco finished second. He played very positive and very attacking football. OK, they had Radamel Falcao and James Rodriguez, but even against Paris St. Germain they played to win and did not sit back and defend. He does demand a lot from his players and had a fall-out with Rodriguez when he left him out when he was unhappy with the player's workrate. But after that he became a key man and got the move to Real Madrid. I see him as good man manager and a man who likes to attack and play his football in the right way. He wasn't afraid to drop James Rodriguez and other players and chop and change formations. Since being at Chelsea, when he got the 'Tinkerman' nickname, football has changed a lot and I don't see it as a particularly big issue. He is an intelligent man and will pick his players on merit; he won't worry about reputations."

Ian Bason, chairman of the Foxes Trust: "I think the reaction will be mixed. He has an international reputation which appealed to the owners and he has Premier League experience. Some fans will always want former Leicester players taking over which I don't think always works out - remember Frank McLintock from many years ago? Things will have moved on since he managed in England but he has a vast amount of experience and it's better to have some experience of the Premier League than none - which was the case with some of the names bandied about and that was causing alarm. One of the interesting things will be the playing style and if that will change. I would like to see us not change too much in what we are doing because the players are used to it and we have a consistency in approach."

THOSE DEFINITELY IN FAVOUR, ANYONE?

However, by searching through Twitter, it was possible to find some positivity from Leicester City fans. Take a bow:

Luke Sullivan: Any manager was an element of risk but I think the owners have chosen well! So long as spending isn't silly then Ranieri could be ok #lcfc

Cooperman: In Ranieri we trust, finally be able to put this whole debacle behind us & concentrate on the football #lcfc

Adam Moore: Quite happy with the appointment of Ranieri, managed some big clubs and big players, and likes to play attractive football! #LCFC

TUESDAY, 21 JULY

After watching his new side secure victory in their first pre-season outing, Ranieri declared himself impressed with the performance of his players.

The Foxes beat Lincoln City 3-1 at Sincil Bank with goals from Riyad Mahrez, Andrej Kramarić and Jamie Vardy.

Fitness was the main goal as the players looked to regain their sharpness ahead of the new campaign.

Ranieri was pleased with what he saw as they overcame a tricky opponent. The Tinkerman tinkered by having 22 players playing 45 minutes - including new signings Robert Huth, Christian Fuchs and Shinji Okazaki.

Speaking exclusively to Foxes Player HD, Ranieri said: "The performance was good, first of all because nobody is injured and that's important for me and secondly because we won the match. The first 20 minutes were very, very hard because Lincoln have already played three matches in pre-season but for us it was a first 45 minutes. But after 20 or 25 minutes I saw the players move better, play on the floor and we scored a great goal. The second half was much better, faster and the strikers moved very well."

While he was impressed, Ranieri still saw room for improvement, as his players gradually get up to speed on their fitness and match sharpness.

He added: "I think we created a lot of opportunities but it's important when you create these opportunities to stay calm in the last 20 metres because we lost the last pass sometimes when there was another team-mate in a good position to score a goal."

AUGUST 2015

SATURDAY, 1 AUGUST

With a week to go before the season opener against Sunderland Claudio Ranieri was one of the ante-post favourites for the sack, while the Foxes were 5000/1 to win the title. That was how little confidence anyone had in the club surviving let alone making any sort of impact, and there was precious little faith in the appointment of The Tinkerman.

Here is a pre-season poll conducted by *The Guardian*: Liverpool had a really tough opening fixture list which catapulted Brendan Rodgers to top of the 'Dead Man Walking' league, followed by the new Watford boss, and then Ranieri close behind. As for who would be the best signing of the season, not one of the Foxes got a sniff. No guessing the three fancied clubs for relegation: Watford, Leicester and Norwich. Vardy didn't even figure in the list of the top 15 most likely Golden Boot winner. Who will win the Premier League? Easy one; Arsenal, second Chelsea, third Manchester United.

MONDAY, 3 AUGUST

Despite all the gloom and doom from virtually every sector of the industry, from the pundits, the media, and the fans pools, there was much optimism within the confines of the club itself.

Like the previous season all 23,000 season tickets were sold out, and the manner of their end of season survival generated some confidence that it might carry on into the new season. Few outside the domain of the King Power stadium and their fans shared such optimism.

The team that had produced one of the most amazing 'Great Escapes' in Premier League history had been bolstered by new signings costing more than £20 million, but that was small change compared to that which the elite could spend with their huge financial resources.

David Chatwani, manager at the JC Sports in Leicester's Market Place, said: "The sales of the new shirts have been excellent so far this year, particularly the black away shirts, we've sold a lot of them. They're very popular, they're a little bit different. We'll have a decent season this year. The fans I've spoken to that have come in here are definitely a lot more positive than this time last year. The furore surrounding Pearson has gone and I think the new manager will make a positive difference."

The confidence was mirrored by Supporters' Club chairman Cliff Ginetta. He said: "To be honest, I think we should be looking at 11th or 12th place or maybe even breaking into the top ten. I think the fans, who are some of the best - if not the best - in the league, can sense there might be something special happening here. The new signings look exciting and there may be more to come in that department. We were never really outplayed in any games last season and with a brilliant run finished very strongly last season." - Did you back them at 5,000-1 Cliff?

Twins Jordan and Jason Becker were even feeling the confidence in New York. Jordan, who maintains the New York Foxes Facebook and Twitter accounts, said: "I would love to see City build on last season and aim for the top 10. I think by the time the transfer window ends, City will be a stronger team than last season."

Jason said: "I hope that the club can build off the successes from the end of last season. So far Ranieri is saying all of the right things and I think he can succeed at the King Power. I also expect that we'll see great things from a confident Jamie Vardy, a full season for Riyad Mahrez, and N'Golo Kanté."

Top ten. Wow! That was aiming high! - Did you back them, guys?

Ranieri adopted a more cautious tone. "In my career, I saw it is more difficult in the Premier League in the second season than the first. Now it is important to maintain and get one more point than last season."

There had been changes in the team:

Ins: Christian Fuchs (Schalke), Robert Huth (Stoke), Shinji Okazaki (Mainz), N'Golo Kanté (Caen), Yohan Benalouane (Atalanta)

Outs: Chris Wood (Leeds), Esteban Cambiasso (turned down contract)

Pearson's departure was followed by that of the previous season's talisman Esteban Cambiasso, leaving a gaping hole in midfield and a daunting job for Ranieri. Japan international Shinji Okazaki had a good record with Mainz in the Bundesliga, but it was widely thought that the team were in need of further strengthening, especially in midfield.

THURSDAY, 6 AUGUST

Ranieri called on his players to show the same resolve as in the final weeks of last season. "We have to fight every match with our character and strength," he said.

The end of season might have been awe inspiring but in reality, Leicester spent longer at the bottom of the table without being relegated than any side in Premier League history (140 days).

However, in Jamie Vardy they had a genuine goalscorer, who might get even better. Last season he provided more assists from open play than any other Premier League forward (8), so much room for optimism there.

Ray Parlour's view was indicative of the pundits' pre-season predictions - pessimistic. He said: "What a great end to the season. Ranieri was a strange appointment, for me, but he's very experienced and he'll have a good coaching set-up around him. They've lost Cambiasso, though, who was very influential. All eyes will be on Leicester in the first 10 games or so to see what they have learned from last season."

Parlour's one to watch: "Riyad Mahrez was excellent last year. He can play either side in the wide areas and he scored some important goals. You want your creative players to be on the ball as much as possible and I think he was a real influence last year."

FRIDAY, 7 AUGUST

The Foxes scored exactly two goals in six of their last seven matches on the opening day, including in the Premier League last term against Everton, so perhaps a good start was predictable.

Ranieri wanted to continue Leicester's end-of-season momentum when they kicked off against Sunderland, especially as their survival was confirmed after a goalless draw at Sunderland on the penultimate day.

Sunderland stuck with the manager that helped them avoid the drop and Dick Advocaat hoped the Black Cats get off to a better start than in their previous season when they won just one of their opening nine games.

New signings Kanté and Yohan Benalouane will be assessed after joining up with the squad this week.

Fuchs and Okazaki could make their debuts after joining before Ranieri's appointment while captain Wes Morgan is available after playing in Jamaica's Gold Cup campaign.

Paul Merson's Sky Sports prediction: "I backed Leicester to avoid relegation last season. Even when they were struggling, I said they would stay up because I saw some good performances from them. I don't have a good feeling for them at the moment after what's happened with the sacking of Nigel Pearson. Saying that, I think they will win this game because Sunderland look as though they have a long hard season lying ahead of them."

Merson's verdict was backed up by the stats: Leicester unbeaten in their last four opening league games since a 3-2 defeat against Crystal Palace in 2010. The last Sunderland manager to win a Premier League game on the opening weekend was Steve Bruce against Bolton in 2009. Sunderland had won only one of the last seven Premier League meetings against Leicester and Sunderland had never won a Premier League fixture at Leicester, failing to score in the last three top-flight games there.

Leonardo Ulloa was a 5/1 favourite to net the opener with Jermain Defoe 13/2 to break the deadlock for the visitors.

SATURDAY, 8 AUGUST

LEICESTER CITY 4-2 SUNDERLAND

Ranieri made a winning return to the Premier League, 11 years after being sacked as Chelsea manager by owner Roman Abramovich, and already Leicester were top, albeit a false position as almost half of the Premier League had yet to play.

Jubilant fans chanted "we are top of the league" after the club's best opening result in 50 years. It may only have been the first match, but the celebrations went on long after the full-time whistle, with their side top, above Crystal Palace, who beat Norwich City 3-1.

Cliff Ginetta, chairman of Leicester City Supporters Club, said: "I was very impressed. They are carrying on from their great form at the end of last season and I think their new manager is letting them express themselves more. The crowd was fantastic on Saturday. It was a great atmosphere in the stadium. We couldn't have asked for a much better start to the season."

Before the match, fans in the Kop created a huge mosaic of a supporter holding a club scarf and another waving a flag. It had the message "Your colours are in our hands, our dreams are in yours." It was organised by supporters club Union FS* and involved thousands of fans lifting up pieces of card. Fan Emma Sperring tweeted: "A privilege to be in the Kop and involved in that display, keep up with the good work."

* Why the name Union FS?

Union FS: Picking a fairly original name was quite a tall order and the founding members took an incredible amount of time deliberating over it. As you might guess the FS is short-form for Filbert Street, but there are two reasons why we settled on the Union pre-fix. Firstly, when the Club moved to the now King Power, then Walkers Stadium in 2002, the fans who had previously stood together in Spion Kop pens 1 to 3 were dispersed across different blocks of the new ground. One of our aims is to 'Unite' those with the old Kop mentality from Filbert Street. Secondly, the Old Grand Union Canal runs adjacent to the new stadium. Local heritage should be important for all football fans and it is for this reason the perhaps conspicuous connection was made.

Source: www.fsf.org.uk

Ranieri's tenure as manager began with a magnificent opening-day victory with three goals in the first 30 minutes, including a deft Vardy header starting the scoring. Riyad Mahrez then also headed home from close range, before scoring from the spot after a Lee Cattermole foul on the Algerian. Jermain Defoe gave the Black Cats hope but, after Marc Albrighton had struck for the Foxes, Steven Fletcher's late header was mere consolation. The ease with which Leicester scored will worry Sunderland fans, but the free flowing goals would have given Leicester supporters huge hope.

Albrighton's pinpoint crosses from the left found two of the smallest players on the pitch. Leicester gained confidence as Sunderland failed to cope with the home side's quick, crisp movement. Leicester could have scored more, with Shinji Okazaki missing one glorious chance in the second half. Mahrez, too, hit the woodwork after the break and forced a fine save from Costel Pantilimon.

Already it was widely suggested that should Ranieri's new team continue to perform with such attacking verve, his first season with the Foxes will be trouble free, which meant avoiding relegation and even being a comfortable mid-table side.

Albrighton remarked: "Claudio Ranieri has come in with fresh ideas to add to the way we were playing. He didn't want to change too much but he has new ideas and we are taking them on board." It may be a side built by Pearson, but Albrighton says Ranieri is already putting his stamp on it. Albrighton, who scored one and set up two goals, said Ranieri had made some tactical changes that were already bearing fruit. "He noticed we did well towards the end of the season, so he has not changed too much," said Albrighton. "But he has put his mark on the side and come in with a couple of fresh ideas. We are working on them and it showed against Sunderland. We felt confident attacking and felt like we could create something and get goals every time we were going forward. When you feel like that and are in a confident mood, it is only good for the team."

Albrighton revealed that the game plan was to get out of the traps quickly. "We were renowned at the end of the season for quick starts and putting teams under pressure early on," he said. "We have continued that this season. It is a great start, but like every club, there is going to come a point when things don't go your way. That is when we need everyone to stick together," added Albrighton.

Albrighton dedicated his goal to his partner's mother who was killed in the Tunisia terror attack. Chloe Fulford's mother Sue Davey and her partner, Scott Chalkley, were among 30 British tourists killed in the terrorist shooting in Sousse, Tunisia, in June. The dedication came following a request from his partner's brother Conor Fulford, and he thanked the club and all the City fans for their support. "At the minute we have my girlfriend's brother Conor living with us," he said. "He was getting into me last night saying you need a celebration, you need to do something for my mum. We were wracking our brains and couldn't think. Chloe has been saying her mum has been up there putting a few things right and she has definitely helped me out today. I can't thank everyone enough for the way that myself and especially my family have been treated. The support we have had has been unbelievable from all quarters and there are no words to thank people for the support. Obviously I wouldn't wish it on anybody at all. When you have support you need to know people are there because there is nothing they can say or do. We have had that in bundles."

The tragedy put life into perspective and playing football helped them all cope with their grief. "Yeah you look at life and everything in a different light and different way," he said. "You think about what is important and what is not important. If I can play football then it is taking my mind off things and if I am doing well my family are happy and that is all I can ask for. I will see them now and they will all be happy, when you see them smiling it is the best thing in the world." Roy and Angela Fisher, from Leicester, also died in the terror attack.

NO TINKERING

Ranieri described his side's performance as "outstanding". The 'Tinkerman' declined to tinker at all, relying on the players who secured top-flight survival by winning win seven of their last nine games to finish 14th, with only one summer signing - Okazaki - in his starting line-up. Of the familiar Leicester faces, Vardy and Mahrez particularly excelled with their creativity and pace causing Sunderland all sorts of problems. Sunderland were fragile on the right side of their defence and 42.2% of Leicester's attacks came from that flank. Marc Albrighton caused damage in the first half with his crosses from the left wing and combined well with Jeff Schlupp and Okazaki for the second goal, which Mahrez scored.

It might have been a surprising start for many, however the stats showed it shouldn't have been such a shock. Since the start of April, Leicester had won more points than any other Premier League side (25). The Foxes won six and lost just one of their last seven league games at the King Power Stadium. Vardy had five goals and four assists in his last 11 league appearances. Albrighton ended last season with three assists but already had two after the opening game.

Ranieri commented: "It was a very good start and I am very happy with my players in the first match, which is so important in front of our fans. I told my players to be the warriors for them. The performance was outstanding from the beginning. Okazaki played very well but I don't like to just say that because the whole team played well. If I talk now about Mahrez I can also remember Shinji Okazaki, or Vardy, or Albrighton, everybody. We played like a team and that was what I wanted. There were one or two not 100 per cent but the team supported the others. Mahrez made something good but because the others supported him, Albrighton, Vardy and Shinji. Everyone worked so hard."

City picked up where they left off last season, and he challenged his players to be inspired by Kasabian's *Fire*, which follows every City goal on home soil. "It was important to start well," said Ranieri. "I told my players that they finished well last season and I want to see them restart at the same level and the performance was very good. The first half was outstanding, the second half was normal. You make mistakes but when you win you are more confident and I say 'hey, you make mistakes, this, this, this' and I show them and I think they are more receptive now when they win. The atmosphere was fantastic, amazing. The crowd were very noisy. Fantastic. I said to them before the kick-off there is a band, a strong band, rock band and when they score the song comes on, and it was fantastic. I told my players, 'when you go on the pitch and you hear the song Fire from Kasabian, that means they want warriors.' I want to see them as warriors for the fans."

Advocaat said: "After 10 minutes there were three crosses and three goals. At this level this cannot happen. You have to show every minute away from home and we didn't see that in the first half. We have to wait (for new players). We struggled again. Everybody can see that we need more."

Man of the match Mahrez's pace and invention caused havoc and the Algeria international could have had a hat-trick before receiving a deserved standing ovation from the Leicester fans as he was substituted towards the end of the match.

SUNDAY, 9 AUGUST

Vichai Srivaddhanaprabha made decisions in the best interest of the club. The billionaire said, in his annual opening day address in the official City match day magazine, that he has a vision for the club and vowed to take the right steps to continue the progress:

"Since the day we took ownership of Leicester City Football Club, our primary ambition has been to support the club's upward growth of bringing pride and success to its supporters and to the great sporting city of Leicester," he said, "It is a great privilege to be part of a chapter in the rich history of this wonderful football club but also a significant responsibility, which is why we have always put the best interests of the club above everything else in every decision we have made in the last five years. It is our duty as custodians of the club to ensure it is held in good stewardship to hold its good name and to continue in the pursuit of sustainable success that can be passed on to future generations. The paths we have taken have always been what we feel are the right decisions for the club's current situation and for the growth and stability that we mutually desired. Despite winning the Championship with a record number of points and victories, there were many people that doubted our ability to compete in the Premier League, particularly during the difficult periods. However, together we proved the doubters wrong and showed that Leicester City deserves its place among football's elite. Last season was an achievement not of individuals but of a team that showed the power of trust in each other and we should all be extremely proud. Our vision has always been one of sustainable long-term success. It is impossible to satisfy everyone but I know myself what we are working towards and I'm sure our fans know that the club is in my heart. Everything we have done and will continue to do is out of love for Leicester City."

MONDAY, 10 AUGUST

New signing Yohan Benalouane played the entire 90 minutes, in front of a good-sized crowd, in the under-21s against reigning champions Manchester United in their season opener. The £5.6m signing, who made his first team debut as a substitute during victory over Sunderland, played right-back.

Record signing Ulloa led the attack. Ranieri, who watched on from the stands as City drew 1-1, previously said on two occasions the Argentine needed more match fitness and Ulloa was given the entire 90 minutes.

Benalouane, who was booked 17 times at Atalanta in Italy last season, was booked for a trip on United winger James Weir and he clashed with the youngster on several occasions, but he also showed his ability on the ball with some exciting touches. Coach, Steve Beaglehole, was pleased with the start the under-21s made. "We dominated in the first 20 minutes and we looked a class act," he said. "As the first team did last Saturday, we had to make that possession and those chances count. We're disappointed not to win, but Manchester United are the champions. But that shows how far we've come, to say that we're disappointed with a draw."

TUESDAY, 11 AUGUST

Ranieri vowed to keep opponents guessing, staying true to his "Tinkerman" reputation, but promised not to make too many changes to the style of play, building on the "fantastic foundations" of Nigel Pearson.

But he wanted to impart his "tactical Italian way" on the side.

TALKING TACTICS

He opted for a 4-4-2 system on the opening day despite having stuck with three at the back for much of pre-season.

It was a fluid formation, though, with players often switching into other systems. This was one of the reasons he bought Yohan Benalouane, who could play centre-back and full-back so he could change formation during a game without needing to make any substitutions.

Benalouane is in the same mould as Huth, said development squad manager Steve Beaglehole, who was impressed with Benalouane's attitude and said that when he is fully fit he will be an asset for Ranieri. "He looks a good acquisition," said Beaglehole. "Considering he is a centre-half playing at right-back and he isn't 100 per cent fit yet, I thought he showed some great attributes. He is strong, brave and had some lovely touches on the ball, and I liked his attitude. I liked his physicality and his all-round game. I don't think he will shirk anything. I think he is another one in the Huth and Wes Morgan mould, which is great."

According to Ranieri, switching tactics during a game is a vital weapon for a manager, and Bayern Munich manager Pep Guardiola is one of the new breed of tinkermen.

"When you play a Guardiola team you do not know if they play three, four or five at the back," said Ranieri. "It is difficult when you play against a team like that. It is easier if you can explain to your players 'they play 4-4-2, 4-3-3, they do this, this, and this' but when you don't know, or you change something, the opponent has more difficulties. There are lots of tinkermen in the Premier League now. I was the first, I am the tinkerman. I carry the flag."

"When I started in Italy, people asked me why I changed the system, but I saved Cagliari when I changed system. Teams were used to playing against me with three at the back. When I changed to 4-4-2 suddenly during the match, they didn't know what happened. My players did, but the opponents didn't. Now lots of managers change system during the match."

Ranieri has moved to the area with his wife and has already been trying out the range of cuisine Leicester has to offer. "I have been to three restaurants in the city centre," said Ranieri. "It's not bad. Not just Italian but Indian and English. I love to change food. I am tinkerman there as well."

Ben Hamer completed his loan switch to Bristol City, but Leicester City can recall him at any time. The 27-year-old joined the Championship new boys on a season-long loan. A deal had been done with Nottingham Forest but their current situation regarding Financial Fair Play penalties meant Hamer had to return. Hamer was third choice at City following the arrival of Mark Schwarzer and the return to fitness of Kasper Schmeichel. Hamer made ten starts for City last season, eight in the Premier League, conceding just nine goals and keeping four clean sheets.

WEDNESDAY, 12 AUGUST

Ranieri believed Vardy was a "fantastic" on-field example, his strength of character and attitude lifts the performances of the rest of the side.

Ranieri was speaking before reports emerged accusing Vardy of racially abusing a man in a Leicester casino. Vardy apologised and the club were investigating the incident.

It came after Vardy made a blistering start to the Premier League campaign, scoring after just 11 minutes, and set the tone up front, pressing from the first whistle and never giving the Sunderland defenders a moment's rest.

"He is a fantastic man," said Ranieri. "He is an example for the other team-mates. He is a strong man, and has a very strong mentality. He impresses everyone. He is a hard worker and I love these kind of people. He continues to press, to press, to press. I love this. He shows this to his team-mates and they look at him and say, 'Come on, we can do this together, as a unit'. That is important. He is a nice boy, very funny, but when he is on the pitch, he is different. He is strong."

Vardy scored five goals for City last season, with four of those coming in the last 10 games as City marched to survival against all the odds. His influential performances in City's end-of-season survival elevated Vardy to an England player, as a substitute in the friendly against Ireland.

Ranieri believed Vardy should be looking to double his goal return this season. "He can improve," said Ranieri. "Last season he scored five goals. I think his target this season should be 10. His England debut was good for him. The door to the national team is open to him, so he must keep it up. The door is open so it is important for it not to close."

David Nugent, Vardy's strike partner for much of his time at the club, was moving to Middlesbrough, as City accepted a £4m offer for the 30-year-old with Nugent set to undergo a medical ahead of a reported three-year deal.

THURSDAY, 13 AUGUST

Jamie Vardy held clear-the-air talks with Japanese team-mate Shinji Okazaki following a video, showing him being rude to a Japanese man in a casino, which had been made public a week earlier. He was in the casino with fiancée Rebekah Nicholson and fellow Leicester players David Nugent and Ritchie de Laet. As they played poker in the early hours of 26 July, Vardy apparently became agitated when he thought the man behind him was looking at his cards.

Just minutes later, Vardy got involved in another row when a customer pointed out to him that watching the action on a poker table *is* allowed, as long as you make no comment on the hand being played. He became angry and asked the customer "outside" to settle the argument. De Laet then held Vardy in a headlock to prevent him going. De Laet and Nugent are seen in the video trying to calm Vardy down, and neither were accused of any wrongdoing.

Vardy apologised but escaped being sacked despite Leicester sacking James Pearson, Tom Hopper and Adam Smith at the end of last season.

In a statement released by Leicester last Sunday, Vardy said: "I wholeheartedly apologise for any offence I've caused. It was a regrettable error in judgement I take full responsibility for and I accept my behaviour was not up to what's expected of me."

Instead Ranieri backed Vardy and Okazaki to form a lethal partnership. He said: "Shinji took no offence, no. I know they spoke together and looked at how they trained together. They could be a very good combination. There is a good relationship with Shinji and Jamie and it is closed. No, Jamie will not be sacked. It is not my matter but he won't be."

Vardy was fined and ordered to undergo a programme of diversity awareness training by Leicester City. "Leicester City Football Club has concluded its investigation into claims made against Jamie Vardy in the national media last weekend," City said in a statement. "Having established a full account of the incident in question and taken into consideration Jamie's prompt apology, the club has issued the player with a substantial fine and prescribed a programme of diversity awareness training. Jamie has been reminded of his responsibilities to the club, his profession and the Leicester community. The fine will be donated to local charities. The club will make no further comment on the matter, which it now deems to be closed."

Ranieri added: "The club has made a statement and everything is okay. Jamie has apologised and it was a mistake," he said. "There is a good relationship with Shinji and Jamie and for me it is closed."

FRIDAY, 14 AUGUST

West Ham vowed there will be low-priced tickets for all supporters when they make the move to the Olympic Stadium, but on this occasion Leicester fans were required to pay £45. Last season, City fans were asked £25 for the same fixture. The price hike angered many. Ian Bason, chairman of the Foxes Trust, said despite attempts to strike reciprocal deals between clubs to lower the cost for away supporters, more needs to be done. "The final opportunity to visit their current ground is our first away game of the season, but it comes at a staggering £45 per adult ticket price compared with £25 last time," he said. "Only Chelsea (£50) and Manchester United (£46) were more expensive last season. City's management have consistently told our own fans' consultative committee the difficultly they have in striking reciprocal deals with other clubs to charge £20 for away fans. This is the amount consistently suggested by the Football Supporters' Federation's (FSF), the 'Twenty is Plenty' campaign. Just nine of the 20 clubs last season took part in any reciprocal deals. Our club funded £10 off per ticket for the Swansea and Sunderland games, but these weren't reciprocal deals."

SATURDAY, 15 AUGUST

WEST HAM UNITED 1-2 LEICESTER CITY

Foxes favourite son and *MOTD* anchorman Gary Lineker was clearly as chuffed with Leicester's start as was Ranieri. So much so, Gary even mentioned Leicester possibly targeting Champions League football…purely tongue-in-cheek banter.

Ranieri's response?

"Oh, thank you Gary…but is not possible."

So long as Gary doesn't suggest his team will win the league and he'll present *MOTD* in his underpants we will all be ok!

The 100% winning start as the club won their opening two games for the first time since 1997-98 had Lineker drooling. In fact, Leicester had won nine of their last 11 Premier League fixtures - one more than they managed in their previous 55 top-flight games.

Okazaki put the Foxes ahead, heading home the loose ball after goalkeeper Adrian blocked his volley. Mahrez made it 2-0 before half-time with a powerful finish for his third goal of the season.

West Ham improved after the break and Dimitri Payet pulled a goal back, but Schmeichel denied Diafra Sakho as they searched for an equaliser. Schmeichel had escaped punishment for colliding with Sakho inside the area before half-time but his opposite number Adrian was not so lucky late in the game. The Hammers keeper was sent off for a challenge on Vardy after he went up for a corner in stoppage time.

Leicester looked to break quickly and both their goals came through neat build-ups and clever final balls from first Vardy and then Albrighton.

West Ham saw most of the ball in the first half - enjoying 63% possession with an 83% passing accuracy - but did little damage with it and did not manage a shot on target before the break.

The Hammers enjoyed even more possession as the game went on but Leicester defended deep and in numbers and held out thanks to Schmeichel's key save from Sakho, one of three good stops he made after the break.

Ranieri: "We are working very hard with the defensive line. I have very good players in front, very fast but it is important we all stay together. I didn't want to defend too deep but when you see your players go deep it is better to help them with their mentality."

West Ham manager Slaven Bilić: "We lost the game in the first half. Two-nil down is very difficult to come back from. We are very disappointed. We scored a goal early enough in the second half to play our normal game but with more aggression. I was expecting us to score a second, but we didn't."

Maybe Gary Lineker needed some diversity spelling awareness training?

 Gary Lineker @GaryLineker · 2h
Leicester lead at West Ham through Okazaxi. The Japanese forward scores from an assist by Vardy... Oh the irony.

FRIDAY, 21 AUGUST

Claudio Ranieri was enjoying his return to English football at the top end of the table after a sensational two wins in his first two outings, but knew he was never going to be given the chance to win titles at Stamford Bridge. Speaking to *The Telegraph*, he said: "I understood from the beginning that Roman wanted to change things. He wanted to take Eriksson. It didn't happen. He said, 'OK Claudio, continue with your job'. But I knew at the end of the season my job would be finished."

Ranieri was enjoying contrasting fortunes to Mourinho right at the start of this season, with the Portuguese boss lingering at the bottom of the table with just one point from his first two games. Yet, he was gracious enough to welcome Ranieri back to the Premier League. The Italian said: "When I came back, Mourinho was the first one to send me a message saying 'welcome back'. We clashed in Italy but that was good for everybody. When I was in Inter every week he sent me a message, he's a nice boy."

Ranieri was considered the tenth choice by some to end up at Leicester, and on his appointment, Gary Lineker famously tweeted: "Ranieri? Really?" But the 63-year-old has no issues with the famous Foxes strikers' comments. He admitted: "Everybody forgot about me. I respect everybody, I spoke with Gary last weekend and it was very funny. I am an old manager. I forgive everything. Why? Life is very short."

SATURDAY, 22 AUGUST

LEICESTER CITY 1-1 TOTTENHAM HOTSPUR

Mahrez's fourth goal of the season quickly cancelled out Spurs' opener, maintaining the unbeaten start.

Spurs broke the deadlock with nine minutes to go when Dele Alli converted Nacer Chadli's cross from close range. But Mahrez, who had earlier hit the post, replied just 90 seconds later with a fierce left-footed finish.

The Foxes went closest to victory when Hugo Lloris saved Wes Morgan's header, but they still retained top billing, above Manchester United on goal difference. Manchester City and Liverpool could leapfrog them later this weekend.

Roy Hodgson named his squad for September's Euro 2016 qualifiers against San Marino and Switzerland next week and was at the King Power Stadium to check on Kane and Vardy. They were both involved in their side's goals, with Kane helping to start the move that ended with Alli heading home from close range, and Vardy's header giving him an assist even if Leicester's goal owed much more to Mahrez's magic. Vardy was his usual energetic self, causing Spurs plenty of problems without ever looking like finding the net himself. Kane, who is yet to score this season after notching 31 times in 2014-15, had a poor first half but showed flashes of his old self in the second period, notably when he forced his way past two defenders and forced Schmeichel into a save.

It was Mahrez who was the game's star performer. The Algerian's goal capped another fine display on the wing and he always looked dangerous when he came inside and ran at the Tottenham defence.

Spurs' coach, Mauricio Pochettino, said before the game that his need for another striker to help Kane was "obvious". There was also a lack of creativity with Christian Eriksen absent with a knee injury.

40 POINTS

Ranieri commented: "Tottenham kept possession of the ball but we created the same chances and 1-1 is the right result. I am happy. My players have a fantastic spirit. It was an outstanding goal and Riyad Mahrez is a very good player. It is important to maintain our place in the Premier League. Seven points, 33 less, that is important for us."

Pochettino observed: "It was 50/50, a very difficult game for both teams. Second half we played much better. I am disappointed with the draw. Last game against Stoke we lost a 2-0 lead and we did it again. We deserved more again but it is a shame. I am angry and disappointed, not frustrated. The mistake we made today is difficult to explain."

TUESDAY, 25 AUGUST
BURY 1-4 LEICESTER CITY
LEAGUE CUP - SECOND ROUND

Youngster Joe Dodoo hit a hat-trick on his debut as the Foxes reached the Capital One Cup third round at Gigg Lane.

England Under-19 international Dodoo also set up the second on 41 minutes for Andrej Kramarić. Bury netted when Tom Pope set up Danny Mayor four minutes after the break. Dodoo fired a right-foot shot into the bottom corner from six yards on 86 minutes, and then scored from just inside the area right on full-time.

SATURDAY, 29 AUGUST
BOURNEMOUTH 1-1 LEICESTER CITY

Little did anyone know but the Vardy phenomena had started on the south coast.

Jamie Vardy was fouled in the box and picked himself up to smash in a late penalty despite the Polish goalkeeper getting a hand on it, to rescue a point and preserve the unbeaten start to the season.

Callum Wilson's bicycle kick opened the scoring for Bournemouth after Max Gradel's deflected header fell kindly. The Cherries were forced to make three substitutions through injuries as goalkeeper Artur Boruc was a spectator for much of the game.

Vardy's hard running was the brightest feature and he tricked Steve Cook into bringing him down with some neat footwork. Vardy was picked for England for the first time a day later.

So, Ranieri remained unbeaten in his first four matches going into the international break with eight points from their first four games in the top flight, but really there was little to no thought that this was to be the record-breaking Vardy run of consecutive goals or, for that matter, that this team had any hope of maintaining what was a superb start but universally viewed as a flash in the pan.

Mahrez was the stand-out performer of the season so far, scoring four goals in the first three games, but against Bournemouth he was taken off at half-time after a poor display. He was clattered into by Max Gradel almost immediately from kick-off and Ranieri said after the game the Algerian winger had struggled to recover.

Eddie Howe, Bournemouth Coach, speaking to BBC Sport: "I'm a bit disappointed not to have got more points. I thought we could have got three today, but sometimes you have to be a grateful for a point."

Ranieri, also speaking to BBC Sport: "We conceded the goal and until then we were playing well. After the goal we slowed down the tempo and had no great personality. There were 10 minutes when Bournemouth played very well. In the second half we put them under pressure and made some good chances. I think at the end we deserved to draw. It's important to take one point from a difficult match."

Leicester City went five away games unbeaten for the first time in the Premier League, but dropped back to third, and let's be honest most pundits would have expected that slide to continue after the International break.

Ranieri added: "We have a week now where the players go to their national team and when they come back we must re-start with the same mentality."

Barclays Premier League Table at the end of August 2015:

POS	CLUB	P	W	D	L	GF	GA	GD	PTS
1	Manchester City	4	4	0	0	10	0	10	12
2	Crystal Palace	4	3	0	1	8	5	3	9
3	Leicester City	4	2	2	0	8	5	3	8

SEPTEMBER 2015

SATURDAY, 5 SEPTEMBER

England confirmed their place at Euro 2016 after the expected 6-0 goal glut against minnows San Marino. Wayne Rooney scored a record-equalling 49th goal with an early penalty but was surprisingly substituted with history beckoning and the San Marino defence out on its feet.

There was still plenty for England to celebrate, though, as they made it seven wins out of seven in qualifying to ensure they will be in France in the summer of 2016. Barkley nodded in his first England goal after the break and England romped clear with two goals from substitute Walcott and Kane's clever lofted finish. Hodgson gave opportunities to players in the relatively sedate surroundings of San Marino. It was a tougher night for Vardy, who struggled to get into the action and, for a short while in the second half, became embroiled in a running battle with defender Giovanni Bonini.

TUESDAY, 8 SEPTEMBER

Substitute Harry Kane pierced the deadlock with a crisp finish after 67 minutes and Rooney rewrote the record books, breaking Sir Bobby Charlton's all-time England goalscoring record, with a thunderous penalty six minutes from time, earning a standing ovation from the Wembley gallery, ensuring England completed eight wins out of eight, securing top spot in Group E.

SUNDAY, 13 SEPTEMBER

LEICESTER CITY 3-2 ASTON VILLA

City staged a thrilling second-half comeback to recover from 2-0 down to beat Aston Villa and move second in the table, maintaining the unbeaten start.

Jack Grealish curled in a deserved opener from 20 yards, his first goal, for a dominant Villa early on and Carles Gil swept in a second. Ritchie de Laet volleyed a lifeline and Vardy prodded Leicester level. Nathan Dyer scored the winner with a brave late header on his debut. The winger had only signed from Swansea on loan on deadline day but made himself an instant hero and left Villa reeling with just one win from five matches. He beat Guzan to a chipped pass from the impressive Mahrez before taking a blow to the head and staying down injured as the ball rolled into the net.

At this stage there was no hint that Villa, one of the Premier League's once elite, were on the way down, or that Vardy, who hardly got a mention in dispatches, had continued with successive goals.

Mahrez was the inspiration behind Leicester's second-half recovery as he continued his impressive start to the season. He had scored four goals already, coming to life after the break with a stunning display of pace and skill, having a hand in all three of rejuvenated Leicester's second-half goals. His improvement, and his side's, came when Ranieri 'tinkered' with his tactics, switching to a 4-2-3-1 from a 4-4-2

Leicester had now gone nine Premier League games unbeaten, winning six, and joint level with Manchester City as the Premier League's form team since 4 April, picking up 33 points from 14 matches.

Ranieri told BBC Sport: "It was a fantastic second half. We know they played better early on but after 2-0 we started to play with our spirit and it was a very fantastic match. We scored a good first goal that gave confidence to everybody and maybe Villa players were wondering what could happen now."

Tim Sherwood added: "I've never felt this bad. Ever! There was a lot of bad play there in the last half hour. The only way you can stop the momentum is to stop the opposition. We turned it over stupidly. What can I say? I'm gutted for everyone who's associated with the football club. We have to stop letting in soft goals. Who cares if we played well? We lost. Totally lost!"

The recognition was now just about starting. BBC Radio 5 live pundit Martin Keown commented: "This Leicester team is incredible. The energy of it all. Jamie Vardy just knows there's going to be an opening for him."

WEDNESDAY, 16 SEPTEMBER

Vardy was recorded as the fastest player in the Premier League this season, with the Foxes claiming the top three speeds this season. According to Sky Sports, Vardy reached a speed of 35.44km/h, equal to just over 22 miles per hour, in the Foxes 2-1 win at West Ham in August. Schlupp (35.26km/h) and Albrighton (35km/h) were second and third respectively.

Vardy also clocked the fifth fastest, hitting 34.95km/h against Bournemouth.

Top 20 fastest speeds clocked this season:

1.   Jamie Vardy (Leicester) 35.44 km/h vs. West Ham
2.   Jeffrey Schlupp (Leicester) 35.26 km/h vs. Bournemouth

3.　Marc Albrighton (Leicester) 35.00 km/h vs. Bournemouth

4.　Mame Biram Diouf (Stoke City) 34.97 km/h vs. Norwich

5.　Jamie Vardy (Leicester) 34.95 km/h vs. Bournemouth

6.　Carl Jenkinson (West Ham) 34.89km/h vs. Leicester

7.　Carl Jenkinson (West Ham) 34.80km/h vs. Bournemouth

8.　Wes Morgan (Leicester) 34.76 km/h vs. Bournemouth

9.　Cedric Soares (Southampton) 34.74 km/h vs. Watford

10.　Mame Biram Diouf (Stoke City) 34.71 km/h vs. Tottenham

THURSDAY, 17 SEPTEMBER

Ranieri told his players that he will buy pizza for the whole squad if they kept a clean sheet against Stoke.

Ranieri said: "Coming back from behind might be exciting, but it is not good. I told them, if you keep a clean sheet, I'll buy pizza for everybody. I think they're waiting for me to offer a hot dog too."

Leicester were now unbeaten after five Premier League games - conceding seven goals - and second in the table, four points behind leaders Manchester City.

Vardy, Schlupp and Albrighton were named as the fastest player in the Premier League as Ranieri compared them to fighter jets. He said: "I say my team is like the RAF, it's fantastic - whoosh whoosh! - I love it."

Stoke had yet to win this season and Ranieri warned his side that they would have to work hard to continue their fine start. "We have to be careful," he said. "My players have been incredible but I have warned them they can't continue to give teams a start because one day you will get punished. There is a very good spirit. They are characters. But I'm very curious - I want to see what they are like when something goes wrong. Every man can go to the ground, but I want to see when they pick themselves up. That is my focus."

SATURDAY, 19 SEPTEMBER
STOKE CITY 2-2 LEICESTER CITY

Leicester came back from two goals down to maintain their unbeaten start to the season.

Vardy held off the home defence to equalise after Mahrez scored his fifth goal of the season from the penalty spot. Bojan, making his first start of the season, gave Stoke an early lead from Marko Arnautović's reverse pass. Jonathan Walters doubled the advantage when captain Wes Morgan was badly at fault for Stoke's second goal, attempting an ill-conceived backpass that fell perfectly into the path of Walters.

The BBC sports website commented: "Claudio Ranieri's Leicester have been one of the stories of the season so far, as three wins and three draws have taken them into third spot in the Premier League, with only Manchester City having gained more points. Last Sunday they scored three times in the last 20 minutes to win 3-2 against Aston Villa and while they could not quite match that feat, their skill and spirit secured them a deserved point."

THREE IN A ROW

Arnautović allowed Leicester a route back into the game, forcing down Danny Drinkwater early in the second half for the penalty converted by Mahrez. Vardy's equaliser was his fourth goal of the season and reward for how he unsettled the Stoke defence after the break, but it was also his THIRD IN SUCCESSION - something that again didn't hit the headlines. Instead, Mahrez had now been involved in eight goals and was being highly acclaimed in the media.

Ranieri remarked: "The first 12 minutes before Stoke scored we played very well but after that they scored a very, very good goal and we were making too many mistakes, losing a lot of balls in the middle of the pitch. We need to start games better so we are not always fighting back." His team were third and the Italian manager added: "The spirit is good. It is good for the table and important for us to work during training."

Mark Hughes commented: "We were good value for being 2-0 up and talked at half-time about not letting Leicester back early in the second half and that's what happened. We made a mistake on the penalty and at 2-1 we had to deal with their momentum. We then made a mistake for their second goal but maybe we were distracted by the foul on Jonathan Walters at the other end. We picked up a point but should have had three."

Leicester are the first team since Everton in 2012 (6) to claim at least a point from being behind in four successive Premier League fixtures. Leicester are unbeaten after six games for only the second time in a PL season (they were unbeaten after eight in 2000-01).

TUESDAY, 22 SEPTEMBER
LEICESTER CITY 2-1 WEST HAM UNITED
LEAGUE CUP - THIRD ROUND

Unbeaten Leicester ended West Ham's three-match winning run on the road to progress into the fourth round with an extra-time winner.

West Ham keeper, Adrian, produced several brilliant saves but Andy King's header with four minutes left won it. Twenty-year-old striker Joe Dodoo, who hit a hat-trick in the previous round, opened the scoring with a fine finish from 10 yards. Mauro Zárate levelled midway through the first half with a 25-yard drive. The tie looked destined for a penalty shootout until King guided a Fuchs cross into the top corner.

Ranieri said: "We made a fantastic performance. I think we made 10 great chances to score, their keeper was man of the match. I am very pleased, we were fantastic. We changed 10 players but they played at the same level. They're a great group and they work very hard. I'm very happy. Some of the players have not been used in the Premier League but I believe in them. I told them that I want to go through the rounds and I pick you to play because I believe you can win."

SATURDAY, 26 SEPTEMBER
LEICESTER CITY 2-5 ARSENAL

Alexis Sánchez rediscovered his goalscoring touch as his hat-trick ended Leicester's unbeaten start and there was a huge danger reality would bite, if not within the camp, then certainly outside where all the 'told you so' pundits had a wry smile at this set back.

FOUR IN A ROW

Vardy had put the Foxes ahead with a superb finish from a tight angle after a clinical counter attack, and while it was his FOURTH IN A ROW, the first time in his career, again it was not the big talking point, far from it.

Walcott equalised when Leicester were themselves caught on the break. Sánchez then took control with his treble - the pick his third from long range - as Vardy and Giroud netted late on.

Sánchez, who scored 25 goals last season, had failed to find the net in eight games across all competitions before this contest, and his performance naturally grabbed all the attention and headlines.

Leicester were now without a win against Arsenal in 18 Premier League games, stretching back to November 1994.

It was true enough that Leicester had ridden their luck somewhat in their impressive start to the season, but against one of last term's top four it ran out. It was another pointer that their lofty position was a false one and wouldn't last, and there were few to argue with that theory.

Even when they were winning Ranieri was complaining about how his side must learn to keep clean sheets, offering pizza as an inducement for his players to increase their number of shut-outs.

Arsenal made a poor start the campaign - collecting four points from their first three games - which saw them written off as possible challengers to Manchester City and Chelsea. Back, though, was the attractive one-touch football as they cut through Leicester's back line - albeit one that has now leaked 14 goals.

Wenger side moved up to fourth, three points behind new leaders Manchester United, as Leicester dropped down to sixth and probably now due to slump further. The league table was beginning to have a more familiar feel to it with most pundits sure they were right after all that normal service was being resumed. By the end of the month Leicester had slipped to eighth and were maybe heading towards a relegation battle.

Ranieri remarked: "We must begin again now and repeat this start to the season. We fought and tried everything to score and the match was very open in the first half, but in the second half when Sánchez scored it was finished."

BBC Final Score pundit Jermaine Jenas, to his credit, did find a word of praise for Vardy's goalscoring exploits: "It's such a difficult place to play at Leicester because of all that pace. Jamie Vardy just runs the channels non-stop."

Barclays Premier League Table at the end of September 2015:

POS	CLUB	P	W	D	L	GF	GA	GD	PTS
1	Manchester United	7	5	1	1	12	5	7	16
2	Manchester City	7	5	0	2	13	6	7	15
3	West Ham United	7	4	1	2	15	9	6	13
4	Arsenal	7	4	1	2	10	7	3	13
5	Everton	7	3	3	1	11	7	4	12
6	Tottenham Hotspur	7	3	3	1	9	5	4	12
7	Crystal Palace	7	4	0	3	9	7	2	12
8	Leicester City	7	3	3	1	15	14	1	12

OCTOBER 2015

SATURDAY, 3 OCTOBER

NORWICH CITY 1-2 LEICESTER CITY

At a Carrow Road stadium bathed in Indian summer sun, the home side fell to their second home defeat of the campaign - in front of a record attendance of 27,067 for an all-seater match. The largest ever crowd there on standing terraces was 43,984 back in 1963, when Canaries fans also experienced defeat...to Leicester City.

Leicester bounced back from last weekend's heavy defeat against Arsenal and have now lost just once in their last 10 Premier League games dating back to last season.

FIVE IN A ROW

Vardy struck another penalty as Leicester returned to winning ways, despite Ranieri revealing the striker was playing with two broken bones in his wrist suffered in the match against Villa. Man-of-the-match Vardy was not inhibited in the slightest. He scored one, would have had another but for a fine stoppage-time save by John Ruddy and caused Norwich problems throughout with his pace, movement and endeavour.

Schlupp had put the Foxes in control by slotting in a second, before Norwich's Dieumerci Mbokani scored. Redmond struck the post with a rising, angled drive in the closing minutes, but Leicester held on.

Despite the late flurry, Norwich slipped to 13th place. Leicester moved up to fourth.

Leicester had won more penalties (4) than any other Premier League team this season and Vardy was clearly benefiting.

Ranieri took the bold decision to leave out Mahrez, one of his most influential players. It was met with murmurs of discontent before the game, but the Italian was rewarded for his bold move. The Algerian playmaker's mantle was assumed by Shinji Okazaki, who was a pest to the Norwich defence in tandem with Vardy.

The Japanese forward - signed from German Bundesliga club Mainz in the summer - could not polish his fine performance with a goal, heading over a cross inside the opening seven minutes and skidding a low shot narrowly wide. But he was integral to a wonderful counter-attacking display.

Schlupp commented: "Everyone has seen that we don't lack the fight and team spirit. We can dig deep when we need to. We can adapt to any situation. Jamie Vardy up front terrorises the defenders. He is a pest and always in the defenders' faces."

40 POINTS

Ranieri added: "We responded very well after our defeat against Arsenal. We showed good character and it was a good performance. We have 15 points, 25 less than we need to. After we get that, we will see what happens."

Norwich manager Alex Neil reacted: "Today, for us in the way we played, it did not work. Our use of the ball was not good enough. The lads will be disappointed and did not do themselves justice in the first half. In the second, they tried but it is difficult being two goals down."

THURSDAY, 8 OCTOBER

Mourinho aimed a dig at former Chelsea boss Ranieri.

Ranieri, who spoke very limited English at the time, took charge at Stamford Bridge back in 2000, but was replaced by Mourinho four years later after failing to win a trophy despite heavy investment. Mourinho led Chelsea to two consecutive Premier League titles and three domestic cups following Ranieri's reign before leaving for Inter Milan in 2007. Ranieri went on to coach Valencia, Juventus and Roma before returning to English football in the summer to replace Pearson. Ranieri's great start failed to stop criticism coming from Mourinho, who has come under increasing pressure himself as the reigning champions, Chelsea, languished in 16th place.

He mocked the 63-year-old's grasp of the English language and lack of trophies. "Ranieri? I guess he's right with what he said I am very demanding of myself and I have to win to be sure of things. This is why I have won so many trophies in my career. Ranieri on the other hand has the mentality of someone who doesn't need to win. He is almost 70 years old. He has won a Supercup and another small trophy and he is too old to change his mentality. He's old and he hasn't won anything. I studied Italian five hours a day for many months to ensure I could communicate with the players, media and fans. Ranieri had been in England for five years and still struggled to say 'good morning' and 'good afternoon.'"

FRIDAY, 9 OCTOBER

England made it nine wins out of nine in their Euro 2016 qualifying campaign with a comfortable 2-0 win over Estonia at Wembley. Hodgson's side had already qualified for France, and even without Rooney were able to dismiss Estonia with barely an anxious moment. Rooney received a Golden Boot from Sir Bobby Charlton before kick-off after breaking his England goalscoring record with his 50th goal from the penalty spot in the last qualifier against Switzerland at Wembley.

There was barely a moment of note in the first 45 minutes until man-of-the-match Ross Barkley picked out Theo Walcott with a superb pass to score with the last kick of the half and England sealed it in the dying moments when substitute Vardy unselfishly set up a second from close range for Raheem Sterling in front of the Wembley crowd of 75,427.

MONDAY, 12 OCTOBER

Jamie Vardy proudly wore the No 9 shirt as England beat Lithuania 3-0 in Vilnius to finish with a 100 per cent record in European Championship qualifying for the first time in their history.

Roy Hodgson's side led 2-0 at the break after a strike from Barkley and an own goal by Lithuania goalkeeper Giedrius Arlauskis. Alex Oxlade-Chamberlain added a well-taken goal just past the hour-mark.

SATURDAY, 17 OCTOBER
SOUTHAMPTON 2-2 LEICESTER CITY

Here we go again - two goals down again. No problem.

SIX IN A ROW

Step up Vardy yet again, the Premier league top scorer. He pulled a goal back with a header and blasted home the equaliser in injury time his ninth of the season. The point left the team in a more than reasonable fifth position, still thinking of points for safety not for anything else, not even a Europa League place.

As the incredible sequence of goals continues virtually unnoticed, Ranieri commented: "Jamie Vardy is very important for us. I believe in this team. When we are desperate we make more, more and more."

The Foxes scored in every Premier League match this season and, sparked into life by the half-time introduction of Mahrez and Dyer, they earned an unlikely point with a stunning final 45 minutes. Southampton were in complete control at half-time but, with the trickery of Mahrez and the clinical finishing of Vardy, the Foxes again showed they should never be ruled out.

Vardy was playing with a double fracture to his wrist, but now had three more goals than any of his Premier League rivals. He scored twice from four shots on target, having nine shots in all.

The introduction of substitutes Mahrez and Dyer at the start of the second half changed the pattern of the game. Mahrez created numerous chances playing just behind Vardy. His pass created the equaliser while Swansea City loanee Dyer made a big impact on the wing, crossing for Vardy's opener.

Southampton should have had the game out of sight, with Sadio Mané delaying after rounding Schmeichel when 2-0 up.

The draw was the seventh point Leicester have earned from a losing position this season.

Vardy became just the fourth Englishman to score in six consecutive Premier League matches this century when he headed home to give the Foxes hope after the break. Before he hammered in the late equaliser the striker shot over from close range and was a constant threat after the break.

Ronald Koeman, Saints manager, on BBC Sport commented: "It was a difficult game. Defensively we did well in the first half and we scored from set pieces. But I expected a difficult second half because we know one of Leicester's strengths is unbelievable spirit and we have to be more clever. They deserved at least one point. They did two good changes after half-time. Mahrez created difficulties for us."

Ranieri added on BBC Sport: "We have fantastic spirit. We believe everything could be possible. We created a lot of chances. It is important to have good players on the bench and I have very good players who can change the match."

SATURDAY, 24 OCTOBER

LEICESTER CITY 1-0 CRYSTAL PALACE

Vardy is known for his all-action style of play, but here he demonstrated he also has the technical ability. He showed composure by nicking the ball over the goalkeeper and slotting in the winner as Leicester moved up to fourth place.

SEVEN IN A ROW

Vardy scored in his seventh successive Premier League game when he pounced after Brede Hangeland's error, nicking the ball over keeper, Wayne Hennessey, and blasting home from all of three yards. His goal settled a poor game with Palace coming closest to an equaliser through Scott Dann's looping header.

Wilfried Zaha was booked late on for a dive in a tangle with Christian Fuchs as The Eagles had a second late penalty appeal waved away by referee Mike Dean when Fuchs appeared to handle in the box.

Crystal Palace manager Alan Pardew was angered by the time it took Ranieri to return the ball from the sidelines for a throw-in in the second half.

Pardew commented: "It was a tight game, Leicester weren't really going anywhere and it was a mistake that cost us the game. I thought Claudio Ranieri was goading our players and he didn't shake my hand at full-time, which is disappointing. But it's a long game and they've got to come to our place and we'll remember that."

40 POINTS

Ranieri countered: "I took the ball because it was our ball. Maybe now I meet Alan Pardew in my dressing room. It was a more Italian than English match apart from the last 10 minutes. We battled well and deserved to win. We are taking it step-by-step. It's important to achieve 40 points, that is our first goal."

Leicester claimed their 100th Premier League win in this match. Drinkwater recorded 88 touches; no Leicester City player has managed more in a single PL matches this season.

Ranieri had promised his players that he would buy them pizza to reward their first clean sheet of the season. After conceding in all 11 of their matches in league and cup, they finally forced their boss to pay up.

Vardy joined a select group of seven - including Thierry Henry, Alan Shearer and Ruud van Nistelrooy - to have scored in seven straight Premier League games. He scored 14 in his last 20 Premier League games, having managed only one in his previous 24 top-flight appearances. His latest goal showed his best qualities - an electric turn of pace and composure in front of goal. He also matched it with a high workrate; one of four Leicester players to cover more than five kilometres during the match and registered his team's second-highest number of sprints behind Albrighton.

Vardy's strike put him top of the Premier League scoring charts with 10, four more than any other player.

He'd had a hand in 19 goals in his last 20 Premier League appearances with 14 goals and five assists, and became only the fifth different English player to score in seven or more successive Premier League games after Alan Shearer (7), Ian Wright (7), Mark Stein (7) and Daniel Sturridge (8).

Ranieri was full of praise for his relentless goalscorer: "Jamie Vardy is fantastic because every ball could be good for him. The spirit is fantastic and is one of our strengths, we never give up."

TUESDAY, 27 OCTOBER

HULL CITY 1-1 LEICESTER CITY (HULL WON 5-4 ON PENS)

LEAGUE CUP - FOURTH ROUND

Championship side Hull shocked high-flyers Leicester winning on penalties to move into the quarter-finals of the League Cup.

David Meyler struck the winning fifth penalty as the Tigers scored all their efforts, with Mahrez hitting the post. After 90 goalless minutes, Mahrez put Leicester ahead in extra-time, tapping in after Vardy's shot was saved. Hernandez levelled on 106 minutes, taking the game to a shootout.

Ranieri had made 10 changes as his priorities were in the league. Hull goalkeeper Eldin Jakupović was the hero in the shootout, denying Mahrez as Hull progressed to the last eight of the competition for the first time in their history.

Ranieri commented: "It was important to use all our players tonight. In the end we lost to one penalty so well done to Hull City. Of course I'm not pleased with the result, but the performance was good. We wanted to go through, but it was one mistake."

Hull boss Steve Bruce: "We made eight changes and beat a Premier League team, which was terrific."

THURSDAY, 29 OCTOBER

The pre-match routine, ahead of the trip to West Bromwich Albion, was slightly different than normal.

Following the clean sheet against Crystal Palace, Claudio Ranieri kept his promise of a pizza as a reward and treated the team to a lunch, but with a twist. Arriving at Peter Pizzeria, the players soon discovered that they were free to enjoy their lunch, but only after they'd made the pizzas themselves.

Boss, Ranieri told lcfc.com : "I pay! I think they deserve this pizza and today we will eat. It's good to stay together for something good (other than) football. I think also this could help to make a very good spirit for each other. I hope they enjoy it today. The most important ingredient for us is team spirit. The second is that they enjoy the training sessions. That is important when they come, they know they can work hard but also enjoy."

SATURDAY, 31 OCTOBER

WEST BROMWICH ALBION 2-3 LEICESTER CITY

On an unseasonably warm day, Leicester Tigers' fans were probably more interested in the Rugby World Cup Final. But for the football fans of Leicester it was all eyes on The Hawthorns.

EIGHT IN A ROW

Vardy's incredible goalscoring run almost came to an end against the Baggies when he went down injured - but after treatment he returned to the pitch and netted his side's third goal taking the team into third place.

Ranieri commented: "It's important Jamie Vardy continues to work for the team. The record is good for everybody."

Vardy scored for the eighth game in a row to help inspire a thrilling come back from a goal down as the team remained unbeaten on their travels. It was all the more impressive as West Brom had not conceded a goal in their last two outings.

Mahrez's two goals in seven minutes provoked a strong reaction from Albion, but Vardy's strike looked to have secured a comfortable win for Leicester. Late substitute Ricky Lambert forced a save from close range in the dying seconds after grabbing his first goal since moving to The Hawthorns.

Minutes before he had extended his scoring streak, Vardy's participation in the rest of the game looked in doubt as he went down clutching his right ankle, and had extensive treatment on the pitch, but the magic sponge did the trick with his 11th goal of the season arriving only a few seconds later.

Leicester had forced the pace in the opening half-an-hour, with Vardy hitting the post after just seven minutes. But they did not take several other chances, and West Brom made the most of their first real opportunity when Salomón Rondón's powerful header beat Schmeichel. Albion's defence had held firm in their two previous outings, but they were caught by teasing crosses from Albrighton from either side of the pitch for both of Mahrez's goals.

Vardy's pace tested the back line, and he used it to good effect when slicing through to make it 3-1.

West Brom manager Tony Pulis commented: "Leicester did really well, it was a good game and in Jamie Vardy they have an exceptional player. His pace frightened us all afternoon. But the referee should have given us a penalty and sent their man off. It shouldn't happen at this level - the standard of refereeing should be better. (Referees' chief) Mike Riley should be on the phone asking why we weren't given two penalties. I've had a go in the tunnel with him and I apologise about that. I should be writing my report but I do hope they look at it."

Ranieri added: "We fight to the end. We have a very strong character and play good football. I told my players they were playing very well at half-time, to be careful at set-plays, and it was important to move the ball quickly and put them under pressure. We did that well."

Interestingly, 15 of the last 17 goals had come in the second half as Leicester City claimed 10 points from losing positions; a league-high.

Barclays Premier League Table at the end of October 2015:

POS	CLUB	P	W	D	L	GF	GA	GD	PTS
1	Manchester City	11	8	1	2	26	9	17	25
2	Arsenal	11	8	1	2	21	8	13	25
3	Leicester City	11	6	4	1	23	19	4	22

NOVEMBER 2015

THURSDAY, 5 NOVEMBER

England manager Roy Hodgson selected Vardy for the prestigious friendlies with reigning Euro champions Spain and Euro 2016 hosts France, then warned him to forget about demanding to play as a centre-forward for the Three Lions, despite his current red-hot form for his club.

Vardy was the Premier League's 11-goal top scorer and wants to play through the middle after his two starts for England so far came on the wing. But Hodgson said: "When you have only played two games, you are in no position to go to the coach and say, 'I will play for England but only in this position.' That is the point I am trying to make. I am just trying to defuse hype and make one very important point which is very, very obvious to anyone who has been following England for a long time. That is: An England shirt is a very valuable commodity. I think Jamie Vardy can play in any of the front three positions. Jamie has only played a couple of games from the start. He should be happy at the moment a) to be in the squad and b) even happier if he makes the team. His job, I think, should be definitely to try to convince that he has got the ability to play as a forward in an England team and not get too hung up like some people if he only plays *here* (in a certain position)."

Vardy was on the brink of making Premier League history after scoring in eight consecutive games, two short of Ruud van Nistelrooy's record; a remarkable success story for the 28-year-old, who only got called up for the first time in May, having restarted a career that stalled when released by Sheffield Wednesday as a 16-year-old and subsequently played in non-league with Stocksbridge, Halifax and Fleetwood before his £1m move to Leicester in 2012.

The unflappable England manager was surprised by Vardy's remarkable rise, but did not want him to get carried away.

Hodgson added: "I would be lying if I didn't say I was surprised, pleasantly surprised. When we selected him, I don't think there were a lot of people in the room saying 'Fantastic - that is a great idea as Jamie Vardy is the obvious man'. He wasn't actually playing as a 100 per cent regular for Leicester not so long back - he had some spells on the bench. Now he is their main man. Now he is the top goal-scorer in the league. Now he has got a record at his fingertips. There is no doubt the qualities he has a football player are very useful. (And) They may be useful qualities for an international team."

SATURDAY, 7 NOVEMBER
LEICESTER CITY 2-1 WATFORD

Another injury scare for Jamie Vardy, this time going down holding his groin.

NINE IN A ROW

But nothing was going to stop Vardy on his mission, though, and he demonstrated that he can hold his nerve. Another from the spot, another win. Vardy had scored for a ninth successive Premier League game as Leicester went level on points with Manchester City and Arsenal at the top.

BBC Sport pundit John Hartson commented: "Jamie Vardy's form is incredible. If he is fit and raring to go, he should start for England."

Vardy got Leicester's second from the spot, converting after he was tripped by Watford goalkeeper Heurelho Gomes. Gomes, impressive so far this season, inexplicably gifted the hosts the lead with a comical error that gave Kanté his first goal for Leicester. The midfielder showed good skill inside the area, wriggling away from three defenders, but could only manage a tame shot. Gomes allowed the ball through his hands, under his body and into the corner of the net.

Vardy had been kept quiet by an organised Watford defence in the first half and was even the subject of an injury scare after Leicester took the lead. Jumping to control the ball with no other player around him, Vardy landed awkwardly and was in discomfort as he lay on the ground, holding his groin. After receiving treatment he produced a moment typical of his season. Running clear of the Watford defence, he latched on to a through ball and was only stopped by a clumsy challenge from the onrushing Gomes, bringing him down edge of the 18-yard box for a penalty. Vardy, handed the ball by regular penalty-taker Mahrez, smashed the spot-kick high into the net.

Only Ruud van Nistelrooy, with 10, scored in more successive Premier League games than Vardy. Vardy is the only player to score in nine consecutive games in the same Premier League season, as Van Nistelrooy's goals came between March and August 2003.

A Troy Deeney penalty in the 75th minute gave Watford hope, but a seventh win of the season took Leicester behind the top two on goal difference alone.

The 25 points from 12 games is as many as they managed in their first 31 last term.

Leicester once again improved after the break - 17 of their last 19 league goals have come in the second half.

After the two-week international break, Leicester went to Newcastle where Vardy looked to score for a record-equalling 10th successive game...

40 POINTS

Ranieri commented: "We could not have imagined this, but it is only November. It's not May. We still have to achieve 40 points first. Jamie is fantastic. He'll be fit for England. After the goal he continued to run and fight - he's OK. It is important to continue the momentum. It's not easy for us, but we are very ambitious."

Watford manager Quique Sanchez Flores remarked: "We have to accept that there are accidents in football sometimes. Heurelho knows he has our support, it is the style of this team. He feels he is guilty, but the rest of us don't feel that way. We are really happy with his performance in general. We had lots of possession of the ball. Leicester were playing for the counter-attack and we didn't always use the possession of the ball in the right way."

THURSDAY, 12 NOVEMBER

Vardy was Hodgson's only injury concern as he picked up a knock in the Foxes' victory over Watford and was doubtful.

FRIDAY, 13 NOVEMBER

England slumped to their first defeat in 16 games as they were comfortably beaten by Spain in Alicante 2-0. Roy Hodgson's side breezed through their Euro 2016 qualifying campaign but this friendly was a reality check as their flaws were exposed by the reigning champions. England held out for 72 minutes until Mario scored with a superb acrobatic finish from Fàbregas' cross before Santi Cazorla slotted in a late second.

Vardy, due to injury, was not in the squad for this game nor for the game against France on Tuesday.

TUESDAY, 17 NOVEMBER

England beat France on an emotional night as more than 70,000 fans honoured the victims of the Paris attacks. Fans united to sing La Marseillaise - the French national anthem - in front of the Duke of Cambridge and Prime Minister David Cameron at Wembley. The French Football Federation chose to go ahead with the fixture despite Friday's attacks in Paris that left 129 people dead. Roy Hodgson and his France counterpart Didier Deschamps embraced after joining Prince William, President of the Football Association, in laying flowers for those killed and there was a perfectly observed minute's silence, with both sets of players standing in solidarity.

Alli scored on his full England debut, a fine 25-yard finish, before Rooney's volley sealed victory. England's 10th and final game of the calendar year brought a seventh victory yet this was a night when the result, tactics and performance were secondary.

SATURDAY, 21 NOVEMBER

NEWCASTLE UNITED 0-3 LEICESTER CITY

With the international break over, all eyes were once again focused on the League and, in particular, on Jamie Vardy.

TEN IN A ROW

Vardy joined Ruud van Nistelrooy in the record books by scoring in 10 straight league games after netting just before half-time. Better news was to come as Manchester City and Arsenal lost, leaving Leicester top of the table following an impressive sequence of four wins in a row in the league.

A delighted Ranieri commented: "It is fantastic for Jamie Vardy. He is a great champion and did well in training. I am glad because we played like a team. I also had Gabriel Batistuta at Fiorentina score in 11 consecutive matches and I hope Jamie can achieve this."

Vardy latched on to a Leonardo Ulloa pass, cut inside Sissoko and drilled in a low shot. Newcastle barely registered a threat and let in a second when Ulloa headed in a Mahrez cross. Okazaki bundled in a third after Simpson's shot was saved.

Manchester City lost at home to Liverpool, and Arsenal were beaten at West Brom.

Vardy was in fact a doubt for the match, having missed England's two games during the international break with a hip injury. He was passed fit and went close when Mahrez played him through on goal only for keeper Elliot to rush out and block the forward's shot. Shortly afterwards, Ulloa played the ball into his angled run from the left flank and he clinically finished for his 13th goal.

"The physios have done brilliantly to get me fit," said Vardy, who also grazed the crossbar with a shot before Ulloa's effort. "We know we can cause teams problems and are solid at the back too. We have a never-say-die attitude and will fight for each other until the end."

Robert Huth pushed Mitrović in the throat during the first half, with the Magpies forward falling to the ground. Referee Mike Jones gave both players a talking to but no cards. Huth was later booked for a foul on Sissoko when the Magpies tried to launch a counter-attack from a Foxes corner.

It was Newcastle's first defeat in three league games after a win and a draw in their previous two outings had suggested signs of slow progress being made under McClaren, but there were boos at the final whistle from the ones who had not left early. The home side suffered an early setback with Tioté going off injured but they were poor. Schmeichel was rarely troubled, apart from when a Wijnaldum header was cleared off the goal-line.

Leicester had now scored in 14 successive Premier League matches. This was Ulloa's 44th Premier League appearance, but the first time he scored and assisted in the same game.

Vardy had to "pinch" himself. "There's a lot of hard work gone into it and long may it continue," Vardy told BBC Sport. "My feet are on the ground. I've not set myself any targets. I just wanted to improve on last year, which I've done."

40 POINTS

Leicester's eighth win in 13 games - 15th in 22 dating back to last term - took the Foxes top but Vardy insisted achieving safety remains their priority. "We have to keep picking points up and as soon as we get to 40 we can reassess. When we get there, we'll look at what we can achieve."

That approach was shared by Ranieri, who said he wants his team to "be safe".

THURSDAY, 26 NOVEMBER

Leicester were serious title contenders, according to Louis van Gaal, as recognition of their team ethic and individual brilliance had caught the eye of the United boss about to tackle them for himself.

The Foxes were top of the table, one point ahead of second-place United. When asked if Ranieri's team could win the league, Van Gaal said: "It is possible, I think."

Van Gaal called Vardy, the league's 13-goal top scorer, a "nasty" player to face.

Vardy had marked his first Premier League start by making four goals and scoring the other as the Foxes beat United 5-3 back in September 2014. He now equalled Van Nistelrooy's record of scoring in 10 successive Premier League games, and could break it on Saturday. "He was already a very nasty player for us last year," Van Gaal said of Vardy. "He scores, he provoked a penalty, now scoring 10 goals in a row, he is a great player. I only know Dennis Bergkamp as a player who did the same with Ajax. It's not so easy to do that."

40 POINTS

Wenger said Leicester "cannot be ruled out" as contenders but Ranieri says survival is the immediate aim. "Thank you to Arsene but he's a joker. He knows the truth very well. The league is very strange and open but our goal is 40 points." Ranieri added: "Our goal at the moment is this but let me see the next two months and then maybe I change the goal. Like everybody else I am also curious in these days to watch my team, and to see how we respond in these big matches."

Ranieri might have called Wenger "a joker" for suggesting that Leicester were title contenders, but Van Gaal thinks they can sustain their form. "Normally these kind of clubs can compete for long time, then at the end it becomes more difficult, but in England because of the quality of the teams, because every team has the money to buy players - and they have bought players - the difference in the Premier League between the clubs is not so high."

At a news conference before Leicester hosted second-placed United, Ranieri was asked about Leicester's ambitions for the future - and whether he would understand if Vardy wanted to leave to further his career as he stood on the threshold of breaking Van Nistelrooy's record. "I hope for him he can break it. Jamie deserves it. I think we are building a very good construction. Jamie can continue to show his strength with us. Him, Riyad Mahrez, and everybody. I believe that next year Leicester's role is going to go up and (will) become a battle with the top. I spoke to the owners in July and this is our project. It is an ambitious project but I said: 'OK, I am ready'. People believe in me - I believe in me too."

Van Gaal was criticised, with former coach René Meulensteen following ex-midfielder Paul Scholes in bemoaning the side's style of play. Ranieri had come up against Van Gaal seven times in his career as a manager - losing four, winning three - but gave his backing to the Dutchman's work at Old Trafford. "He is a fantastic manager. The respect is very big. Under him United are slowly, slowly getting better, he is building. From last season to this season, now the defence line is fantastic and it is difficult to break their lines. When you play against great teams, you have to see how your team reacts. For us this is another match to know where we have to improve."

Leicester confirmed they would enforce strict security measures following the Paris attacks. There will be a no readmission policy, no storage within the stadium will be available for baggage, while fans must have photo identification to collect tickets. The club asked supporters to arrive early at the King Power Stadium and no cans or bottles would be allowed into the ground.

FRIDAY, 27 NOVEMBER

Jamie Vardy was planning a new academy to seek the next stars of non-league football. Vardy was at Fleetwood in 2012 when they were a non-league side but was now the Premier League's top scorer.

The aim of Vardy's 'V9 Academy' is to discover hidden talent and stop players drifting away from the game. "I know there are players out there in a similar position to where I was that just need an opportunity," he said. "More and more players are dropping out of the system early. For me, it was at Sheffield Wednesday when I was 16 because they thought I was too small. I remember how that felt and it's difficult to come back from or even think about the professional game."

The former Stocksbridge Park Steels and Halifax forward, whose goals helped Leicester to the top of the Premier League, told BBC Football Focus: "I want to give people the shot I was given because there are some talented players in non-league. There are a lot of teams which won't take the gamble and probably will rather pay over the odds to get a player who has the experience but they might not do it either. With teams taking a risk on non-league players it will only benefit the game and make the English game altogether a lot better."

He will accept applications for his academy in May 2016 and, after a selection process, 60 non-league players will be given the chance on a week-long course in summer 2017.

SATURDAY, 28 NOVEMBER
LEICESTER CITY 1-1 MANCHESTER UNITED

Yes. He's done it! Vardy became a record-breaker, getting on the end of Fuchs' through ball and slotting past David de Gea. No guessing the man-of-the-match, then.

Former Leicester defender Matt Elliott: "Oh my word! The whole stadium is up on its feet, myself included! It was an inch-perfect ball in behind the United defence, and Jamie Vardy was onto it in a flash. What a finish, what quality!"

ELEVEN IN A ROW

Vardy wrote his name into Premier League history by scoring for the 11th successive game - but both teams missed the chance to go top with this draw.

Vardy, wearing golden boots, went into this game hoping to eclipse former United striker Ruud van Nistelrooy's record, set across two seasons in 2003 and he savoured his moment in the 24th minute, running on to Fuchs' pass to send a low, powerful finish past De Gea. Fuchs registered his first assist in the Premier League for Vardy's goal, becoming the seventh Austrian to provide an assist for a Premier League goal.

Vardy, who four years ago was playing for Fleetwood in the Conference in front of 768 people, said he was "taking each match as it comes". He added: "The record was not in my mind, it would have affected my performance and the team's, and that's the last thing I wanted to do. I can think about it when I am home but as soon as I cross the white line all I should be concentrating on is my football. That's what I have been doing and exactly what I will continue to do."

Ranieri said Vardy's record was "an incredible achievement. We had two objectives - to win the match and try to help Vardy break the record," he said. "Jamie made the record, it is fantastic for us. Five years ago he played in non-league, it is difficult to grow up so quickly and this fantastic man is not only our goalscorer but he presses, he works hard, he is important."

Louis van Gaal also praised Vardy's "amazing and fantastic" feat, saying: "The goal he scored is also amazing because it is not so easy. I can say our organisation is bad but he is provoking that also. It is a fantastic record to have, 11 matches in a row. Not many players will do that."

Bastian Schweinsteiger headed United's equaliser right on half-time and despite plenty of energy from both sides after the break, the stalemate left Manchester City at the Premier League summit.

Man of the day - and of the season so far - irrespective of the result was Vardy as he scored the goal that wrote his name in the Premier League record books. There was not a trace of nerves as he darted between two United defenders and on to Fuchs' pass to race clear and beat goalkeeper De Gea with a precise finish. As the King Power Stadium rocked to a crescendo of noise and Vardy took the acclaim, it was time to reflect on the sort of finish that has become his trademark in a golden season for the striker who has made his way from Stocksbridge Park Steel in the non-league to England recognition and history maker. Vardy's 14 goals make him the highest scoring Leicester player in a single Premier League season, one above Tony Cottee who scored 13 in 1999-2000.

What a story - and what an example to any youngsters or non-league players fighting their way up the ladder. It was in stark contrast to England captain Rooney, on £300,000-a-week, who suffered another game of toil and struggle before he was substituted by Louis van Gaal after 67 minutes.

There were just two passes in the counter attack that led to Vardy's record-breaking goal as Vardy took Fuchs' pass in his stride and fired an unerring low finish past De Gea - and the tributes came instantly from the football world. In fact, in the minute after Vardy scored there were 26,839 tweets mentioning the Leicester striker's name - not surprisingly he was 'trending'.

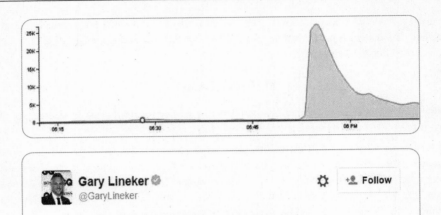

Gary Lineker ✅
@GaryLineker

⚙ +👤 Follow

Vardy! He scores when he wants.

Tottenham defender Kyle Walker, who is from the same city as Vardy:

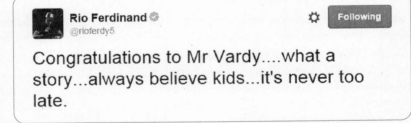

Kyle Walker ✅
@kylewalker2

⚙ +👤 Follow

Take a bow @vardy7 #recordbreaker #Sheffield 👏

Rio Ferdinand ✅
@rioferdy5

⚙ Following

Congratulations to Mr Vardy....what a story...always believe kids...it's never too late.

Paul konchesky ✅
@konch3

⚙ +👤 Follow

Absolutely buzzing for my man @vardy7 breaking the record! Fully deserved pal keep it going m8! #JAMIE Vardy having a party ⚽⚽🍺🍺🍺

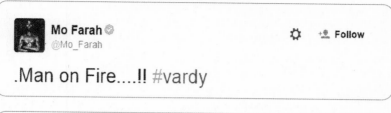

Ruud van Nistelrooy was setting his 10-game record in 2003, as the then 16-year-old Vardy was being released by hometown club Sheffield Wednesday.

Vardy now needed to score in his next two games to equal the all-time record of consecutive goals scored at the top level of English football, set by Jimmy Dunne back in 1931-32. Playing for Sheffield United, Dunne scored 12 goals in succession. Stan Mortensen hit 15 goals in consecutive games for Blackpool in the 1950-51 season, but he missed matches during that run because of injury, recovering to continue scoring when he returned to the side.

If Vardy is the man of the season, then Leicester were the team of the season, yet question marks persisted whether they would last the distance.

40 POINTS

Ranieri added: "The whole team are in very good physical condition and they have a good mentality. They want to do their best until the end, and if the opponent is better than us on the day then well done to the opponent. Our first priority remains 40 points - that is our goal, to keep us in the Premier League. As soon as we get there we can look to take another step."

Van Gaal said: "I am very disappointed. It was a feeling that we could have won this game and we didn't. We gave the goal away and the other chances we had we gave away as well. We could have lost as well in spite of our dominance and I think when you want to be the champion at the end of the season, and the players, managers and supporters all want that, you have to win these kind of games. We created not so many chances but that was also because there were many chances in a very compact pitch."

MONDAY, 30 NOVEMBER

FLEETWOOD TO HOLLYWOOD

The story of Vardy's rise from non-League striker to Premier League record-breaker could be made into a Hollywood blockbuster. Vardy's remarkable story was being considered for the big screen with British writer Adrian Butchart, who co-wrote the first and second parts of football trilogy *Goal!*, set to discuss a deal in Los Angeles. "It's the kind of story that if we made it up, people wouldn't believe it," Butchart commented, "His achievements are incredible and to break the Premier League record with such a sublime goal against the biggest club in football pushed him to the top of our agenda. It's amazing to think he was playing non-League football and making medical splints for a living until so recently before breaking the record. It is the kind of role actors dream of."

Butchart touted Hollywood stars Robert Pattinson, Zac Efron and Andrew Garfield to play the role of Vardy.

The record breaker had been playing with broken bones in his wrist since September and following his strike for the 11th successive Premier League game with Manchester United he now needed to freeze a sore foot. Ranieri had suggested Vardy sit one out or take a breather on the bench. The rebuttals are immediate. "I think it's just getting common knowledge now, I'm getting an injury every week," said Vardy. "I never want to not play, it's as simple as that. I want to play as many games as I can and help the team out in as good a way as I can. We got a point against United which is good. I took a little knock on top of my foot. I've had it iced and I'm sure it will be fine by next week. As soon as you start running again it warms up so you don't really feel it that much."

Ranieri added: "Jamie, he forgets everything when there is a ball. He had a pain during the match, maybe he got a kick on some bone. I said to him, 'Are you ok, do you want me to change it?' because I saw him a little tired. 'No, no, no, I am good.' Then he is a great threat for the opponents."

During the escape from relegation Vardy kept playing through the use of pain-killing injections in the hours before kick-off, having damaged tissue in his foot that affects sprinting. The same method was used before the encounter at Newcastle - when Vardy scored for the 10th game in a row - to help him recover from the hip injury that kept him out of England's friendlies against Spain and France.

Contrast that to Jürgen Klopp on Daniel Sturridge last week. Sturridge had appeared 22 times for Liverpool since August 2014 and Klopp, while advocating patience, also said: "You have to learn what is serious pain and what is only pain."

Ranieri believes the spirit of his squad will be a factor in any decision Vardy needs to make despite being linked with Chelsea. "The camaraderie is fantastic," said the Leicester manager. "I think this is the secret; the players fight for each other. I just put my Italian tactics, my knowledge, and they respond very well. It is a very, very good group, one of the best I've found in my career. Now they believe everything is possible. We have to build."

In the House of Commons Leicester East MP, Keith Vaz, proposed an 'Early day motion* 792':

JAMIE VARDY'S 11TH SUCCESSIVE PREMIER LEAGUE GOAL

Session: 2015-16

Date tabled: 30.11.2015

Primary sponsor: Vaz, Keith

Sponsors: Day, Martyn. Thomas, Gareth (Harrow West). Meale, Alan. Robinson, Gavin. Vaz, Valerie.

That this House congratulates Jamie Vardy on becoming the first player in Premier League history to score in 11 consecutive matches; considers that this historic achievement brings credit to himself, Leicester City Football Club and the City of Leicester; and urges him to continue with his goal scoring success which has made 2015 an outstanding year for all at the King Power Stadium.

*Early Day Motions (EDMs) are formal motions submitted for debate in the House of Commons. However, very few are actually debated. EDMs allow MPs to draw attention to an event or cause. MPs register their support by signing individual motions.

Barclays Premier League Table at the end of November 2015:

POS	CLUB	P	W	D	L	GF	GA	GD	PTS
1	Manchester City	14	9	2	3	30	14	16	29
2	Leicester City	14	8	5	1	29	21	8	29
3	Manchester United	14	8	4	2	20	10	10	28

DECEMBER 2015

SATURDAY, 5 DECEMBER

SWANSEA CITY 0-3 LEICESTER CITY

Riyad Mahrez's hat-trick propelled Leicester to the top as they beat Swansea to increase the pressure on manager Garry Monk.

Mahrez headed the Foxes in front after five minutes and then fired in calmly for his second, although he seemed offside. Ki Sung-yueng headed against the bar after the break for Swansea, but Mahrez finished an incisive counter-attack to seal his first ever hat-trick.

Manchester City's defeat to Stoke had presented Leicester with the opportunity to reclaim their place at the top of the table and, as Ranieri's men have done so often this season, they seized the opportunity. Mahrez became the first Algerian player to score a Premier League hat-trick. He had now been involved in 16 Premier League goals this season (10 goals, 6 assists) - a record only team-mate Vardy can match (14 goals, 2 assists). He became only the third Leicester player to score a Premier League hat-trick, after Ian Marshall and Stan Collymore. The Foxes have lost just one of their last 19 top-flight games (W12 D6) as Ranieri's side were the only team to have scored in all 15 games this season.

The pre-match attention was inevitably focused on Vardy, who had set a Premier League record, but instead had to be content with a supporting role as Mahrez took centre stage. The Algerian's first two goals were fortuitous, but they were no more than Ranieri's side deserved for a dominant first half. Mahrez's opening goal was a scrappy one, the ball flicked on from a corner, hitting his head and arm before trickling over the line. The second was confidently swept into the bottom corner, but he should have been offside from N'Golo Kanté's pass.

Leicester were now two points clear at the top and, with the busy festive period looming, they find themselves in the unlikely position of being genuine title challengers.

Monk commented: "It was a poor first half from us. Those first two goals were extremely soft. The first one was clearly handball, the second was clearly offside, but the results haven't been good enough in this period."

40 POINTS

Ranieri was still insisting safety was the priority: "We are thinking about ourselves, to take points and make good football. That is our first goal, to achieve 40 points, to be safe. It was a tough match because Swansea play very good football. We started very well, we scored three goals, and had a minimum other four clear chances and I'm very pleased. Our fans they must dream, but we must stay calm and keep our feet on the ground."

MONDAY, 7 DECEMBER

Sir Alex Ferguson believed Leicester City can win the league. Such a public declaration of faith, from someone like Sir Alex had many starting to believe the impossible was possible. Sir Alex, though, felt it was vital they invested in January to ensure they had a strong enough squad to last the course.

Currently two points clear, Ranieri maintained that reaching 40 points - they had 32 - remained their priority.

Fergie, in contrast though, thought they should set their sights much higher now they have got themselves in contention. "I was listening to Peter Schmeichel last week and what he was saying was fantastic talking about how people are under-estimating Leicester City. This is a team with fantastic vitality, speed, energy. Peter was saying at the moment Leicester are the best team in the league, without a doubt. But, the question is, how long will it last? Have they the resources to continue throughout the season? For instance, back in 92-93 when we won the league for the first time, Norwich led the league until the middle of March, the whole season. But we beat them at their own ground and won the league. So, for a small club historically as Leicester City, they have a challenge, how far can they go with this present squad, can they last the whole season? If I were him (Ranieri) I'd want an investment in January because this is a big opportunity. They could win the league, the way they are playing at the moment, and they have goals in their team. The problem for the owners is have they got the money? I think they have. If he wants to win the league I think he should add to it. And I think there may be a great chance."

He warned that their success could come at a price - their star players becoming wanted men; top scorers, Jamie Vardy and winger Riyad Mahrez, were Leicester's two biggest assets, scoring 24 league goals between them already.

Speaking at the TechCrunch Disrupt (since you ask: "TechCrunch Disrupt is the world's leading authority in debuting revolutionary startups, introducing game-changing technologies, and discussing what's top of mind for the tech industry's key innovators") conference in London, Fergie said: "When Aberdeen won the European Cup Winners' Cup it was the greatest moment for Aberdeen in their history and it was the worst moment too because five players left within a year because they wanted to better themselves. Gordon Strachan went to Manchester United, Mark McGhee went to Hamburg. It is going to be a big decision at the end of the season, not so much for the owners but the players themselves. Miller and McLeish stayed forever (at Aberdeen) because they loved being there. And they may have a situation where they love being at Leicester City and don't want to move and they will have some who do want to move to Manchester United, or they want to play for Liverpool or Real Madrid. It is natural, it is progress. People want to achieve the most they can do."

Fergie had praise for 14-goal striker Vardy, who was linked with a move to Old Trafford and had set a new Premier League record scoring in 11 consecutive games. He added: "Vardy is a great example of never giving in and keeping a great belief in himself. He has got certain assets that suit modern day football, particularly at a club like Leicester City - he is aggressive, he is quick, he has got energy and he got a goal in him. He has proved that."

MONDAY, 14 DECEMBER

LEICESTER CITY 2-1 CHELSEA

Ranieri guided his team back to the top and increased the pressure on Chelsea manager José Mourinho to intolerable and unstainable levels.

Before the match they were selling half-and-half scarves...Claudio Ranieri "The Tinkerman" versus José Mourinho "The Special One".

Ranieri came out on top as the Leicester fans chanted: "We're going to win the league." Leicester City were an astonishing 20 points clear of the champions Chelsea. It was to be a lose too far for the Roman Empire who had, of course, kicked out Ranieri to replace him first time around with Mourinho.

Ranieri still refused to dream along with his fans.

40 POINTS

The Premier League trophy was on the sidelines before the game and Richard Scudamore, the League's Chief Executive, was in the crowd but for Ranieri it was realism first.

"For our fans we are top of the league, for my players we need another five points," he said in the press conference room. Cue chuckles from the hardened hacks. "Don't laugh. It's true," he added. "I don't know when we can achieve these five points. Now there is Everton away, Liverpool away, Manchester City at home and Bournemouth, who are a fantastic team, at home - four very tough games. Let me achieve 40 points, then I'll think about what is the next goal. But until 40 I think only 40 points."

Vardy's 15th goal put Leicester ahead before half-time and Mahrez's brilliant curling strike just after the break sealed the win.

Substitute Loic Remy pulled one back but Leicester survived in relative comfort to move back ahead of Manchester City at the top, while the reigning champions, in contrast, were just a point off the relegation zone in 16th place with Mourinho fighting for survival and his team in free fall.

How ironic. Ranieri had been in Mourinho's shadow from the time he was succeeded at Stamford Bridge by "The Special One" in 2004 and relations between the pair have often been fractious. They are more cordial now, but the hugely popular Italian enjoyed the sweet taste of victory against his former club.

The dramatic and surprising collapse of the champions was endemic of a season of shocks. While Chelsea were in crisis, Leicester City were the remarkable title pacesetters. Surely that wasn't possible? The grand order of the Premier League had been stood on its head.

The pace and movement of Vardy and Mahrez exposed John Terry in particular, although, to be fair, the style of play troubled many teams on Leicester's remarkable rise to the top. Terry being replaced by Cesc Fàbregas after only 53 minutes was a sign of the times. The sight of Terry making his way to the bench so early on in the second half emphasised the urgency of Chelsea's defensive plight and was in stark contrast to the verve of Leicester City's attack. It was an attack which had scored in every Premier League game this season with Vardy scoring or assisting in 14 consecutive Premier League games; compare that with the subdued Diego Costa. Only Borussia Dortmund's Pierre-Emerick Aubameyang (18) had netted more goals in Europe's top five leagues this season than Vardy (15).

Ranieri's side were high on confidence and adrenalin whilst the reigning champions fearful and tentative; barely believable that only seven months ago Chelsea were crowned champions and Leicester were pulling off an unbelievable escape from what looked certain relegation.

Here was the remarkable role reversal; Leicester's best start to a top-flight season in their entire history, and Mourinho on the verge of the sack. Leicester deservedly inflicted a ninth loss in 16 games on Chelsea at a thunderous King Power Stadium and pushed Mourinho to the edge of an impending exit. Hardly surprising this was too much for Abramovich to bear.

THURSDAY, 17 DECEMBER

José sacked! And the irony of the timing was not lost on Ranieri, as he had inflicted the last defeat on his adversary that turned out to be the final nail in his Stamford Bridge coffin.

The pair shared a notoriously feisty relationship with Mourinho famously, back in October, mocking the 63-year-old's grasp of the English language and lack of trophies.

FRIDAY, 18 DECEMBER

Ranieri believed Mourinho feared him ahead of their meeting at the King Power Stadium. The Foxes inflicted a ninth League defeat on the defending champions, a game which turned out to be Mourinho's last as Chelsea manager.

Despite their 'history' Ranieri, ever the gentleman, responded to Mourinho's jibes by taking the moral high ground, admitting his disappointment at his dismissal.

Ranieri said: "Do you want to know the truth, the whole truth? I am truly disappointed for him. He said those things because he was afraid of me. That's what Mourinho does, it's his method with the opponent he wants to beat. Then, when I arrived here at Leicester, he was the first to send me a welcome message. When I embraced him at the end of the match, I was sincere. At this moment we are the anomaly, thanks also to the fact none of the big clubs are playing at the right level, but it cannot last. I am convinced, for example that Chelsea will climb back up quickly and I am also impressed with my friend Arsene Wenger's Arsenal."

SATURDAY, 19 DECEMBER
EVERTON 2-3 LEICESTER CITY

Riyad Mahrez scored the first of two penalties after Funes Mori held back Okazaki. Lukaku levelled, but Howard tripped Vardy to allow Mahrez to again convert from the spot. Okazaki fired in a third, and Leicester held on despite Kevin Mirallas' late strike.

TOP (NOT BOTTOM) AT CHRISTMAS

Leicester City ensured they will be top of the tree at Christmas. Only 11 of the previous 23 teams to have been top at Christmas went on to win the title, although five of the past six did.

So, another energetic, controlled performance had left the doubters waiting at least one more week for any signs of a collapse.

Vardy clutched his hamstring while being replaced. The team couldn't afford to lose him even though Mahrez took his tally to 13 with two well-taken penalties.

Roberto Martínez lamented: "Leicester will always make it a game that will suit them. That's real credit to them. They tried to take as long as they can with every restart and it seems that frustrated our play a little bit. We had a sense of control and that allowed Leicester to get goals from disappointing positions. We need to learn and get a lot better."

40 POINTS

A delighted Ranieri commented: "I am satisfied because we were against a fantastic team. We worked so hard to concentrate during all the match. It only gets harder when you are down the table. For our fans and everybody it is a dream. We have to concentrate now and clear our mind. Our target is 40 points and I want to speak to my players. It is important to understand what they believe they can achieve and also I will say my ideas about them. If some players relax they go out the team. That is my philosophy and they know that."

Leicester were now the only team in Premier League history to be bottom on Christmas Day one year and top the following Christmas.

Ranieri's side would go into their game at Liverpool on 26 December as leaders, regardless of the result of Monday's match between second-placed Arsenal and third-placed Manchester City.

The day was rounded off perfectly, as well as hugely emotionally, by a caller on Radio 5 live 606, speaking to Darren Fletcher and, in particular, Robbie Savage.

Throughout the season, up to this point at least, Robbie Savage had never fancied Leicester for the title. I'm sure he'd always said something along the lines of "…they could, but they won't." Which, to be fair, is what most other fans and pundits were also thinking. Cue, Leicester fan, Lee…

"Hello boys…now you've brought me in I'm welling up right. What you've got to realise, we're five points clear. I've been a season ticket holder for near enough 20 years…this is the first time, the first time that I have ever seen anything like what I've seen this season. This season is just unbelievable pal and I mean that Robbie. Listen, with all due respect Robbie, loved you to bits, loved you to bits, but I'll tell you something…Kanté, Drinky and all the boys are putting it on the next level, and it shows in the league table, we're now five, we're now five…hold on a minute (clearly tearful)…we're now five points clear, five points clear. I went to Atletico Madrid, I went to Red Star. I have brought my son up…when he was in school…Manchester United, Manchester United, Arsenal, Liverpool, Manchester United, Arsenal, Liverpool…and I, and I stuck by my guns, said 'listen sunshine, wear the fox, wear the blue…we will come through', and all of a sudden my son's turned round and said to me, and looked me in the eye today, looked me in the eye and turned around and said to me 'Dad, Dad, amazing, absolutely amazing'. He's seen players, he's seen class players like Robbie, like aaah, honest to God, now tell me, you cannot, you cannot, you cannot tell me, we have not got a chance of winning the league Robbie? And listen, and this is, (voice breaking) this is, this is, and I grew up with you Robbie, you cannot tell me, you cannot believe we cannot win the league…please?" To which Robbie softly replied "Lee, Lee how can I tell you can't win the league after that."

Lee Wells, is a 43 year old, season ticket holder, making an incredible 360-mile round trip from Lampeter for each game. Lee later told the *Leicester Mercury* that he was not embarrassed at showing his emotion on the radio.

He said: "I wear my heart on my sleeve and my Leicester City shirt with pride. I was a bit tipsy and got very emotional as I talked about the team I have loved since I first went to see them at the age of 10."

Lee confirmed, not surprisingly, that he's had a lot of ribbing from his mates about his performance.

He added: "I walked into the pub on Sunday and they put 'Crying' by Roy Orbison on the jukebox. I love it. The banter is good."

Jason deVos, @jasondevos - Football is nothing without its brilliant fans - Leicester City fan reduced to tears on phone-in show.

Gary Lineker, @GaryLineker - There's nowt like football.

Piers Morgan, @piersmorgan - When people express bemusement that I get so emotional about football, I will now play them this.

MONDAY, 21 DECEMBER

The "People's Choice" for the title, Ranieri declared, having shaken up the established top order and guaranteed to be top of the charts for Christmas Day.

The Premier League was a closed shop for the past 20 seasons, with only Arsenal, Chelsea, Manchester City and Manchester United lifting the trophy. Ranieri believed English fans were cheering on his little minnows against the traditional heavyweights. "This is good for English football," said Ranieri. "I think if we go through this fantastic moment - because now we have Liverpool, Manchester City and then Bournemouth, who are in great form, then Tottenham - maybe if we are still top, not only Leicester fans are behind us, but a lot of English fans as well. Because Leicester, I think, are a likeable team. Maybe the people say, 'If my team doesn't win, I'm very happy if Leicester win.' And this is a good thing. But, there is no easy match because if Leicester, Bournemouth, Watford and Crystal Palace are top of the form table, that means everyone wants to win. The other thing is the big teams are thinking about other things, because it's not normal that the big teams aren't at the top. If there is one year strange, that's ok for us."

Although Ranieri believes City are the fans' favourites for the title, he insisted the club were not in the hunt for the trophy, and has backed Arsenal to be crowned champions after Arsenal defeated Manchester City 2-1 on Monday night to move within two points of Leicester at the top.

KIDOLOGY OR MIND GAMES?

"I agree with these people, when they say Arsenal is the favourite or Manchester City is the favourite, I agree with them," Ranieri added. "For me, Arsenal is the favourite. They have so many fantastic players. Our team is a young team, it's the first time we're top of the league. We aren't used to staying there, and for this reason it's important for me that they don't think about it. It's like a climber. If you look below, Ah, my God! I sign now, I want to stay above Arsenal at the end of the league. Then, if not the top, we will be very close."

TUESDAY, 22 DECEMBER

Ranieri may add to his table-topping side in January but only if some of his current squad leave, such as Andrej Kramarić or Gökhan Inler. Kramarić, who signed for £7million in January, has played just 12 minutes of Premier League football this season while £5.6m signing Inler found his game-time limited. Inler's agent was quoted as saying the Switzerland captain did not want to leave but needs regular football if he is to be ready for Euro 2016 this summer.

"Maybe now I tell you one thing, but tomorrow I think another," Ranieri said. "That is football. Football is like a volcano, every day something changes. I would like to maintain everyone but I understand if someone wants to go," said Ranieri, who added that he would "hope" to sign a replacement for anyone who leaves.

Ranieri added that star winger Riyad Mahrez was like "a king" at City and would be going nowhere amid rumoured £30m bids from Manchester United and Tottenham.

Hundreds of fans took the chance to be served by members of the table topping first team squad at the club shop, the local *Leicester Mercury* reported. Fresh from the 3-2 away victory over Everton Shinji Okazaki and Nathan Dyer helped at the tills and signed photographs and other merchandise at the King Power Stadium. They were joined by Gökhan Inler and reserve goalkeeper Ben Hamer.

Among the customers looking for Christmas gifts was fervent fan Gemma Parkin, 27, from Shepshed. She visited with her baby daughter Maisie with the match shirt worn by Dyer in Saturday's win at Goodison Park. She said: "Nathan threw the shirt to my brother Daniel after the game. Daniel, a season ticket holder, is working and wanted Nathan to sign it. I apologised because the shirt was still covered in mud from the game. But Nathan was great and signed it." She said they are hoping to get the shirt framed. "I also got Daniel a surprise present."

Also helping out was Shinji Okazaki who scored one of the goals which guaranteed Leicester were top of the table at Christmas. Student Tom Cant, 18, queued for about 30 minutes before getting into the shop. He said: "It was great to see members of the first team at the shop. The atmosphere was great." Tom, who travelled to Leicester from his home in Grantham, said "My granddad comes from Leicester and we are all Leicester fans. I had my picture taken with Shinji Okazaki and he signed it and I also bought a retro football."

WEDNESDAY, 23 DECEMBER

Leicester had the Premier League's two fastest players this season but it was not Vardy and Jeffrey Schlupp that Ranieri mentioned when asked whether the surprise leaders could last the distance. His response invoked an image of Forrest Gump, the Tom Hanks' hero in the 1994 Oscar-winning film who ran across the United States. Ranieri suggested that his side would "run, run, run" all season long as evidence of their staying power. Their strong finish last spring when they won seven of nine fixtures to avoid relegation was the point of reference. "Look, I am very confident because if Leicester last season saved themselves in the last two months, that means the stamina is fantastic, and why can't we continue to run, run, run? We are like Forrest Gump. Leicester is Forrest Gump. I give you the headline there!"

He has been in this position before - a Christmas-time leader in promotion-winning campaigns with Fiorentina in Italy and Monaco in France - and, as he recalled, has also been in a title race right to the last day in Italy, when his Roma side lost out to Internazionale in 2010. "In the last 30 minutes Inter Milan scored a goal and won the scudetto (title)," he remembered.

In the inaugural Premier League campaign of 1992-93, Norwich City led by four points yet finished third. In 1995, Kevin Keegan's Newcastle United had a 10-point lead but ended up as runners-up. In 1998, Aston Villa were top but fell to sixth - the only Christmas Day leaders to have slipped out of the European places altogether post-1992.

SATURDAY, 26 DECEMBER

LIVERPOOL 1-0 LEICESTER CITY

The nine-match unbeaten Premier League run was ended by substitute Christian Benteke's second-half winner.

The Reds dominated the first half at Anfield, but failed to fully test Schmeichel. They were rewarded when Roberto Firmino's pull-back from the left was steered in by a stretching Benteke after Liverpool peppered the Leicester goal with 26 attempts, 5 of which were on target.

Leicester offered little threat, Nathan Dyer going closest as they failed to score for the first time this season, and suffered their first league defeat since losing 5-2 at home to Arsenal on 26 September; which left them vulnerable to be overtaken by the Gunners later on Saturday. But Wenger's men failed to capitalise after a 4-0 humiliation at Southampton, leaving the Foxes still two points clear.

Now the emphasis was on whether Ranieri's side reacted positively to defeat or would finally capitulate as most of the pundits thought they surely would.

After a toothless display, managing just three shots on target, Leicester would have to recover to maintain their lofty position. "We have to clean this result away and restart," said Ranieri afterwards.

Two of the brightest stars, Vardy and Mahrez, who had contributed 29 of Leicester's 37 Premier League goals, as well as providing 10 assists for each other or their team-mates, made little to no impact, with Ranieri revealing afterwards that Vardy played with a fever and Mahrez was "very tired".

As a team, they lacked their usual energy, managing just seven attempts at the Liverpool goal. Benteke had six touches in the Leicester penalty area, while Vardy only managed one in the Liverpool box.

Liverpool's revival under Jürgen Klopp had shown signs of slowing down in recent weeks, with the Reds picking up just one point in their three previous Premier League matches. Following the 3-0 defeat at Watford, Klopp decided to recall Belgium striker Divock Origi to provide more pace and movement as the focal point of his attack. Origi's speed caused problems for the Leicester defence in the opening half an hour. A hamstring injury curtailed Origi's afternoon, with Benteke summoned from the bench. Benteke, a £32m summer signing from Aston Villa, had not scored a Premier League goal in six appearances and wastefully headed over an early second-half opportunity. However, he clinically finished when it mattered - sliding in the winner as Liverpool moved up to eighth.

Ranieri's side had lost their first away match of the season, last losing on the road in the Premier League in March (4-3 at Tottenham). Leicester had won just one of their past 11 top-flight Boxing Day fixtures, drawing three and losing seven.

Jürgen Klopp was ecstatic: "After four games with no result, that was very important today. Everybody knows of the quality of Leicester and what we had to do today was play simple football. The first half was really good and then we had to change. Christian Benteke was not warm, it's not easy to come into the game. We made the goal, it was a brilliant situation where the boys showed their quality in small situations. We were never really under pressure."

Ranieri observed: "We started to play too late. Liverpool pushed from the beginning and for this reason they deserved to win. We tried to do our best but maybe in the first half we were too nervous to play our football. The second half was much better."

MONDAY, 28 DECEMBER

Ranieri urged his players to enjoy their football and not be daunted by their place in the upper echelons ahead of Manchester City's visit.

The Foxes had a superb first half of the campaign and will have the chance to end 2015 top of the pile with a win over City after Arsenal knocked them into second place with their victory over Bournemouth.

Ranieri wanted to avoid a repeat of what he saw at Liverpool on Boxing Day, where his side were over-anxious. "'You know my idea about this (the title) - we are dreaming. We are in good condition and in a good position with 38 points. Now we can continue, but I want to see my players enjoy it. I don't know why we were so nervous at the beginning. Why? Play football, don't worry. If you lose, lose. That's it. We have the time."

Manuel Pellegrini was convinced Leicester had what it takes to stay the course as the Manchester City boss warned his players they must approach the trip to the King Power Stadium as they would any other top-of-the-table showdown despite the Foxes' loss at Liverpool, only their second defeat of a campaign – City, meanwhile, had already been beaten five times.

Pellegrini did not believe one bad result would prompt a Leicester slump. Pellegrini's side had moved to within three points of Leicester by thrashing Sunderland 4-1. He said: "Before that they beat Chelsea and drew against (Manchester) United. We must consider Leicester not thinking that they lost on Saturday and could collapse, but as a team that will have options to be fighting for the title until the end. With that mentality we must try to play the game. They are top of the table because they deserve to be. They have important players in a very good moment with high performance."

Ranieri assessed Vardy before finalising his team with the striker yet to fully overcome the fever that affected him in the loss at Liverpool. Vardy was off his usual intensity at Anfield due to the effects of a strong virus and was replaced by Ulloa in the 69th minute despite Leicester being a goal down.

Manchester City monitored Vardy's record-breaking exploits and would inevitably use this match to study the player once again. Pellegrini was thought, in the media, to be giving serious consideration to a January bid, despite Leicester's assurances that no sales of Vardy or Mahrez would be considered.

Marc Albrighton insisted their bubble had not burst following the loss to Liverpool and backed Leicester to return to winning ways against Manchester City and regain the Premier League top spot. Leicester had not lost back-to-back league games all season and Albrighton was confident they were not about to start now. "We see this as a test. There will probably be a lot of pundits and media that might think now we are going to lie down and relax with our 30-something points. We're not a side to do that. We look forward to bouncing back against City. To be honest, I don't think we will play another game this season with pressure. We've got ourselves in a brilliant situation and we are doing fantastic. Everyone was tipping us to be down there at the start of the season, but we're right in the mix and we deserve to be where we are. No one likes losing, we showed that from the end of last season and we will fight to the end. We always believe we can win every game and that's not going to change because we lost. The manager said to us to keep going and we have a great team and squad. City are a great team, the players they have got are world class but there's nothing better than to come up against some of their players at home after a defeat. We'll react in the right way. I know the kind of players we have in our dressing room. I'm pretty sure the fans will see us from the whistle on Tuesday getting straight into them."

Danny Simpson also expected a response with Leicester welcoming back Drinkwater after a hamstring injury. "No one likes losing, we showed that from the end of last season and we will fight to the end. We always believe we can win every game and that's not going to change because we got beaten. The manager said to us to keep going and we have a great team and squad."

The Foxes had spent considerably less than their title rivals and were desperate to continue to prove the doubters wrong following the Boxing Day defeat by Liverpool, especially as Pellegrini's City could leapfrog Ranieri's side.

COMPARE AND CONTRAST

The combined cost of Leicester's probable starting line-up was £21m. This was less than David Silva alone, who is *only* the eighth most expensive Manchester City player at £24m. Their total team cost being £292.9m.

Leicester: Kasper Schmeichel (£1m); Danny Simpson (£2m), Robert Huth (£3m), Wes Morgan (£1m), Christian Fuchs (free); Riyad Mahrez (£400,000), N'Golo Kanté (£5.6m), Andy King (free), Marc Albrighton (free); Jamie Vardy (£1m), Shinji Okazaki (£7m).

TOTAL: £21m

Manchester City: Joe Hart (£600,000); Bacary Sagna (free), Nicolas Otamendi (£28.5m), Eliaquim Mangala (£42m), Gael Clichy (£7m); Fernandinho (£34m), Yaya Touré (£24m); Kevin De Bruyne (£56m), David Silva (£24m), Raheem Sterling (£49m); Sergio Agüero (£38m).

TOTAL: £292.9m

The £56m City paid Wolfsburg for De Bruyne in August is their biggest outlay, while a month earlier they received £22m from Valencia for Alvaro Negredo.

Croatia striker Andrej Kramarić - at £9.7m from HNK Rijeka in January - is Leicester's record signing. The £11m sale of Emile Heskey to Liverpool in 2000 is the club's biggest fee received.

Pellegrini's £3.4m salary is modest compared with Europe's top clubs, but is still three times as much as the £1m Ranieri earns in a year. Ranieri pockets £100,000 for every position Leicester finish above 18th, a sign of just how low expectations were at the start of the season.

City struck oil when they were taken over in 2008, and boast the richest owners in the Premier League. Mansour bin Zayed Al Nahyan (Sheik Mansour) is chairman of the City Football Group, worth an estimated £20bn.

Leicester's owners are the ninth richest in the division and Vichai Srivaddhanaprabha, the founder and CEO of King Power International, is said to be worth *only* £1.4bn.

Manchester City's Etihad Stadium's record attendance was on Boxing Day with a crowd of 54,523 to see a comfortable 4-1 victory over Sunderland. It was opened in 2002 for the Commonwealth Games before being converted into a football stadium one year later. The total cost topped £150m.

Leicester's King Power Stadium holds just 32,262 - relatively small by top-flight standards - and cost £37m to build in 2002, a sum which in part contributed to the club entering receivership shortly after their move to the new home.

City's £200m Etihad Campus was unveiled last year and is the best training facility in the world; 16 football pitches, six swimming pools, three gyms and the third floor is entirely reserved for bedrooms.

Leicester were met with resistance from local residents who opposed the club's plans to install a floodlit five-a-side pitch at their Belvoir Drive training ground.

City won the Premier League twice in the last four seasons and have another two top-flight crowns from 1937 and 1968. They lifted eight domestic cups and the UEFA Cup Winners' Cup.

Leicester had never won England's top division; their best finish was second in 1929. They have never lifted the FA Cup and their last domestic trophy was the League Cup in 2000, a competition they also won in 1997 and 1964.

TUESDAY, 29 DECEMBER

LEICESTER CITY 0-0 MANCHESTER CITY

Leicester fans were able to toast a memorable 2015 with a free beer on arrival at the stadium. The Foxes' owners arranged for partner Singha Beer to provide a bottle for each fan as a thank you for their support during a year which began with the club adrift at the bottom of the Premier League but now challenging at the top.

In his programme notes ahead of the match, vice chairman Aiyawatt Srivaddhanaprabha said: "There have been so many highlights from 2015 - the amazing escape last season, the fantastic start to this one, club records broken, Premier League records broken and moments that will live with us all for a long time. You have been a huge part of it and Leicester City heads into 2016 in better shape than it has ever been. As a thank you for the role you have played in such a great year, our friends at Singha Beer will be buying the first round tonight. Enjoy it, you've all earned it!"

Water was available for supporters under 18 years old.

It was the question that has been asked all season - how will Leicester City react to a defeat? The visit of Pellegrini's expensively assembled squad was both a test and an opportunity. The club's groundsmen had mown the grass into a dazzling geometric pattern as it looked in perfect condition.

They answered the question with a performance of spirit and energy, roared on by the trademark vibrant atmosphere at a packed King Power Stadium. Manchester City kept their first clean sheet of the season in games without Vincent Kompany. Kompany was in the stands to watch the game, making the trip despite the calf injury he suffered on Boxing Day. But Leicester missed the chance to return to the top as they played out a goalless draw. However, Ranieri's side took heart from an impressive response to only their second league defeat of the season - but Arsenal remained top on goal difference.

Both teams had chances in an entertaining encounter, with goalkeepers Schmeichel and Hart excelling. Leicester failed to score at home in the Premier League for the first time in 15 games.

Vardy missed the best chance when he shot over the top after racing clear in the first half while the normally lethal Sergio Agüero was off target from inside the six-yard box as both sides pushed for the win. The outstanding Kanté almost broke the deadlock with a flashing 25-yard shot just wide then showed remarkable pace to catch Sterling in a race to halt a City attack. Kanté ran over 11km in the match, only Albrighton covered more ground.

Wes Morgan was once again a powerhouse in defence alongside Huth, while Fuchs ran a marathon down the left, almost creating a first-half goal for Albrighton with a superb cross.

While Manchester City were formidable at home, their poor away form was costing them the chance to be champions again.

Ranieri commented: "I think we made a very good match. It was difficult. We played well, we created some chances. I wanted to see how my players responded after the Liverpool defeat and they responded well. Every match is difficult for us. This league is very crazy...nobody wants to win the league. It's very strange. We're the basement and the other teams are a villa with a swimming pool. It's not easy for us but we want to fight with everybody. It's a miracle what we're doing."

Pellegrini observed: "I think we did more than Leicester to win the game. We had more possession, more attempts, more options but it was a tough game against a tough team playing away. This is a crucial period. I think at the end of January we will know exactly what position we are in."

Ranieri's side could have leapfrogged leaders Arsenal with a win but missed their chance, instead moving level on points with the Gunners while Manchester City were three points behind.

Arsenal were now favourites for a first title in 12 years despite their 4-0 defeat at Southampton last week. Leicester, though, remained surprise contenders at the half-way point after 19 games.

Ranieri says everything is starting to fall into place for the side that he inherited from Nigel Pearson as the window comes down on a brilliant 2015 for the Foxes.

Barclays Premier League Table at the end of December 2015:

POS	CLUB	P	W	D	L	GF	GA	GD	PTS
1	Arsenal	19	12	3	4	33	18	15	39
2	Leicester City	19	11	6	2	37	25	12	39
3	Manchester City	19	11	3	5	37	20	17	36
4	Tottenham Hotspur	19	9	8	2	33	15	18	35

JANUARY 2016

FRIDAY, 1 JANUARY

Ranieri would rest star striker Jamie Vardy when the time was right after a successful but gruelling 2015. He was prepared to give the club's 15-goal top-scorer a break after he played through injury and illness this season.

Vardy shook off a recent virus but also played with a broken wrist and an ankle problem this term.

He was set to start against Bournemouth with Leicester second in the Premier League, but Ranieri says he would give the 28-year-old a breather soon. He commented: "Yes, when I think it's the right moment to give him a rest I'll give it to him. At the moment he doesn't need one yet. Now it's important to carry on with him. Jamie had a little problem for one or two months and of course he didn't train every day. The last days he's had a fever and he's not 100 per cent. This is another aspect, everyone is saying 'top of the league, top of the league' but we are running a lot. Now we must continue at this top level because when we put the other teams under pressure we are very dangerous but we have to run. We can continue at this level but one thing is to not be relegated and one thing is to be at the top of the league."

Title rivals Manchester City and Arsenal face Champions League ties with Dynamo Kiev and Barcelona respectively when that competition resumes in February, while City also have a League Cup semi-final against Stoke to contest. Leicester, meanwhile, were free to concentrate on the league and forthcoming FA Cup. Ranieri wants the games to pile up on their competitors. He added: "This is good for us because big teams play in a lot of competitions: the Champions League, the FA Cup, League Cup and Premier League. I want them to continue to win in the Champions League until the end."

PAIR TO STAY

Vardy and Mahrez would not be leaving in the January transfer window, insisted Ranieri. The in-form duo played key roles for the high-flying Foxes which led to speculation linking the free-scoring forwards with big-money moves.

Vardy was the Premier League's joint-top scorer with 15 goals, and Mahrez was involved in more goals than any other player in the top division scoring 13 and laying on 7 assists.

Newspaper reports claimed Chelsea and Manchester City were keeping tabs on Vardy while Mahrez's displays reportedly attracted the interest of Arsenal, Barcelona and Manchester United.

Despite the speculation Ranieri was adamant that the pair would be staying and speaking at his press conference ahead of Saturday's clash with Bournemouth, he again insisted neither player were looking to leave the King Power Stadium. "Nobody goes from Leicester," said Ranieri. "They have said they want to stay and fight until the end and build with me and the chairman and our fans a big Leicester. We are a solid team and we want to continue together with everybody."

Ranieri preferred to leave talk about possible contract extensions for the pair - who between them have scored 28 goals in the Premier League - to one side. Vardy's current deal lasts until the summer of 2018 while Mahrez is under contract until 2019. Ranieri added: "They are concentrating, they must be very professional. It is not important now the contract. They have their agents but it is another thing to play. For this reason they pay their agents to think about the contract. If they think about too many other things and not the real job, they will not continue to improve."

Bournemouth boss Eddie Howe warned his defenders to be on red alert when they come up against the "unique" talents of Vardy. The Cherries saw their six-match unbeaten run come to an end with a 2-0 defeat at Arsenal on Monday, while Leicester drew 0-0 for the first time this season against Manchester City on Tuesday night, a result which meant the Gunners would top the table heading in 2016.

The form of Vardy and his fellow Foxes has been the story of the first half of the campaign, although he was now without a goal in three games.

Many managers considered whether the one-time Stocksbridge Park Steels frontman was worth the gamble, and had declined. "I was aware of him a few seasons ago (when I was) at Burnley and he first made his move to Leicester," said Howe. "It is a hard journey to make and you really do have to excel to be noticed to move and carry on that momentum. To succeed at this level is incredibly difficult and he deserved all of the plaudits for what he has done."

Howe continued: "Jamie Vardy has unique strengths, he combines an incredible work ethic with real pace, determination, and fight to score his next goal. We handled him quite well here in the first game (in August) and our defenders will need to be alert because he is one of those players who only needs one chance to have an impact on the game."

Howe believes Leicester's remarkable progress under Ranieri was "no fluke", as he argued, "Leicester have certainly been the surprise of the season, in terms of the positive aspect of being at the top of the league. They have been outstanding, they really have. They have a way of playing and a hard-working group of players, the attitude and commitment of their players in every game has been second to none and they have got match winners in their squad, so it is full credit to them, the players and coaching staff for what they have achieved so far this season. It is no fluke, they deserve to be where they are."

Sky Sports pundit Paul Merson's prediction: "This is a big game for Leicester. They have gone two games without scoring, albeit against good opposition, but they changed the way they played at home to Manchester City. I was disappointed with that, instead of playing 4-4-2, they played one up front and I just don't think it worked. They need to win this game to get back on track, but it's a hard one for them. When you're in a relegation battle like Bournemouth are, the run they have just been on could keep them up. If you get nine points out of nine in three games, that's a quarter of your needed points over three games. It was a nice run, but they may need another before the end of the season."

SATURDAY, 2 JANUARY

LEICESTER CITY 0-0 BOURNEMOUTH

Mahrez saw a second-half penalty saved as Leicester fell two points behind Arsenal at the top.

Moments after Bournemouth captain Simon Francis was sent off for denying Vardy a goalscoring chance, Artur Boruc denied Mahrez with a two-handed save.

Vardy struck a post when well-placed in an even first half, but the red card left the Cherries hanging on. Boruc again denied Mahrez late on, but the visitors deservedly earned a point.

Vardy has won seven Premier League penalties since the start of 2014-15, two more than any other player in this period. After a run of scoring in 18 successive Premier League matches from May-December 2015, Leicester now failed to score in each of their past three. Bournemouth did not attempt a single shot on target in this match - the 11th occasion that a side have failed to attempt one in a Premier League game this season and the first time Bournemouth have failed to do so. Though the stats said Leicester led 16 shots to nine, the home side failed to make their one-man advantage count. A paltry two attempts on target underlines the fact many of their efforts came from long distance or were half-chances.

Ranieri's side had missed a golden opportunity to stay level on points with Arsenal; instead they were left with just two points from three games, in which they have failed to score a single goal.

Questions were inevitably asked whether this was finally the start of a decline expected by many.

CELEBRATION

Leicester, however, had the 40 points Ranieri targeted to ensure Premier League survival! "Champagne for my players" said the manager.

He was also celebrating a possible new signing, with talented Birmingham winger Demarai Gray having a medical. But the acquisition of Gray would not be sufficient in itself to get out of their first sticky patch of the campaign. Vardy and Mahrez needed, though, someone to share the burden of goals as, if they could not deliver, no one else looked like doing so.

Ranieri commented: "We knew it was a difficult match and we started playing too late. Bournemouth moved the ball very quickly but in the second half we were much better. We hit the post, we missed a penalty and had some good chances. We have not scored for three games but we have had chances. Sometimes everything is right but now some things are wrong. The performance was good, a fantastic effort."

Bournemouth manager Eddie Howe confronted referee Andre Marriner on the pitch after the game in a protest against the sending-off of Francis. It was a close call, with the central defender getting a slight touch on the ball as he made contact with Vardy right on the edge of the area. "I didn't think it was a foul from my angle - he definitely touched the ball. It was a great recovery tackle. It's not a foul, a penalty or a sending-off. It was a very even game before that point, a high-tempo game and very high quality. We had some great chances in the first half but when we went down to 10 men we showed character and it's a great point for us. We won't appeal the red card as it's a one-game ban and the FA Cup is coming up." added Howe.

MONDAY, 4 JANUARY

Vardy will be out of action for up to 10 days needing minor surgery on a groin problem. It would be a big test for the team to operate without his selfless running and eye for goal despite having not scored since the 2-1 win over Chelsea on 14 December. Leicester have timed the operation so that he misses Sunday's FA Cup tie with Tottenham, but he is expected to be available for the Premier League game, also against Spurs, on 13 January.

Ranieri had revealed on Saturday that he would rest the club's 15-goal top-scorer when the time was right after a successful but gruelling 2015.

The Italian said ahead of the goalless draw with Bournemouth: "Jamie had a little problem for one or two months and of course he didn't train every day. The last days he's had a fever and he's not 100 per cent."

The club signed Birmingham City winger Demarai Gray after meeting a £3.7m release clause in his contract. Gray had a medical on Saturday and signed a four-and-a-half year deal. The club had a bid turned down for the 19-year-old in August.

He was available for Sunday's FA Cup tie at Tottenham. "I watch a lot of football. The way Leicester play suits my style," said the England U-20 player. Bournemouth were also interested in the highly-rated teenager, who burst onto the scene with a hat-trick against Reading in December 2014. Gray came through the Blues' youth system and made 78 senior appearances for the club, scoring eight goals.

Demarai Gray on Instagram: "Small message to Birmingham for everything. Been at the club since 10 years old and loved every moment there. Forever in my heart and thank every member of staff that I've worked with." Birmingham manager Gary Rowett had confirmed Demarai Gray was in talks with a Premier League club after the Blues' 2-1 win over Brentford on Saturday.

SUNDAY, 10 JANUARY

TOTTENHAM HOTSPUR 2-2 LEICESTER CITY

FA CUP - THIRD ROUND

Harry Kane's controversial late penalty kept Spurs in the FA Cup as the striker's equaliser earned a third-round replay.

Kane scored from the spot after Nathan Dyer had been penalised for handball, much to the visitors' anger. Christian Eriksen put Spurs ahead with a low drive after Schmeichel parried Chadli's shot. Marcin Wasilewski's header levelled before substitute Shinji Okazaki weaved into the box and fired Leicester ahead.

Schmeichel was booked in the aftermath of referee Bobby Madley awarding Tottenham a penalty in the 89th minute. The ball struck Nathan Dyer's hand as he turned to attempt to tackle Danny Rose in the penalty area. Pundit Kevin Kilbane told BBC One: "It is harsh but it was hand to ball - Nathan Dyer has flicked his hand out at the ball going past him." Alan Shearer and Martin O'Neill both disagreed. "I think that's a very poor decision - it's not a penalty at all, Nathan Dyer doesn't even know where the ball is. It's very harsh," said Shearer. O'Neill added: "I agree with Alan, it's a very harsh penalty - Nathan Dyer has just turned round and doesn't know where the ball is. Doesn't it have to be deliberate?"

Wednesday's forthcoming Premier League meeting between the sides, however, was far more important than an FA Cup third round tie, with both still in contention for the title. Leicester are second in the table and Tottenham in fourth, four points behind. Consequently, for this cup tie, Ranieri did his 'Tinkerman' bit with eight changes while Spurs made seven from their last league outings, but there was no lack of desire from the players involved. Despite Spurs missing Kane and Alli initially, and Leicester being without Mahrez and Vardy entirely - they produced an enthralling contest.

Tottenham's intent was clear as they brought on top scorer Kane with 24 minutes left and Alli followed soon after, while Leicester's anger at the final whistle was again evidence of how much it meant.

Spurs had 74% possession but, despite having 24 shots to Leicester's 10, they rarely threatened Schmeichel's goal.

Leicester went into the match having failed to score in their last three matches - after netting in each of their previous 21 games in all competitions - and with just two points from their last three league games. With top scorer Vardy injured and playmaker Mahrez rested, the visiting fans must have feared the worst, especially when Eriksen put Spurs ahead early on. Fortunate to be level at the break through Wasilewski with lone striker Ulloa isolated, the Foxes were rewarded for a more adventurous second-half approach.

New signing, Demarai Gray, created Okazaki's equaliser and almost scored with a 20-yarder. His 64-minute display showed glimpses of the pace that will cause Premier League defences problems. But it was the half-time introduction of Okazaki that added more attacking threat, although for the majority of the game Leicester were content to soak up pressure and hit Tottenham on the break.

Tottenham manager Mauricio Pochettino commented: "I am happy because it was a draw and this is an important competition for us. A defeat would not have been fair, a draw is a bit more fair but if you analyse the full 90 minutes then we deserved more. I'm happy with the performance and we made a great effort."

Ranieri added: "I didn't see the penalty, there were two players in front of me, but the more important thing is that the referee gave the penalty so it is a penalty. I'm very pleased with our performance. We had eight players who had not been playing for some time, but now they played and they deserved a positive result - 2-2 is a positive result."

WEDNESDAY, 13 JANUARY

TOTTENHAM HOTSPUR 0-1 LEICESTER CITY

Robert Huth scored a late winner in a hugely significant victory over their top-four rivals. A string of saves from Schmeichel kept Spurs at bay as the visitors ended their three-game winless run in the Premier League. The Foxes were now level on points with leaders Arsenal.

It clearly meant an awful lot to the players as Christian Fuchs tweeted, @FuchsOfficial - That's how we do it!! Big header by the big man @robert_huth. #Foxesneverquit @LCFC

Leicester looked like having to settle for a fourth league game without a goal until unmarked Huth headed home Fuchs' corner.

Kane had Spurs' best chance when his effort was touched on to the bar by Schmeichel. It was one of only five shots on target by Spurs. Huth's role in keeping a clean sheet combined with a goal with one of his only two touches in Spurs' half made him the star man.

Vardy returned from groin surgery but had a quiet game. Since breaking the Premier League record for goals in consecutive games, Vardy has scored just one goal from six shots on target in seven games.

There had been fears a slide was beginning after three games without scoring, and they looked like making that four in a row before Huth's late goal. But this win took them seven points above fourth-placed Spurs and eight clear of West Ham in fifth. It generated hope of finishing in the Champions League places, if not higher.

They were characteristically short of possession with only 39% - their average of 40.62% was the third lowest in the league - but they proved that they were far from a two-man team with Mahrez and Vardy, subdued.

Alan Shearer commented on BBC *Match of the Day*: "It's a remarkable story for Leicester. Only Manchester City have scored more goals than them. It was a good old-fashioned proper plant your feet, arch your back and get your neck muscles going header from Huth. Look at the power. Boof!"

Ex-Germany midfielder Dietmar Hamann: "It's a blip for Spurs. They're still in a good position and favourites to reach the Champions League. The worry is the lack of form from Christian Eriksen, who hasn't scored in the league since October. They are over-reliant on Harry Kane. If he gets injured they'll be in trouble."

Ranieri told *Match of the Day*: "We wanted to win but we knew it was a difficult match. Tottenham started very well and put us under pressure but we didn't lose our confidence or shape and it was difficult for them. In the second half it was an open match. We both had chances and we scored the goal. Unfortunately it's January, not May. There's so much work to do. We have to remain calm and believe in what we're doing."

Interestingly, Ranieri tried to sign Spurs coach, Mauricio Pochettino, for Atletico Madrid during his playing days.

Ranieri continued his mantra that he was still not dreaming about the title despite going level on points with Arsenal at the top. "It's ok, it's good. We must continue to work hard and remain grounded. This is a crazy league this year. I hope I can help my players. I want them always if we win or lose to clear their minds and think about the next match. Because, what we did has passed and now it's important to focus on Aston Villa. Yes, they won their match, they want to fight and don't want to be relegated. It will be another good battle on Saturday. A lot of people ask what Leicester can do; I don't know what we can do. We are very solid and we want to continue. There's a very good atmosphere, good lads because they are very friendly. I want this to continue."

Pochettino commented: "I'm disappointed. We created the better chances. You need to score. We need to keep calm and try to improve. All the stats are positive for us. It's difficult to explain - we deserved more and to win the game. In football you can get punished for one little mistake. We are going to try to analyse the game. We were unlucky tonight."

Leicester had secured more points this season (43) than they did in the whole of the 2014-15 Premier League campaign (41). Huth's goal ended Leicester's run of 374 minutes without a goal in the Premier League. The Foxes earned their first league win at White Hart Lane since October 1999. Ranieri has never lost a Premier League match as a manager against Tottenham (W7 D3).

FRIDAY, 15 JANUARY

Ranieri smiled a lot, laughed even more, but below the surface there was a steely determination.

Occasionally there are flashes of anger as he patrols the touchline, demanding more form his players. "If I am angry you can see I am angry," he says. "I am not an actor and I cannot hide it. It is...you call it, a Latin temper. Sometimes I am angry with myself for not explaining things to my players very well but no I cannot remember this year. When I am happy you can see it in my eyes. My eyes are laughing first always."

Ranieri remembered being on holiday in Calabria, Greece last summer, having been out of work since an unhappy and short experience with their national team, when he received the call that Leicester were interested. "Of course I thought I was signing up to a relegation battle," he says. "But they asked me whether I could maintain the Premier League and build a good team. I said I am used to building a good foundation."

His dignity throughout a difficult final season at the Bridge, attracted sympathy and affection from fans up and down the country and prompted a memoir, from which he donated all profits to *Great Ormond Street Children's Hospital*, called 'Proud Man Walking'. "I wanted to call it 'Tinker Man'," he says laughing again. "But the publishers said no. For me Tinkerman was good. A tinkerman finds the right solution. Now I see a lot of managers change a lot and also they are tinkermen - but there is only one with the flag. I have that flag and they are second."

For all the theatricality, his authority there as manager is unquestioned. "Slowly we are improving tactically," he says, looking serious. "This team shows my character. When I was a player I wasn't a champion but I was a hard worker and I was a fighter. The one thing makes me crazy is if you make a mistake but you slow down," he adds slumping his shoulders. There have been no signs of that.

Ranieri laughs when it is put to him that he has not stayed at any one club for a great length of time - his four years at Fiorentina and Chelsea a personal best. "I move a lot of course but in Italy four years in a team is like a Ferguson or Arsene Wenger! If you achieve one year there you are 'aaaargh'," he says, shouting loudly and raising his fists in the air. "It is unbelievable what happened."

Something similarly unbelievable is happening here in Leicester. The proud man is still walking, tinkering and, most importantly, has not stopped smiling since he arrived.

SATURDAY, 16 JANUARY
ASTON VILLA 1-1 LEICESTER CITY

Leicester returned to the top with a draw at bottom-of-the-table Villa.

Shinji Okazaki opened the scoring, reacting quickest to poke home after keeper Mark Bunn had athletically clawed out Vardy's lob. Vardy was afforded time to get onto the end of Schmeichel's long clearance. Bunn may have backtracked well to keep out his lob, but his defenders were too slow to the rebound, letting Okazaki in for the opener.

Mahrez missed a chance to double the lead after Leicester were awarded a controversial penalty for handball. Villa's Aly Cissokho had dived in to block Mahrez's shot from a couple of yards, but the ball struck his arm up by his face with the defender facing the other way.

The home side had their own strong claim for a penalty in the second half when Huth wrapped his arm around Kozak's head to get to a cross first, but the referee turned down the appeal. Gestede levelled after his second-half shot deflected past Schmeichel, ending the run of six hours and 11 minutes without conceding a Premier League goal.

Leicester were now a point clear of Manchester City and Arsenal at the top, but the Gunners would go back to the top if they got a point against Stoke on Sunday. The Foxes had now been top of the table for 33 days, the same number of days that Spurs had been top of the Premier League table since its inception in 1992 (based on end of days).

Vardy had just come back from a minor operation and did well for his goal, but he did not look as sharp as he might and missed a chance to win it in stoppage time when he fired over from a tight angle.

Mahrez's weak penalty - his second missed penalty in a row - was a frustration to his manager. Ranieri commented: "Yes, we lost two points. We started very well and scored a goal but after the missed penalty the Aston Villa players took a new energy. If we score a second goal, we close the match. We are very sad but also I say to the players 'if we make the performance the result is not important'. It's one point, it's OK, it's a derby - but we are disappointed." Ranieri further added "If I remember well, this is the second or third mistake from Riyad; I want to speak with him. If he is calm, if he wants to continue to shoot the goal, he can continue. He was very sad. I will speak with Riyad and Jamie because they are two of my penalty scorers."

Mahrez suffered, perhaps, an inevitable dip in form after setting incredible heights and Ranieri wanted a response, but also protection from officials. "He was fantastic at the beginning and now a lot of people are around him, trying to take the ball or trying to take the legs, that's difficult.

It's important the referees are very close to him and say if the opponent goes to take a normal tackle or goes to take the legs. It's important he understands this new thing on the pitch, that everyone wants to stop him with the right way or the wrong way and he has to be very clever."

FISH AND CHIPS

Okazaki, on the other hand, had now scored five goals in all competitions, all of them coming away from home. "All my goals have been away and I hope to score at home soon. Vardy is still our main striker and it is a big thing he scores goals for us. But if he is not scoring then I hope to help the team and Vardy as well. He created some chances against Villa and so I am not worried about him at all."

His run of contributing important goals is being fuelled by a fortnightly diet of fish and chips. He found the net for the fourth time in nine games and then remarked on how his English acclimatisation had been helped by regular portions of deep-fried cod. "I like fish and chips!" said Okazaki. "I have them sometimes, maybe once every two weeks, then I am happy. Now I have scored I want some fish and chips, it is better than pizza!"

In a period when Vardy has not scored in six games, Okazaki's goals were crucial. Against Villa he followed up Vardy's audacious chip to convert, although for a brief few seconds he was unsure HawkEye would come to his aid as Mark Bunn saved his shot behind the line. "I saw it was in but I was a bit worried about it," said Okazaki. "The technology confirmed it. I was happy."

SUNDAY, 17 JANUARY

Chelsea want Ranieri back! Well, that was according to a report in Italian newspaper *Tuttosport* which claimed owner Roman Abramovich was considering the Leicester coach after interim Guus Hiddink left in the summer. Ranieri was sacked by Abramovich back in 2004 following four years at the club and was replaced by José Mourinho, and the notion that Abramovich would want another former boss back after the experiences with Mourinho was the kind of speculation that often dominated the media agenda without the slightest substance. Chelsea had their short list, and it didn't contain the name of the Leicester City coach!

WEDNESDAY, 20 JANUARY

LEICESTER CITY 0-2 TOTTENHAM HOTSPUR

FA CUP - THIRD ROUND REPLAY

With Tottenham pairing Kane and Alli, and the Foxes' Vardy and Mahrez starting on the bench, it was clear that Ranieri saw the priority in the league. But so too did Spurs, as they made eight changes.

CONCENTRATE ON THE LEAGUE

In what was the third meeting between these two sides in 10 days, Son Heung-min scored a stunning goal and set up another as Spurs booked their place in the FA Cup fourth round and left Leicester with only one thing to worry about - the league.

Spurs were barely troubled and took the lead in the 39th minute when Son's 18-yard strike beat Schmeichel. Chadli made it 2-0 when he converted Son's precise through ball. The north London side travel to League One strugglers Colchester United in the fourth round, a distraction that Leicester would not have now.

Son penetrated the powerful Leicester backline when he shifted past defender Ben Chilwell before scoring with a ferocious dipping strike, and his assist for the second was also a thing of beauty. After collecting substitute Kane's pass from the left, Son nutmegged Yohan Benalouane with his ball for Chadli, who fired beyond Schmeichel.

'Tinkerman' Ranieri repeated much of what he had done before the first match by making nine changes from the previous league match. As in the first game, his side were content to let Tottenham dominate possession in the hope of catching them on the break.

However, the plan failed. The Spurs midfield quelled the threat of wingers Demarai Gray and Nathan Dyer, and in doing so cut off the supply line for lone striker Ulloa. Okazaki and Albrighton were brought on after the break, as in the match at White Hart Lane, and improved matters. Albrighton had the Foxes best chance when he forced a good low save from the otherwise redundant Michel Vorm. In defence, Chilwell should perhaps have closed down Son for the opener, but he was Leicester's best player. The youngster was exceptional as an attacking full-back - the highlight a mazy first-half run that won his side a free-kick.

But with only one win in seven games in all competitions this was a blip most had anticipated.

Pochettino commented: "We have also the Premier League and Europa League and I think it is very important to keep the squad fit and working hard, and the FA Cup is very important for this. We are having a fantastic season, we are at a fantastic level. It is difficult to be fair to players but there is fantastic spirit in the changing room and in the training ground. I don't like to speak about change. For me, when you have 24 or 25 players they all work very hard and some players deserve to play and can't - you can only pick 11 and seven on the bench."

Ranieri remarked: "Tonight, Tottenham deserved to win. Our priority is the Premier League. The FA Cup, I wanted to see all my players and they played at their maximum. I'm very, very pleased with their performance."

SATURDAY, 23 JANUARY
LEICESTER CITY 3-0 STOKE CITY

Leicester moved three points clear at the top with an impressive victory to put to an end to any talk about a blip.

CRISIS WHAT CRISIS

Jamie Vardy struck straight at Jack Butland early on before Danny Drinkwater lashed in from the edge of the area close to half time. Drinkwater's goal was the first of his Premier League career. Leicester had scored 42 goals, but this was the first time they netted from outside the box.

Vardy rounded Butland and slotted into an open net as Ulloa added a third from close range late on.

Stoke's best chance falling to Joselu, whose header was pushed away by Schmeichel.

Leicester had won just one of their last five league games going into this fixture and there were question marks about whether they could stay in the hunt for the title, but they answered the critics with a performance full of energy and industry.

Even with their so-called blip, they had conceded just one goal in their last five games, patrolled at the back by a tough looking centre-back pairing of Morgan, who made seven clearances, and Huth. In front of them, Kanté's Makelele-like dominance epitomised the team's performance.

Question marks about Vardy disappeared as he netted his first in six league games, before Ulloa struck after sublime skills from Mahrez. Vardy had, thankfully, ended his personal goal drought of 10 hours and 17 minutes without a goal in the Premier League. Ranieri had been telling Vardy that if he continued to work hard then his goal drought would end - and he was proved right. During his six Premier League matches without a goal Vardy was typically industrious, despite his fitness being tempered earlier by a minor groin operation. Ranieri confirmed "It was not a problem. Jamie I tell every day it is not important, although I know goals for the strikers is important and maybe now he has more confidence, and when I speak with him I say it is important you continue to work hard because you are the main man and if you start to press then everyone follows. Then sooner or later you score a goal, I tell him this. You have to work and make it happen and then the goal will arrive."

Despite Leicester having won just one of their last five league games, it could quite easily be viewed as an impressive record of one defeat in their last 16 league games, and one which would be firmly put to the test in the next three matches against Liverpool, title rivals Arsenal and Manchester City - games which will define whether they were indeed title pretenders.

Ranieri commented: "Nobody can believe it. Our fans are dreaming and I want them to continue to dream. I don't know if we are a contender at this moment. February is a big month and after that month I can say something more realistic." He added "Now the players will have three days off, to clear the minds. And when they come back we restart to work hard because the league for us is very exciting. You know how much I love the clean sheet but it was also very important to score the three goals because Stoke City is a very good team - solid, strong and taller than us. The first half was very difficult but fortunately we find the goals. We made a fantastic performance and I am very pleased with my players."

Mark Hughes observed: "We are a lot better than we were able to show but that's credit to Leicester, who work exceptionally hard and press you in all areas of the field. We couldn't deal with that and we couldn't retain the ball in key areas of the pitch because of the pressure we were put under, which was disappointing."

MONDAY, 25 JANUARY

Back at the Premier League summit, Ranieri outlined their desire to stay in the title race by bringing in another striker before the transfer window closes in a week's time. Ranieri let Andrej Kramarić join German club Hoffenheim on loan last week. He said: "I'd like another striker to give support to the other three, because our strength is playing at a high intensity and it's not possible to play at high intensity for all the season. Everyone is reinforcing or taking (new) players because they want to save their season or want to win something. We want to maintain our position. I know it's difficult but we must try."

Leicester's display against Stoke was an impressive return to form for a team who had scored just twice in their preceding five league matches. It lifted them back to the top ahead of a "crucial" February: Liverpool, Manchester City and Arsenal, the next three opponents. According to Ranieri "I told the players February is very, very tough, and it's important to be top because, if a bad moment arrives, we'll be in a strong enough position to get over it."

The importance of one of Leicester's unsung heroes, Danny Drinkwater, who scored his first top-flight goal and set up Vardy's strike with an outstanding pass, began to materialise. He preferred to praise his team-mate though: "There was never any doubt in the dressing room that Vards would get his goals again," Drinkwater said. "That is his strength - you can hit a 50-50 ball and he changes the odds with his pace and hunger."

HISTORY ON OUR SIDE?

Ranieri could take inspiration from Blackburn Rovers' exploits over two decades ago. The Ewood Park outfit are the only other team outside of the top five to lead at this stage of the season, after which they went on to win the Premier League title in 1994-95. And history shows that the teams who lead the league after matchday 23 tend to go on to lift the title. Since 1992, only five teams have failed to secure silverware after leading their rivals at this stage. The first to throw away top spot was Newcastle, who somehow blew a 12-point lead to hand Sir Alex Ferguson his third league title as Manchester United manager.

United bounced back again the following season by finishing above the St James' Park outfit once more although Liverpool led the way after 23 matches. A campaign later and it was United's turn to surrender the lead as Arsene Wenger secured his first Premier League title as Arsenal manager. The same pattern occurred during the 2001-02 season when the Red Devils occupied top spot before their rivals pipped them to the league. However, Ferguson got his revenge the following season when United secured league glory - the last time a team failed to win the league after leading the race at this stage of the season.

TUESDAY, 26 JANUARY

Planning for the Hollywood film about Vardy's life progressed with screenwriter Adrian Butchart due in the UK for talks and research.

Butchart aimed to spend time with Vardy and those closest to him, and visit Stocksbridge Park Steels and the medical splints factory where the England international worked before joining Fleetwood Town as a full-time professional.

Butchart would also like to speak to England manager Roy Hodgson, and former Leicester boss Nigel Pearson, the man who took a chance on Vardy by bringing him to the King Power Stadium.

British-born Butchart was eyeing a star name to play the lead role, including *One Direction's* Louis Tomlinson, who follows Vardy on Twitter and sent him a message when he broke Van Nistelrooy's Premier League scoring streak. Butchart said: "We are looking at a few actors. Zac Efron and Robert Pattinson are two favorites, however *One Direction's* Louis Tomlinson is also very much on our radar, he's apparently a great footballer, he can act and he's from South Yorkshire so the accent won't be a problem for him. In fact we hear he's a Jamie Vardy fan, he even tweeted Jamie when he broke the goal scoring record in November." Tomlinson, who once turned out for the reserve side of boyhood club Doncaster Rovers, went to acting school as a kid and had small roles in ITV's *If I Had You* and BBC's *Waterloo Road*.

Butchart, who lives in Hollywood and makes movies with his production company Knightsbridge Films, wrote the scripts for the first two movies in the *Goal!* film trilogy that were released in 2005 and 2007. They made more than £23m at the box office around the world and featured cameos from stellar names including Zinedine Zidane and David Beckham. Richard Halsey, who won an Oscar in 1977 for best film-editing for the original *Rocky* film, agreed to team up with Butchart on the Vardy film having been inspired by his rise from non-league to Premier League top scorer. Universal, Disney and Warner Brothers were all interested in financing the project.

Butchart planned to watch Leicester's match against Liverpool on 2 February from Vardy's private box.

COACHING INSIGHT

Vardy felt he was now fully recovered following his minor operation. He elected to go under the knife in order to speed up his recovery, and is now "fully pumped up" ahead of Tuesday's visit of Liverpool. "You go through a spell where you don't score but thankfully I've scored a goal," said Vardy. "It's just one of those things that happens to strikers. It was well-documented that I had to have an operation and I was playing with pain-killing injections. But I could have literally gone straight back into training after my operation. I think this is the best my groin has felt. It was just a case of the pain from the operation which made me sit out a few training sessions, but other than that I'm fully pumped up and ready to go."

Vardy's success in front of goal has been one of the surprise stories of the season and conditioning coach Matt Reeves disclosed the sort of work that Vardy does behind the scenes to maintain his peak physical condition.

Vardy's game relies heavily on explosive bursts of pace which, according to Reeves, means he requires more recovery time than other players. "'Jamie is an extremely explosive player who plays at full tilt every game," Reeves explains during an interview with *The Times*. "As a result the medical, sports science and coaching departments are in agreement that he requires slightly longer to recover after each game than his team-mates. Immediately after a game the focus is on a good meal, milk and protein supplement, while players are sent away with recovery pack including Cherry Active* for its anti-oxidant properties and Leucine tablets to support muscle repair. When back in at the club's training ground, he utilises a combination of modalities, using common methods such as spin bikes, foam roller release, contrast bathing and massage, while also making the most of Leicester City's new Cryo Chamber unit in which players are exposed to temperatures of -135C.'

* Cherry Active offers a range nutritional supplements that are high in antioxidants, which are needed to fight off naturally occurring 'free radicals' that can cause damage to your body. A 30ml serving of Cherry Active concentrate is the antioxidant equivalent of eating 23 fruit & vegetables.

SUNDAY, 30 JANUARY

Claudio Ranieri talked briefly about the signing of Daniel Amartey. The Ghana international signed earlier in the window on a four-and-a-half year deal, costing £6m from Copenhagen. Ranieri admits the 21-year-old was not ready for the visit of Liverpool, when they'll be looking to defend their three-point lead at the top.

Amartey, who can play in midfield and defence, could be in contention to face title contenders Manchester City though at the weekend. Ranieri said in his pre-match press conference: "Daniel Amartey is not ready for Liverpool but I think he could be ready for Man City. His position is centre midfield, but I've seen him play in defence, right back and on the flank."

Leicester were keen to sign a new striker before the transfer window closed tonight, with CSKA Moscow's Ahmed Musa, Chelsea's Loic Remy and Crystal Palace's Dwight Gayle on their wish list. Leicester had a £15m bid rejected for the Nigeria captain earlier this week as CSKA Moscow held out for at least £19m. The agent of Musa believed the pacy forward, who had scored 10 goals, would remain at the Russian club as time was running out in the window. "There is little time left in the transfer window," representative Tony Harris said. "We are waiting for developments. "Sometimes the situation is changing in the last few hours. But Ahmed will most likely remain in Moscow. Playing in England is tempting for each player, and Musa is no exception. He would willingly go there. But it is necessary for his club to agree to the proposed terms. However, there is no urgency. Ahmed is happy in Moscow. But if there is a suitable offer, he would certainly consider it. I can only say that the interest is from a number of clubs, not just Leicester. Once a proposal is acceptable to all parties, we will consider it."

Ranieri, as usual, was more focused on the game ahead, "Always I'm positive but now, believe me, I am very focused on the next match. There are other people involved in the negotiations. Everything is done (identifying players) and now it is their job. My job is thinking about the team. (The squad) is enough because my team is so strong. It doesn't matter. If a player arrives or doesn't arrive, it's the same. If someone arrives I'm happy because these kind of players can help us. That's it. I am always confident."

Barclays Premier League Table at the end of January 2016:

POS	CLUB	P	W	D	L	GF	GA	GD	PTS
1	Leicester City	23	13	8	2	42	26	16	47
2	Manchester City	23	13	5	5	45	23	22	44
3	Arsenal	23	13	5	5	37	22	15	44
4	Tottenham Hotspur	23	11	9	3	41	19	22	42

FEBRUARY 2016

MONDAY, 1 FEBRUARY

Claudio Ranieri's men had had 10 days to prepare for the visit of Liverpool to the King Power, which marked the start of a pivotal run of fixtures for the club; tricky looking trips to both the Etihad and Emirates over the next fortnight, before returning to finish February at home to struggling Norwich City.

On the day of this game, Leicester would have spent 43 days at the top, only Manchester City (100 days) had been top for longer. Vardy had touched the ball in the opposition box more often than any other player in the Premier League so far this season (146).

The last 11 teams top of the table at the turn of February went on to win the title that season.

Ranieri shook his head and smiled when asked whether he could envisage himself hoisting the Premier League trophy at Stamford Bridge on the final day of the season. "I am a positive man and a positive man takes everything step by step," Ranieri said. "But you are moving too fast, like a Formula One car."

With 15 games to go, Ranieri's 'Improbables' were three points clear at the top, and a very useful 10 points ahead of fifth-placed Manchester United.

Ranieri urged his players to fulfil their destiny - and his. "This has been a crazy league, very strange, but the players know that we can now do something good." Ranieri said. "This is the right moment to push a lot, to fight, because next season will not be the same. This season, we can fight because it is David against Goliath, but next season will be the truth. I said I wanted us to reach 40 points. We did that and I am happy. If we take more, I will be even happier, but now we face Liverpool and I want my players to look at the game as being the last game that finishes our season. We must be focused."

Liverpool and Arsenal were the only two teams to have defeated Leicester in the Premier League this season and the outcome of the return fixtures, plus the trip to City on Saturday, would largely define the season.

"If you say to me that we will lose two more games between now and the end of the season, I will sign for that now," Ranieri said. "But yes, the next three games are very crucial. Every time I have said, 'Look where we are in a month,' we have stayed in the top positions, so now I say let us look where we are at the end of February. I like positive energy. If you believe positively and talk with positivity, then you can do much more than if you are negative."

With City confirming that Pep Guardiola will replace Manuel Pellegrini as manager in the summer, Ranieri dismissed the prospect of Leicester's title rivals at the Etihad being distracted. "Of course, I feel sorry for Pellegrini, but this is our life. I am old man, nothing in football surprises me. I knew from the start at Chelsea that I was finished at the end of the season. Abramovich tried to hire Sven-Göran Eriksson, but could not get him from the English (Football) Association. Then (Chief Executive) Peter Kenyon spoke to say, 'If Claudio does not win the title, it will be a disaster', so I knew and I understood the situation. But everybody at Chelsea stayed very focused, we got to the Champions League semi-final and finished second behind the unbeatable Arsenal team. So I don't think it will affect the focus of the Manchester City players."

Sky Sports pundit Paul Merson predicted: "The next three games define them, and if they win all three they will be Premier League champions. If they lose all three they will be fighting to stay in the top four. If Leicester are not talking about winning the league now surely that makes you lackadaisical and makes you think you've got a free swing at it. It's not a free swing. We are 23 games in, not five. However, I do see them winning this game. They can beat this Liverpool side, who I think are a bit all over the shop at the moment. I'm going for a 2-1 home win and I'm also backing Jamie Vardy to be first goalscorer. I just cannot see how Liverpool will cope with him."

TUESDAY, 2 FEBRUARY

LEICESTER CITY 2-0 LIVERPOOL

Merson wasn't far off - Vardy scored twice as Leicester beat Liverpool to stay three points clear at the top.

Ranieri insisted his side held no fears in the race for the title as Vardy scored twice, including a wonder strike to beat Mignolet on the hour-mark. Leicester now move on to fixtures against Manchester City and Arsenal at the top of the Premier League

When asked whether his side hold any fear, Ranieri told Sky Sports: "No because we enjoy when we play. It's not important if we lose because we are doing it in our way. Anything can happen and we'll continue to fight until the end. We have to take it step-by-step and now there is another fantastic match in Manchester against City. It's important for us to recover our energy because it is our football to press and to play very quickly. It's important the lads recover very well."

"Do you believe Leicester can win the Premier League, Claudio?" asked a reporter, three points clear with 14 games remaining. Ranieri responded: "What is this thing about which you speak? The title? I don't know what you mean. We are playing Manchester City next, a big game. That is all I can tell you. You understand the message."

UNBELIEVABLE

Ranieri was full of praise for Vardy as the striker took his tally to 18 Premier League goals for the season in front of the watching England coach Roy Hodgson. "Unbelievable," Ranieri said, when asked about Vardy's opener. "How Riyad Mahrez passed the ball to Vardy, and Vardy had the time to look at the goalkeeper and see him out of the goal and score? Unbelievable, unbelievable. There is a very good feeling between Drinkwater, Vardy, Mahrez and Okazaki because everybody understands the movement before they are doing the movement. That is unbelievable. Amazing.

The first goal was unbelievable. Jamie is very fast and can create a lot but it was unbelievable how Mahrez found him and how he had the time to see the keeper out of the goal and score a fantastic goal."

There was a feeling the next two weeks would define Leicester's season and they came through the first of those three games in style. Vardy opened the scoring with a brilliant, goal-of-the-season contender, 25-yard strike over Mignolet from Mahrez's long ball forward and he sealed the victory when he turned home Okazaki's deflected shot from close range 11 minutes later. Mignolet touched an Okazaki header onto the bar in the first half. Sakho brought down Okazaki and Leicester were unlucky not to win a penalty.

Drinkwater said: "We're staying on the ground but if we carry on the way we are then why not have the belief? It would go down in history surely."

In the Sky Sports studio Iain Dowie can't hold in his excitement after Vardy scored his wonder goal. Dowie called it one of the best goals he has ever seen! Vardy had 18 league goals, only one fewer than Cristiano Ronaldo and Luis Suarez. Vardy had never scored a Premier League goal from outside the box. He let Mahrez's long ball bounce before smashing it over Mignolet. After the game he revealed he had seen the keeper stray off his line on previous occasions and decided to try his luck. Drinkwater told BBC *Match of the Day*: "His first goal was incredible. You think he's going to square it but he hits it top corner. It sums his season up. He can turn an average ball into a great ball."

Vardy planned to stay at Leicester for a long time after agreeing a new three-and-a-half-year deal. He had more than two years to run on his current deal having joined Leicester from Fleetwood for £1m in 2012. Speaking after scoring twice: "It's nothing people don't know. I'd like to be here for a long time."

Leicester's next game is now their biggest of the season to date, when they visit second-placed Manchester City on Saturday lunchtime, knowing they could either be knocked off top - or go six points clear. "The team is in good condition," said Ranieri. "Now it is important to recover the energy because we have to run a lot against Manchester City. We are free of pressure. The players have a good feeling. In training sessions I saw my players refreshed. After Christmas we were a little tired but now they're getting better. Now I'm curious because on Saturday we have to run, run, run a lot. Against City it will be another tough match but it was important to start this month well. For me it's important to see my players fight and try to win. Sooner or later we'll lose a match but that's not important. What's important is how we lose. If there is a great goal from an opponent, well done - but we have to fight. If Man City fight more than us, well done to them."

WEDNESDAY, 3 FEBRUARY

Ranieri jokily promised John Arne Riise a coffee for favourable coverage on Norwegian television.

Riise was covering the game at Anfield in December for a Norwegian sports channel and he admitted the pair chatted before kick-off. "I actually spoke to him before Leicester's game against Liverpool because I was covering it for Norwegian television," he told *Goal.com*. "I told him that I would say good things about him and he replied by saying that he would owe me a coffee. In fact, I am still waiting for that coffee!"

Since losing that game, Leicester went on a formidable run dropping just nine points in the last eight games to top the Premier League. Riise believes Ranieri's man-management skills are the reason for the Foxes drastic change in fortunes this season. "He is a fantastic person and a coach who really connects with his players," he added, "He jokes with the players, he is always there to help them and that is why they give 100 per cent for him."

THURSDAY, 4 FEBRUARY

Jamie Carragher is always worth listening to and writing in his *Daily Mail* column the serial title winner with Liverpool, sagely commented: "What do you look for from the Premier League champions? The first thing you expect them to have is one of the leading scorers in the division, a man who has made the difference in the big moments. Next you would anticipate them having the best player in the country, someone whose performances have lit up the campaign and inspired those around him. After that, you would assume they would have the fewest losses and win the games that matter. Leicester City tick every single one of those boxes. Jamie Vardy has been the striker of the season, his 18 goals being worth an extra 18 points to his team; Riyad Mahrez - 13 goals, nine assists - must be a contender for the PFA Player of the Year while they have only lost two of their 24 matches. Those are the numbers of champions. So why are they not being taken seriously still? How come opposition fans are thinking 'It's only Leicester', as if to imply they should be beating them easily? They wouldn't be that way before a game against Manchester City or Arsenal, so why be like that before facing the league leaders? Look at how Liverpool played at the King Power Stadium on Tuesday. Would Sergio Agüero or Alexis Sanchez have been given the space to run into that Vardy was afforded for his first goal? No. If City's defenders don't show Leicester respect, Vardy will tear them apart. Teams keep treating them without the respect their position in the table demands.

I remember being on *Monday Night Football* in November after Leicester had been to Newcastle and won 3-0. They blitzed Steve McClaren's team on the counter-attack and took full advantage of the fact Newcastle wanted to go at them. What I couldn't understand was why Newcastle had been so cavalier when, only a few weeks earlier, they set up against champions Chelsea at St James' Park as if they were the away team. I've read a number of articles this week about Claudio Ranieri's squad and the general conclusion is that they will, at some point, fall away. Everyone loves the romance of their rise but very few genuinely believe they will see this through. It is a dangerous assumption. Leicester are not going away. When they beat Tottenham with that late Robert Huth goal last month, that was the first time I thought 'This could happen' and the more I look at things, the more I see how many advantages they have got over Arsenal, Manchester City and Tottenham. For starters, they have the most straightforward fixture list. We all saw in 2013-14 how that benefited Liverpool when their sole focus was the Barclays Premier League. When the workloads of their three rivals are increasing, Leicester will be able to stay fresh and focused. Another big factor is the absence of Sir Alex Ferguson and José Mourinho. Can you imagine if they were involved in this title race? The mind games would have started long ago, with questions about Leicester's psychological strength and remarks that would increase scrutiny on the squad.

Arsene Wenger and Manuel Pellegrini will not do the same. They are both nice men and don't use their press conferences to launch verbal grenades in the way Ferguson and Mourinho would. It isn't their style to apply that kind of pressure. If anything, the pressure is all on Wenger and Pellegrini, who are carrying the weight of expectation. Should Arsenal come up short, Wenger's argument about title winners having the best financial resources would become redundant. How would he explain 5,000-1 shots Leicester, who have spent longer (47 days) at the top than Arsenal (27 days), as champions?

What really impresses me is that every time a question is asked of Leicester they answer it firmly and emphatically. When everyone said the Christmas period would find them out, they responded with a sequence of results that has taken them three points clear. When questions were asked about their defensive record - Leicester went 11 games in all competitions at the beginning of the season without keeping a clean sheet - Ranieri addressed the issue by changing his full backs and the results are there to see. Danny Simpson has taken over at right back from Ritchie de Laet, Christian Fuchs took over from the injured Jeffrey Schlupp on the other flank and Leicester have now only conceded one goal in their past six Premier League games. Huth, signed 13 months ago, has also played a huge role.

Recruitment is the downfall of so many managers but Leicester's has been outstanding, spearheaded by Steve Walsh. The team has been put together superbly and the prices they have paid for excellent players, such as N'Golo Kanté (£5.6million from Caen), puts others to shame.

So now comes their next big assignment and Saturday's trip to the Etihad Stadium. The biggest obstacle to Leicester becoming champions is Agüero staying fit until the end of the season, but even if he fires in this match and Pellegrini's side win, it won't be the end of the world. A Manchester City win would only see them go level with Leicester. They have still got lots of games to play and there will inevitably come a point when their workload impacts on results.

Can you imagine what will happen, though, if Leicester win again? Having a six-point cushion at this stage of the campaign would be huge and leave Manchester City under massive pressure. Ranieri and his men, by contrast, can enjoy every single step along the way. Over the past 38 games, stretching back to this weekend 12 months ago, Leicester have collected 74 points. That total would see them comfortably reach the Champions League. If they keep up this pace, it might just take them to the ultimate prize."

FRIDAY, 5 FEBRUARY

Vardy's choice of bag, as he arrived in Manchester with the team, was heavily featured online which only further illustrated that every tiny piece of 'happening' suddenly became of interest to the media. He was pictured wearing a black *MCM Honshu Tantris* backpack, which is made from canvas and cowhide and features metal stud decoration. The bag, apparently, retails at £1,000, but he could afford it as he had been offered a new three-year deal worth £80,000-a-week. Of the contract, Vardy said: "It will be sorted, I'm leaving all of that up to my agent."

Leicester were taking on City at the Etihad, at the Saturday lunchtime kick-off slot, looking to extend their lead at the top to six points with just 13 games remaining. Vardy told *Foxes Player HD:* "It's going to be tough, we know that. They've got absolutely world class players but we know that we can give any team a game and we'll be trying our hardest to come home with the three points. It doesn't matter how they play because they'll come out, attack teams and expect to win. It's up to us to show that we're not just going to be pushovers and put in a performance that deserves the victory if we can get it. I think that day (the 0-0 draw in December) we gave them a bit too much time on the ball and let them play their game instead of us doing what we know best. So we'll be going to the Etihad with a different mentality and hopefully put in a performance that brings us the points."

Joe Hart knows Vardy's game but insisted Sergio Agüero is more lethal and had some advice for his opposite number Kasper Schmeichel who will be all too aware of what Agüero is capable of. "Sergio is a phenomenal player, he's a killer. He got one chance at Sunderland (1-0 win) the other night, stuck it in the corner and won us the game," Hart said, with perhaps more than a hint of mind games. The Argentina striker had scored 13 goals in the league this season despite missing most of October and November due to a heel injury.

Leicester had a three point gap over second-placed City and Vardy's first goal against Liverpool was a stunning, dipping volley from 30 yards. "Vardy's a top player and he's really on top of his game at the moment, but we've got the same (with Agüero) and we look forward to the challenge," said Hart. "Vardy's doing well, but we're going to look to stop him, the same way we dealt with him when we played at their place."

Asked for his views on the Midlands club's rise to prominence, Pellegrini suggested it had already made this season the best of recent memory and predicted that it could start a trend. "I think it's very good for the Premier League and probably next year another new team will be involved in the fight for the title," said the City manager. "Here in England all the teams have a lot of money to spend and a lot of them have very good players. For me this is the best season because we have such a small difference between one team and another that every game is like a final. Of course the big teams will continue trying to bring the best players but I think that other teams can bring different players and all of them are very good players. We have seen this season that maybe for some it can work."

Having taken Villarreal to the heights in Spain and Europe between 2004 and 2009, Pellegrini knows how it feels to upset the established order and can recognise Leicester's momentum building from afar. "Of course Leicester can do it, and they are demonstrating they can do it this season," he said. "I don't think we can keep talking about them being a surprise and I don't think we can keep thinking Leicester won't be involved in the title until the end. They will."

SATURDAY, 6 FEBRUARY
MANCHESTER CITY 1-3 LEICESTER CITY

Wow!

Leicester had already beaten third-placed Tottenham at White Hart Lane in January but this resounding result against Manchester City was their most significant in a remarkable season.

Robert Huth met Riyad Mahrez's free-kick to give the Foxes an early lead. The hosts rarely looked like breaking down the visitors' defence, while their own back line appeared vulnerable. Mahrez made it 2-0 with a neat step-over and finish, and Huth found space to head home a Christian Fuchs corner before Sergio Agüero scored a late consolation.

Manchester City boss Manuel Pellegrini said he had "no complaints" about the result but insists his side's hopes of winning the title are not over.

Pellegrini told BBC Sport: "Leicester played better than us. Conceding a goal from a set piece after two minutes was very important for the game. We had chances but it was a difficult game. I expected more from the beginning because it was very important, we are at home and playing top of the table, but we couldn't do it. There are 36 points to play for, nothing is finished. It is important for us to recover our players and I am continuing to not give up because we got an unexpected defeat but we must continue."

Claudio Ranieri saluted his side's defensive discipline at the final whistle, telling BBC Sport: "We played very, very compact and believed everything could be possible. We play without pressure because we don't have to win the league. We must enjoy. This league is so strange and now it is important to think about Arsenal. I want to wait until the end of April because I know the last matches are very tough. This is a fantastic moment for the Premier League, nobody knows who can win it."

FAVOURITES

Leicester City were named as several bookmakers' favourites to win the League after beating Manchester City 3-1 at the Etihad, the first time they had been named favourites to win the league outright and those who backed them at the start of the season could find themselves very rich come May. Sky Bet, Bet365, Coral and William Hill all slashed their odds on the Foxes winning their first League title minutes after the full-time whistle in Manchester.

The most commonly offered odds for that to happen were 15/8 - a far cry from the 5000/1 some punters were offered in mid-August.

Arsenal, who don't play until Sunday against Bournemouth at the Emirates, could be backed at 10/3, while Tottenham were at 9/2.

"After being as big as 5000-1 at the start of the season, Leicester are the new favourites to win the Premier League title in what would be an incredible story if they were to lift the trophy," said Coral's John Hill.

"Several small-stake punters could be set to win big on the back of the Foxes' remarkable campaign, leaving Britain's bookmakers set for a £50 million industry pay-out," added Hill.

Sky Bet would stand to lose 5.25m if Leicester claim the crown.

Andrew, 52, will win £33,333 if Leicester win the title, or £8,333 if they finish runner-up. The Foxes fan told *Sportsmail*: "Every year I place a bet on Leicester to win the league they are in. When they won the Championship I won £140 and so when they were promoted to the Premier League, I placed the same £5 each-way bet at 5000/1. I also put on a bet Leicester finishing in the top four (£5 at 500/1 to make £2,500). I am very confident at that bet coming in but as to winning the Premier League, well let's just see."

AL (THINGS) BRIGHTON BEAUTIFUL

Marc Albrighton might have been heading for the Championship, instead he was on course for the Champions League. Unworthy of a new contract at Aston Villa, he was picked up by Leicester for nothing, and turned into one of the most effective wingers in the Premier League, scoring only once, but providing six assists, integral to the high energy, quick-moving side under Ranieri. He tracks back to win balls and whips crosses into the box at every opportunity, totaling 140 for the season at a rate of nearly six per game.

The boyhood Villa fan, who attended the club's FA Cup semi-final against Liverpool at Wembley last season, believed arrogance was their demise. "I don't think it's right that a club as big as that could be playing in the Championship" he says of the Premier League's bottom-club. "It just goes to show that you are never too big to go down and a bit of arrogance has probably cost them in the end. I think that's something that needs to be addressed but that's down to them."

Albrighton confirmed he paid for train tickets for Villa fans heading back from London last April. "We were on the train and in first class. There were no seats in the normal section. There were five or six of us in there and I think it was ten pound to upgrade. We were enjoying the company. We were all enjoying it, so I sorted them out." That period coincided with him earning his place back in the team, having been omitted for most of the season by Nigel Pearson. But the former manager brought Albrighton on as a half-time substitute against West Ham on 4 April and Leicester went on to win.

Albrighton retained his starting place for the final eight games of last season, operating as an offensive wing-back, as Leicester mounted their great escape, and in total he has only tasted defeat three times in 33 Premier League matches. "It's pretty strange," he conceded. "But this time last year, it was the total opposite. I wasn't playing. We were bottom of the league by a long way. I probably appreciate it more being where we are at this stage than anyone because I know how I felt this time last year. I know how I felt."

Albrighton spent 16 years at Villa. "Where Villa are at this minute, it's not nice at all. I wish for them to stay up but it's not looking likely," he said. "I hope they can be one of the clubs that bounces back straight away, but that will be difficult. It's such a tough division to get out of. My first hope is that we can do something big but then I hope that something can get sorted at Villa Park."

SUNDAY, 7 FEBRUARY

Writing in his *Mail on Sunday* column, the former England, Spurs and Chelsea manager Glenn Hoddle said: "Leicester were simply stunning on Saturday. In a season of great performances, that must surely rank as their best. If that had been a team coming from Europe to play at Manchester City, we would all be saying: 'What a fantastic side this is. Look at the pace they have, the way they pass the ball, how tactically smart they are.'

Having all got it so wrong at the start of the season, myself included, it's time to give Leicester their due credit. They clearly can win the Premier League. Of course the pressure will build up in the last few games. And Manchester City, Arsenal and Tottenham still have a good chance as well. But Leicester, under Claudio Ranieri, will be there right at the end. They are the real deal. They were better than Manchester City and the belief and confidence they have accumulated means they are playing better than almost anyone. Combined with a reasonable run-in, they have every chance.

There are some players, such as Danny Drinkwater and Marc Albrighton who are now achieving levels you perhaps might not have expected. They were excellent in possession and hitting balls I wouldn't have thought were possible."

MONDAY, 8 FEBRUARY

Gary Lineker tweeted that Arsenal recruited the wrong scout when they poached Ben Wrigglesworth.

Wrigglesworth became an unusual transfer saga before confirming his move via Twitter by thanking his current employers. He tweeted: "After three-and-a-half unbelievable seasons, working with amazing people, I am now starting a new chapter. It was a very difficult decision, leaving Leicester, but I had to take an opportunity that doesn't come round often. I only wish the best for Leicester in the future and will always be eternally grateful to them for getting me to where I am."

The young scout was credited with the success of Leicester's recent recruits, including being the man to have discovered Riyad Mahrez before Leicester completed the £375,000 from French side Le Havre.

Steve Walsh, however, was the source, as Lineker said: "I love how Arsenal nicked the wrong scout! Steve Walsh is the guy who found these players and bought them in. I know when he found Mahrez he was sent to watch someone else and came back with Mahrez. He's done a brilliant job and that's been the large key to Leicester's success. As in all clubs, it's about the people you bring in and they've done it on a relatively small budget compared with the giants. Christian Fuchs is another for sure. He's so underrated, we got him on a free transfer."

Gary Lineker, @GaryLineker - Oops! Think you'll find that Steve Walsh was largely responsible for spotting Mahrez et al.

TUESDAY, 9 FEBRUARY

To be fair, Gary Lineker was delighted Ranieri has proven him wrong in taking his old club five points clear with 13 games to go. He fears, though, he really *will* have to present *Match of the Day* in his underpants in August.

Lineker is a former Filbert Street season-ticket holder, who cried on his way home from their 1969 FA Cup final defeat by Manchester City. Then he was a promotion-winning striker there. And in 2002, he was the figurehead for a consortium which saved the club after it had plunged into administration.

Lineker was regretting promising he would present *MOTD* in undies. "I stupidly said I would present the show in my pants - but at that stage I absolutely categorically knew that they *weren't* going to win the league. Now the nation is in trouble - I'm hoping to get a really good (sponsorship) deal! I'm hoping to get some very large pants that will go over my head to stop me blushing. At the start of the season they were 5,000-1 for the title, now I think it's about 7-4. I was just pleased that they managed to keep the whole squad together for the January window. I'm not worried about any danger in the summer - if they win the league that'll do me! They could cease to exist and it wouldn't matter. It's just magical what's happened - but we're trying not to get ahead of ourselves. It wasn't my first thought when I got the job with BT Sport last summer that I can follow Leicester in the Champions League! But, they are in a great shape to get a Champions League spot now, there is a massive (12-point) difference between them and (Manchester United in) fifth-place. A couple of serious injuries and things can change, when you haven't got the depth of other teams. But the fact Leicester are not in any other competitions will limit the possibilities of bad luck in that sense. It would be a great adventure for Leicester to be in the Champions League. They are actually quite well equipped to play European football because of the nature of the counter-attacking style Leicester play and the pace they play on the break, but we are probably getting ahead of ourselves here…"

Ranieri proved him wrong. "We were all wrong. Ranieri has changed things, because Pearson had been playing five at the back and Ranieri went to a back four. He did tinker a bit, but he kept the pace on the counter-attack, he's clearly got the backing of the players, he's respected and liked, he's done a fabulous job. Those of us who were critical or not overly excited by the appointment have wonderfully been proved wrong."

Lineker would include at least four Leicester players - Vardy, Mahrez, Kanté and Fuchs - in his Premier League team of the season. "They have a wonderful spirit and a great dynamism. Fuchs is an excellent player, I haven't seen anyone better in midfield than Kanté this season, in terms of the role that he plays. Vardy has been sensational, Mahrez unbelievable and Marc Albrighton has done brilliantly too. Vardy thinks about his game a lot, he works really hard and has exhilarating pace. His finishing has improved a lot, which was the one part of his game a couple of years ago you'd have said was his weakness. The two centre-backs, Rob Huth and Wes Morgan, are in many ways journeyman pros but they have that wonderful attitude and never-say-die spirit that has culminated in them being top of the league. I was a season-ticket holder at Leicester with my Dad and Grandad aged eight and I cried all the way home from the 1969 Cup final, so what is happening now is just unbelievable."

WEDNESDAY, 10 FEBRUARY

Ranieri did not want to be woken up from his title dream, and no one seemed to be able to do so, with all the big boys showing remarkable inconsistencies.

Five points clear of Spurs at the top, following the win over Manchester City at Etihad Stadium, Ranieri insisted his players were not feeling the tension even though his team were now the bookmakers' favourites to win the title. "It's a great story so why the pressure? Let's enjoy," he said. "I hope the bookmakers, this time, are right but I am very pragmatic. Give me points and not words. We want to continue to dream - nobody wake us up, please."

Leicester lost only two out of 25 games in the League, as Ranieri agreed a top-four finish would be "fantastic" for a club who were 5,000-1 shots to win the League before the start of the season. "It's a 12-point gap (to Manchester United in fifth place) and for us to achieve the Champions League would be fantastic," he said.

Leicester next meet third-placed Arsenal at Emirates Stadium on Valentine's Day, followed by a 13-day break before a home fixture against Norwich City.

THURSDAY, 11 FEBRUARY

Danny Drinkwater was in line for an England call-up following his outstanding performances. He was not among the 40 players attending the get-together at St George's Park but was under consideration for the squad for next month's friendlies against Holland and Germany.

Hodgson attended the win against Liverpool at the King Power Stadium, where he was also running checks on Vardy and Jordan Henderson, and there are plans for his staff to look at Drinkwater in the coming weeks. The 25-year-old faced stiff competition although there are doubts over the fitness of Michael Carrick and Jack Wilshere in the key central midfield area. Drinkwater represented England at under-18 and under-19 level but has been overlooked at a higher age group since 2009.

FRIDAY, 12 FEBRUARY

Thirteen games to go and, in part of north London there was much hope it would be Arsenal taking the honours. Arsene Wenger, so often complaining of fixture congestion, offered a perverse suggestion that Ranieri's team might suffer down the home straight because, absent from all cup competitions, they will not have played enough games. "Time to think (in between games) can be a disadvantage if you are not thinking in a positive way and the pressure is on," argued Wenger. "It is true that sometimes the less time you have to wait for the next game, the better it is."

Ranieri delivered the perfect response: "When they are playing in the cups we will go to the sea, make some swimming and sit in the sunshine," placing his hands behind his head in deckchair pose.

No pressure evident form an ultra-relaxed Ranieri. As always, he began his media briefing by shaking the hand of every journalist in the room, a task that takes longer every week. "I am superstitious," he said, "but yes, this was easier when there were only five people here."

No, he insisted in numerous different ways, there is no strain, only the thrill and romance. "Listen, I think the pressure is about the other teams, not us," said Ranieri. "You mention the money, the big guy. We are the little guy, but Arsene spends big money every year. Tell me why I must feel pressure? We are close to continuing to dream with our fans and we want to dream. Nobody wake us up, please. We know very well that we need to make points in every match, but we know we can (afford to) lose against Arsenal. But it is important to continue, we don't have pressure. We did our job (stayed up), our goal is OK, so everything we can do now is fantastic. I know that slowly, slowly people want to build pressure, they say we will go down but now people are thinking we can win, it is important for them to say something because they spend a lot of money and, if they don't win, it is a disaster. I don't have pressure and I try to take pressure out of my players, but let us see how we play."

Ranieri felt little anxiety visiting a stadium where Arsenal had not scored in their last two games.

Asked if Leicester could win the title, Wenger said: "I'm not sure. I believe that there is still a long way and it is still too early. Leicester today are in a strong position and they have certainly silenced all the doubters since the start of the season because at Christmas people were saying they would not be there and now we are at Easter and they are still there. In the last week they have shown solid potential to win the league with two positive results against Liverpool and Manchester City away. Of course, it is very romantic and I understand the whole country (being behind them). That is human. It is good for football and it goes against the usual practice in our game, which is spend, buy big stars. It is important to know that with quality work, quality scouting and quality management you can have great results. I believe they are still in a position where they think they have nothing to lose but once you are top of the league, you can also think about losing what you have. That is where the nerves come in a little bit. I do not know how they will respond to that."

Louis van Gaal said Leicester can lead from the front and claim a historic title as they sit five points clear at the top of ahead of their showdown with rivals Arsenal on Sunday. Van Gaal believed Gary Lineker, the former striker and club favourite, could be made to regret his bet. "They are the favourites because they are five points away from the rest. Is it possible? Why not?" Van Gaal told the *Independent.* "Maybe their players can cope, but that you do not know and that is a question that both Leicester and Tottenham must answer."

Van Gaal later added: "Maybe you remember that I have already said that Leicester can be the champion?' The Godfather, Gary Lineker, was laughing about that, but he has to undress himself if they win it, is that right? Well, I am waiting for that."

SUNDAY, 14 FEBRUARY

ARSENAL 2-1 LEICESTER CITY

Danny Welbeck threw the Premier League title race wide open when he scored a dramatic winner, in the 95th minute, with only seconds remaining as Arsenal beat leaders Leicester City.

Ranieri and his men were left desolate after an outstanding backs-to-the-wall performance, exemplified by the brilliance of keeper Schmeichel as he kept Arsenal at bay, with one late world-class save from Giroud especially notable.

Gary Lineker, on Twitter, reflected the pain that the Leicester fans were no doubt feeling:

Gary Lineker, @GaryLineker - There is nothing quite like football for filling you with joy one minute and tearing your heart to shreds the next.

Leicester still led the table - but Arsenal's win leaves them only two points clear.

Jamie Vardy gave the Foxes the lead with a hotly-disputed penalty on the stroke of half-time after he tumbled over Nacho Monreal's outstretched leg.

Substitute Theo Walcott then set up a frantic final 20 minutes with a side-foot finish from Olivier Giroud's superb knockdown.

The Foxes looked set to hold out for a vital draw, as a thrilling game went into injury time, despite being reduced to 10 men after Danny Simpson was sent off for a second yellow card early in the second half...enter Danny Welbeck who, playing his first competitive game since April last year, glanced Mesut Özil's free-kick past the magnificent Kasper Schmeichel to spark wild celebrations at the Emirates Stadium. Leicester had lost in the league for just the third time this season.

Arsenal boss, Arsene Wenger, spoke to BBC Sport: "The effort, energy, intensity was all good. Leicester defended very well but we had bad luck to be 1-0 down at half-time. We were relentless after that - we should have scored more goals. It was a pivotal moment today because the mathematics meant it could be eight points or it could be two points. That is a great change."

Claudio Ranieri told Sky Sports: "It was a fantastic match, very fast. I don't know if in a normal match that our two yellows cards was a sending off. They were normal fouls, but not yellow cards. I think the referee was too severe to us for the sending off. 11 v 11, I'm sure we win the match. The match was full of fouls so why send off a player? Come on. We know Arsenal are a fantastic team, they move the ball quickly and have skill, but we had to concentrate. We tried to counter-attack and we controlled the match very well. We are still top of the table, got two points more - we must carry on and smile. We lost to our opponents - we must say well done."

FRIDAY, 19 FEBRUARY

Wes Morgan did not make his top-flight debut until he was 30, but was now captaining the leaders in one of the most incredible seasons the Premier League has ever seen.

Just over 18 months on from finally making it into England's top division, Morgan talked to BBC East Midlands Today. He was released by Notts County as a youngster in 1999 but after a couple of years in non-league, he was given a second chance across the River Trent. John Pemberton, then Forest's academy director, remembered having to keep Morgan away from manager Paul Hart when he first joined because he simply wasn't fit enough. "His socks didn't go up to his knees because his calves were too big, his legs rubbed together and his shirt was skin tight. He was well overweight," Pemberton said. "Paul saw him in the car park and said: 'Who's that lad?' We said he was a trialist and Paul said: 'We don't want any trialists looking like that'. So we hid from the manager - and we actually hid him for about eight months."

Morgan explained: "Getting released wasn't nice. It was hard to take. But I remained positive and I got a trial at Forest and that was an opportunity to get back into it and that's where it all started." Morgan thanked Hart as he made his debut as a 19-year-old in August 2003. "I came on trial and did well and was kept on for the season," Morgan said. "I wasn't in the best shape possible and had to work hard. There was a lot of conditioning work to get to the point where I needed to be. You have to be at a certain fitness level and I needed to put in the work to get to that point. I have nothing but good things to say about Paul Hart. He gave me my first professional contract and my debut. It all began with him."

Hart told BBC Sport: "When I first saw him he was quite big and I said I am not putting him in our kit until that changes. But he worked extremely hard. You always saw a good footballer; he always had the basics. I gave him his debut at left-back and he was excellent. Wesley was very aware of his strengths and weaknesses, and when you have that you have a great chance."

Morgan's move across the East Midlands after 10 years with Forest came as a shock in 2012, but Nigel Pearson was desperate for a dominant centre-back. "He's as good a defender as there is at this level and has been since he's been here - never mind just this season," Pearson said.

Morgan remained one of the many Pearson players to figure in a central role in their astonishing season under Ranieri. Morgan remarked, "To be in the position we are in is an achievement in itself. Anything that happens now is definitely a bonus. People tipped us to be relegated at the start of the season and we are competing at the top of the league. We are just delighted with how things have gone so far. We have a real confidence and belief and know that on our day we can be as good, if not better, than anyone out there in this league."

Morgan spent much of Leicester City's fixture-free week at a half-term football school, MB Coaching, coaching youngsters with his lifelong friend and former Forest team-mate Julian Bennett. The pair grew up together in The Meadows, one of Nottingham's toughest areas. The council estate has a reputation for gun crime, drugs and gangs and Morgan has always said his love for football could well have saved from a very different path. "It has always been a dream of mine to play in the Premier League and I have done," Morgan said. "I am very thankful for that and I am glad to be able to give something back with the coaching alongside my good friend Julian. From as early as I can remember I used to see Jules - he used to live two or three minutes away from me and playing football on the streets was a big part of growing up. We have always had that passion. I thought the opportunity to play in the Premier League had passed me by. Everyone wants to play at the highest level and it took a lot longer than I anticipated and wanted, but I got there eventually. I am enjoying it a lot!"

Morgan's biggest fan is his mother. His mum added a few extra kisses to her post-game text messages to mark the Foxes' remarkable season. "Right now things are going well so I'm getting extra kisses on the end of the text message after games. She is obviously delighted. But win, lose or draw she is happy for me and what I have achieved. I know she is very proud of me and it's good to have that support."

Morgan had not started talks about a new contract with a year to run on the three-year deal he signed in 2014. Morgan told BBC East Midlands Today: "I love it here and would love to stay. But now I am focusing on what we can achieve as a group and trying to get over that finishing line. First and foremost I need to concentrate on the pitch and see what happens after that."

The Foxes now had 53 points, two points clear at the top with 12 games remaining. Arsenal and Spurs had 51 points, with Manchester City in fourth place on 47 points.

FRIDAY, 26 FEBRUARY

Leicester were back and refreshed felt Wes Morgan. Having lost agonisingly in injury-time at Arsenal on Valentine's Day, the squad were given a week off training by Ranieri as their title rivals fought in cup competitions.

The Foxes were due to host relegation threatened Norwich hoping to maintain their two point cushion over Spurs and Arsenal.

The players appreciated Ranieri's offer of a week break, especially after the loss at the Gunners. "The manager came in the dressing room and he was full of praise for our performance (at Arsenal) and the way we went about our jobs," Morgan told the *Independent*. "Then he turned round and said, 'you've got a week off'. So the boys were delighted with that and I think quite a few of them booked a break away pretty quickly."

Morgan was adamant they can steal a march on their rivals having relaxed for a week whereas Manchester City, Arsenal and Spurs all battled in European fixtures. "To have a two-week period without a game, I think it's wise to take advantage of that and have a mental break as well as a physical break - recharge the batteries, spend some time away from the grass, if you get a chance to get some sun, go ahead and do that. Then come back refreshed and raring to go for the final part of the season."

The players ignored the incessant hype. "I know the pundits and the media are talking about a run of easier games for us now, but it's the Premier League - no games are easy. Some of these teams are fighting for their lives, just as we were at this time last season; sometimes they are even tougher games than playing against the top sides. I think we need to keep the same mindset and the same focus that we've had for every single game," declared Morgan. "We're not getting carried away with what people are saying."

A fan convinced his partner to name their unborn child after Jamie Vardy by launching an online petition.

Ashley Marriott, from Leicester, will give his daughter the middle name Vardy after he hit a target of 5,000 signatures, reaching the total on Thursday after the story was originally featured in the *Leicester Mercury*.

The "massive" Foxes fan said he has had support from all over the world. "Jokingly the other night she (Mr. Marriott's partner Daisy) said to me, 'I've been following your campaign, it's not really got anywhere', and the day after...it went everywhere," he said. "I'm happy and I think she's taken to it now - there's no way you can back out from it now." He was in awe of Vardy's achievements, including scoring in 11 consecutive matches plus the Foxes were two points clear with 12 games remaining, despite being bottom of the table at the same stage last season. His girlfriend was initially not convinced by his idea and took a lot of persuading. He added: "I kept saying about it and she thought I was joking, but I was serious. I wanted it to happen so I had to do something to show I was serious." He started the petition last week and said she finally "gave in" after the target was broken.

One of the comments on the petition page is from *a* Jamie Vardy, but it was unclear if it was the player. It said: "Follow your dream mate, support us all the way!! Thankful to you for being so loyal and a true fan to dedicate her middle name to me."

The baby is due in June.

SATURDAY, 27 FEBRUARY
LEICESTER CITY 1-0 NORWICH CITY

Leonardo Ulloa's 89th-minute goal extended the lead to five points.

The Foxes were facing the prospect of losing top spot if either of Arsenal or Spurs win on Sunday - instead they were guaranteed to stay at the top with 11 games left. Cameron Jerome should have scored when he climbed highest to meet a first-half corner, while Redmond fizzed a shot past the post from long range with Schmeichel beaten.

Ulloa's late winner was further evidence of the momentum and belief that has carried Ranieri's men this far. Leicester did not record a shot on target until the 58th minute. Two of Ulloa's three Premier League goals this season have come as a sub, and Leicester have conceded only four goals in their last nine Premier League games.

As the clock ticked down, the hosts had only managed two shots on target, both from distance, both dealt with by John Ruddy. Enter Ulloa, who arrived at the back post to convert into an empty net after Albrighton's low cross had crucially been poked past Ruddy by Vardy.

Champions notoriously find a way to win when they are not at their best, as Norwich devised a plan to prevent Leicester from the pacy counter-attacks that have carried them to the top. Vardy was given no space behind the defence and was largely anonymous, while Mahrez, bar a couple of jinking runs, was often crowded out.

It was only the third time Leicester had the most possession in a Premier League match as Norwich were happy to concede the ball in order to not leave the sort of space in which Vardy and Mahrez thrived.

In their final 11 fixtures, Leicester would face only three clubs in the current top nine.

Ranieri commented: "It was a difficult match. Norwich played well and closed the space, but we believed until the end. This victory was very important to restart after the Arsenal defeat. I said before the Arsenal match that Norwich would be more difficult. Both teams could have scored a goal in the final 20 minutes. The conclusion I have drawn from this is that my players believe until the end. That, for me, is very important. If the other teams start to win, they can win all the matches. But for us, the next match is always the final match. That is our mentality."

Norwich manager Alex Neil: "I don't think we deserved that. In the game we had good chances and defensively we were solid. We kept Vardy and Mahrez quiet and we certainly deserved something."

Barclays Premier League Table at the end of February 2016:

POS	CLUB	P	W	D	L	GF	GA	GD	PTS
1	Leicester City	27	16	8	3	49	29	20	56
2	Tottenham Hotspur	27	15	9	3	49	21	28	54
3	Arsenal	27	15	6	6	43	26	17	51
4	Manchester City	26	14	5	7	48	28	20	47

MARCH 2016

TUESDAY, 1 MARCH

LEICESTER CITY 2-2 WEST BROMWICH ALBION

Leicester missed the chance to go five points clear at the top as West Brom came from behind to claim a thrilling draw.

Salomón Rondón shrugged off Huth to give West Brom the lead, but a Danny Drinkwater deflected shot levelled it. Andy King finished a wonderful move to put Leicester ahead only for Craig Gardner to equalise with a free-kick after Mahrez needlessly handled.

Leicester twice hit the bar at a raucous King Power Stadium, but could not find a winner. The draw left the Foxes three points ahead of Spurs, who could go top with victory at West Ham on Wednesday, and six ahead of Arsenal, who faced Swansea.

Albion conceded possession, defended deeply, and they were bombarded by wave after wave of Leicester attacks, mainly down the flanks through the excellent Mahrez and Albrighton. The Foxes had 22 attempts, with headers from Vardy and Okazaki hitting the woodwork. Foster also saved from Schlupp and Morgan, while Ulloa could not repeat his weekend heroics when the ball flashed across the face of goal in the very last minute.

However, even with nine red shirts behind the ball, Leicester still found a way to lead, meaning West Brom had to make more of the play in the second half. It worked to their advantage as, after Mahrez needlessly handballed, Gardner curled in a sublime free-kick. Rondón could even have won it but somehow turned over from inside the six-yard box. The Baggies overall, however, needed some fortune to hang on at the end of a breathless night.

Leicester became the first Premier League team this season to score 50+ goals in the competition. Mahrez has had a part in a league-high 25 Premier League goals this season (14 goals, 11 assists). Two of Leicester's three top-flight goals from outside the area this season have been scored by Drinkwater. Leicester's record as the only Premier League side not to concede at home in 2016 ended.

King was making only his seventh league start of the season, in the side for the injured Kanté. The Welsh midfielder is the only member of the Foxes squad remaining from their time in the third tier seven years ago and has winners' medals from both League One and the Championship. He was moving toward adding a Premier League medal when he met Mahrez's athletic back-heel to finish sharply past Foster. King is the fourth Welshman to score on St David's Day in Premier League history (the other three being Mark Pembridge, Dean Saunders and Jack Collison).

"Little Leicester" were ready to fight for the title, according to Ranieri. "There are Tottenham and Manchester City in the race to fight for the title and there is little Leicester to fight against them," said the Italian. "We are confident. Why not win it? Be positive."

"Four points from two difficult matches, it is fantastic," said Ranieri. "We are alive and our spirit is ready to fight again. I am happy, not that we didn't get the three points because you can't always get the three points, but our performance was fantastic."

Leicester had lost only three times in the first 28 games. "We can repeat last season," said Ranieri. "We try to do our best. Today we were not so lucky, but perhaps in the last 10 matches we will be. I am very pleased with our performance. They played so well - there was no panic after the first goal. We played much better than against Norwich. I am satisfied with the performance. Just sometimes you can do everything but the ball doesn't want to go in. I want to create a lot of chances and sooner or later we score. Tonight wasn't the right moment but we are alive and we fight to the end. Everybody is ready to fight, to play well, to create chances. Only the victory was missing. We tried to do everything and well done to my players. We never, never give up. We always try the best in every situation. Every team plays football and we have to find the solution and try to win. It is important not to lose the match too as they could have counter-attacked."

West Brom manager Tony Pulis: "Leicester are a good side. They ask questions of you. It's another point on the way for us. It's important for us to get to 40 points and we are happy with the way things are going. We need the hunger and desire to get to 40 points. We should have kept the ball better tonight. I'm really pleased with the players though. I'd love to see Leicester win the title."

It wouldn't be the last time Tony Pulis would make such a statement.

SATURDAY, 5 MARCH
WATFORD 0-1 LEICESTER CITY

Leicester beat Watford to move five points clear at the top as Mahrez scored his 15th Premier League goal, and after second-placed Tottenham drew with third-placed Arsenal, the Foxes took a step closer to English football's most unlikely title win.

Mahrez almost set up Vardy for an early goal as the Foxes started well and a similar start to the second half saw the Algerian rifle high into the net after José Holebas cleared to him. He had scored or assisted 26 goals this season, but caused no little concern after he seemingly pulled his hamstring late in the game and was substituted. Fortunately, Mahrez later said it was only cramp.

Despite good chances for Troy Deeney and Odion Ighalo, the visitors held on and now there were *only* nine games between them and a historic first title triumph. The victory also took them 11 points clear of fifth-placed West Ham as the Foxes closed on a Champions League spot, and they were a massive 41 points better off than they were at the same stage last season when they were bottom of the table.

Each week the pressure is ramped up, but since the Foxes drew with West Brom on Tuesday, rivals Spurs and Arsenal were both beaten, before the two north London sides drew in a fiercely contested derby earlier on Saturday.

Watford, admittedly, did not offer the toughest opposition, but an opportunity to take a five-point lead presented its own examination. Morgan had a running battle with Ighalo, who missed a close-range header late on, with Amrabat and Holebas both having shots saved by Schmeichel. Aké also clipped the top of the crossbar with a header but the hosts rarely threatened the Leicester goal.

Leicester had won 31 points away from home this season; five more than any other team. Eleven of Mahrez's 15 Premier League goals came away from home. Leicester scored 33 goals in the second half of Premier league games - two more than any other side.

Ranieri commented: "It was an important win, a big battle. Now there will be only battles for everybody not just for us. A tough match. We created four or five chances, they created two or three. We are so happy now. The title is not ours. We have to fight a lot, step by step and keep our feet on the ground. At the end we can see what happens. I'm sorry, we know every team can win or lose so it has to be slowly, slowly."

On Mahrez' hamstring, the manager added: "No injury, he was tired and had a little cramp so I changed him in the late minutes. His goal was so important."

Watford manager Quique Sanchez Flores said: "It was very difficult, they defended very well, lots of intensity through the middle. We created some attempts, we make one mistake and when they score first it is very difficult."

Leicester now had a nine-day break until Newcastle at home.

MONDAY, 7 MARCH

A fan who stood to win £250,000 from a £50 bet cashed out for £72,000. The Warwickshire man, who chose to remain anonymous, bowed out of the 5,000-1 wager on Saturday.

Hours later his stake would have been worth £91,000 after the Foxes beat Watford 1-0, said Ladbrokes. The winner said: "It will mean so much if we win, so there's no point in being greedy." He was "ecstatic" and looking forward to the rest of the league whatever the outcome. "The odds are constantly changing, even Chelsea could sneak into the top four at the last minute," he said. "A holiday to Spain is a certainty followed by paying off the mortgage with the winnings." Jessica Bridge of Ladbrokes said: "It's a life-changing amount of money and we congratulate our customer for holding his nerve this long."

Odds on winning the title were now 5-4, said Ladbrokes. It comes a week after Leicester City fan, John Pryke, who last August placed a bet after "fancying the look" of the odds, cashed out his bet for nearly £30,000. For lifelong fan John the money at stake was all getting a bit too much and the thought of a £100,000 windfall should the Foxes be champions was dominating his thoughts at every match. He cashed out his £20 bet, taking home a useful £29,000, although it means he has had to give up on his dream of buying an Aston Martin. "It was ruining the game, to be honest," he said. "I just want to enjoy the time when Leicester actually win the Premiership. I knew that anything could happen (when the bet was placed) and it has." He had hoped to buy a bungalow but settled for redecorating the family home after getting nervous about recent results. "It's been a crazy season, I'd be silly not to take my money and run. I've also backed Leicester to finish in the top 4 at 400-1, so I can enjoy the rest of season knowing I've got my winnings early." That extra bet could net him the tidy sum of £4,000.

The BBC Sport website featured self-employed DJ Nathaniel Whessell who had placed a 60p "investment" that could net him £3,000. The 20-year-old had pennies left over in his William Hill account and thought, "why not Leicester? I've never followed Leicester - I'm a Brighton fan. I considered putting some money on them but with odds of 16-1 it didn't really seem worth it. I wasn't planning on putting 60p on anything, I just thought let's back an outsider for a laugh."

Bookmakers were now frantically offering gamblers a chance to cash out their bet early for a reduced sum. But Nathaniel was holding out for the end of the season; the last three games, against Manchester United, Everton and Chelsea, made him a little nervous. "If the odds get really good I might take the money. But I'm only losing 60p if I don't win anything. What can you get for 60p?"

Keval Nakeshree had already made a healthy £5,000 after putting £5 on Leicester being top at Christmas. If the father-of-two from Gloucester holds his nerve he stands to trouser another £33,000."This time last year Leicester were bottom of the league. Lots of people said they were going down so that inspired me to place the bet. The last seven or eight games of last season really showed they were on form and I genuinely believed they could win."

Keval is a Leicester fan, having grown up in the city and watched the likes of Emile Heskey and Muzzy Izzet at the club's old Filbert Street ground. He had no plans to cash out early, but after a recent flurry of gamblers panicked and picked up their winnings he was now considering it. And what to do with the money? "I think my wife might have spent it already!"

Another Leicester fan - who did not want to be named - cashed out his ticket on Monday, pocketing £29,788, after pressure from his wife. Staff at the William Hill shop in Leicester said he had been in and out of the shop regularly asking about his bet's cash-out value.

At Ladbrokes, there were still 23 gamblers resisting the temptation to cash out early, with one punter in line for a potential £100,000 win. Spokesman Alex Donohue said: "Around half of the 5000-1 backers have cashed in their chips, while the rest hold their nerve. Record sums have already been paid out on a bet yet to be a winner and for many fans the lure of a life-changing sum of money is too much with several difficult games still to go."

One of those sticking to his guns was 38-year-old Leigh Herbert, from Leicester, who was hoping for a windfall of £25,000. He put £5 on the Foxes while on holiday in Cornwall after news of Claudio Ranieri's appointment. "I watched them last season and they didn't play that badly. When he was appointed I thought he might bring something," he told BBC Sport. "The first thing I thought the next day was that I'd lost that fiver. I'm not a betting man, apart from a pound or two on the Grand National." The carpenter added he was trying not to think about the money - instead focusing on his beloved team's success.

Even some Nottingham Forest fans were rooting for Leicester, as well as most of the football loving nation. Not so the bookmakers. Joe Crilly, from William Hill, said: "Leicester are the neutrals' pick to win the Premier League this season, yet for the bookies, it is anyone but. At the start of the season, 25 people backed them with William Hill at 5000-1 and those bets, totalling just £68.55, cost over £300,000. A Premier League title would cost us alone £2.5m."

TUESDAY, 8 MARCH

An "earthquake" caused by football fans celebrating a goal has been recorded for the first time in the UK.

A University of Leicester team installed a seismometer near the King Power stadium and reported a minor quake with a magnitude of 0.3. The tremor was attributed to a "sudden energy release" made by Foxes fans when Ulloa scored a last-minute winner against Norwich, in February. The event has been labelled the "Vardy Quake". A seismometer was installed by geology students, and the British Geological Survey (BGS), at Hazel Community Primary School, 500m (0.3 miles) from the King Power Stadium, as part of a project to detect earthquakes around the world.

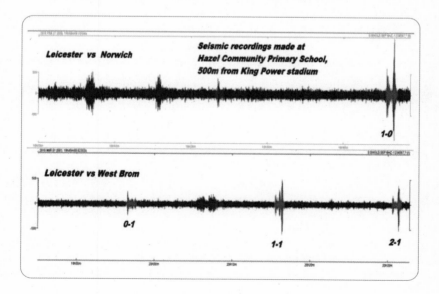

Paul Denton, a seismologist from the BGS, said the team wondered if football fans would affect the detectors. He said: "The seismometers were actually closer to the Leicester Tigers (rugby) ground and so we were expecting stronger signals from there but we can't find anything. It says something about the nature of football, it's so tense and then we get four or five seconds of unexpected magic. (In Leicester's case) it was in the 89th minute, the game was practically over. It wasn't just a case of cheering or clapping, it was 30,000 people standing up at the same time - an awful amount of energy." The scientist, who recorded similar results at the Reading music festival and freight trains passing through the city, said he would like to see how Leicester compares with other football clubs. He said it could inspire children to get more interested in science.

Leicester City have been the surprise package in the Premier League this season and are clear at the top by five points with nine games left to play. The students continued to monitor the Foxes' home games and will provide updates via the @VardyQuake Twitter account.

VardyQuake, @VardyQuake - We are a team of #UniofLeicester geoscience students measuring the seismic signals of #LCFC games. Follow us for live updates.

SUNDAY, 13 MARCH

Former Chelsea captain Marcel Desailly, who played under Ranieri at Stamford Bridge, did not think that they would be caught. "(Leicester) have a few games left and it's not just about them. It's also about Arsenal, Tottenham and Manchester City. They don't have that consistency to put a run together to catch Leicester. No one expected Leicester to go this far. Other teams were hoping that one loss would suddenly put them into some difficulty, but Ranieri is an experienced coach. He is also a leader, sometimes too much, to the point where he scares players. But, this time, it looks like his communication with the players has been very good."

Gary Lineker put his name to a 'first person' article which would appear on the front page of *The Guardian* on the day of the big game against Newcastle United who, themselves, would have the extra motivation of trying to impress a new manager and the momentum that inevitably creates.

This is the article in full under the banner headline at the foot of the front page: "My Premier League cup runneth over; a football fairytale." The sub headline read: "Against the odds, Leicester City has raced up the table from bottom. Will the club he's followed since boyhood make sporting history, asks Gary Lineker"

"Something extraordinary is happening in the world of football. Something that defies logic. Something truly magical. Something that makes me well-up with emotion, because this something is happening to my team. It is the team I have supported since I was the size of a multipack of crisps. I watched Leicester City lose in the 1969 FA Cup final with my dad and grandad when I was eight and cried all the way home. I have seen them get promoted and relegated. I played for them for eight years. I even got a group of like-minded fans and friends to stump up a few quid to salvage the club when they went into liquidation. But nothing compares to this. Nothing. Things like this just do not happen to clubs like mine."

Lineker had to confess that he did not welcome the appointment of Ranieri: "At this point I feel I should come clean and say that, like many others, I felt it was a pretty uninspired choice. His previous appointment saw him manage a Greek national side that lost to the Faroe Islands. Not that I could have got away with not coming clean anyway - Twitter would never allow that to happen. Oh, how wrong I was, how wonderfully, spectacularly, blissfully wrong. The bookies agreed with me: Leicester were the overwhelming favourites to be relegated. Who then could possibly have envisaged what would transpire?"

"What we are witnessing, should Leicester go on to win the title, is quite possibly the most unlikely triumph in the history of team sport. A collection of individuals who couldn't win a football match for love nor money a year ago have turned into an invincible force. A team with a spirit and togetherness the like of which the game has seldom seen. All beautifully held together by the canny, inspirational - yes inspirational - Tinkerman."

"So how do we fathom the unfathomable? It couldn't, as has been mooted by some, be down to the fact that Richard III was buried in Leicester around the same time as the Foxes revival began, could it? A Premier League crown? Superstitious nonsense, surely?"

"Players that struggled in their first season in the top flight began to find their feet, encouraged, of course, by the staggering climax to that campaign. Jamie Vardy started to score the goals that his lightning speed of foot and monstrous effort always promised he might. Riyad Mahrez, the twinkle-toed, twiglet-legged genius, was conjuring up his magic - week in, week out. The addition of the ubiquitous N'Golo Kanté alongside a fitter Danny Drinkwater provided a midfield duo unrivalled by any in the Premier League this season. Elsewhere, there is an outlandish energy to the side supplied by the likes of Marc Albrighton, Shinji Okazaki and Jeffrey Schlupp. Kasper Schmeichel has been outstanding in goal as well as possessing obvious leadership qualities he may have inherited. Then, and this is the most astounding aspect of this side, there is an ensemble of journeymen defenders who have come together to form a back four who have bonded with a 'thou shalt not pass' mentality that appeared beyond them earlier in the season. In that back four, though, there is experience and calm heads. It is not a team that relishes possession, this is a team that exploits the opposition's possession, or rather their loss of it. Perfectly organised, fabulously competitive, they counter with electrifying brilliance. They are an exceptionally good side. It remains to be seen whether Leicester can see this through. It could all fall apart in the home stretch. This most unreal of dreams could turn into a miserable reality. I hope not."

"I don't think I have ever wanted something to happen more in sport in my entire life. It is utterly joyous observing the delight that my three Leicester-supporting boys are feeling. Even my eldest, George, a lifelong Manchester United fan (he has always been contrary), is enthused by the Foxes' charge. As for my dad, well he recently tweeted: 'I've waited over 70 years for this. F***ing brill.' I get a real sense too that football fans the world over feel the same way. The pressure will mount with every passing week. With expectation comes danger. They have, though, shown no fear thus far. No sign of wavering under the magnitude of what they might achieve. They are on the edge of sporting immortality."

"Don't be afraid, my team. Make it yours. As Shakespeare's Richard III said: 'What do I fear? Myself?'"

MONDAY, 14 MARCH

LEICESTER CITY 1-0 NEWCASTLE UNITED

The lead was five points, yes five points! The title was no longer a possibility but a probability providing the team kept their nerve, and there were few signs that the pressure was affecting them other than they were having to grind out the results. So much for the Tinkerman, just 25 changes to their starting XI, fewer than any other side. This was the 10th time Ranieri had named an unchanged starting XI.

Rafael Benitez's first match in charge of Newcastle was sunk by Okazaki's spectacular overhead kick, a great goal, and enough to continue the impossible dream.

Before the match, Ranieri refused to accept his team were favourites, insisting that qualifying for the Europa League was the target, but as the manager gesticulated manically on the sidelines in the closing minutes, urging the fans to increase the volume, his actions suggested that he and his team knew it was possible.

Leicester lost just one of their last 18 Premier League games at the King Power Stadium, keeping a clean sheet in six of their last seven Premier League home matches, scored in 27 Premier League games, more than any other team. They had now won 12 games by a single goal, more than any other Premier League team and they scored with their only shot on target of the game.

Man-of-the-match was surely all-action Kanté, in my view, even though the Sky Sports co-commentator surprisingly gave it to Drinkwater, whose touch seemed to desert him in the later stages of the game as he gave away possession far too cheaply at times.

The bookies' favourites to be relegated were on the home straight, unbeaten in four matches, 12 points clear of much fancied Manchester City, 11 ahead of one time favourites Arsenal, leaving the once disbelieving pundits believing the title was a two-way fight with second-placed Tottenham.

Leicester were to next travel to Crystal Palace to face a side who had not won in the league in 2016 but had progressed to the semi-finals of the FA Cup. They had a kind draw with Watford and perhaps were dreaming of the Final, with their manager Alan Pardew in the stands casting his eye over his next opponents, hoping his team could keep their eye on the league rather than focus deflected to the Cup.

Ranieri: "It wasn't the best performance from us but we showed fantastic spirit. We defended very well. It wasn't nervy in the second half, the team was so close and compact. I feel now that I am just concentrating on the next game against Crystal Palace. We are so strong, we think only one game at a time. Step by step, that is our philosophy. Their players showed Rafa their attitude and the Newcastle players are very good. I am sure that they will be safe."

Asked if only Leicester or Spurs could be champions, Ranieri responded: "No, the race is open."

He explained: "There are so many people who are dreaming, but we have to continue to work hard. I want to fight every match. Now our concentration is about Crystal Palace, another difficult match. We will go to battle there."

Ranieri continued to avoid looking at the table. "Our fans are dreaming and continue to want us to win, but I don't look at the table. I just look at the next match - Crystal Palace. We want to enjoy and we want to continue, but we have to maintain calm, be normal. All of the city is behind us and pushing, but we must stay calm and enjoy. There is so much noise around the world, they are all talking about Leicester, but we must keep concentrating on football. It was not a classic, but it was a thriller. We won three points and at this stage of the season, how you win is more important than how you play."

THE ANGRY MAN

Ranieri delivered a furious rebuke to his players at half-time. Leicester were winning through Okazaki's spectacular bicycle kick but struggling to assert their authority over a side fighting relegation. Ranieri demanded more composure; his usual calm demeanour disappeared during a fiery interval. Okazaki said: "We've got a five-point gap again now so it was a very important match to win, but the manager was so angry at half-time. He is smiling most of the time but when we came in at half-time he was mad. He is always joking but maybe to see him angry like that is good for us. He doesn't throw things though!"

Okazaki believed a usually relaxed dressing room and light hearted team spirt were behind the calmness and lack of pressure. Squad jesters such as Mahrez and Vardy often lightened the mood.

"I think one of the things about this team is that it is so simple so that helps us to not get pressure," said Okazaki. "Our spirit is very good for each game - nice and simple. No pressure. It's not easy to switch off but maybe the character of the players is what is good. Vardy, Mahrez, they are so relaxed. They are laughing and joking all the time. I don't know how I've fitted in with all of them. You'd have to ask them. But I like a joke. When they make jokes, even if I don't understand it, I just smile!"

Okazaki sent the King Power Stadium into raptures with his fifth Premier League goal, a perfectly executed overhead kick from six yards out. "I have scored one like that before in the Bundesliga against Hannover but it was a completely different situation. This was a far more important game and because it was the winning goal it makes it a lot different. I don't practise overhead kicks but I like direct shooting. One touch - then shoot. The goal was just instinctive. That is my character."

Benitez told a different story from his perspective: "I wasn't happy with the goal because there were too many balls bouncing in the box. I would like to think about the positives. We reacted well and were pushing well. I thought that we could get a result and I was convinced we could do it. But they worked really hard and are pushing and their tempo is not easy for any team."

Michael, a Leicester fan on the 5 live social media: "We're going to win the league. I'm a teacher at a prep school near Leicester and now the kids are arguing about who wants to play for Leicester. They want to be Leicester - they don't want to be Arsenal or Manchester United. I've never seen anything like it. It's absolutely fantastic."

Alex Storey on Twitter: It's actually just hit me...Leicester will play the likes of Barcelona, Real Madrid and Bayern Munich next season.

Champion Opeyemi: Irrespective of whether Barca win another treble, Leicester and Ranieri has to be the world club and manager of the year.

Gavin Harris: Did Roy of the Rovers wear Leicester City pyjamas? He must have, right? Biggest upset ever in British football if they win.

Robbie Savage, at last, confidently predicted his old club would now be crowned champions. "It's ridiculous to think of Leicester being so far ahead," he told BBC Radio 5 live. "It's a two-horse race, no doubt about it. You can't rule out Spurs, but City and Arsenal have no chance of winning it now. You can't see them winning four or five in a row." The former Fox and Wales international said the current team was better than the one he played in under O'Neill that won the League Cup in 1997 and 2000, securing qualification for the now defunct UEFA Cup. They also finished in the Premier League's top 10 for four straight seasons from 1997 to 2000. "This team is easily better," said Savage. "If they win it, I believe this is the greatest football achievement we've ever seen."

JASBIR RUPRA

Soon after the match had ended it was reported that a supporter was being treated in hospital after suffering a heart attack outside the stadium. He had been at the King Power Stadium with his son and was walking back to his car on Aylestone Road nearby when he collapsed shortly after full-time.

As later reported in the *Leicester Mercury* the gentleman was named as Jasbir Rupra, 67, of South Knighton, and had been a Foxes fan for more than 40 years. His son, Perminder, was with his father when he collapsed. He said fans gave CPR and mouth-to-mouth resuscitation and formed a human cordon round his father to allow the ambulance to get to him straightaway, after which he was rushed to hospital.

Sadly, though, Jasbir died in hospital after his family had taken the heartbreaking decision to turn off his life-support machine, following advice from medical staff. Perminder said doctors at Glenfield Hospital told the family that his father had suffered severe brain damage after the heart attack, and confirmed, "There was no hope for him. His ventilator was switched off at 5pm on Sunday and he passed away at 5.55am the next day."

As the tragic news was announced Foxes fans from all over the world took to Twitter to send condolences to Jasbir's family and to try to organise a minute's applause at the next home game:

LCFC Away Days posted: "In memory of him, Jasbir Rupra, let's get a 67th minute applause going for him for the Southampton home game. Please spread this. #LCFC"

Leicester City Japan tweeted: "Japan is far from Leicestershire, but foxes in Japan also support your activity. RIP to Jasbir."

New York Foxes posted: "Our deepest condolences to the family of Jasbir Rupra. Sending out love from New York."

Leicester City ambassador Alan Birchenall said everyone at the club sent their best wishes to Jasbir's family. He said: "Our thoughts and prayers are with his family at this sad time."

Season ticket holder Perminder, also of South Knighton, Leicester, said his family owed the caring Foxes fans a huge debt. He said: "Leicester City fans proved on that night that they are the best in the world. They all helped us out and gave us the best chance to save dad's life. Their swift action enabled us to get the right treatment for dad as soon as possible and to get him to hospital quickly. Those precious days we had with him while he was in hospital allowed all the family to come to see him to say our goodbyes."

Perminder said that his father had been a Foxes fan after moving to Leicester from Uganda with his parents and seven siblings in 1972. The Newcastle game was the first time his father had ever been to watch Leicester City play. "My seven-year-old son Giaan has a season ticket but the night game was too late for him. I persuaded dad to take his ticket and we went along. Dad had the most amazing night. He could not believe how friendly everyone was. We left with ten minutes to go as dad has trouble with his knees and can't walk too far. Jeevan, one of my brothers, was waiting near Freeman's Common to pick us up. Even though we left early, we had seen that great overhead kick by Shinji Okazaki and dad was delighted to have seen that goal. He was convinced Leicester are going to win the league. Dad was so excited he did not stop banging those clappers they give out at the ground. He had such a good time, he wanted to go along to another game as soon as he could."

Perminder confirmed that he will be at the Southampton game with his son Giaan. He said: "We are overwhelmed with this suggestion but we would rather focus the one minute applause towards the fans that helped rather than dad. We cannot thank the fans enough. They deserve the applause. We don't want Leicester City to win the league for dad, we want them to win the title for their fans - without doubt the best supporters in the world."

Following the emotional tribute to his father on the 67th minute at the game versus Southampton, on 3 April, Perminder recalled, "When the applause happened it sent shivers down my spine. It was an incredible gesture," he told the *Leicester Mercury*. He added, "The minute's applause was mentioned during the Sky Sports coverage which was amazing too. This just shows there is still a lot of good in the world."

Jasbir leaves a wife Parmjit, three sons - Perminder, Jeevan and Ranjit- and four grandchildren, Giaan, Ajuni, Amari and Darshan.

TUESDAY, 15 MARCH

Emile Heskey won the First Division play-offs and two League Cup finals with Leicester City although he will be, arguably, most remembered for scoring in the historic 5-1 England win in Germany.

"We, as a team in my day, were driven on by the thoughts of getting to cup finals and doing well in the league, but this team are blowing that away," Heskey told *Sportsmail*. "This group of players has taken it to the next level and can actually dream of going all the way and winning the Premier League title. It's incredible."

Heskey watched Leicester secure a narrow victory at home to Newcastle, "They've got the momentum at the minute and they're playing with phenomenal confidence. The real top teams have consistency, they keep doing it they keep playing well and it's great," he added. "They don't care whether they are underdogs or not, or whether they are favourites or not. They just want to go out there and play football and entertain the fans and that's what they are doing. We've always been in the shadow of the rugby team - and quite rightly too because they have been exceptional for years. But this side is putting the football team back on the map. Leicester winning the league would be massive not just for the club and the fans but also for the Premier League. It would be really good, because it shows that the league is not just all about the money. It's about the team and the spirit and the willingness to perform and put a game plan together as well. Good managers install confidence in lads and that's been shown this season with how Leicester play the game. Vardy's showing that he's good enough to go to Euro 2016. His performances in the Premier league just go to show he is capable of terrorising any defender and playing at the highest level. Clubs are out there paying a lot of money for players with Vardy's pace because the top strikers always have an abundance of pace. I'm guessing he will be on a lot of transfer lists this summer because at the end of the day he's had a fantastic season and he's grabbed a lot of headlines."

Martin O'Neill, regarded as one of the most successful managers in the club's history, heralding an era of consistent top-10 finishes, two League Cup triumphs and UEFA Cup qualification in the late nineties, confessed that he doubted their title charge - until January. Ranieri went several steps further, already eclipsing Leicester's previous record points tally (55) in the Premier League era, with Champions League football increasingly seeming an inevitability. The Foxes have never reached European football's elite competition but were now 14 points clear of fifth-placed West Ham, who had played an extra game. "I could not believe that they could have done it at Christmas time even in January," O'Neill said at the League Managers Association (LMA) president's dinner. "The first time I felt they had a chance was when I heard the Manchester City manager say after he qualified for the League Cup final that he had nine games that month and another nine in February. At the same time there were 15 games left in the league. Leicester were out of everything else. That was the first time I thought they could and since then I have not changed my mind. It has been a fantastic effort."

It has been rare in the Premier League era for a team to have such a big lead in the closing stages of the season and not win the title. In 1997-98, Manchester United were six points clear of eventual champions Arsenal after they had played 33 games, but the Gunners had three games in hand. Four years earlier, Sir Alex Ferguson's team lost an eight-point cushion to Manchester City in the final six games of the season. Two seasons earlier, Liverpool were five points clear of second-placed Chelsea with three games to play only for Manchester City to win the title.

WEDNESDAY, 16 MARCH

Hodgson called up Danny Drinkwater as well as Jamie Vardy for the double header of friendlies against Germany in Berlin and Holland at Wembley.

On Drinkwater, the England manager commented: "What he's done has been pretty evident to everybody. He's had a fantastic season in a team that's having a fantastic season, but even last year we were aware of him. In that area of the field the competition is quite fierce, but this is an opportunity to bring him in and see if he can reproduce the quality of football he has achieved with Leicester."

It was reported that Leicester City had signed the nephew of the Sultan of Brunei, one of the world's richest men. Faiq Jefri Bolkiah, a 17-year-old winger, had been at Chelsea since 2014 after earlier spells with both Arsenal and Reading.

Ranieri, meanwhile, reflected on this achievement in an extensive interview with leading Spanish newspaper *MARCA* (marca.com).

What's your Leicester side's secret?

There isn't one. Our success is based on a combination of circumstances. The Premier League's big boys aren't having the season they should be and we're having a year that no one had expected. When I joined Leicester last summer, the chairman told me that my job was to keep us up for the first two seasons of my contract (he signed a three-year deal). The chairman is an ambitious, but down-to-earth guy; he knows that you can only reach for big things if you put the foundations in place first.

But it's all come together this season.

Yes. After those two years to establish ourselves, then the idea would have been to think about Europe. But everything has changed this season. I have a tight-knit, wonderful dressing room and a team that works. However, we know we haven't done anything yet. Everyone is rooting for us to win the Premier League. It's incredible that a small club are punching above their weight like this in the big-money era. If we were Chelsea, Arsenal, City or United we'd be thinking about the title. We're not, though.

So, the million-pound question: do you think you'll withstand the pressure and win the Premier League?

Leicester are a small club and we have to take things slow. We've achieved our most important target: we've already won because next season we'll be in the Premier League. Now we're going to fight to qualify for Europe. And if we stay up there, we'll try to get into the Champions League and then go for the title. But we have to take it one step at a time.

How do you turn a team who were bottom of the table a year ago into title favourites?

We've changed the system. I'd watched several games before I came in, I knew how they played and I've made some tweaks. I felt that certain players could play better in different positions and it's paying off.

Daydreaming about the future, could your Leicester compete with Real Madrid or Barcelona?

I don't even know if we can beat Crystal Palace in our next game! One thing I'm sure about is that we won't change our style. We want players with heart and spirit. That's the way we are.

THURSDAY, 17 MARCH

Inter Milan coach Roberto Mancini would prefer to see Leicester City win the Premier League than Manchester City win the Champions League. Mancini, who played five times for the Foxes in 2001, led Manchester City to a first league title in 44 years in 2012. Leicester were five points clear with eight games remaining, while Manchester City have reached the Champions League quarter-finals for the first time. "If I could only choose one it would be Leicester," he told BBC Sport.

Mancini and Carlo Ancelotti are the only Italian managers to win the Premier League, and the Inter Milan boss hopes Claudio Ranieri can join the club. "Ranieri is a good man," said Mancini. "He knows football very well. I hope he will be the third Italian to do it. For a team like Leicester to win the Premier League against the biggest teams like Manchester United, Chelsea and Arsenal, it would be incredible."

FRIDAY, 18 MARCH

Ranieri's pre-match press conference was interrupted by a pair of Italian comedians. He was ambushed in bizarre scenes outside the King Power Stadium as he arrived to speak to the media ahead of Saturday's Premier League clash with Crystal Palace. The pair of Italian TV presenters, who appear to be Italy's version of Ant and Dec, proceeded to kiss Ranieri's feet before conducting an impromptu interview. They also presented Ranieri with a miniature bull's horn, which is reputed to ward off evil. Ranieri, who played along with the pair before conducting his normal media duties, will hope the trinket helps his side keep their title challenge on track. And he has insisted they will not see him back in his homeland any time soon by pledging his future to Leicester - even if his country comes calling.

CAN HE KANTE

Leicester's success was rewarded again when midfielders Danny Drinkwater and N'Golo Kanté received their first call-ups for England and France respectively.

"I am pleased for 'Drinky' and all his team-mates are pleased," said Ranieri. "It's good because that means we are working well, and he deserves it because during all the season he's playing very well, very solid, good quality, now he also starts to score goals, that's good. There is a very good partnership with Kanté, they switch together, they understand together, and it's solid and strong. I like him when he goes to the tackle, he wins the tackles, for me that is important. Also there is a very good balance from when we go forward and when we defend, he's very attentive. I'm happy about Kanté because Didier Deschamps (France manager) has very good midfielders, but I think he also wants to understand what Kanté can do."

N'Golo Kanté insisted his focus was a good finish to the season and he paid no attention to speculation about a possible summer move. He was a revelation since a £5.6million move from Caen, tipped to challenge for Player of the Year awards. His dynamic displays triggered interest from other clubs, notably Arsenal, but the 24-year-old was committed the cause at Leicester. "I am focused on Leicester, I don't think about people saying something else. Just Leicester," he confirmed.

Kanté is vital to his side's style, breaking up play and intercepting possession, and a major factor in Leicester leading the League by five points. But he insisted the squad are only looking at Saturday's match against Crystal Palace. "We don't know who will win the title but what we can do is just fight for every game. This is the only thing we can do," he said. "Claudio Ranieri is positive. He is happy at the way the team is going and we have to stick together. There are eight games left. We go game after game."

Kanté provided a humble response to the suggestion he was phenomenal this season. "It is all the team. We do good work and we hope to keep going," he said. "I just try to do my best and anticipate the action. Against Newcastle we didn't play very well but we won and that is the most important thing, the three points. We're happy if we can keep doing this. Hopefully we will have a good finish."

Alan Pardew believed his Palace side could derail another title challenge. Despite being winless in 12 league matches, they made a habit in recent seasons of upsetting the favourites in the home stretch. In 2014, they came back from three goals down with 11 minutes left to hold title-chasing Liverpool to a draw and last season they beat Manchester City 2-1 to all but end their hopes.

The Palace boss, however, reserved praise for Danny Simpson, the defender who he managed at Newcastle but released under the assumption he could improve in that position. "They're not star names, most of them. Danny Simpson, I had at Newcastle - we released him thinking we could get someone better and here he is in a position to win the league. I take my hat off to him and a number of their players. Now the run is clear for them, they are the clear favourites, even Alex Ferguson said they're going to win it. For us, it's envy a little bit for what they've done and also admiration. They've got to keep perfect but the margins are really tight. Don't expect this one to be any different, don't think they'll run away from us. It's only natural, it's human instinct that when you're trying to achieve something magnificent like they are, you're going to start worrying and doubting. It is almost the perfect season, but it doesn't always come all the way through that perfect run, so maybe their blips are still to come."

Ranieri warned his leaders to beware of Palace without a win in their last 12 league games with their last victory coming at Stoke in December as Pardew's side dropped to 15th in the Premier League. But, with Leicester expected to win in London, Ranieri is cautious against their out-of-form hosts. He said: "Yes, it's very strange. When we played here it was a very difficult match, I was so happy the last time because we made the first clean sheet if you remember. Also at the end of the match I didn't say hello to Alan Pardew - I made a mistake. I was so happy I went to the pitch because I recognised it was a very, very difficult match to beat them. It will be the same on Saturday, it will be a very, very tough match."

The clean sheet had famously prompted Ranieri to deliver on his promise to take the players out for a pizza, and at his press conference, when it was pointed out to Ranieri that a local butcher had named a sausage - containing fennel, garlic, chilli and "a hint of Champions League" - after the Leicester manager, Ranieri laughed, "I pay for pizza, you pay for the sausage. I am the sausageman."

Ranieri was convinced more points than the target he set in January were now needed, as he warned his players not to take their foot off the gas as Spurs, Arsenal and Manchester City still had designs on the title.

The Premier League title had only been won three times with 79 points or fewer and the previous season Chelsea finished top with 87. "If we make 79 points I am happy because I said 39 in the first part of the season and 40 in the second so we improve, so I would be happy. But if we can do something more I am happier," he said. "I think we need a little more, we need an extra. We have to put a turbo behind us and push a lot. We are not the favourites, there are the others. Tottenham are a very, very strong team. Arsenal now lost in the Champions League and now are free. There are behind us teams who can win all the last eight matches and get 24 points."

As usual Ranieri maintained a cautious approach. "I don't look at the table, believe me. I don't see which teams the other favourites are playing against. The others are words and with words you don't achieve points. Now, we want to fight - but we are very focused, not on the title, we are focussed on the Crystal Palace match. They are strong, they are tall, they are very, very solid. And there is another tough match, there will be another battle. That is our mentality."

"If results are good it's good. If not good it doesn't matter. We've done our job - to save the team. Now it's to enjoy the matches, make our fans proud - then we can do something more. But not the nightmare, the obsession, to make something different. No. Continue, let's play. Now we are very close to the Europa League and it's important in the next two to three matches to continue in this way to be also in the Champions League. It would be a great achievement but I want to go back to my focus on Crystal Palace."

SATURDAY, 19 MARCH

CRYSTAL PALACE 0-1 LEICESTER CITY

Arsenal were in superlative form in the early kick off game, keeping up the intensity they had shown even in defeat in the Nou Camp as they romped to an impressive 2-0 win at Goodison Park.

Arsene Wenger on the title race: "We are still in it in our minds and mathematically, yes, and we want everyone to be behind the team to give us a chance. We are ready for a battle. Why should it be a two-horse race with one team three points in front of us? Let's focus on performances and after that we will see how we finish."

In his programme notes, Pardew said the "stars have aligned" for Leicester profiting from "very few injuries, the top teams falling well short and some tight games going their way" and City had been awarded double the number of penalties than any other season.

Clive Allen, the former Tottenham and England goalscorer was at Selhurst Park for 5 live Sport. He commented at kick-off. "You can start to believe, if you're a Leicester City supporter. They are within touching distance, and a victory here today will certainly put them in the driving seat. Crystal Palace have had horrendous form in the league in 2016. Now they are up against the league leaders, who are in scintillating form."

Martin Keown, the former Arsenal defender on Final Score, remarked: "I think Tottenham will win the title. A point at Palace today would be good for Leicester, and that could be the game of the day, end-to-end action. Tottenham are at home tomorrow and I can see them beating Bournemouth. Following that it's Liverpool away, and if they can get anything there then I think they'll have the form to win the league." Martin was big enough to admit by the end of play that he might well have got it all wrong as Leicester moved eight points clear at the top after Mahrez's goal saw off a stubborn Palace in an exhilarating contest.

When Ranieri walked along the touchline to take his customary place in the dugout Palace fans in the Main Stand spontaneously applauded the Italian. Ranieri acknowledged them, and as he did, several rose to their feet in appreciation. Not often is the opposition manager applauded all the way to the bench.

At the end, despite their bitter disappointment, many Palace fans waited for the Leicester players to finish their celebrations on the pitch and make their way to the tunnel, applauding their opponents off the pitch.

Leicester City had become the 'People's Champions', should, they indeed, become champions, and Ranieri made reference to the warmth he and his players are feeling across the country.

Of course, the Palace fans wanted to see their team topple the team of the moment, but for a while now it has been muted that Leicester City had become everyone's second favourite team after their own.

As for the action, it somehow had become inconsequential to the actual result.

One-nil wins are reminiscent of the George Graham era at Arsenal, not pretty but a nice winning feeling of satisfaction. To be fair, Ranieri had entertained all season, now at the business end it was results. Three one-nils in the last four games is evidence of a new way of winning.

Ranieri has a difficult balance - to maintain the carefree atmosphere that got them this far, but to now focus on results through the run-in. "Just to manage them softly," he said. "And kill them softly when they make some mistakes."

Mahrez missed an early chance after being put clean through but made amends when he turned in Vardy's cross. Damien Delaney hit the bar in injury time but the Foxes held out to clinch another vital win. While The Foxes marched on The Eagles, who might be in the FA Cup semi-finals, were without a league victory since 19 December.

Leicester enjoyed success using a 4-4-2, a formation considered unsuited to the modern game. Their compactness from back to front allowed them to flourish despite routinely being outnumbered in the centre of the park, but Drinkwater and Kanté's ability to cover large amounts of ground and break up opposition attacks has been important. "I think they showed in the first half why they're top of the league," Pardew conceded afterwards. "They were strong, disciplined and hard to get through, and we couldn't make much of an impact on them."

Pardew admitted City were deserved winners. "We needed to get crosses in the box, take a few more risks and I thought we did that well against a good side. We hit the bar. Whenever I have seen Leicester, you don't get a load of chances against them. They are a very organised team. I don't think there was much wrong with our performance against a team with massive momentum and confidence and a team that is fighting to try to get their results to win the league. Both teams gave a good account of themselves. They just shaded it."

Pardew would be happy to see Leicester go on to win the title. "From what I have seen, against my team, who had a bit of momentum from last week (FA Cup quarter-final victory over Reading), they will be worthy champions. Of course I would like them to win the title. It is something we would be thrilled with as a neutral but you are probably asking me on the wrong day. They have done a great job from chairman to the kit man. Good luck to them."

Kevin Kilbane on BBC Final Score commented: "Claudio Ranieri is quick to get off the pitch, he shows his respect to the supporters and he lets his players get on with it. It's about them, it's not about him. That shows what Leicester are all about. Ranieri wants to free himself of all the limelight, he wants his players to take all the plaudits. How many managers in this position start to believe their own hype? But he's quick to praise his staff, he's quick to praise the club itself for what they've achieved and he's quick to praise his players."

Palace fans, to their credit, applauded Leicester off despite their own disappointment and Ranieri acknowledged that the entire nation was behind them. "Yes. I have felt this. A lot of people are like this.   Also teams of fans in the race with us say: 'If we don't win, I hope Leicester can win.' I think because a lot of people say Leicester play with heart, with spirit to try to do something unbelievable. Now everybody is speaking about us, not just in England but in all the world. Everyone is pushing behind us and that is a great energy we feel. If in the end someone is better than us, we still had a fantastic achievement."

AND NOW YOU'RE GONNA BELIEVE US

Leicester fans refused to leave, standing in their enclosure repeatedly singing: "And now you're going to believe us. We're going to win the league." The fans sang about winning the league for 20 minutes, prompting the Selhurst Park announcer to, politely, ask them to leave.

Ranieri insisted he was "not dreaming" of the title just yet, but Champions League qualification was "very close". Speaking after the match, the Italian said: "It sounds good, our fans are singing a very good song about that but we are to stay calm because the Premier League is the same as every match, you don't know what will happen. We have to continue to push a lot because the Champions League is very close to us. Maybe in the next two matches I can say something more. Concentration is very important for us. Now the others have to do something. I think now we are close to achieving the Champions League, that is a great achievement, step by step. I'm not dreaming (of the title), I make a comparison between the race for the title, and each match. You don't know what will happen until the end."

Ranieri, however, knew his side were "on the home straight" with seven games remaining. "We have to be focused," said Ranieri. "Sometimes I've said we are at the last turn and now we are on the final, home straight. Now I want to see my horses, how they run."

Ranieri revised his points target, moving upwards from 79 points to 82 points, which was now the most Spurs could manage if they won all their remaining games. Whatever Spurs did, Leicester knew that if they won six of their last seven to reach 84 points - nobody could catch them.

Roy Hodgson was in the Selhurst Park stands observing how Drinkwater responded to his England call-up. Drinkwater snaps into tackles, covers an inordinate amount of ground, and always looks for the early pass forward; qualities that attracted the England coach. He started the move for the winning goal, with a decisive touch 20 yards out, supplying Vardy instantly on the left on the box. Vardy took on his man then hit the ball low and hard and straight into the path of Mahrez.

Ranieri's side had won 13 games by a single goal, more than any other top-flight team. They had the best away record in the Premier League with 10 wins. Mahrez was involved in more Premier League goals than anyone else (16 goals, 11 assists), two more than Vardy (25). Mahrez scored more away league goals than any other player (12). Mahrez and Vardy set each other up for eight Premier League goals (five Mahrez assists, three Vardy assists), a joint-high along with Arsenal's Mesut Özil and Olivier Giroud.

Nigel Clarke was convinced the side he has been watching for 38 years, will triumph in just a few weeks' time after a lifetime of ups and downs following his beloved Foxes, which includes seeing his side relegated, losing to non-league Harlow and now on the cusp of greatness. Speaking to the *Leicester Mercury*, he said: "Everybody laughed at us when in November we beat Newcastle and we started to believe. The pundits all wrote us off and are now having to eat humble pie, and while the fans are taking it game by game, just like the players, we feel like it's going to happen." Having spoken to former midfielder Robbie Savage on the BBC radio show 606, Nigel was laughed at last year, but when he spoke on Saturday's show, Savage changed his tact, admitting he thought City would win the title. "Its great fun", he added, "how can you not enjoy the ride, the way the team are playing? They have 100 per cent trust in themselves and each other. Claudio Ranieri hasn't changed much, he's given the players freedom to enjoy themselves and play their game. It's funny to hear the Spurs fans chanting that they're coming for us, and when Arsenal beat Leicester a few weeks ago, their fans were celebrating like they'd won the league and then the players were posing for celebratory pictures in the dressing rooms afterwards. Is that really what it's come to?"

He had some special words of warning for current European Cup holders and favourites, Barcelona. "The team from the Nou Camp won't know what's hit them when they come up against Jamie Vardy and Riyad Mahrez. Barcelona, we're coming for you!"

But he was also showing signs of nerves: "It is just a nightmare to have this break at the moment, so I just hope the players return OK."

Ranieri's team were closing in on the most-extraordinary title win since Brian Clough's Nottingham Forest won the old league title in 1978 having been promoted the season before. Yet he knew that his side could still throw it away. With Leicester going eight points clear of Tottenham, who had a game in hand, Ranieri said: "We have seven matches and it is not easy for us. We are Leicester. We aren't a team like United, City, Chelsea. If they were five or eight point clear it would be finished. With us, no. We have to fight every match."

SUNDAY, 20 MARCH

Spurs cut the lead to five points as Harry Kane again inspired his team to an impressive win over Bournemouth. Kane turned in Walker's cross after 43 seconds and then latched onto Alli's pass to finish left-footed past Boruc to double the lead. The England striker was now the Premier League's top scorer with 21 goals, over-taking Vardy.

Eriksen tapped in Tottenham's third from close range after Boruc had pushed out Kane's shot from 25 yards. Mid-table Bournemouth, who had won three successive league games before their trip to the Lane, rarely threatened as Pochettino was delighted when he said: "I'm very happy with the collective performance, I thought we were fantastic today. It was important to score early, and then we showed a strong mentality in the way we managed the game. We played well against a very good team - we showed a mature performance. It's important to get some time to analyse - 90% of the squad will be with their national teams and I think it's a good moment to analyse during this period."

Kane's hat-trick at Bournemouth in October ended a poor run of goalscoring for, but now his brace against the Cherries took his tally to 23 goals in his past 30 appearances.

Pochettino urged his players to continue "to fight and believe", Leicester can be caught. "It's true that we need to reduce the gap Leicester have with us, Arsenal and Manchester City, and it's true they have a good advantage, but we need to keep fighting and believing. We need to believe we can catch them. We have to keep our standards up and go into the next game looking to perform like this again. Today was complete. It helped us to score early in the game, in the first action, and we controlled and managed the game very well after that. But we'll go into a different period now from recently. After the international break we'll play one game every week and we'll have time to prepare in a different way, to training, to improve and do a lot of things that were impossible before. We are in a moment where we need to see our future in a very good way. It's important to keep working hard and fight in every game."

Kane insisted Spurs are not growing tense. "With Leicester and Arsenal winning, there was a lot of talk about us having to get a result but we were very calm," he said. "We played well and looked comfortable, and, if you score early, it always settles the nerves. We wanted to come out of the blocks flying and get that early goal, and we controlled it from then on in. All we can do is keep winning games and see where it takes us. There is no panic, no rush. Hopefully Leicester will drop points, but all we can do is keep doing what we're doing. We'll see where we are come the last two games of the season, but of course we believe we can win the league. Why not? We are playing well and are very confident. We just have to focus and see what happens."

After the international fortnight, Spurs travel to Liverpool and could trim Leicester's lead to just two points before the Foxes played again. "All we know is we deserve to be in this position," Pochettino added. "Liverpool at Anfield will be difficult, every game will be very tough."

Frank Bruno, the former world champion, was in Leicester to help raise funds for local youth charity, Community Giants. He entertained audiences at Symphony Rooms, in Burnmoor Street, Leicester, and told the *Mercury* how he respected the way City showed the footballing world how to succeed on a budget. "I love the fact Leicester are standing up against the bigger clubs. Maybe now it can be a more even playing field pouring multimillions into a club doesn't guarantee success, and I take my hat off to the directors and management of the club for showing some of the other clubs a different way of gaining success." He stopped short of predicting title success. "As a West Ham fan we would rather be where Leicester is, but we have had a good season so far. Will Leicester win the premiership? What do I know? Would I like them see them win? Yes, I suppose, but after West Ham!"

MONDAY, 21 MARCH

Ranieri visited his family in Rome during the international break to avoid pressure building on him and his Leicester team. His laid-back approach contributed to his team's sense of freedom. Asked how he will take advantage of the international break, he responded: "I go to Italy now. I go to the family, maybe I go to watch some matches but I am not sure. I go to the family in Rome. (The squad and I) don't speak about the title. We are speaking about our performance, how we play the last match and how we must play today. That is our focus. When I say my players are very concentrated before the match, during the match, I am very calm. Okay, we can win, we can lose, but our performance is good. And then when our performance is good, you can't tell them anything because if they make a mistake, it is normal."

But he'll be back if Drinkwater is picked for England. "I'm very happy for him because he has worked hard from the beginning," Ranieri said of Drinkwater in his post-match news conference. "It's a great honour to be called for the national team. Maybe if he plays I'll go to watch the match!"

Sky Sports pundit Niall Quinn feared Leicester could trip up, as he didn't believe their favourable run-in matters at this stage. Quinn says the nerves could hit home if they slip up just once. "I watched the game live and it was up and down. It was unbelievable. You didn't know who was going to get the breakthrough. In absolute truth Crystal Palace could have won the game. You can be sure of one thing, they will go out and try and score goals. When they start to get picked off - if it happens - then we'll see what Ranieri has to do. He's just letting it flow at the moment, but when that one result goes wrong we'll know a lot more. All day long, Spurs have a tougher run-in, but I'm not so certain it's a matter of who you're playing against. It's a matter of how you deal with this incredible challenge that's ahead of you. I'm just convinced that Leicester are going to hit some kind of banana skin. I hope it doesn't happen and I'm with everybody else on that. I want Leicester to win the title. But that's the time we'll see what they are really made of. I really hope they win it. I think there are games there that Spurs could trip up in. Leicester, on paper, have an easier run-in, but that goes out the window with what is at stake."

Graeme Souness believed Spurs with their young side will push Leicester to the wire. Souness echoed Quinn's belief that one defeat could rock Leicester, but says a Foxes title win would be great for the game. "I want Leicester to win the league. I think it would be great for football. There is still a doubt in my mind: will they choke? I just think the nearer they get to the finishing line…I've got it in my head, maybe because it's never been done before. We shall see, but you have to say what a job the manager has done and what a job the players have done. Tottenham are a team that weren't fancied and all of a sudden they have come into the race with no one fancying them. They are not talking about winning it and will be delighted with Champions League football. Tottenham have got a youthful group that will keep going. I think they will push them all the way. If Leicester slip up once then you will see those nerves jangling."

Sky Sports pundit Jamie Redknapp's observations in his *Daily Mail* column: "That's four 1-0 wins out of the last five games for Leicester. They have the look of champions about them. Last season Chelsea started the season with all guns blazing before knuckling down to grind out the title. It looks like Leicester are learning to do the same. In 2016 they have scored fewer goals per game than in the first half of the season but have still won more games. Of course, it helps when you have players like Jamie Vardy and Riyad Mahrez. They have scored 35 goals between them and set each other up for eight of those. The dream gets closer"

So who will win the title, Jamie? "I think Leicester might just get across the line. I'm not saying I trust them to do it because they've never won it before. If they had an in-form Man City or last season's Chelsea breathing down their necks I don't think they'd hang on but with Tottenham, who have not been in this position either, their nearest challengers, they may well do it. I do worry about all their 1-0 wins, though. It's great to grind out results but that may come unstuck eventually. The thing I like about Tottenham is how many managers say they are the best team they have faced - that's no coincidence."

The nation was urging Leicester City on. "After games the last few weeks I have had lads that send me messages saying good luck and they hope we do it," Danny Simpson said. "Darren Fletcher said it after the game against West Bromwich Albion and some of my old mates at Newcastle. Yohan Cabaye said it today after the game. I know he was disappointed but it was still nice. I used to be his team-mate and he said go on and win it, good luck. Yes you do notice the support. It is nice to hear that and get that feeling from them."

The support from their own fans was becoming the talk of the Premier League. "They are class, especially when you come away from home and there are so many of them here," said Simpson.

But, at this stage, there was a pragmatic approach developing in the dressing room. "We have that no-nonsense approach," said Simpson. "We don't mind booting it into row Z. We don't try to mess about. We make it as difficult as we can for the opponents. We love defending, we love clean sheets."

Kasper Schmeichel attempted to play down the chances of winning a first Premier League title. The 29-year-old goalkeeper was on international duty with Denmark and had been instrumental in helping Leicester reach the top of the table.

Schmeichel - who was named as the Danish FA's player of the year on Monday - is keen to keep the pressure off his teammates. He said: "We haven't won anything yet. I think people need to relax a little. There is still a very long way to go. We keep our feet firmly on the ground and do what we've done all season, namely to take one match at a time. There's no pressure on us. We just enjoy playing the games. I probably hadn't expected that we'd be so high at the moment, but I have always believed that we could do something special as to guarantee us a place in the European tournaments. We have great players, but most of all we have a great team spirit."

Spurs' Christian Eriksen was owed a dinner out at a restaurant of his choice by Schmeichel, after the pair bet on the winner of the Danish FA player of the year award. Schmeichel backed Eriksen to win but the keeper took the crown and, subsequently, will have to treat his national team-mate to a night out. It was also admitted that the pair text each other about who will drop points in the Premier League run in.

Nigel Pearson was the front-runner to replace Remi Garde at bottom placed Aston Villa with the Frenchman expected to be sacked.

TUESDAY, 22 MARCH

Ranieri's two key assistants agreed details of new contracts. Head of recruitment Steve Walsh and coach Craig Shakespeare committed to the club until 2018 after agreeing improved terms. Negotiations began before Christmas but they had stalled recently, sparking fears the two men may leave in the summer. They played huge roles in Leicester's incredible rise. Ranieri's role in negotiations between Walsh, Shakespeare and the club illustrates his own commitment. Walsh was key to the signings of Riyad Mahrez, Jamie Vardy and N'Golo Kanté, and Arsenal had been keen to add him to their recruitment staff at the Emirates. Shakespeare takes a leading role in training sessions and his good humour and intelligent instructions make him a popular figure among the players.

Leicester City were confirmed as one the teams to participate in the 2016 International Champions Cup (ICC). The friendly tournament marks the arrival of Ranieri's side in the big time, with a first step onto the same stage as the European giants of football.

The ICC is played in North & Central America, Australia & Oceania, and Asia.

Fixtures announced confirmed Celtic (23 July), Paris Saint-Germain (31 July) and the European champions, Barcelona (3 August), as their opponents, only four days before possibly featuring in the Community Shield at Wembley on 7 August.

City's exploits captured the imagination of sports fans around the world, as a press conference was held in New York to announce details of three different events forming the International Champions Cup taking place in China, Australia and the United States.

Following their invitation to the tournament, Leicester Chief Executive Susan Whelan told the club's official website: "An invitation to participate in the International Champions Cup highlights the significant impression the Club is making on an international audience. We are delighted to be involved in this year's competition. It will form part of a carefully planned pre-season programme that has worked extremely well in recent years - including a week-long training camp in Austria and selected domestic friendly fixtures. The ICC is a great opportunity to compete with some of Europe's leading clubs and to further promote the Club, and the city of Leicester, around the world."

Leicester ambassador Alan Birchenall added at the tournament's press conference: "This time last year we were last in the Premier League. (To be invited) means everything to our football club, it's a wonderful story. We're really looking forward to this fantastic tournament."

WEDNESDAY, 23 MARCH

Sixteen players were missing for the best part of two weeks during the international break. "The important thing is nobody has an injury, I hope," said Ranieri. "There are maybe around six players who stay with me and the others can go." Ranieri gave the rest of the squad a few days off as they tried to persuade him for more time away. "The players have a few days off now too. They ask me if I can give to them one more day off. They are big bandits."

Kanté was naturally delighted at his first international call-up, with France manager Didier Deschamps rewarding the Leicester midfielder for his stellar performances. He was hoping for his first cap as the Euro 2016 hosts travelled to face Holland before entertaining Russia at the Stade de France four days later. "The rise has been quick," he told the French Football Federation. "I've seen new experiences and new challenges every year. I take them step by step. I will give my best and then we'll see what happens. When I saw my name on the list, it was gratifying. I couldn't see it coming. I was happy. I thought mainly of my journey. Today I've reached that level, and it's really satisfying." Kanté had excelled, making 131 tackles - more than anyone in Europe this season.

Former manager Martin O'Neill says he can see shades of the Nottingham Forest side that became English and European champions in the 1970s in the current Foxes team. O'Neill played for Brian Clough's Forest when they won the top-flight title in 1978, a year after promotion. "I see a lot of similarities," he said in a BBC Radio 5 live special. "There are players I can identify with who are similar in roles they are playing for each side - Riyad Mahrez is a very creative player a bit like John Robertson, your outfield genius, Jamie Vardy looks like Tony Woodcock. They are similar with the two players at the back, with Larry Lloyd and Kenny Burns, you could go right through the side and see similarities. It is remarkable in this day and age - when big clubs with a lot of money to spend are ruling the roost - for Leicester to come and win this championship would be an almighty achievement." Republic of Ireland boss O'Neill, who managed Leicester for five years from 1995, was speaking on 'Leicester: The Impossible Team', a 5 live Sport Special. Forest's exploits are considered one of football's greatest success stories, and O'Neill believes City winning the title would be comparable. "Without question there is romance about the story - people are talking about it all over Europe. I was in France recently for a UEFA meeting and it was the talk of the evening, people are really taking note. It is a great story and if they do it, it would be the story of the century."

West Brom boss Tony Pulis, however, thinks Leicester winning the title would eclipse Forest's 1978 title victory. "This is a bigger achievement because the difference between the finances are massive compared to what they were when Cloughie was managing Forest," he said. "I am hoping and praying they do it for everyone outside the top six football clubs. It gives everyone that bit of hope, that freshness and I think it makes this league the best in the world. It is brilliant for British football, brilliant for the Premier League and brilliant for everyone connected."

The club's longest serving player, Andy King, came through the youth system and the midfielder has played for them in League One, the Championship and now the Premier League. He already has title-winning medals from the lower two divisions. "I can remember playing away at Stockport," he said. "It was the second game of the season in League One and we drew 0-0, Matt Oakley launched a shot late on over the bar and into a river behind the stadium. Ultimately we got promoted that year and the rest, as they say, is history. There's still 21 points to play for this season. It will be a nice story for everyone but we don't want to think about that. We are just concentrating on our football."

THURSDAY, 24 MARCH

Gary Lineker admits watching his old club's title bid is more nerve-wracking than taking a World Cup penalty, as he did in the 1990 World Cup semi-final. "This is actually quite agonising. It turns you into a big bag of nerves," he told BBC Radio 5 live. "I've never suffered from nerves in my life. I've taken a penalty at the World Cup and never felt a thing." Lineker planned to stay away from games to avoid "spooking" their challenge, but he planned to be at the Manchester United game on 1 May.

FRIDAY, 25 MARCH

Jamie Vardy and Danny Drinkwater sit on the podium, facing the media proudly in their England polo shirts. What did Claudio Ranieri say when it was announced that both players had been called up?

"Dilly-ding, dilly-dong," replies Vardy before Drinkwater can answer; the phrase the Italian shouts to get the players attention during training.

"He was chuffed," Drinkwater eventually admits. "N'Golo Kanté got called up the same day, so to have both midfielders have their first call-ups in the same week was a good moment." A moment that brought the training session to an abrupt halt? "There were five minutes of madness, really," Drinkwater says. "Training kind of half stopped and there were high-fives everywhere."

Two years ago, Vardy was reminded, Leicester's pre-season preparations were against Walsall and MK Dons, next season it will be Barcelona in a prestigious tournament for the big boys, in preparation for the Champions League.

"Unbelievable scenes," Vardy says with a grin at the prospect of facing Lionel Messi and Co. "I have just had the picture sent (of the fixtures). It is very interesting."

Vardy and Drinkwater both suffered set-backs in their careers. Drinkwater was let go by Manchester United having failed to make a first-team appearance.

"People like Scholes, so what are you going to do with that?" he says. "You just look at him as an idol. I have watched him since I was a little kid, I'm a United fan. I couldn't have had a much better teacher." Drinkwater was in the same United youth team as Danny Welbeck, who was also in the England squad. "I played reserves for quite a few years and I wanted to take that next step which was a loan move, I spent two years out in total (on loan at Huddersfield, Cardiff, Watford and Barnsley) and I didn't really want to go back into the reserves and dip in and out of the first team. I wanted to play."

Leaving United, after 13 years, was the lowest point of his career. He was on loan at Barnsley but

United accepted an offer from Leicester in January 2012, when Vardy was still playing for Fleetwood in the Conference. "I supported them, they were my childhood club," Drinkwater says. "I just had to concentrate on my new club. It was a low but look what has come of it."

Last season Drinkwater was not a regular for Leicester. He played just two of the last nine games in the run-in. Now no English midfielder had made more tackles this season.

Drinkwater did not consider England a realistic possibility at the age of 26. "But I have worked hard," he says. "I have got into a team where everything ticks, everything works well. It is a good club and it was always going to move forward. It was never, 'Could I get back up to that stage?' It was, 'Get your head down, work hard and see what happens'. You can always have self-belief. Leaving a club like United was huge, but look where we are now."

Vardy says of his team-mate, who did not want to do this press conference alone at his first England get-together: "He has been brilliant." Vardy, along with goalkeeper Kasper Schmeichel, is known as the most vocal in the Leicester dressing room, Drinkwater is a calming, quieter influence.

So what are the midfield player's qualities? "He is the puppet-master," Vardy replies. "He is the one who holds all the strings and makes sure he pulls everyone into the right places. He feeds the ball where it needs to go."

Hodgson said Drinkwater will feature. "That's news to me. Good," Drinkwater says. "I am looking forward to the opportunity and hopefully I take the chance. If it is down to confidence, that is quite high at the minute. I am playing probably the best football I have played."

Meanwhile, Vardy said of British screenwriter Adrian Butchart's plans for a movie, "I asked him if he was mad," Vardy says. "It was in the papers and I didn't know if it was true. It turned out it was. If they want to do that, there is nothing I can do."

SATURDAY, 26 MARCH

Vardy came off the bench to score his first goal for his country as Roy Hodgson's side fought back from two-goals down to claim a stunning and memorable victory in Berlin.

Goals from Toni Kroos and Mario Gomez put Joachim Löw's side in control, before Kane pulled one back just before the hour with a well taken strike following a beautifully executed 'Cruyff turn', just days after the Dutch legend sadly passed away. Vardy, brought on as a second half substitute, flicked home an eye-catching, mouth-watering equaliser, before Dier's stoppage-time bullet header won the match.

Germany coach Joachim Löw hailed Vardy as a "spectacular player".

"We did watch him and he is a spectacular player," Löw said. "A great performance, we did talk about him the last couple of days, not only him, but he is a player who is straightforward and is always looking to find the gap in the defence and get in behind the defence. That is where it hurts the most and I think that is one of his biggest qualities."

Vardy had to settle for a place on England's bench due to the form of Kane, who topped the Premier League scoring charts with 21 - including five in his last three games - and Löw knows the 22-year-old can also cause damage. "Kane could play as well," he added. "I'm not sure if they have played together already. It could really impact our defence and it will be a different game if Kane or Vardy is playing - he is a fantastic player."

Huth had gone without a cap for almost a decade, but Löw said he would have no qualms about bringing the 31-year-old back into his squad if necessary. "I'm very happy about his performances in the Premier League, he has always been a great player and had great performances in our team," he said. "I know if something happens with our defenders we can call him. We do have a lot of defenders in our pocket but we could call him. He is a really good central defender and I would be happy if he wins the Premier League."

MONDAY, 28 MARCH

The Arsenal fan known for his infamous "Thanks For The Memories" banner dismissing Arsene Wenger, is now stuck with a tattoo of the boss after losing a bet on social media. The man, known as "DT", tweeted that if Vardy scored for England against Germany he would get inked-up. DT remained true to his word and a cartoon version of Wenger now has pride of place on his calf. However, always one for the last word, he couldn't get the tattoo without having a sly dig at Wenger. Written beneath the French boss, are the words, "Arsene, Thanks For The Memories."

Mr Marmite DT ©, @DeejayDt - If Vardy scores I'll get Arsene Wenger tattooed on me

TUESDAY, 29 MARCH

Danny Drinkwater turned his attention back to his club after being named Man of the Match on his England debut. He was slightly taken aback to be given the award for his performance in the 2-1 defeat by Holland at Wembley as there were areas where he felt room for improvement.

Asked whether he expected the Man of the Match champagne, Drinkwater said: "Obviously not. It is an added achievement on the moment. I am pleased with that but disappointed with the result. It is back to club football now and hopefully to carry on the form we have shown that got us here in the first place. I am just going to get back in with the lads and pick up where we left off, get another victory on Sunday and see how the run goes. I will share the drink with the family."

Drinkwater hoped Vardy continued his goalscoring form after the striker added to his first against Germany with another against Holland. "He is on fire," Drinkwater said. "He is always a threat against defenders. His goalscoring is two in two so if he can carry on club and country, that is perfect. That's Jamie Vardy. He does it for Leicester. He puts defenders on the back foot and creates spaces for other players and when he gets the ball in behind he is more than likely going to score. I have been training with him for years. He has always had his pace - that has always been a threat while I have played with him. But his quality now and the way he puts the ball in the back of the net is credit to him. I could say he impressed me tonight or Saturday. He is easy to play with. He makes bad balls look good."

Of his own performance for England: "I guess not a bad start. I enjoyed it, loved every minute of it. Hopefully it is the first of many. I saw plenty of the ball, which is good. I could have moved it a bit faster, but it was my debut, so I was happy." Of his club's season: "I don't know if I can believe it but it's happening, so I'm just trying to take it all in as it comes." he said.

WEDNESDAY, 30 MARCH

On the front page of America's *Wall Street Journal* they have been educating readers on how to pronounce the name of the Premier League leaders. "LESS-ter, not LIE-ches-ter," explained an editorial and indeed a web video.

In France, a sports panel show saw two guests declare Leicester to be "somewhere in the suburbs of London."

Jason Becker of the *New York Foxes* - a Leicester City fans' group based in Manhattan - told *Sportsmail*: "My colleagues used to say, 'How did your little *soccer* team do this weekend?' Then it was, 'Did Leicester win and did Vardy score?' Now it's, 'Hey, great win for Leicester and what a goal by Mahrez!' That sums it up. Last year nobody here had heard of Leicester or could even pronounce it. Now every *soccer* fan is pulling for them. They have become the story because things like this don't happen in American sport."

American promoter, Charlie Stillitano, whose Relevant Sports company heads up the International Champions Cup pre-season jamboree in the US, insinuated that Leicester lack cachet and therefore do little for the Premier League brand. But Becker - a Leicester fan since 1998 - said: "Charlie said he was taken out of context but if he wasn't then his words were a bit insulting and the negative reaction showed what people think. In America we don't just watch English football because of the so-called big teams and brands. We watch it for the sport, for the competition. The Leicester story is why people watch sport, isn't it? It's what makes football great."

On US television, NBC were using Leicester on their trailers.

In Spain, the story of Los Zorros (the Foxes) captured the imagination.

In France, where the Premier League is shown live on Canal+, Erik Bielderman, a journalist with French sports paper *L'Equipe*, said: "Every Leicester game is live now. They are treated the same as Manchester United. United are always a story here. Arsenal are always a story. But not a story like this story! There has been criticism of Premier League clubs in France because they haven't achieved in Europe. But we recognise that this Leicester story shows us the Premier League is still one of the most competitive leagues in the world."

Christian Fuchs wants to become an NFL kicker when his life as a footballer is over. "I have ambitions to become an NFL kicker," he told Sky Sports. "Seriously!" Fuchs has experienced throwing an NFL ball. In January, Leicester's players took part in an American football training session after receiving Carolina Panthers jerseys.

Asked how realistic he thought his plans were, he replied: "Depending on the managers in the NFL and if they want a footballer in their team, but I am very much up for it. I know I can kick 60 yards or so, or a 65 yard field goal. Let's see. Dreams can come true you know if you don't dream you won't reach anything." The Austrian-born player will move to America to be with his family in New York. He visits his wife and two children a few times a year and admits he has struggled with them not being with him on a permanent basis. He said: "I have a family in New York. I have a wife and two kids. It's not as easy as having a family that is here all of the time because I am person who needs the family around and I am a family guy. It's pretty tough." While it might be difficult, he does smile when he thinks of his son wearing a Leicester jersey at school while the other children look on in bemusement.

"My son is singing all of the time 'Leicester City we're top of the league'. He's very much into it and he's wearing his Leicester City jersey in the school and everyone's asking him 'why Leicester City? Why Leicester City?' because there are a lot of Premier League fans over there you know from all the other clubs. I'm already thinking about what's after my career. I will be in America and I will move to be with my family. I simply want to do something. I can't just be laying on the couch because that's so not me."

The club struck up a relationship with NFL team the Carolina Panthers, an underdog franchise that recently reached the Super Bowl. The clubs exchanged shirts and share a Twitter hashtag #keeppounding.

Carolina Panthers, @Panthers - @LCFC #KeepPounding

THURSDAY, 31 MARCH

In the club shop at the King Power Stadium, they had only 13 first-team shirts left and they are all

XXX Large, according to a feature in the *Daily Mail*.

"That's it," said a shop assistant. "There will be no more until we get the new one in stock in June."

Council officials at City Hall prepare for unexpected sporting success. Deputy Mayor Rory Palmer entertained visitors from the media of China and America.

Palmer recently opened letters from locals keen to see a road named after Leicester centre forward Jamie Vardy. Moves were afoot to change welcome signs that say: "Leicester: An Historic City" to something reflecting the achievements of the football team.

In the smartly modernised council building at City Hall the officers plan all sorts of things in advance, so they ought to be making arrangements for a victory parade just in case?

Town Hall Square, where 10,000 locals gathered to celebrate City's promotion from the Championship two springs ago, would be nowhere near big enough this time. But, they fear that to plan is to tempt fate. "Imagine," one council worker says, "if an email talking about an open-top bus tour leaked out and then we didn't win it. We'd never hear the last of it."

Requests to interview Sir Peter Soulsby, the city mayor, pour in from around the globe. This last week, CNN, *L'Équipe* and the Japanese Broadcasting Corporation, among a dozen other leading international media outlets, were in Leicester. "We were on the front page of The *Wall Street Journal* last week," said Soulsby, in an interview with *Telegraph Sport*. "A provincial English city doesn't get on the front of the WSJ unless it's doing something amazing."

"The cliché is it's put Leicester on the map," says Soulsby. "But it's true. Now, wherever I go, all anyone I meet wants to talk about is football. This time last year if they spoke to me at all it was on the subject of reburying kings."

Near Lineker's fruit and veg stall, the once family-owned business where a young Gary had a Saturday job selling turnips, Adrian Chiles set up for a BBC 5 live radio broadcast. "I'm loving this," says Chiles, during a break for the news. "I mean, if you'd told Tottenham fans last summer that all they had to do was finish ahead of Leicester to win the league, they'd never have believed you. What a story. You just couldn't make it up."

Ian Stringer, BBC Radio Leicester's football correspondent and one of those waiting in Chiles's queue, commented, "It's like getting a text on your phone from Cindy Crawford inviting you on a date. Not only that, you turn up and it actually is her and not a mate winding you up. And as if that isn't enough, you only go and find six months down the line she's still texting you wanting to go out on dates."

Barclays Premier League Table at the end of March 2016:

POS	CLUB	P	W	D	L	GF	GA	GD	PTS
1	Leicester City	31	19	9	3	54	31	23	66
2	Tottenham Hotspur	31	17	10	4	56	24	32	61
3	Arsenal	30	16	7	7	48	30	18	55
4	Manchester City	30	15	6	9	52	32	20	51

APRIL 2016

FRIDAY, 1 APRIL

Vice-chairman Aiyawatt Srivaddhanaprabha landed his helicopter on the pitch before training at

Belvoir Drive. Srivaddhanaprabha's father Vichai - the owner - predicted Leicester's ascent in 2014. "In three years, we could be there," he said. Srivaddhanaprabha was referring to the top five of the Premier League. His son touched down with something altogether more remarkable to talk about and Ranieri responded with a smile and a hug.

Later, the Leicester manager admitted that Leicester were on the cusp of the biggest six weeks of their 132-year existence. Reminded that Sir Alex Ferguson had tipped his team for the title earlier in the week, he said: "It's good to hear but it would be even better to do it. I can't say we will, but we do have our focus. There's no pressure. That was at the start of the season. Yes, it's important to start thinking like a big club, as before the season nobody knew us. We have opened the hearts and minds (of people) for the other little clubs. But we must concentrate on our matches, concentrate on what we have to do."

Ranieri is overseeing something quite remarkable. Asked by a TV crew from France what it feels like to bring such an incredible story of sporting overachievement to the world, Ranieri replied - in passable French: "I have not written anything yet. We have not won anything. People can say it but we are still trying to win each game. Nobody knows who will be the champions."

Presented with sausages made in his honour by local butcher W Archer & Son - fennel and garlic with a 'hint of Champions League' - the manager peered at the media pack and said: "Here, feed them to my sharks."

At the forthcoming Southampton game, ticket holders will get a celebratory Singha beer and Krispy Kreme doughnut courtesy of Srivaddhanaprabha. Earlier this season the Foxes gave out free limited edition packets of Walkers crisps bearing Jamie Vardy on the front of the bag. The one-off crisps were produced in honour of the striker's record breaking 11 game goal scoring run in the Premier League.

"There are many special bonds that exist at our Football Club - between the players, the staff, the owners and the fans - and that's been vital to the incredible season we've had. Everywhere we go, people are talking about it," said Leicester City Chief Executive Susan Whelan. "We're entering the run-in to the end of the season now, so that bond is going to be as important as it's ever been in the next seven games, and the support of our fans is an essential part of the final push."

N'Golo Kanté can leave Leicester if he insists on a move and a big-money bid is made, according to Ranieri. The 25-year-old midfielder, who starred on his full France debut by scoring against Russia, suggested his future may lie elsewhere with Arsenal and Paris St-Germain interested. Kanté said: "I will fight for Leicester this season, next season we never know and we will see. At this moment I am focused on Leicester. We have to finish well this season but I don't mind about (being linked with) the other clubs."

To maintain a united squad Ranieri would be willing to let Kanté go should the £5.6million signing from Caen grow unhappy. "I think he should remain here. He is working very well." said the Leicester manager. "But if arrive some big teams, who give us a lot of big money, maybe we can think about it, if he is not happy here and wants to go. I don't want sad people here. I want happy people. He is not sad. He is always smiling. It is speculation. There isn't chance, now our focus is on the pitch. After is another season."

Ranieri confirmed that influential assistants Craig Shakespeare and Steve Walsh were poised to sign their new deals. Shakespeare, who helps lead the coaching sessions, and head of recruitment Walsh, responsible for signing Kanté, Mahrez and Vardy, were ready to commit to summer 2018 in line with Ranieri's contract. "I think they are very close," said Ranieri. "I don't know if they are already signed or are signing in the next few days. This is the job of the agent and the club. I told so many times how they are important for us. For this reason I asked them to stay here and for the club to maintain the normal situation here."

Ranieri reported that all players returned from internationals in good health, apart from Jeff Schlupp who was nursing a sore knee after playing for Ghana against Mozambique.

After a fortnight of international football, the Premier League entered its final stretch. It would be a modern footballing miracle should Leicester hold on to their five-point lead as they hosted Southampton on Sunday in a fixture they should win with Vardy and Drinkwater in excellent form and high spirits following good England performances. Ranieri had a run of winnable fixtures. They had the backing of neutrals all over the world, delighted to see the Foxes shatter the established order.

The only realistic challengers now were Spurs and they would trim the gap to two points if they won at Liverpool on Saturday night. Pochettino relied on an English core of Harry Kane, Dele Alli and Eric Dier. The majority of Spurs remaining fixtures were now scheduled before Leicester's.

Pochettino said seven teams still had a chance to win the League, dismissing suggestions the title battle had become a two-horse race as Tottenham aimed for their first league title since 1961, a further six points clear of Arsenal in third, although Arsene Wenger's side had a game in hand, while fourth-placed Manchester City were 15 points off top spot.

"For me, at the moment we compete with different teams - not only Leicester, but Arsenal, Manchester City, United, West Ham and Southampton have the possibility," he said. "It's mathematically possible. Seven games is a lot of points. You never know in football. We need to be focused in every game. It's not just a race between Leicester City and us."

Tottenham's recent record at Anfield was miserable, winning one of their last 21 league visits to Liverpool. Liverpool had won five and lost none of their last six league meetings with Spurs, scoring 18 goals.

Pochettino believed Leicester deserved to be in pole position in the title race but urged his players to focus on themselves. He may have been unable to the halt the leaders, who won four of their last five matches 1-0, but the Tottenham head coach insisted his players cannot get frustrated. "We need to give the credit to Leicester," the Argentinian said. "Today they are top because they deserve to be. From the beginning of the season they were fantastic. We cannot take the credit from them. We are in a very good position but we cannot compare with another team. We need to fight. We have seven games and it's important to fight until the end of the season with the possibility to achieve good things. One is the possibility to win the title and the other is to finish in the top four, which is important for us."

PREDICTIONS

The pundits were out in force summing up the run-in and making their predictions. A host of them appeared on the BBC Sport website. Midlands' reporter Pat Murphy commented: "Trying to predict how the top six will finish is like trying to predict the weather at the moment. My heart wants my old team Tottenham to win the title but my head says Leicester are going to do it because of the way they are digging out results. Either way, it is going to be very close. Spurs have got some incredibly difficult fixtures but, if they go to Anfield on Saturday and beat Liverpool, then Leicester slip up at home to Southampton on Sunday - both of which are entirely possible - then you might get a different one and two from me by Monday. As things stand, though, I am going with the Foxes."

Spurs legend Chris Waddle said: "It is Tottenham for the title for me - their players are bang in form and they have got real momentum."

Another spurs ex had his say, Jermaine Jenas: "Tottenham are in a great position but to win the title they cannot afford to lose another game between now and the end of the season and, with their away fixtures, that is too big an ask. I have watched Leicester a lot recently and the times where I thought they would fall away, they haven't. Far from feeling the pressure, they have actually got stronger and stronger and shown they can win when games are really tight. I don't see them dropping enough points now to let Spurs in, and although they will definitely be champions if they win six of their last seven games, I don't think they will need to do that to finish top. Jamie Vardy's goals had dried up a bit - he has gone five league games without finding the net - but scoring for England against Germany and the Netherlands last week should reinvigorate him. Even if it doesn't, the Foxes have got the quality of Riyad Mahrez, who can make the difference when it matters, and their defence looks solid too. At the start of the season they were leaking a few, and just scoring more goals, whereas now the attack has not really been at it but their back four has carried them and they have won their last three games 1-0."

Chris Sutton observed: "I don't see Leicester being shifted from top spot and the bigger clubs should learn some lessons from the way they have shut up shop recently. Robert Huth and Wes Morgan are old-fashioned centre-halves but they have got the job done as part of a back four who stay in place and defend as a unit - you never see their full-backs bombing on to look for a second goal when they are 1-0 up."

Seasoned summariser Mark Lawrenson remarked: "I said before the international break that Leicester are on course to win the title and I don't see anything in their remaining games to change that. Like everyone else, I keep waiting for Leicester to fall, but the only thing that could possibly upset them now is if they get some injuries. Without Vardy or Mahrez, or both, they would be in some trouble but even then they have got Leonardo Ulloa and Shinji Okazaki, who are capable of coming in and getting them over the line. Yes they have to go to Old Trafford and Stamford Bridge in May, but forget the clubs they will play and look at their team and their league position. Manchester United are ordinary and Chelsea are poor, while Leicester are the best team in the league and have been all season."

John Hartson said: "People who say they did not expect Leicester to slip up are lying, but they have stood up to every challenge that has come their way. If the Foxes do win the league, they will absolutely deserve it - they have played the best football and they will have won it on merit."

With the international break over, Ranieri recognises the magnitude of the final six weeks. He said: "Of course, because never Leicester have been at this level at the end of the season to fight for something unbelievable. For us it is to be focused on the next match, without thinking of the next matches - step by step. The electricity was at the beginning and now continues to be strong. There is a good atmosphere and that is good before the match but after you have to be very focused. The training session today and tomorrow is important to make a group. When the players come from around the world it's important now to compact everything."

SATURDAY, 2 APRIL

Pochettino believed the league title was still within reach after his side cut the gap with a 1-1 draw at Liverpool, but in reality it was two points dropped as Leicester could go seven points clear with six games left, should they win against Southampton the next day.

After Harry Kane's 22nd league goal of the season salvaged a point, Pochettino said: "We dropped two points but with six games, we need to believe and fight. We showed we are ambitious and want to fight for the title. Leicester have a tough game against Southampton and deserve to be in the place they are but in football anything can happen. We have to fight until the end of the season. It was difficult to come here and try and win the three points but we were calm and believe in our quality. We feel disappointed but we still need belief and to be ready for the next game."

Spurs host Manchester United a week on Sunday, by which time they could be 10 points behind Ranieri's side, who travel to Sunderland earlier the same day.

Gareth Bale helped Real Madrid end Barcelona's 39-game unbeaten run and then declared that he was still hoping for the perfect end to the season - Real winning the Champions League and Tottenham winning the Premier League. Asked about his dream double of Spurs catching Leicester and Real conquering Europe again as they did two seasons ago he said: "That would be great. It would be the perfect end to the season."

Glenn Hoddle won the title with Monaco while it eluded him at the Lane. He said in his *Mail on Sunday* column: "Title run ins are strange affairs. They can make you forget all the things you have done well through throughout the season. You start playing it safe when your attacking football is what got you to the top. It's impressive that this hasn't happened to Leicester so far. Their season has been incredible and I think most people, myself included, expected them to struggle at some point. But they have simply kept going, doing all the things that got them into this position. In recent week when teams have tightened up against them, they've managed to sneak those 1-0 wins which are so often the mark of title winning sides. In fact I feel the pressure is more on Tottenham and Arsenal. Spurs haven't won a title for 55 years and know this is a glorious opportunity. For Arsenal it's been twelve years but they know, as Mesut Özil indicated last week, that with the squad they have, they ought to be top of the league. In a year in which Manchester City, Manchester United, Chelsea and Liverpool are so poor, there is a clear opportunity. And in 20 years times, both Tottenham and Arsenal may well be saying: 'That year when there was such a good chance: to win it, Leicester City did it.' Whatever happens to Leicester now it's been an extraordinary season and Claudio Ranieri has been using that feeling incredibly well to take the pressure off his players. Liverpool threw it away from this position two years ago but I feel the weight of history and the enormity of the achievement got to them. They had to win the title to be deemed a success with Liverpool's track record, Leicester don't. Whatever they do, they know this has been a glorious season. And that seems to be playing in their favour at present. It's a year ago that they started their incredible run, winning seven out of the last nine games, to stay up in the Premier League. So it's not like they don't know how to manage the run in to the season. But this season is less tense than last season. Then the pressure of failure meant dropping out if the league. Now they're simply finishing off what has already been a magnificent season and that freedom looks like it will get them over the line."

SUNDAY, 3 APRIL

LEICESTER CITY 1-0 SOUTHAMPTON

It completes a remarkable year for Leicester, who were bottom of the table and seven points off safety last 3 April. "A solid 12 months," is how the club's official Twitter feed described events in mock understatement. They have been top since 14 December.

Before the game they were selling £5 scarves proclaiming "Leicester - Premier League Champions 2016. Presumptuous? Perhaps. Not really. They were living the dream. The scarf-seller is a Chelsea fan!

Leicester moved seven points clear with six games remaining after Wes Morgan's header saw off Southampton. Morgan rose from his sick bed to head Leicester to victory. His goal meant his side needed only four more wins to clinch an historic title. Ranieri said Morgan returned very tired from international duty with Jamaica, adding: "He's strong. The cold passed through him so many times." Ranieri praised Morgan for his leadership and commitment. He spent last summer playing in the Copa America and Gold Cup for Jamaica, but had not missed a minute of Premier League action since. "Wes is fantastic. He didn't have a holiday this season," said Ranieri. "He had the national team in July and he came back here, so I gave him some days off during the season because he needed them. He is a good example for everybody. When he speaks, everyone listens to him."

In the Directors' box, owner Vichai Srivaddhanaprabha gave his thumbs-up. Nice birthday present. Leicester's players sang happy birthday to their billionaire Thai owner, who was 59 today, in the dressing room before kick-off.

Chairman Vichai Srivaddhanaprabha adhered to his birthday promise to the fans: the doughnuts came in a smart box with the club badge and a message "Thank You for Your Support, Vichai". "There is a video floating around," said Marc Albrighton. "But we never saw any doughnuts or bottles of beer! He was after the three points, so that is our gift to him."

Susan Whelan, club's Chief Executive, said Mr. Srivaddhanaprabha arrived in the UK from Thailand for the game. "Just to be with us and to support the team. There are many special bonds that exist at our football club - between the players, the staff, the owners and the fans - and that's been vital to the incredible season we've had. Everywhere we go, people are talking about it. We're entering the run-in to the end of the season now, so that bond is going to be as important as it's ever been in the next games, and the support of our fans is an essential part of the final push."

Leicester weathered Southampton pressure, as their possession dropped from 52.5% in the first half to 40% after the interval. Once again their back four proved impregnable, with Wes Morgan and Robert Huth making 20 clearances between them.

Southampton slipped to only a second defeat in six away games, but manager Ronald Koeman felt his side were on the receiving end of two bad decisions; Simpson's first-half block was a handball, and cited a similar infringement in the second half when Huth blocked a cross. "For the third match in a row we don't get a 100% penalty - Stoke City away, Liverpool at home, and today two penalties," Koeman said. "The big one is when Sadio Mané's shot hits Danny Simpson and it is a red card and a penalty. If it is not a handball, it is a goal. I don't know what they are doing. The second one was when Robert Huth handled. I don't say (Leicester) don't deserve the victory, but if it is a penalty and a red card, they don't win."

Koeman did add: "They deserve to win the title. I hope they do."

Ranieri, however, suggested the right decision was made as Simpson's arm was kept close to his body. "They had a fantastic chance in the first half, but we worked so hard," he said. "It was a normal run by Danny Simpson, with the arms close to the body. If the ball does not hit his arm it hits his body."

Ranieri insisted Leicester remained professional, "We are dreaming, if we fight we can do something and we must continue. It's important to stay very calm and maintain our feet on the ground," he told Sky Sports.

Ranieri added to BBC Sport: "Everyone is expecting something more for us and we are in the clouds, but we have to keep concentrating. We want to stay there and continue. If the others are better than us then congratulations. We know it will be hard - in the next match Sunderland will be fighting to survive. I don't want to think about champions, I want to focus on the match. There is a chance for us to be champions this season, but we have to be professional."

Ranieri has explained how Leicester have improved since the start of the season. "We are (training) the same way since the start of the season," Ranieri said. "Slowly we improved a lot, and now we defend altogether; we close the space very well. Sometimes the opponent has a good chance, but at this moment everything goes well and I hope (it does) until the end."

Ranieri knows it is a one-off, a once in a life time chance, and it won't be the same next season. "We believe it's a magical season and next season won't be the same. We try to do our best. Other teams can win 3-0, 4-0. We have to fight to win 1-0. We must be focused in our way."

For sure the genial Italian is also showing a ruthless streak few believed he possessed. "What is choke?" When asked if his team would wilt, "choke", he said, putting his hand across his throat before making a throttling sound.

Leicester would now clinch the title if they win four of their remaining games, having won five of their last six matches by a 1-0 scoreline - they became the first team to register four 1-0s in a row in the top flight since Liverpool in May-September 2013. Only two of the Foxes' first 26 league games were 1-0 wins, but at a crucial stage of the season, they found the knack of grinding out narrow wins based on defensive solidity and clinical finishing, finding vital goals from unlikely sources - with Danny Drinkwater, Andy King and Leonardo Ulloa all having chipped in in recent weeks - and this time it was Morgan who outmuscled Jordy Clasie from a cross by Fuchs - the Austrian's fourth assist of the season.

Betfred, @Betfred - Our breaking news this afternoon is that Betfred Boss Fred Done has declared the race for the #BPL Title over! #LCFC

So, the Premier League title race was over, at least according to one bookmaker Betfred boss Fred Done. The bookmaker was already paying out on what was now universally being described as the biggest shock in sporting history. Done said: "Today was a very significant win and Leicester have impressed me all season. I have a number of punters who incredibly backed the Foxes for fivers and tenners at very fancy prices and it will cost me a million pounds. I want those punters to get their dough now. I am delighted because Leicester have been an absolute breath of fresh air this season." Done was the first ever bookmaker to pay out early in 1998 on his beloved Manchester United only for Arsenal to win the title. He also paid out early on Manchester United in 2012 only for Manchester City to win the title on goal difference. He added: "I've been wrong before but this time I can't see Spurs or Arsenal catching Ranieri's men. They were 5000/1 before a ball was kicked at the start of the season and it's been a remarkable turnaround for Leicester City."

Betfred, @Betfred – 1 shop punter had £20 at 2000/1 on #Leicester winning the League – he came to claim his £40,000 winnings at about 5.15 today !!!

Jubilant fans were, once again, tweeting away:

Gary Lineker, @GaryLineker - WOW! Just WOW! 7 points.

@joerobbs - One of the top three keepers in the league, solid defence, best central midfield in the league, best wide player in the league and one of the top strikers.

@gavdicko - Absolutely massive performance from @dannysimpson today. Won us the game.

@lcfcawaydays - Exactly one year ago, we were seven points adrift from safety. Today, we're seven points clear of 2nd at the top of the league! Mad. #LCFC

@Rav_Kooch - It's great that my children can see first-hand what you can achieve with hard work, passion and team spirit. It's not all about money

@Riddy94 - Leicester are honestly deserving champions ,every week people doubt them yet they keep winning.

@AdamRayPalmer - Good performance from #saintsfc but happy to have witnessed a live game from the soon-to-be champions. A historic sporting achievement #LCFC

@HipsterAllah - Gray looked like a senior player when he came on. Closed the game down with superb game management as if he was a seasoned pro

@Mattallica - So happy for Big Wes. Going to be awesome seeing him lift the Premier League trophy at the end of the season.

@benlapworth - 'Leicester aren't the best team' 'Spurs have the better stats'. The most important stat? League points. How's that looking?

@wreckyourworld - Thank you, @LCFC, for helping all football fans believe again in the face of 'modern football'. Well done.

@RobHall1984 - This football club. I've known heartbreak, relegation, Wembley visits, glory, cold Tuesday nights in awful grounds, but this is new.

Bruno Berner was back after four years.

When he announced his retirement and waved goodbye to the fans who had chanted his name throughout his four years at the club, City were 12th in the Championship. The fans and many of the people around the club hadn't changed, but something significant had.

"Can they win the title?" club ambassador and resident cheerleader Alan Birchenall asked him at half-time as City led Southampton 1-0 and were on their way to opening up a seven-point gap at the top. "It was amazing," said the 38-year-old. "I had goosebumps. When Birch called me out at half-time that was a special moment for me. It was four years since I had last stood on that pitch, when I announced my retirement and said goodbye to the club and supporters. Four years later I am back talking about Leicester winning the Premier League with Birch. It is incredible. I really enjoyed it. The club may be competing at a higher level but it still has that family feel. I saw lots of people who have been at the club for a very long time and were so nice to me when I was playing. It was just a lovely day for me." Nigel Pearson signed Berner from Blackburn in 2008.

"Credit to Ranieri that he has come in and identified that not a lot needed changing," said Berner. "He saw that he had inherited a club on solid foundations laid by his predecessor. He has such a big football knowledge anyway, tactically. He has worked with some of the best in the world, but he knew that what Nigel left behind was potentially the start of something special. I am so happy he is being successful because that means the club is successful." Berner visited the training ground during the week, meeting up again with Shakespeare and Walsh, "These two guys have been such a big factor, not just in this season but over the past few seasons. Walshy's recruitment has been outstanding. Even when you are in League One you still need to bring the right players in for that league, and that is what he is so good at. It was the same in the Championship and now the Premier League. Walshy's experience and eye for complete players is amazing. He always seems to get it right. Shakey is a fantastic guy with a great knowledge of football and knows how to get the best out of players. He is a very important link between the players and the manager. Good assistant coaches are rare and he is one of the best I have ever played under. Both of them have been vital to City's success this season."

Berner said it was the same back home in Switzerland, as it was around the world, where he is often asked about the club and how it is possible that they have been able to break the stranglehold of the established elite of English football. "People are taking notice in Switzerland more and more," he said. "They recognise there is a fairytale going on in England. There were a few interesting articles that were well researched by the writers. Plus Gökhan Inler, our captain, has been a topic because he was recently left out of the Swiss side as he isn't playing at City, so Leicester has been an interesting topic in recent weeks. I am helping them out with a little insight."

The *Sunday Times* reported that Vardy's agent John Morris of Key Sports Management, was negotiating a £250,000 book deal for his life story. The Sunday paper reported: "Vardy's life story, which is remarkable even by the standards of a sport that is no stranger to superlatives, was the subject of a fierce bidding war between several of Britain's best-known publishers. Four years ago, Vardy was playing in front of average crowds of less than 2,300 for Fleetwood Town in the then Conference Premier, the fifth flight of English football."

I had intimate knowledge of the process that brought the offer on the table to a quarter of a million. Through my connections with Christian Smith, former commercial manager at the club, I was told in February that the most Vardy had been offered for an autobiography had been £75,000 - a relatively low amount, I assumed because the publishers didn't believe that Leicester would last the course, as most people and pundits didn't. Having written nearly 80 books and worked for all the publishers in my time, I was confident of finding someone with the vision for the Vardy book. I negotiated a £250,000 deal with a leading publisher. The challenge was that by hitting £250,000 I could get the book deal over the line. However, the publisher couldn't come up with the full advance without some strings attached. A proportion of the advance would be based on bonuses, such as winning the league, finishing top scorer, winning an individual award, and scoring in the Euros. I met John Morris with Christian at a bar in Kings Cross Station on Monday, 7 March at which point the Orion offer was far superior to anything that had gone before. Clearly, though, as the realisation grew that the team were not about to blow the title, there was renewed interest at the higher level.

MONDAY, 4 APRIL

Harry Redknapp was full of praise for the 'People's Team' writing in his weekly Monday *Daily Telegraph* column, but didn't think the title race was cut and dried. He said: "Judging by the scenes at full time in Leicester it is clear that some of their supporters think they have already won the league. They reckon that with a seven-point lead they cannot be caught, and that the Premier League can start putting blue and white ribbons on the trophy. Well I am afraid it is not that simple - this title race is not over, not by a long chalk. At the moment, Leicester are doing just enough to win. Each of their last four games has ended 1-0, but grinding out a result week after week is so hard to do. They have also got a really tough run of games coming up, and I would not be at all surprised if their lead is cut to just four points by this time next week. On paper their trip to the Stadium of Light looks simple enough, but at this stage of the season I cannot think of many tougher teams to play than a Sunderland side fighting for their lives. They are absolutely desperate for points and Sam Allardyce will have them well prepared. Sunderland seem to have been written off, too, and I really do not know why. The title race may well come down to the final day and I think the relegation fight definitely will. I would not like to call which two of Newcastle, Norwich and Sunderland will join Aston Villa in the Championship, I really would not. The stakes are huge for both teams. Leicester will be doing really well to win that game, and I would not be shocked if they come unstuck. If they do and their lead is down to four points then the heat really will be on. Claudio Ranieri will be telling his players that it is all to play for, too. He will know that Spurs and Arsenal will be looking to strike at any sign of weakness, and I think both north London clubs are still in the hunt. Arsenal are a long way back, but there is no reason they cannot win every single one of their games to put the heat on. Tottenham are still most likely to challenge, though, and they looked good in their draw against Liverpool. They can go on a run, that's for sure."

As for the managerial nerves, 'Arry feels Claudio is hiding it well. "I did not envy Claudio one little bit during those last 20 minutes. Don't get me wrong, he is having the season of his life - but the stress of watching the clock tick down is one every manager knows all too well. If you are one goal ahead the clock just doesn't move. If you are losing it feels like it is going at 100 miles per hour. The last 20 minutes of Sunday's match must have felt like an eternity for Claudio. You kick every ball, and his players kept giving away silly free-kicks that allowed Southampton to pump the ball into the box, which absolutely does your head in as a manager. When he got back to the dressing room Claudio would have been calming them down, though. He knows Leicester will never have a better chance of winning the title than this. Chelsea, Manchester United and Manchester City will be a lot better next season. This is Leicester's chance, and they are in a position that no one ever thought possible. With the exception of parts of north London, everyone in the entire country is willing them over the line, desperate for the underdogs to beat the big boys - something I did not think would happen again in the Premier League. But they are not there yet. If Southampton was tough then Sunderland will be even tougher. It is not over, that's for sure."

MORGAN FOR ENGLAND?

Redknapp was full of praise for Morgan, "If Kane is important for Tottenham then Wes Morgan is doubly so for Leicester," writes Redknapp. "He was immense, as he has been all season…and I think he is very unlucky not to have got an England cap by now. It is almost certainly too late for him to make it into England's Euro 2016 squad but I do not think he would let anyone down if given the chance."

Hmmh, what a rum do! Captain Morgan made his debut for Jamaica in September 2013, for whom he has already won 25 caps.

Redknapp's blunder was the topic of much social media amusement and mickey taking before *The Telegraph* had the mistake corrected.

Son of 'Arry, the slicker Jamie, wrote in his *Daily Mail* column: "I'm a big fan of Wes Morgan - he has epitomised the whole story at Leicester. I wonder how many managers have looked at him over the years and thought he's not quite good enough for the Premier League. My dad sent scouts to watch him loads of times. While they told him Morgan was good, they weren't sure how he would cope against quick players, or if he was mobile enough for the top flight." So, yet another 'Arry gaffe!

Jamie went on to point out that the lack of pace hasn't been too much of a handicap as he continues to rattle up the clean sheets. "That certainly hasn't been a problem for him this season as he's proved his critics wrong. He and Robert Huth have been so solid and they clear their lines well. The Leicester defence is a real band of brothers and not only are they brilliant in their own box, they've chipped in at the other end, too. Huth scored vital goals to see off Spurs and Man City and Morgan joined the party on Sunday - his winner against Southampton was his first Premier League goal of the season."

Watford striker Troy Deeney, who battled against the Foxes defence twice this season, gave a fascinating insight on *Match of the Day 2*, explaining what is feels like attempting to break down their back line - surplus at Chelsea and then Stoke, Robert Huth fought back to become one of the most effective defenders in the league. Morgan was let go by Nottingham Forest for £1million in 2012, a bargain now. "I have played against every Premier League defence this season for Watford, and Leicester's Robert Huth is the toughest opponent I have faced. Huth is the sort of centre-half who will let you know he is there, so to speak, with a challenge or two early in the game. But when I got my chance, I made sure I let him know what I was about too. To be fair, he did not seem to mind," Deeney told *MOTD2*. "Like his team-mate Wes Morgan, who I had many battles with in the

Championship earlier in our careers, Huth is old-school - an out-and-out defender who really enjoys the physical side of the game. That is normally the side I thrive on too, but I did not have much joy against the German. He is horrible to play against, in the most complimentary way. He heads it, he kicks it, and he kicks you - anything - he does not care, as long as the ball does not go in. Huth is not a player who gives you verbals when you are out on the pitch - in both games against him this season, he hardly talked to me."

He highlighted the success of the Leicester foundation is a vocal matter. "In terms of talking to each other, the whole Leicester defence never stopped for the entire game, including Kasper Schmeichel in goal. And if Danny Drinkwater did not hear the right call then he was always going back from midfield and asking what was what too. That is one of the reasons they are so well organised at the back."

Deeney struggled to impose his game on the league leaders, as the Leicester back line is so well regimented that it is a monumental task to try and move the defenders out of position. "Part of my job leading the line for Watford is to occupy centre-halves - by that I mean those battles with Huth, say, to try to win headers when the ball is played forward. But I also look to bring centre-halves out of position to the flanks and make space for my team-mates in the middle. It is difficult to do that against Leicester because their centre-halves, Huth and Wes Morgan, never put themselves in danger of being isolated. When Watford had the ball in wide areas they kind of left us to it, and concentrated on dealing with the cross rather than stopping it being put in. Huth and Morgan take two positions - one takes the near post and the other takes the middle of the box near the penalty spot as if to say 'go on, cross it, and we will deal with it'."

Deeney highlighted how the full backs buck the modern trend of continuously surging forward, that they understand their collective role and defensive responsibilities too. "The other thing that makes it harder to break down Leicester than the other top teams is that both their full-backs are very switched-on defensively. Most full-backs in the Premier League bomb on now, and I don't want to be disrespectful to them but it is often a lot easier when you are up against a right winger who has been switched to a right-back. It seems to be more about how good they are going forward, and there are not many who are as solid as Danny Simpson and Christian Fuchs are for Leicester. Yes, they can join the attack too, as Fuchs showed with his cross for their winner against Southampton, but if he is forward down the left then you know Simpson will drop in rather than getting up the pitch down the right too. The whole team all know their jobs, from front to back, and they all work very hard too."

Ranieri's side lost in the Premier League only to Arsenal and Liverpool and Deeney was adamant it was because of their mindset, cohesion and trust in the plan that the Italian formulates. "I am not surprised to find out that Shinji Okazaki is the most substituted player in the Premier League this season, because he runs himself into the ground every time. It would be easy for the likes of Riyad Mahrez and Jamie Vardy to say 'we are too good for this' but they don't. Leicester are still playing the same counter-attacking football they were playing home and away in the first half of the season, but they are getting better at it and I can see why they have only lost three league games out of 32 so far."

Drinkwater and Kanté in the engine room are as effective as the back line. "When the ball was played forward to me against Leicester, I had to try to bring it down and hold it up with Huth behind me grappling with me and putting me under pressure. Then you have also got N'Golo Kanté and Danny Drinkwater buzzing around you too. Kanté was just everywhere against us - I was watching the Southampton game in the *Match of the Day 2* production office and he was the same in that match too. If he is taking a breather, which is not often, then Drinkwater is there doing exactly the same. You don't know where they are coming from, but you know they are coming, so when you have got the ball you are thinking 'I need to lay it off quickly'. It works so well because they are both so energetic. If one of them gets forward, then he knows the other has got the legs to cover for him. If teams want to come through the middle, they have to get past those two first. And, as we saw against Southampton, you don't just have to get past Kanté, you have to keep him behind you, which is the hardest part. He has been the best midfielder in the Premier League this season."

Deeney explained how they manipulate their opponents to build in confidence and stature before pouncing with their attacking speed. "With Kanté and Drinkwater in the middle, in front of their centre-halves, they kind of funnel teams wide, and invite them to cross. As I said earlier, Huth and Morgan are waiting for the ball to come in but what makes Leicester different from a lot of the top teams is that their full-backs are prepared for it too. Dealing with crosses at the back post might be a weakness with some of those sides who have wingers at full-back because they are less likely to win headers, but Simpson and Fuchs tuck in and know what they have to do. They are very effective when the ball comes in and it means that, as a striker, you cannot pull on to them to avoid the big centre-halves either. Allowing teams to cross is part of their attacking ploy too," added Deeney. "Leicester are the kind of team that want you to get a little bit confident when you come forward, thinking you are on top. Then, when you commit men forward and are getting excited because you are having all these crosses and think the momentum is with you, that is when they pounce with a quick break using the pace of their forwards."

It is a party atmosphere at the King Power Stadium. "The support that Leicester get at the King Power Stadium is the kind of thing that will help them get over the line. If the team is nervy, like they were at the back end of Sunday's game, then their fans are not stupid - they realised their team needed them and raised the noise levels again. Part of that is down to the thousands of cardboard clappers the club leave out on the seats for fans before games. I think that actually started in the Championship play-offs in 2013, when we beat them in the semi-finals. I remember it being a bit annoying in the first leg at their place when their fans were using them but, now I am playing in the Premier League, I actually appreciated the noise when we went there. I don't want to sound too critical, but a lot of fans at some grounds I go to have got cameras in their hands, taking pictures of anything rather than generating any atmosphere during the game. At Leicester, it was all about getting behind their team."

TUESDAY, 5 APRIL

Kasper Schmeichel dismissed the 'pressure' theory and instead suggested they are relishing the challenge, even enjoying it.

Last season's desperate fight to avoid relegation was what represented "real pressure" as he argued "we are under no pressure at all. This is great. The pressure was last season when your backs are to the wall, you're fighting for your lives; relegation means everything to a club, to a city, to a whole community. People lose their jobs. That would have been catastrophic for us. That was real pressure. This is just great. We are enjoying this."

The team were also benefiting from the experience of winning the Championship title two seasons ago. "Granted it was in another league but we've done this before," the Dane said. "We've done it in the Championship. A lot of us were there in that period, we know what it's like. You have to take one game at a time."

Schmeichel aimed for his 11th clean sheet in 15 league games at relegation haunted Sunderland. "We defend as a team, we are tough to break down," he added.

Marc Albrighton called for one final push from his team-mates or the season will be 'worthless'.

"It has been going on so long that we keep saying a year ago today. Where we were to this, it is a massive transformation. We will never get away from that fact. But we have got to concentrate on where we are now. Although it is fantastic it will be worth nothing if we don't see it out."

One of the unsung heroes, playing in all 32 league games, he believed the squad had what it takes to handle the pressure of the run-in given their brush with relegation last campaign. "There was a lot more pressure last season but I haven't felt any pressure this season," he added. "I can't see why there is any on us. We are in a position no one expected us to be in. If we don't go on and achieve something now then don't get me wrong, we would be disappointed."

Wes Morgan leaned on the experience of winning the Championship to help them negotiate a tricky set of remaining fixtures. Morgan, Drinkwater, Schmeichel, Vardy, King and Mahrez were in the side that won the Championship with two games to spare in 2014. "The experience of going up from the Championship will help us this time round," the Jamaica international commented. "We are approaching it one game at a time, not getting carried away thinking, 'If we win the next three or four games, we've done whatever'. That's the way we probably looked at it in the Championship. It's much different this time round. We don't want to get carried away, we want to stay focused. It was just momentum (in 2014). We kept winning games, in fantastic form, full of confidence. We went into games knowing we could win and we were doing so by big margins. It is hard to compare that to the Premier League. The games are much tougher, and they are not as frequent. There is a lot of preparation going into games, a lot of thought. We approach games in the way to maybe stop the opposition first, then try to win in different ways. The experience of going up from the Championship will help us this time round. The lads are full of confidence to keep it going. We try to take it one game, right that's ticked off, then prepare for the next one. We're not thinking we need to win the next three of five. That's the way we probably looked at it in the Championship."

The improvement in the defensive record from earlier this season elevated them to an unimaginable position in the Premier League. As Ranieri said his side had become "more Italian" after their victory against Southampton.

Morgan and Huth are solid in central defence, full-backs Simpson and Fuchs, not regular starters at the beginning of the season, excelled at the back and in attack. Morgan explained, "We understand each other, we know each other's jobs. It is a lot easier when you have a sense of each other's roles and abilities, strengths and weaknesses. I have to say it is more of a team defensive performance. It is not just us two at the back keeping clean sheets. We have full-backs in the right positions at the right times, making important blocks, interceptions, and headers. Simmo was unbelievable at that against Southampton. He was in some key positions to clear the ball. You might look at me and Huthy as the reason we are keeping clean sheets but it's definitely a team effort. I had no rest in the summer (after playing for Jamaica in both the Copa América and Gold Cup), constant football. I came back, had two days training and was back into the new season. It has been constant ever since. I try to get my rest in when I can. The gaffer looks after me. He gives me extra days off throughout the week if possible. You have to keep going. It's been tough but I feel OK and I'll keep going."

Leicester are a "magic team" deserving of a spot in Europe's top competition, proclaimed the businessman who initially opposed their place in a proposed breakaway. Charlie Stillitano, co-founder of the International Champions Cup, met with Premier League clubs in March about a new format. Leicester have since been included in the pre-season Champions Cup. "I would not want a closed league," Stillitano told BBC Radio Leicester. "I would want these magical teams, like Leicester, to be a part of this. Can you imagine if they were left out of the (Champions) League after what they've done? It would be absurd," continued the American. "They are maybe the (best) sports story ever. If they win the Premier League this year, I cannot think of any accomplishment bigger than what they're doing."

After last month's meeting with officials from Manchester United, Arsenal, Chelsea, Liverpool and Manchester City, Stillitano said the change to the Champions League format was "being discussed all over Europe".

At the time, he was quoted as saying: "What would Manchester United argue: did we create soccer or did Leicester create [it]?" Stillitano claimed his comments were "really unfairly treated", and that the opinions of Juventus president Andrea Agnelli and Karl-Heinz Rummenigge, chairman of the European Clubs' Association, will shape the Champions League debate. "I was very clear that I am not the architect, I am not behind it in any way, shape or form," Stillitano said. "I was just commenting that different people are saying different things. You've had the real leaders of football talking about it, not me - some guy from New Jersey. All I was commenting on was that the conversation was out there, it's not mine. I think, honestly, that I was misquoted."

WEDNESDAY, 6 APRIL

Prince William arrived at Wembley Stadium for a special lunch to celebrate his 10th year as president of the FA. He was accompanied by his wife, the Duchess of Cambridge, and joined Roy Hodgson, FA chairman Greg Dyke and board members. Prince William concluded the event with a speech looking forward to the future of the game's governing body. During his speech, the Villa fan, revealed he was "dying" for Leicester to win the Premier League. "It will be good for the game," he commented. FA board member Ian Lenagan, a director of Oxford United, said of William's comments about Leicester: "He felt it would be good for football - it would be great for the game." He cheekily added: "He's rather more worried about the prospect of Championship football from his own point of view."

Ranieri considered Vardy as a horse! "This is not a footballer. This is a fantastic horse," Leicester's manager said. "He has a need to be free out there on the pitch. I say to him, 'You are free to move however you want, but you must help us when we lose the ball. That's all I ask of you. If you start to press the opposition, all of your team-mates will follow you.'"

Leicester's owners told the new manager that the target this season was survival and that he responded by telling them he would "try" to reach 40 points. Instead, he guided his squad into potential champions rather than try to avoid relegation. "Perhaps you have heard their names now," Ranieri added in his blog for *The Players' Tribune*. "Players who were considered too small or too slow for other big clubs. N'Golo Kanté. Jamie Vardy. Wes Morgan. Danny Drinkwater. Riyad Mahrez. When I arrived my first day of training and I saw the quality of these players, I knew how good they could be. Well, I knew we had a chance to survive in the Premier League. This player Kanté, he was running so hard that I thought he must have a pack full of batteries hidden in his shorts. He never stopped running in training. I tell him, 'One day, I'm going to see you cross the ball, and then finish the cross with a header yourself'. He's unbelievable."

Ranieri promised his players he would buy them pizza if they kept a clean sheet against Crystal Palace in October and, when they obliged, the Leicester manager duly took them out. They were taken to Peter Pizzeria in Leicester city centre but told they had to make their own - in a bid to teach them a lesson about hard work. But the boss made them another promise if they win the title, as he said: "Who knows, maybe at the end of the season, we will have two pizza parties."

THURSDAY, 7 APRIL

Football fans were given the chance to present the Premier League Trophy to the champions. A competition was launched to find the lucky supporter to be on the podium to join the celebrations. The free-to-enter competition was launched by Leicester footballing legend Gary Lineker, former Spurs star Ledley King and Arsenal favourite Ian Wright, representing the three teams in the hunt for the title.

Lineker said: "This is the most extraordinary season in the history of the Barclays Premier League. You might have expected Tottenham to compete for the title, but for Leicester, after battling relegation last season, to challenge for the title this time is amazing. Of course, for a fan to hand over the trophy to the winning captain in any season would be fantastic but this season it is in the realms of fantasy football, and Barclays are making that dream possible." The three joined last year's trophy presenter Rachel Key with the trophy as it prepares to make the journey to either the East Midlands or north London this May. It will then set out on a tour of the winning home city on an open top bus.

John Terry revealed his PFA votes, which includes a plethora of Leicester City stars.

The former England captain, who is unable to vote for his team-mates, took to Instagram and showed his choices. Leicester dominated with Kasper Schmeichel, Robert Huth, Wes Morgan, Riyad Mahrez, Danny Drinkwater, N'Golo Kanté and Jamie Vardy. Mahrez also earned his vote in the 'Men's Player's Player of the Year'. PFA votes which includes seven Leicester City players

Claudio Ranieri was named Italian Coach of the Year. The 2016 National Enzo Bearzot Award recognises Ranieri's brilliance in the dugout at the King Power Stadium, with Leicester having only lost three league games all season and destined for a Champions League berth at the very least. The accolade, named after Italy's 1982 World Cup winning coach, was picked by a jury including Italian Football Federation President Carlo Tavecchio and representatives from Italian media outlets. Established in 2011, previous winners of the award include Cesare Prandelli, Walter Mazzarri, Vincenzo Montella, Carlo Ancelotti and Massimiliano Allegri.

Ranieri also picked up the (sometimes dreaded) Premier League Manager of the Month award for the second time this season following an unbeaten month which cemented their place at the top of the table, leading his side to victories against Watford, Newcastle and Crystal Palace as well as an entertaining 2-2 home draw against West Brom. He saw off competition from West Ham manager Slaven Bilić, Swansea boss Francesco Guidolin and Bournemouth's Eddie Howe.

Fans called for big screens to be put up in the city to show the climax of this season's historic title chase. An online petition was launched calling on the club and Leicester City Council to make arrangements so supporters unable to get tickets for matches can come together.

Kris, 26, a life-long City fan, was quoted in the *Leicester Mercury*: "It would be great to get some sort of pop-up fan zones where we could go and see the matches. This is an historic time for the club and the fans and it might be a once-in-a-lifetime opportunity. It's hard to get tickets for the matches and when you have kids the pub might not be the best place. I just think it would be brilliant if something could be sorted out. Imagine the atmosphere. We've even got people who would volunteer to clear up the old Filbert Street site near the King Power Stadium. If you did something there it would be a great way of linking the club's past with its amazing present. The fans have been like a 12th man for the team this season."

Donna, 34, said: "We've been blown away by how many people have got behind the idea. We are really going to press this because so many people want it to happen."

A Leicester City spokesman said: "Our supporters have been an integral part of the team's success this season and we're looking at a number of options to involve as many of them in the run-in as possible." City mayor Sir Peter Soulsby said: "It (showing matches on big screens) has been considered before and I seem to remember there were some issues with broadcasting rights which are very strictly controlled. I will look at it again but it is more likely a matter for the club."

The city's mayor unveiled plans to honour the region's title-chasing team. Sir Peter Soulsby suggested that the squad members will get the same treatment as Gary Lineker and golfing greats Lee Trevino and Tony Jacklin in having streets named after them - should they end the season top of the table. When Leicester won promotion to the Premier League in 2014, a civil reception in the Town Hall Square brought 10,000 fans together in celebration but Soulsby feels larger recognition would be due if Claudio Ranieri's side complete the most remarkable of title triumphs. "Town Hall Square will not be big enough this time," he said. "Leicester has honoured its sporting stars in the past. There is an area named after golfers and there is also a Lineker Road. It has been a real team effort, so as well as Vardy Vale we would need to have Schmeichel Street, Drinkwater Drive and Ranieri Road."

One paper suggested the club had held secret talks with council chiefs about a title-winning open-top bus parade; although refusing to set a date for celebrations as they do not want to jinx their title bid.

A council insider was quoted as saying: "With the club being top of the table we have spoken to the club about a parade. But they made it clear that they don't want to think about setting a date just yet. They are fully focused on winning football matches and it is something they will look at closely once they need to." Leicester were top of the table in 1963 before collapsing dramatically and missing out on the title. So they were anxious to avoid taking the title for granted - despite some fans buying "champions" scarves.

For the first time since 1963, the Foxes will finish as the highest-placed team in the Midlands after closest challengers Stoke - in the west of the area - drew with Swansea as Leicester beat Southampton. Leicester were the best side in the Midlands 53 years ago, when, after leading the First Division with five games to go, they slipped to fourth after losing four and drawing one of their final games. Aston Villa have dominated Midlands football as Premier League ever-presents - though they look certain to lose that title with relegation looming as they sit rooted to the bottom of the table, 15 points adrift of safety - and have taken the crown locally for 22 of the 53 years since Leicester last topped the charts. Nottingham Forest are second with 14 'titles' thanks to the glory years under Brian Clough during which they won two European Cups. West Brom are third in the list having finished highest on six occasions since 1963 with Derby next having finished above their Midland rivals five times. Wolves and Stoke have come out on top just twice while Birmingham have managed to finish highest on just one occasion.

Harry Panayiotou, 21, became the Foxes' top international scorer last month - breaking an 85-year-old record - to eclipse Vardy's achievements with England. Panayiotou, currently on loan at Raith Rovers, had six goals in 10 games for Saint Kitts and Nevis, beating Ernie Hine's four goals in six caps for England between 1928 and 1931. Vardy scored twice for England against Germany and Holland but Panayiotou was determined to stay ahead of his team-mate, "No one is taking that off me. It's nice to know you've broken an 85-year record, it means a lot to you," he said, after Caribbean Cup goals against Aruba and Antigua & Barbuda set the record. "I just score goals for myself and my country. The main thing is getting the three points and going through. I love scoring goals, I feel so relaxed. In the Caribbean everyone is so relaxed, the manager just tells me to play with freedom." Panayiotou scored a last-minute winner against Leeds United on his debut in 2012 which remains his only game for the club but he has still learnt from Vardy and the others at Leicester. "What I like about Vardy is he knows when to run, when to turn off the shoulder and he is brilliant at that," he said. "You take something from everyone. He is still the same guy he was last year. He's not turned big time and done anything different but (Claudio) Ranieri has played Vards more than (Nigel) Pearson has." He scored his first goal for Raith in Saturday's 3-3 draw with Rangers - to temporarily deny the Gers the Ladbrokes Championship title until they sealed it on Tuesday. His Leicester contract expires at the end of the season and he was enjoying life in Scotland but has one eye on the Foxes' title challenge. He added: "I'm not just a player, I'm a Leicester fan. I hope they can do it because it would mean a lot to everyone in Leicester."

FRIDAY, 8 APRIL

Vardy, on 19 league goals, failed to find the net in their last six but Ranieri's men stayed unbeaten despite his mini-drought. Five chipped in with six goals to ensure the Foxes notched five wins and a draw over that period as their main rivals dropped points. Even Wes Morgan scored for the first time, and Danny Simpson reflected on how important his captain's contribution had been. "Wes does feel like a big brother," he said. "You can probably see how we were at the final whistle. We knew it was a big moment and we all pulled together. Every single one of us is giving 100 percent for each other and for the fans. We've just got to keep going, take it game-by-game and keep knocking those games off. We've still got a long way to go and hopefully we'll keep working hard and pick up some more wins."

Ranieri was not concerned about his strike force's lack of goals. For all the brilliance by Vardy and Mahrez, with 35 goals between them this season, they hit a dry patch. Vardy had scored only one league goal in his past eight games, Mahrez contributed three in 15 going into Sunday's game with Sunderland. The duo have been instrumental in Leicester's stunning season and Ranieri was adamant that their recent scoring issues are "not important". He said: "Every time I tell the strikers it's not important if they score a goal. Of course it's their job to score. But look at Jamie, in the last two matches he didn't score but he made the final pass. That is fantastic. I look always at the performance - if everybody links together and fights together and helps each other. That is my performance."

Ranieri's team made a habit of narrow 1-0 wins, with each of their past four games won by that scoreline. Ranieri added: "I ask every time the same things - we create chance and in the end we score one goal. More or less we are creating the same chances as before. If we don't concede, one is enough."

CHAMPIONS LEAGUE

Ranieri's stance has been to consistently dismiss questions of winning the title in favour of lesser milestones, such as "40 Points." Ranieri said the emphasis is now on securing Champions League football for next season. "Everybody is looking at what happens in the last six matches, that's normal. Me too, I'm very curious. But we have to wait and play the matches. It is important to maintain the right things and keep the feet on the ground. We had little children at the training ground in the rain today, saying 'Hi Claudio'. It's amazing. Now we go step by step, like from the beginning. Now Europe is done, now we are fighting for the Champions League. Let me play another three matches and I may tell you something different."

Leicester's lead could stretch to 10 points if they beat Sunderland on Sunday and Tottenham lost to United. Ranieri admitted for the first time the finishing line for the title was in sight and he allowed himself to imagine what it would be like for little Leicester to face Europe's elite in the Champions

League. Qualifying for that competition in itself would be "unbelievable" Ranieri said. "The Champions League would be fantastic," Ranieri said. "Can you imagine if next season Bayern Munich, Barcelona, Real Madrid and so on come here? That would be unbelievable for our fans and for everybody. It's a good experience. We must understand very well that this year is a strange year. The next year you have to restart. Next year we will have to work harder because what is happening this year cannot always happen."

Ranieri was so close to the trophy that he cannot ignore it. It was put to him that his underdogs are doing rather well heading into Grand National weekend, to which he replied: "We are in front but we have to run a lot now. We have finished the last corner and we can see the line. We have to hold on tight and stick our elbows out to make sure nobody gets past."

Leicester's achievements allowed other clubs to dare to dream that the top four, even the title, is not the preserve of an established super-wealthy. "I think now we have opened the heart to everybody, the little normal teams and the normal players. How many of our players were playing in non-league or small leagues a few years ago? And that is good for football. It's good publicity for everybody."

An example of that, Ranieri felt, was the reaction of the Crystal Palace supporters to him before victory at Selhurst Park last month as he walked down the touchline prior to kick-off. The main stand stood and applauded. "It's amazing because at Crystal Palace they clapped me at the beginning, not at the end. Why did they do that? I think," he added, "because they can imagine that Crystal Palace can do this (challenge as Leicester have) next season. That's it." Tony Pulis, Ronald Koeman and Alan Pardew declared they want them to now go on and win the league.

Last season Leicester went to the Stadium of Light to gain the goalless draw, in the penultimate match, that secured their Premier League status. This season they go to try and gain a 10-point lead at the top. "We must understand very well that this year is a strange year," Ranieri said.

Vardy was in a relaxed mood on Friday night when he appeared with girlfriend Rebekah Nicholson at the 2016 British Asian Awards at The Grosvenor House Hotel in London. Leicester fan and TV presenter Manish Bhasin posted a picture on Twitter of himself and Vardy.

SATURDAY, 9 APRIL

Former Barcelona 'pass master' Xavi Hernández told *FourFourTwo* how he hopes Leicester City can get over the finishing line. Speaking exclusively in the May 2016 edition of *FourFourTwo*, he says: "Can you imagine if Leicester won the league? Let's hope they don't blow up and get ahead of themselves, because it's easy for perceptions to change. The thing is, Leicester have a good team. They're very compact, Jamie Vardy is so quick on the break and Riyad Mahrez has great quality. Did you see that volleyed backheel assist (in the 2-2 draw with West Bromwich Albion)? Outrageous. I flicked over from La Liga just to watch it. N'Golo Kanté is a phenomenon in midfield and Danny Drinkwater and Christian Fuchs, the left-back, are very solid too. Robert Huth is huge at centre-back."

Jamie Carragher in his *Daily Mail* column observed: "So, they are nearly there: four more wins and the Leicester fairytale will be complete. Another 12 points and the tributes will begin to flow. The first place everyone will look is to the dynamic and gifted forwards Jamie Vardy and Riyad Mahrez. After that the fantastic efforts in midfield, led by N'Golo Kanté and Danny Drinkwater, will be hailed, so too will the rock solid defence. There will even be glowing praise for the scouts.

But what about the manager? Claudio Ranieri has been responsible for making sure all these elements have come together so spectacularly...but here are Leicester, on the brink of one of the greatest achievements in football, and it feels like he is not getting the credit he deserves. Is this because of what happened when he was appointed last summer? There was a lot of criticism that Leicester chose to bring in a coach in his 60s whose previous job in charge of Greece had ended in the calamity of a home defeat by the Faroe Islands. I include myself among those who were surprised that Leicester turned to Ranieri but, looking back, I am disappointed about the way I reacted. Why couldn't we have just looked at his CV and accepted here was a very good manager? It has made me think about the way we view managers nowadays and how difficult the profession is. It seems that unless you are one of the serial winners - Sir Alex Ferguson, José Mourinho or Pep Guardiola - you don't really get rated. The truth is that Ranieri has a distinguished pedigree. He showed early on, when guiding Cagliari from Serie C to Serie A, what he could do, while, with the likes of Gabriel Batistuta, he led his Fiorentina team to the Coppa Italia and Italian Super Cup in the mid-1990s.

My first encounter with Ranieri was in 1998 when Liverpool knocked his Valencia team out of the UEFA Cup. Then he went to Chelsea, who finished second in the title race on his watch and got to a Champions League semi-final. Among the players he signed was Frank Lampard. His work continued to be solid after leaving Stamford Bridge and he won the European Super Cup when returning to Valencia and finished second in Serie A with Roma and Juventus. He also took Monaco out of the French second division as champions and guided them into the Champions League.

When you are not universally appreciated, however, it shows how hard the job is. All it takes is one failure and a sacking and your abilities are dismissed. That is what happened with Ranieri and that is what Gary Neville will find now. Thinking about the way Ranieri and Neville are perceived has made me wonder about management and the career path I have gone down.

One thing is certain, you don't go into management expecting to receive plaudits. Claudio Ranieri provides proof of that. Now, he has just won his second manager of the month award after guiding Leicester to the brink of history and the LMA prize for the season will surely follow. Finally it feels like Ranieri will be accepted for what he has been all along, ever since he set out on his journey in the late 1980s. He is a very good manager. It is a shame it has taken so long to get that recognition."

After watching Morgan head the winner against Southampton Harry Kane switched over to the World Twenty20 final. He said: "Leicester kick off before us in their next four games, so if they start losing it will give us a bit more urgency. The title race is a bit like watching cricket - we are batting second and the team that bats second knows what they have to do."

It was now Leicester's to lose and Kane, like the rest of the country, was on the edge of his seat watching them last Sunday. He was convinced Sadio Mané would put Saints ahead when he was clean through but he was denied when Danny Simpson threw out an elbow to divert his effort. Kane said: "When Mané went around the keeper I was on the edge of my seat, but unfortunately he didn't score. Leicester went on to win 1-0 again but they have some tough games coming up. All we can do is control our games and try to win them."

Spurs face Manchester United, walking out at White Hart Lane immediately after Leicester's game at the Stadium of Light has finished. No more margin for error after they were held to a frustrating draw at Liverpool last Saturday. Kane said: "Getting a 1-1 at Anfield is not a bad result and there is a lot of football to be played yet. Manchester United are always a threat but we are in good form and we don't fear anyone. We will play attacking football and try to keep clean sheets. If Leicester win all their next six games then there is nothing we can do. People are more patient with us because going for the title is a new experience for a lot of the crowd. We enjoy our football and because we have so many English players in the team it's like playing with your mates. If we finish second it will still be a good season and it will show progress. Well done Leicester if they win it."

Arsene Wenger had not given up on the title, 11 points behind with a game in hand. "As long as it is mathematically possible, there is a strong chance. Every game is tight." But his bold comment in the build up to the West Ham game looked pretty sick after going 2-up, then losing 3-2 and just about grabbing a point at 3-3, victims of a Carroll hat-trick, leaving them 10 points adrift of the leaders. Arsenal needed the unlikely collapses from Leicester and Spurs as Wenger admited, "It leaves us third in the league on 59 points and that's not where we want to be, but we've made it much more difficult for ourselves to win the championship but we have to keep going and hope. You never know what can happen. And we have to look behind and the clubs chasing us, be serious and focus on finishing as high as possible."

SUNDAY, 10 APRIL
SUNDERLAND 0-2 LEICESTER CITY

Alan Birchenall, who works out of the club's Belvoir Drive training ground, has a lifetime contract as he is such a popular institution at the club. When City's participation was recently announced in this summer's International Champions Cup, alongside many of Europe's elite, Birchenall represented them at the New York launch. He said: "It wasn't until I went on to that stage and I saw the backdrop of the clubs' badges that it really hit me. I've been around for over 40 years at Leicester and seen everything from promotion, relegation and administration. But that stage really brought it home what the season has been like. There was Barcelona, Real Madrid, Bayern Munich, AC Milan, Inter Milan, Celtic, Liverpool, PSG, Chelsea and then our badge. It was only a few years ago we were languishing in level three (League One). When you think about it, it is quite amazing. But I sat on stage that day in New York and looked at all the great players - Edgar Davids, Italian internationals, and then me at the end. I had to say a few words and started off explaining this time last year we were seven points adrift of survival, looking dead and buried, and now we are leading arguably the best league in the world. Perhaps we are the first club to break the mould? We are not where we are because of money because we have only spent about £22-23million."

With the movie chiefs planning a movie about Vardy, Birchenall laughingly demanded Hollywood heart-throb George Clooney play him in it. He said of the Foxes' hitman: "Jamie bangs on my door down the training ground and pokes his head in and asks how the coffin dodger is!"

Birchenall paid tribute to Ranieri, who previously bossed 15 teams including Fiorentina, Valencia, Atletico Madrid, Chelsea, Juventus and Inter Milan. Birchenall, 70, told *Mirror Sport*: "I watch Claudio and I see an artist at work with the players, the press, the fans. It is great because everything is going well but it is going well because he has helped it go well. Claudio was one of the early favourites to lose his job but can you think of anyone else who can get manager of the year now? I said to one of the players pre-season, 'How is the new man?' He said, 'Birch, he just stood there for a week watching us and has hardly said anything'. That made me think he was having a good look to see what he'd got, what he'd inherited. You can't be in control of all those clubs and not accumulate a wealth of experience. What I have seen is a manager who has gathered all the experience from the big clubs he has managed and put it all in one bag, fortunately for Leicester City. He came in after the win on Sunday over Southampton and said, 'Well done, we move on to the next one'. That is what it has been like."

Leicester named an unchanged side. The 'Tinkerman' is dead, now the 'Thinkerman'. He named the same starting line-up 12 times this season, seven more than any other team.

Ranieri: "Everyone is looking at what happens in the last six matches, me too, I am very curious, but we have to wait. There are a lot of people pushing behind us and that's important but it's important to keep our feet on the ground. Sunderland are desperate and it will be a big battle.

Sometimes there is pretty football but I am waiting for a battle."

Vardy turned up at the Stadium of Light, with energy drink in hand, big tunes in ears and a tennis ball for a bit of keepie-up.

Ex-Sunderland defender Gary Bennett at the Stadium of Light told BBC Newcastle: "There is a mood here around the Stadium of Light, much more positive than it has been in recent weeks. Sunderland fans believe they can cause an upset here this afternoon, but Sam Allardyce's players will have to play with their heads, win their individual battles."

Vardy scored twice as leaders Leicester moved to within three victories of their first top-flight title and Ranieri was spotted sobbing at the end.

Match of the Day's Alan Shearer tweeted: "Do Leicester know they are about to win the Premier League the most incredible story in football history? No nerves. No wobbles. Amazing."

Vardy coolly slotted in the first, before outpacing the opposition defence and tucking home a second deep into injury time. Drinkwater and Vardy combined for the striker's 20th league goal, the first Leicester striker to reach the milestone in the top flight since Gary Lineker in the 1984-85 season. The Foxes legend scored 24 goals that season and got a big money move to Everton the following summer. "It is massive for me personally, but the main thing is the team. We knew it was going to be hard but we've dug in and taken the three points. It's brilliant (my name is alongside his). But hopefully it will be up there with who knows at the end of the season, maybe a title. There is nothing wrong with looking at the fixtures, the table or watching the games of your rivals. The team that we have got, they are not a bunch that are going to let it go to their heads. None of the boys are like that."

"Coming off the Sunderland fans were clapping us as well which is brilliant," Vardy told Sky Sports. "It was a great game, we knew it would be tough but managed to grind it out. It's a step closer to possibly winning the league. We'll enjoy this for the rest of the day and then get back to training for the next week."

The supporters stayed inside the ground well after the final whistle chanting "we're gonna win the league, now you're gonna believe us" as only an astonishing collapse would stop them.

Drinkwater supplied Vardy's first with a trademark ball over the top. Vardy explained: "Me and Drinky had a little chat in the first half and saw that one of the centre halves was always going to attack and one was dropping off, so if I was on the last man the ball was there to be played over the top. Luckily in the second half it has worked a treat."

Ranieri challenged Vardy to beat Kane in the scoring charts, but he said he will not set a total, adding: "To be honest I couldn't care if don't score any more as long the team wins (games). We are just enjoying ourselves and picking up points when we can. We will be back on that training field now and hopefully pick up three points next week as well (against West Ham)."

Ranieri pleaded with Vardy during the interval. "I am very happy because in the last weeks he didn't score but he made a great assist for his team-mates and they score a goal. At half-time I said to him 'Come on Jamie, I need you, we need you.' And he scored twice."

Summing up at the press conference Ranieri said: "It is fantastic when you see before the match, an old lady with a Leicester shirt outside the stadium. I say 'Unbelievable'. They come from Leicester to support us. This is my emotion. It is fantastic. That is football. I was on the bus. I saw unbelievable and I want to say thank you for the support. They are amazing. They can continue to say this. It is important we stay focused on the next match. I said this to the players, well done. We won today but now we have two matches at home, the first against West Ham United, a very difficult match because they are a fantastic team with good players, everything right. And then after that it is Swansea, another very difficult match. But now we must stay focused. The fans must continue to dream but we must continue to be concentrated and focused. Now we have two tough matches at home, the Champions League is on the table and we have to keep it. We haven't achieved anything yet. You make this job for the emotion you feel inside, but it is difficult for me to tell what kind of emotion. It was a tough, tough match, very difficult. They could have drawn the match. We had the chances to close out the match, but we could not score the second. And three points was very important for us. We made a normal performance, but our opponent was very desperate and that is normal. And for this reason I told my players it would be a tough match. We had the opportunity to finish the match, but we made mistakes. We wanted to win, of course, while Sunderland were a little bit more anxious. They wanted to score, of course, but not to concede a goal. But we played normally, we wanted to score a goal. And in the second half I told my players to keep going as it was important to maintain a high tempo. Maybe slowly, slowly we read the match better and we tried to play better, but I am satisfied. But now we have to play another good match at home against West Ham, which will be another difficult match as they play very, very well and they are dangerous. Nobody could believe this (at the start of the season), but now we are in this position, we have to fight and fight until the end. I told my players we have everything in our hands and we have to only think about ourselves."

Vardy hoped the season finishes with the fairytale of winning the Premier League. That film about his life is, as we've been promised, in the pipeline, but the final script will not be written until this summer with producers waiting to see if Leicester can win an historic title. Vardy said: "They are hoping for a fairytale ending so let's hope it goes that way."

'We've got a few games left. It's a step but a very big one," Drinkwater said. "If this puts more pressure on them (Spurs) then perfect but I can't see Tottenham putting too much on this. It's up to them now. The fans here are brilliant, and credit to the lads we deserved that."

All five of Drinkwater's Premier League assists were for Vardy. Vardy's 21st in injury time was superb, leaving Patrick van Aanholt floundering after breaking from the half way line before going round Mannone to slip the ball into an open net. The double couldn't have come at a better time with Ranieri being quizzed before the game about the lack of Vardy goals. So often a match-winner this season, he turned provider in recent weeks but had not scored since converting the penalty at Arsenal on 14 February, seven games ago. "It is good, he scored with his national team and now he scores with us and that is important as the goalscorer wants to score a goal," Ranieri said.

The day ended with United held up in traffic as Spurs eventually won the game at the Lane, determined to cling to Leicester's coat tails, as they maintained their own title challenge with a thumping 3-0 victory.

Victory, combined with Manchester United's defeat at White Hart Lane, made it impossible for Leicester to finish outside the top four, meaning qualification for Europe's elite competition. "'This is an amazing season for us, for our fans, four our chairman, for me, for everyone," Ranieri said. "Our goal was to be safe. Then it is okay. Next I said Europa League and it is there. Now we have the Champions League. Come on, keep going."

"It's the most incredible story of the Premier League's history," Graeme Souness said on Sky Sports. "Such a small team, got themselves so far in front, been top of the league for so long, playing with great resilience, always easy on the eye to watch. It's a type of football we thought was a thing of the past - get it forward as quickly as you can for a striker of 29 (Vardy) it's very unusual he wants to run in behind all the time."

Jamie Carragher was part of the Liverpool side that won the Champions League in 2005 after coming back to win on penalties after being 3-0 down at half-time in the final to AC Milan. He said Leicester winning the league could be an even greater achievement than what Forest managed in the 1970s. "Graeme spoke about maybe the biggest story in the Premier League, is it the biggest story we've seen in football? There's the Nottingham Forest one and they went on to win European Cups. I think it's safe to say I don't see Leicester doing that - but the days of someone coming up, or a smaller team, winning the league was more likely to happen wasn't it, maybe in the sixties, seventies, eighties?" He didn't think a similar feat could be repeated. "Ranieri said before the game this could happen in 50, 60 years' time. The chances of seeing something like this again? I think it could be double that."

Robert Huth was soon on Twitter following Leicester guaranteeing themselves a place among Europe's elite…

robert huth, @robert_huth - Yes! Champions League guaranteed! Better start practicing my Rabonas

MONDAY, 11 APRIL

Tickets to watch the final home game were being offered for £15,000 a pair through an online re-sale website.

The match which could see the Foxes become champions, sold out in 90 minutes. Within hours, individual tickets were being advertised for more than £3,000 each and a pair for much more. The club said it would "take action against any ticket touting" or attempts to "resell tickets above face value". One fan who contacted BBC Sport said he had missed out on a ticket, despite having a membership package and having been to all but three home games this season. "This season is something we never expected and will probably never happen again in our lifetimes," said the supporter, who wished to remain anonymous. "Now I won't be there to potentially celebrate us winning the Premier League. It is a bit of a 'here's what you could have won' moment. The club have been brilliant with fans these past couple of seasons. But I think there will be a few questions for them to answer as to how this has happened. I can't see how ordinary fans could afford to pay £15,000 for two tickets - looking at some of them, it's the price of a second-hand car."

Leicester posted on their own website that the Everton game had seen "unprecedented demand" and sold out in "record time", with the "vast majority" of higher-tier members able to get a ticket. Membership does not guarantee a ticket, the club told the *Leicester Mercury*. "The unauthorised sale of football tickets is a criminal offence under UK law," added a club spokesman.

A number of disappointed fans responded to the club's Facebook post with their complaints:

David Lea: "Very bad when they are on ticket sites at anything from £495 to £5,000. Who's giving the touts these tickets? What's the point of being a gold/silver member? I'd like to hear the club's views on this."

Ben Dunkley: "Absolute joke, what a waste of money spending £75 on a gold membership."

Peter Schoneveld: "I made 85 calls since 9am as I have to book by phone because I have a family membership and was unable to get through. The system is rubbish. I have only been able to get tickets to one match all season!! Why am I paying over £100 for a membership (plus however much on phone calls sitting through an automated message to then be cut off) to get priority on tickets and still unable to get any! I am gutted… and angry."

Emilia Woch: "The shameful fact of the matter is half these people who got tickets will go on to sell them off for thousands of pounds, whilst us TRUE fans (who find it hard enough to afford £50 a ticket, let alone thousands of pounds) miss out. If the club truly cares about its fans, it would void every resold ticket and sell them back to the fans who don't want to make money off Leicester's success and who actually want to go to their last home game of the season."

Adie Wheat: "Gutted. Been all season, 1968 my first game never miss a season. Silver member can't get a ticket for the most important game - winning the league."

Gemma Kott: "Gold membership! Was trying to get a ticket since 9am only to be told all sold out! Never had that problem before. People selling their tickets for a massive profit should be banned from buying tickets again."

Philip Goodchild: "Gutted. You would have thought paying £40 per season would get you a ticket. The club should have capped the memberships at the beginning of the season."

With 23,000 season ticket holders and more than 3,000 tickets handed to away fans at the 32,000-capacity King Power Stadium, around 6,000 tickets were available via the club's various membership schemes on a match-by-match basis. The first choice of seats is offered to Family Fox and Gold Fox members who, respectively, pay £100 and £75 per season for priority access to tickets. Tickets are then offered to lower level Silver Fox and City Fox members.

The ticket story gathered pace with BBC Sport Online later taking up the story, interviewing numerous fans:

Adie Wheat has watched Leicester City since 1968. He has a club membership and said he hasn't missed a home game all season. But now he will watch the game that could potentially see his side lift the Premier League trophy on television. Other fans have expressed "disgust", "frustration" and "disappointment" at missing out on tickets, only to see some reappear on ticket resale sites for way over their face value.

Chris Hubbard, from Market Bosworth, failed to get tickets despite having a Silver Fox membership. "It's just disgusting" he told BBC Radio Leicester. "We go and watch night games, we went when they were two tiers down, it's just gutting that proper fans can't afford these prices to go and watch the last game. You just feel like you've been robbed, you pay for the privilege to have this ticket and then not even have the chance. Then you see them online for those stupid prices, it's just gut wrenching."

Gordon Ward, who has been supporting Leicester City for 50 years, said he feels the problems for this game are just the "tip of the iceberg. Is this going to be the same next season during the Champions League?" he said. "It has been sell-outs all season, but we've never had this problem. We think this could just be the tip of the iceberg, we think it's so unfair, but it's so unfair for so many."

Gemma Kott said she had tried phoning from 9:00am but was told about an hour later that the tickets had all been snapped up. "I'd not had a problem getting tickets before," she said. "All the big games, Manchester United, Liverpool, absolutely fine. It's frustrating that we've paid for priority but what can you do? Maybe I was naive, but I didn't realise the club had sold more memberships than tickets." She was upset that some tickets are being sold online for thousands of pounds. "If these tickets are allocated, why doesn't the club know who they are selling them on to?"

Liam Underwood has been supporting the Foxes for 13 years and has not been able to get a ticket with his silver membership. "It's disappointing, but I didn't think it would sell out as fast," he said. "It has been fine all season trying to get tickets and you've sometimes been able to get them the week before a match. More people have been getting memberships as we've got closer to the title and even some gold members have missed out. "It does beg the question - where have all the tickets gone?"

One person who was not disappointed on Monday was Leicester's mayor Sir Peter Soulsby, who tweeted that after an hour and a half wait he had secured a ticket. The Labour leader of the city council said he has only missed one home game in the past 12 months.

The Italian media lead with Ranieri's success on the front cover of Monday's newspapers. *La Gazzetta dello Sport* headline read "Italian Style" with a picture of a jubilant Ranieri as he and

Leicester "march to the throne. Another victory, tears, the Vardy miracle: we reveal the secrets of the Coach who at age 64 put his hands on the Premier League title at Leicester," the paper adds.

Corriere dello Sport report on the Foxes with a more philosophical approach. "Ranieri's lesson" is their headline as they add that he has proved "you can bring an outsider to within touching distance of the title as Leicester soar and enchant England."

Alan Smith in his *Daily Telegraph* column felt there had been "the defining moment in this incredible season". He said of Ranieri: "Judging by his emotional reaction, the Italian seemed to think so too. How had he brought about that change after a flat first half? Some tactical tweak that confounded Sunderland? An inspirational substitution that turned the match on its head? No, neither. Granted, Leonardo Ulloa's introduction did lend an improvement, though it did not directly lead to Jamie Vardy's opening goal a couple of minutes later. You can only conclude it must have been Ranieri's words in that away dressing room at half-time that led to the Leicester manager 'finding a way'.

Over the course of this campaign, we have all tried to work out what Ranieri has done from a tactical standpoint to turn a near-relegated team into likely champions. It has not been easy. Not even his players can really pinpoint the reasons for the staggering turnaround. Some of them, though, might remember a moment that would have a huge impact in the months to come. They might think back to a September day at the Britannia Stadium when Stoke were leading 2-0 at half-time. The visitors hadn't got going. The shape wasn't working. At this point, Ranieri decided to take off Gökhan Inler, the midfielder he had gone out of his way to sign in the summer. Inler wasn't one of Steve Walsh's inspirational finds. Leicester's head of recruitment could not claim this one. Walsh's new boss had specifically earmarked the Napoli player to replace the recently departed Esteban Cambiasso. Yet it clearly was not happening on that afternoon in the Potteries. Inler was struggling to keep up with the pace. As a result, the highly decorated Switzerland international was swiftly replaced at half-time by Marc Albrighton as N'Golo Kanté moved inside from his wide position. Leicester subsequently fought back to draw 2-2 with a new-look midfield that has more or less stayed together for every game since.

This story has a bearing on something the genial Roman said last week. Paraphrasing, he insisted you have to be tough on the big players. His experiences at Chelsea, Valencia, Inter Milan and Juventus had taught him how to handle the well-known names. Maybe that's why he acted so decisively with Inler. With the other Leicester lads, however, he claims it is different. 'I only encourage' he said with a smile. True or not, Ranieri has practically turned water into wine over the last nine months. Whatever the challenge or situation, he has 'found a way' to get the job done. As a result, this campaign will be mulled over incessantly in the years to come. For City fans, a sunny day on Wearside will surely never be forgotten. Neither will a manager set to gain this club a place in football folklore."

As for the former Leicester City striker's "Moment of the Weekend", he added: "The final whistle had long since sounded but the Leicester City fans refused to go home. 'We shall not, we shall not be moved!' Their songs from the top tier at the Stadium of Light could clearly be heard below stairs as the managers gave their interviews. For those wearing blue and white this was surreal stuff. Virtually this time last year, at the same ground, they were celebrating safety. Now they were singing about title glory."

A fan has quite literally captured the spirt of the team in a bottle. Foxes season ticket holder and writer Dom Roskrow (who, on his Twitter account, describes himself as a "Freelance whisky writer, Leicester City and All Blacks fan, & Fortnum & Mason Drink Writer of The Year. Likes bad heavy rock music and has dodgy political views") has had six bottles of Leicester City Football Club whisky produced at £65 each. The 54-year-old plans to keep five of the bottles for himself and to hand one over to the Leicester City billionaire chairman Vichai Srivaddhanaprabha.

Dom had the special spirit produced by the English Whisky Company in Norfolk. He said: "After Jamie Vardy and Danny Drinkwater's England call up I decided it had to be an English whisky. I live in Norfolk close to St George's distillery and know the team there very well. The managing director Andrew Nelstrop was only too happy to help out."

The single malt whisky has been made with malt that has been matured in an ex-bourbon cask and finished in a virgin oak cask. It is bottled at its natural strength of 59.7% ABV.

Dom has been a season ticket holder at the King Power Stadium for three years, along with his teenage sons, Jules and Louie. He said: "The plan is to drink one bottle during the rest of the season to toast each of our remaining six games, no matter what happens in them, and to open two of them for a barbecue and party to celebrate the extraordinary few months we've had. That leaves just three unopened bottles so they are going to be real collectors' items." Dom hopes to give one of the remaining bottles to Leicester City chairman. He said: "It's partly to say thank you for the amazing support he and his family have shown our club and turned it in to such a wonderful and warm place, and partly to say thank you from the fans for the free beer and donuts."

English Whisky Company MD Andrew Nelstrop added: "This is a genuinely unique whisky and if the Leicester City chairman likes whisky he will love this stuff."

The Foxes cannot finish lower than fourth but could still miss out on a place in Europe's premier club competition if: Leicester finished in fourth place and Manchester City won the Champions League and finished outside of the top four.

Head of Media Anthony Herlihy confirmed to me that he was a "guest" at Manchester City on Monday and Tuesday to go behind the scenes for a Champions League match.

TUESDAY, 12 APRIL

José Mourinho expressed his admiration for old adversary Ranieri, hoping the Italian he has ridiculed in the past can win the Premier League.

Ranieri is in pole position to succeed Mourinho as Premier League champions and he would be happy if that happens.

"When Prince William is saying he would love Leicester to win it, I am nobody to say anything," Mourinho told Sky Sports News. "I think his (Ranieri's) career deserves that. He is a good man who I respect. In spite of bad words, he knows I like him very much and I would like him to win. But I like Mauricio (Pochettino), I have a great relationship with him and his work at Tottenham is very good. Let's go for the simple one, the one with more points deserves to win."

The players showed they were staying humble as numerous fans grabbed selfies and autographs. Dozens of Leicester fans waited patiently outside the training base following their daily session in the hope of meeting their idols and coming home with a memento. Vardy arrived in his blue Bentley, he was the man most wanted and they were delighted when he got out of the car to join them, posed for snaps with a number of fans as well as signing pictures. Mahrez also signed autographs, as did Drinkwater, Fuchs, Ulloa, Dyer, and many others.

Hard to stay grounded when Italy and Juventus goalkeeping legend Gianluigi Buffon welcomed Leicester City and his former manager Ranieri to the Champions League. "Leicester is no more a fairytale, now is reality. Welcome in Europe Mr. Claudio Ranieri," tweeted Buffon, who was coached by his fellow countryman at Juventus from 2007-09. Ranieri's achievements dominated the front of the Italian sports newspapers, despite a full weekend of Serie A fixtures including Juventus' win against AC Milan. He last managed in Italy in 2012, when he was sacked by Inter Milan, prior to that he resigned after a two-year spell with Roma and was also dismissed by Juventus.

Gary Lineker spoke of the pain and ecstasy of being a Leicester City fan this season "It's a mixture of utter joy and excruciating agony. It's so incredible, and you want it to happen so much that it's become quite tough watching the games. It is Roy of the Rovers stuff. If someone had pitched this as a movie, they'd say it was too ridiculous. I was in Barcelona at the weekend, and took my four boys. Three support Leicester and even George, who's a United fan, has come around a bit. We ended up in this tiny Moroccan restaurant - the only one we could find with a TV in it. And we're 1-0 up and we're all going through absolute hell. It's like a great film or comedy so tense it's hard to watch."

Of course he also pledged to present *MOTD* in his underpants. "I said I'd do it, so I'll do it. Of course, when I said I'd do it, I categorically knew that it wouldn't happen…the possibility that a provincial town could win the League completely bucks the trend. It's still very hard to fathom how it's happened."

Shown a picture of Ronaldo posing in his underpants, he remarked: "I could carry off the body bit, no problem, but I'm not sure I'll be going for a pair like that." What kind, then? "Honestly, I'm not getting ahead of myself on this. At the moment, I still think there's only a 50% chance of it happening." Does he regret that tweet now? "Well it was a bit of fun at the time. And if they do it, I suppose it will bring a bit of attention to the first show of next season." The highest ratings ever? "Or the lowest! I think a lot of people will switch off. Crikey, it's going to be a bit of a cringe."

He's only been to see them three times this season, and they've failed to win a single time. He is now worried he jinxes the team. "I am slightly concerned, because I am planning to go to Old Trafford." He added: "I used to be very superstitious until I realised it's bad luck."

WEDNESDAY, 13 APRIL

Ranieri didn't want to get "carried away by emotion" despite shedding a tear after his side's last game as he praised wife Rosanna for giving him the stability to work his magic in the Premier League. Speaking to *Gazzetta dello Sport*, he said of his family and his tears at the Stadium of Light: "They weren't real tears, they were unshed tears. It was an emotional moment. Seeing all those people around us, entire families on buses in Leicester shirts to follow us up to Sunderland - that struck me deeply."

"In the press room afterwards I wanted to explain the concept but it's already difficult for me to express my feelings in Italian, let alone English. I have a public role and I try to be level-headed. I have to give clear signals to my team, I can't get carried away by emotion. My wife Rosanna is my rock. In July we'll celebrate 40 years of marriage. Then there's my daughter, and my grandson Orlando who is 14 months. I see him on Skype. When he calls me 'Grandpa' that's a really strong emotion."

Ranieri faced a "terrible" last five games acknowledging Spurs will fight until the end. Ranieri's side will be champions if they secured three victories in their remaining matches, starting with West Ham at the King Power Stadium on Sunday, followed by another home match against Swansea before Leicester faced Manchester United, Everton and Chelsea in their final three games. "It's not done yet though. We're in the Champions League, even the preliminary round of the Champions League, but the last five games will be terrible. Tottenham won't give up and we have to stay focused. I never think about what others do but what I have to do and doing our work in the best way. If Tottenham overtake us then we'll compliment them. That's how sport works."

"Our work rate? That's our great asset. I knew right away in the training camp in Austria this team has a special moral strength. They're good lads, facing the story of their lives with great responsibility. In the week they work hard, then when the game comes around they're laughing and joking in the dressing room getting ready to take to the pitch. Nobody saves themselves or stops for breath."

"The attention surrounding Leicester? It's the power of the media. In the 90s when I was in charge of Valencia and we got important results, it didn't unleash this kind of whirlwind. Today there's all this TV which brings games from around the world into your living room, there's Facebook and Twitter, there's the internet."

Ranieri, perhaps surprisingly, banned Vardy from shooting practice at the training ground. Vardy explained, "I don't really get the chance to practise that much on my finishing because we have our shooting drills early in the week when the gaffer's wanting me to rest my legs. So normally, when there's a bit of shooting, the gaffer tells me to go inside! I'll keep doing that if it means I'm saving my legs - and goals - for games."

Vardy revealed that laughter proved a force for positive thinking, "We're always laughing. In training we're always having a laugh and a joke. That's just how we are, everyone's relaxed - and the gaffer wants it to be like that. The good thing about this squad is we're tight-knit. That's how we've been from day one. It's the same group of characters we had at the start of the season and to be honest with you that's the good thing about us. We're only looking ahead to the next game. Next week. That's all we have done all season, one game at a time. We'll be back on that training pitch, looking at ways we can get the win."

German centre-back Huth is often a target for the dressing room jokers. "In the warm up there are sprint contests around different mannequins," added Vardy. "And Huthy, for some reason has ended up in the top group. I don't know how. If he gets turned round the mannequins first and puts his arm out then that's it, you're not going to get past him. So we are always having a laugh and a joke about it. That is how we are, everyone is relaxed. The gaffer wants it to be like that."

Ranieri refuses to underestimate the importance of the chemistry "camaraderie" can produce. "There isn't a secret to us," Drinkwater said. "It's just that we're a bunch of lads that get along. We're all willing to work hard for each other on the pitch. It shows by how well we graft out results. If stuff's not going well, we still manage to win games. Wes Morgan's a great skipper. If a big header or a big tackle's needed, he's going to make it but we all tend to talk and fire each other up. It's not just down to Wes; we've got a few players who like doing that."

Drinkwater's bond with Vardy resulted in a telepathic, understanding on the pitch. "Drinky knows exactly where I'm going to be," said Vardy, whose first goal on Sunday came after his collection of the midfielder's long ball over the top of Sunderland's defence. "He doesn't have to look most of the time. As long as I know the rough area where it's going to go, I'll be on my bike and chasing the ball down."

Drinkwater agreed. "The majority of time you don't need to look for Jamie. You just know he's going to be on the move and that, with his pace, if the pass is right, it's going to cause defenders problem. It works, it scores us goals, so why stop?"

Drinkwater claimed his upbringing in Manchester United's Academy taught him how to cope with the pressure of situations like this, even though he never played a first team game at Old Trafford. "One thing they taught you as a youngster was to keep focused on the job. My upbringing at that club was probably something that is going to stand me in good stead."

Ranieri educated some of the journeymen players. "It's exciting to learn new things from the manager," Drinkwater said. "It's brilliant. It's showing in our performances, where we are in the league. But Claudio Ranieri's a big name in football."

Drinkwater has not forgotten Nigel Pearson's contribution either. "The momentum obviously carried on from last season," he said. "Credit to the old gaffer for starting that off. Both managers, I think, deserve credit."

Paddy Power quoted Leicester at 100-1 to win next season's Champions League…a long way short of their, now famous, previous 5,000-1 Premier League odds. But, the Irish bookmaker are only offering 40-1 on Manchester United winning Europe's top prize in 2017 despite them looking unlikely to qualify. Ladbrokes quoted them at 150-1. Are Leicester are being underestimated again?

Vardy, Mahrez and Kanté were named on the six-man shortlist for the PFA Players' Player of the Year award joined by Özil, Payet and Kane. Kane was also in contention to retain the Young Player of the Year award he won 12 months ago and is named alongside Spurs team-mate Dele Alli. Vardy scored 21 league goals, six assists, Mahrez contributed 16 goals, 11 assists. Kanté made more tackles (146) and interceptions (134) than any other player in the Premier League.

THURSDAY, 14 APRIL

Ranieri gives his side two days off a week because he trusts them to give their all.

"I promised the players that they have two days each week off, that was our pact. I said, I trust you, you explain a few ideas from football, as long as you give everything," he told *Kicker*. "I am happy here and do not think about a change. I think Leicester will be my last stop. I hope they give me a long contract, so about six or seven years. And then I finish my career here."

Clubs performance psychologist Ken Way made little of the so called pressure. "I'm not a busy man at the moment," he told *The Times*. "I was actually busier this time last season. I was even able to take a short holiday last week and not worry about it. I was concerned at one point, earlier in the season, about how (the pressure) might start to affect the players. But it honestly hasn't. It's not a stressful situation. It's only stressful if you allow it to be."

Vardy had 21 goals already but only managed five goals last term and Way revealed he doubted himself after making the leap from non-League to the Championship and eventually the Premier League. "Jamie definitely suffered a little in terms of his belief. He knew he had performed to an exceptionally high standard before, but when a striker stops scoring goals, there's always a question mark in his mind."

Way, who has been in his role there since 2011, added: "With the individual work I do, it's very little with goalkeepers, a little bit more with the defenders and midfielders, but the strikers are often the ones I work with on an individual basis. That's true of football in general. But it would be erroneous for me to take any credit for what Jamie has done or what the team has done. I'm just a very small cog in a very well-oiled machine."

The Premier League removed referee Kevin Friend from the Spurs game at Stoke City on Monday, because he supports Leicester, and Spurs were seven points behind with five games left. The Professional Game Match Officials Ltd (PGMOL) do not pick Friend, who lives in Leicester and has attended games in a personal capacity, to referee matches involving the Foxes. The PGMOL said "the timing and context" of the game saw them replace Friend. "It was felt unnecessary to add extra scrutiny on the refereeing appointment," a PGMOL statement said. Neil Swarbrick, from Preston, will take charge at Stoke, with Friend instead officiating Newcastle's game against Manchester City on Tuesday.

Dutch goalkeeper Diego Coret was on trial. The 16-year-old plays for AZ Alkmaar but was set to leave at the end of the season after failing to agree terms on a professional contract. Coret has also

Saturday, 8 August, 2015. Claudio Ranieri in charge of his first game. But how long would he last in the job?

Saturday, 28 November, 2015.
Jamie Vardy scores
against Manchester United,
to make it 11 in a row!
A new Premier League record.

Tuesday, 2 February, 2016.
Jamie Vardy scores Leicester's
goal of the season - that stunning,
dipping, half-volley vs Liverpool.

Saturday, 6 February, 2016. Robert Huth scores the decisive third goal in the pivotal 3-1 victory at Manchester City.

Monday, 2 May, 2016.
Leicester City fans celebrating Chelsea's second goal in that 2-2 draw with Spurs. Nearly Champions of England!

Tuesday, 3 May, 2016.
The day after the night before. Leicester City fans gather
outside the King Power Stadium. Has anyone been to bed?

Saturday, 7 May, 2016.
There's no backing out
now for Gary Lineker.

Saturday, 7 May, 2016.
It's a carnival atmosphere
at the King Power Stadium.

Saturday, 7 May, 2016. Leicester fans unveil a 'Champions' banner before the match against Everton.

Saturday, 7 May, 2016. Leicester City players and staff celebrate with the trophy.

Saturday, 7 May, 2016.
Claudio Ranieri and
Wes Morgan lift the Barclays
Premier League trophy.

Monday, 16 May, 2016.
Claudio Ranieri with Danny Simpson,
Kasper Schmeichel, Riyad Mahrez,
Andy King, Danny Drinkwater
Leonardo Ulloa, Jamie Vardy and
Robert Huth show off the trophy and
marvel at the overwhelming scenes.

Monday, 16 May, 2016.
Every vantage point is filled as
thousands witness the open top
procession through Leicester.

Monday, 16 May, 2016.
Incredible scenes inside Victoria Park.

had a spell at FC Utrecht but is keen on a move to the Premier League. The club stepped up their youth recruitment, targeting some of the best young talent in Europe as they look to capitalise on their position as the Premier League's leading club. They had winger Serge Atakayi on trial from FF Jaro in Finland and checked on AC Milan's 18-year-old midfield prospect Manuel Locatelli. Atakayi, who has dual nationality, can play on either wing, made his league debut at 16 and is the youngest player to score in Finnish football.

Sky Bet's biggest Leicester backer decided to Cash Out their 5,000/1 each way bet for a profit of over £100k. The punter placed £20 each-way on Leicester in August - and has now won £108,703.41. The windfall would have been just over £133k had they held out. Winnings would have been reduced to £25,020 had Leicester slipped to a second or third-placed finish - and they would have won nothing if Leicester ended the season fourth. "Backers of Leicester have faced a real head-scratcher over the last few weeks," said Sky Bet's Sandro Di Michele. "All these 1-0 wins and even their 2-0 win at Sunderland have come with moments of genuine alarm and I must say bravo to this customer for seeing it through for so long. Presumably the punter was keen to make sure they won six figures for their small each-way play and now that it's job done, they can relax and enjoy the rest of the season."

Vinnie Jones was being lined up to play Nigel Pearson in the Vardy movie. The ex-Wimbledon and Chelsea midfielder, sent off 12 times in his footballing persona, carved out an acting career in Hollywood since hanging up his boots and is seen as the ideal man to take up the role of Pearson in the movie charting Vardy's rise from non-league player to international striker.

Vinnie won a vote on the Pearson casting, ahead of fellow *Lock, Stock* star Jason Statham and Ray Stevenson, from TV's *Rome*, run in the *Leicester Mercury*, and the producers of the movie agree, with Jones, now living in Los Angeles, rated as a favourite for the role. *One Direction* singer Louis Tomlinson was the bookmakers' tip to play Vardy, with Zac Efron and Robert Pattinson also touted as possible candidates. Screenwriter and producer, award-winning filmmaker Adrian Butchart, said he hoped to begin filming later this year. "We have to wait until after the European Championships in the summer because we want his story to play out, but we are going all guns blazing to shoot as soon after that as possible," he said. "As long as everything goes to plan, we would like to see it released in March/April next year."

Drinkers across Leicestershire are toasting the current success with a pint of beer named after Vardy. 'Steamin' Billy's' latest craft beer, from Charnwood Brewery, brewed in celebration of the Yorkshireman was available at pubs in the county owned by the company. 'Vardy's Volley' is a light ale and is already on tap at The Railway pub in Hinckley, whose manager Adam Crump said: "Everything Leicester is going down very well with the regulars, there is Leicester fever at the minute. We will have it until the end of the season, but we will have to see if it lasts until the Champions League final next year!" he told the *Hinckley Times*. Employees at 'Steamin' Billy' came up with the idea in November after Vardy became the first player to score in 11 consecutive Premier League games.

FRIDAY, 15 APRIL

The club handed a number of season-ticket holders "multi-year" bans for re-selling tickets illegally.

"The club has a duty of care to its supporters and is working diligently to prevent ticket touting," said a club statement. "As a result, a small number of season-ticket holders and members have this week received multi-year bans." The club explained this prevents those responsible from attending Leicester games, as well as having their season tickets cancelled "without compensation".

The statement added: "In light of the unprecedented demand that currently exists for Leicester City tickets, supporters are reminded that all Leicester City tickets must be purchased directly from the Club. The unauthorised advertising and selling of Premier League tickets is illegal. If you buy tickets from an unauthorised source, whether that be an unauthorised website, an online marketplace or a ticket tout outside the ground, you risk being denied entry to the match and losing the money you paid. Tickets sold by such methods will become void, which will lead to the bearers being denied entry to, or removed from, the stadium. The Club has a duty of care to its supporters and is working diligently to prevent ticket touting, while also encouraging all fans to report any such activity."

In addition: "Please note that tickets and hospitality packages for all three of Leicester City's remaining 2015/16 Premier League home games against West Ham United, Swansea City and Everton have sold out."

The Foxes took to their Belvoir Training Complex on Friday ahead of one of their toughest remaining games this season, knowing they only need, at most, nine more points to be named champions.

The players looked like there was zero pressure, in fact Albrighton was keen to savour the moment. "For me personally it's an unbelievable feeling that we have secured Champions League football for next season. You put on the TV on a Tuesday and Wednesday night and watch the best players in the world. To know we can be rubbing shoulders with them next season is brilliant."

But the title was in their sights as he added: "We do want to go that one step further. We have this as a cushion and now we can push on. It doesn't feel real. A lot of us have not been in this position before. We've just got to enjoy it and embrace it. As hard as it is, take each day as it comes."

Later, Ranieri broke the habit of the season by declining to shake hands with each and every journalist before the press conference...but only because the international media scrum had become too big.

He insisted he is not superstitious and that he had no worries about breaking the ritual which has preceded all his previous Leicester press conferences. "I'm sorry I can't shake hands today," he said. "But if I did, it would take an hour there are so many people. I'm not superstitious about it. If everything goes right, it's superstition; when they lose it's the manager. That's not the right balance. But this is good because we want this and we want a lot of journalists, not only for one year but during our journey with Leicester. This is the ambition of my owner, my ambition and of our players: to have a lot of people at every press conference, because that means we are being successful."

He added: "We don't achieve anything yet. Football is very strange. If you weren't here in Leicester but somewhere else, maybe City or United, with seven points more, you would say 'it is finished'. At this moment you don't think this. Why? Because we are Leicester. We have to fight and we have to be focused and strong. And you cannot compare us yet to teams like Denmark winning the Euros in 1992 or Greece in 2004 yet because they won. We made a good story but to make something that people remember in 30 or 40 years you have to win. But we fight with a smile because our job is done: we are safe. Why are you laughing? No one remembers the first match when Ranieri was meant to be the first manager to be sacked and Leicester was going to be relegated. I remember it very well."

Ranieri is a fan of the Champions League anthem, "I love to hear the Champions League music. But now it's not true yet. Because we have only made it to the qualifying games. It's two matches, not the Champions League. I want to play six matches. The next goal is Champions League. We have to fight again to achieve the Champions League proper. From the dream arrives the reality, but wait first."

Referring to his three players on the six-man shortlist for the Professional Footballers' Association Players' Player of the Year award, "I am very proud because they deserve it," said Ranieri. "They are doing a fantastic performance in every match and I hope one of them can win. They are three sons for me. If one son wins I am very happy."

He added significantly: "Vardy, Mahrez and Kanté are on the highlights, and everyone watches them, but I think their strength is the strength of the team. If you don't have this team mentality and you are a lazy boy, you stay with me on the bench or the stand. This was my character when I was on the pitch and these players are the same as my character."

Don't cry for Ranieri: "I'm happy when the people that follow us are happy. I didn't cry (at Sunderland). My eyes shine but not cry!"

Albrighton puts it as succinctly. "When you are making your manager cry with pride, then you know you have done something special. We've never seen that emotional side of the manager before but I think it was a bit of everything: the way we played against Sunderland; the way the game went. It wasn't comfortable. Jack Rodwell had a chance at 1-0 and we couldn't get that second goal to put it to bed until the last kick. Then obviously the final whistle went and there was relief walking off the pitch. Our supporters up in the heavens were magnificent. And to be applauded off by the home fans is very rare in this day and age. That touched everyone, especially the gaffer. With what is going on, it is an emotional time. We are in a place where no one - not even ourselves - thought we would be in. We've achieved something special, so it is a credit to us and an emotional time."

All around the country, even globally, fans of all clubs - Spurs apart - want to see Leicester over the line for what would be the most stunning title win since Brian Clough's Nottingham Forest in 1978 and Alf Ramsey's Ipswich Town in 1962. A win against West Ham would put them in touching distance. "I was walking through my local town centre the other day and a guy hit me on the arm and said: 'Go on, win it son!'" says Albrighton, and he lives in Sutton Coldfield in the suburbs of Birmingham! "I think he was a Villa fan. And I think that sort of sums up what we're doing at the minute. People can relate to us: hard-working people, with no airs or graces. We just sort of enjoy our game, our job; and fans can relate to that. I think that's what they like most about it. Clubs will be looking at it thinking: 'That can be us next year. We can do that.' So it's given everyone a chance. The applause from opposition fans started last season when we played Sunderland and that was the one that clinched us staying up in the league. So, we noticed it then and had a few this season. Man City was one of them and then Sunderland again and a couple of others. In football these days it is more getting booed off, it just goes to show you are doing the right things and people are appreciating it."

Beat West Ham and there might be more Claudio tears. "Claudio might be crying again this weekend. Or maybe he has all his tears out now. Win the league, and no one will be holding back. I'm a crier, so I will be blubbing," Albrighton admits.

Ranieri reiterated plans to remain as Leicester boss: "I'd like to stay (for the long term). If the chairman is happy then I'm happy. When you have a very good chairman, sooner or later, you build a good building. Everything starts from the boss."

Ranieri enjoyed being on the front pages of the papers back in his homeland, but it wasn't the only time. Yet, interestingly, being sacked by Greece wasn't the lowest point in his career. Sacked by Valencia in his second stint at the club in 2005 *was* as he explained: "It is good to be on the front pages but a lot of times I have been on the front pages of Italian newspapers and also on the front of the Greek newspapers! Greece wasn't the worst time of my career - Valencia, the second time I went there, was the worst. I explained to the club and the chairman what was going to happen during the season. I said to them: 'I help you now. But after when it goes wrong, you have to help me.' And they said: 'Yes, yes, yes, Claudio.' And when the bad moment arrived: 'Sack Claudio.' That was the worst moment because those people betrayed me. If I tell you: 'Look! Soon it will rain, take something to cover; umbrella, something.' And you say: 'OK, Claudio, OK.' And you don't take the umbrella and after the rain comes and you say: 'It's your mistake! Go away.' I'm the same manager now as then. And in Greece I worked only 15 days in four months. What can I do? I am not a magician. I'm a hard worker."

Despite Mourinho's comments about his lack of language skills Ranieri still can't understand what the fans inside the King Power stadium sing about him. But, with a seven-point gap at the top of the table, he's pretty confident they're on his side. "I'm taking them as positive, but I don't understand them! I don't know English that well. I can hear them saying 'Ranieri' and something else. I hope they're praising me!"

Slaven Bilić accepted Leicester's "unbelievable fairytale" left everyone else's achievements in the shade. West Ham still had an outside shot at Champions League qualification. West Ham had been handed plenty of praise, but the Foxes' achievements were putting his good work "in the shadows". "People recognise we are having a good season, playing good football and praising us," Bilić said. "But what Leicester have done puts our successful season a little bit in the shadows. It's like a fairytale and they deserve all the credit they are getting. It is unbelievable."

Bilić had an inkling months ago. The Foxes won 2-1 at Upton Park in August and the West Ham manager had words with Ranieri about the strengths of his side post-match. "I wouldn't say then I thought they would be in this position, no one would have said that" Bilić conceded. "But what was obvious, even then I said to Claudio: 'You have a team who will be extremely hard to beat.' But I didn't know they would be big-time favourites now to win the league. Nobody did."

West Ham were "quite close" to swooping for Kanté but missed the chance. Bilić said: "He was on our list, we were quite close, quite close. I had watched him in France. He was a good player, the same player he is now at Leicester - a holding midfielder, not very tall but he is one of those players that after 20 minutes you think there are twins. You think there is two of him because of his energy and his intelligence, he is always there. When you watch the television, he is always in shot, he is never out. That is not only big lungs, big legs or a capacity to run, it's also intelligence. He was on our list, but then we got some other players for the same position and it was a bit too many players for the same position."

Tony Cottee, who scored 294 times during his seven-club career which took in Leicester and West Ham, would nominate Vardy for Footballer of the Year award. "Jamie Vardy has been one of the biggest success stories that the English game has ever seen," said Cottee, who will be at the King Power Stadium to watch two of his former clubs. "It's incredible this is a fella who, Sheffield Wednesday said wasn't good enough. Jamie must have been devastated to be told that he was being released. You see a lot of lads just pack the game in when they have gone through that kind of disappointment. But Jamie went playing for a works team and even in the Sunday League - and I think that illustrates just how much he really loves the game. Strikers just want to play and score goals. I can't explain it, it's just in your DNA. And the way Jamie Vardy has rebuilt his career, coming up through non-league to now be playing for England and within touching distance of a title medal, has given hope to every young boy who dreams of, one day, being a professional footballer. He just has to win the player-of-the-year award, hasn't he?"

Ranieri and Bilić proved that clubs don't have to spend millions to build successful teams. Cottee said: "Slaven has proved, with the purchase of Payet, that he can spot a player - just as Leicester have done with N'Golo Kanté, Riyad Mahrez and Jamie Vardy. The players are out there - it's all about getting scouts who can identify their potential and clubs then taking that chance. I think that scouts and the people in charge of recruitment at Premier League clubs have become lazy. They no longer seem to put the hard yards in when it comes to watching players in the Championship and lower leagues. Wes Morgan was playing in the Championship a couple of years ago - now, he could be lifting the Premier League trophy in a few weeks."

Cottee will be dressed in his claret and blue at the King Power today - but he admits that his loyalties will be split. "I'll be there supporting my team, West Ham, but a part of me will be delighted if Leicester win, and I think everyone in the country, outside of White Hart Lane, will feel exactly the same."

SATURDAY, 16 APRIL

A cross-party group of MPs urged David Cameron to reward what will be the Premier League's greatest triumph by handing Claudio a knighthood. Labour MP Jonathan Ashworth, whose constituency is home to the King Power Stadium, said: "What Claudio Ranieri has done, not only for Leicester City but for English football, is nothing short of phenomenal. It has been a beautiful fairytale story and fans would surely agree he deserves the recognition an honorary knighthood would bring. I shall be doing all I can to persuade the Palace to reward him." Labour colleague Keith Vaz, a City season ticket holder, added: "He has united the city and brought together people of different faiths and races. It would be fitting and more than deserved." Ranieri would not be able to call himself Sir, which can only be used if you are British. Pele and US film director Steven Spielberg are both foreigners with honorary knighthoods.

Roy Hodgson used Leicester as an example of why you don't need to be among the big spenders to succeed. "What they have proved is that you don't have to win that battle that Jim White on Sky Sports wants you to win every January and June; the battle of 'we spent the most money.' You don't actually have to do that. You don't have to win that league table where you are vilified because you have only spent £6million but you are fantastic because you spent £75million. What Leicester have taught us is that it is not necessarily a direct correlation between the money you spend and the success you have. At the start of the season if Leicester had put their players on the market and said 'Who wants to buy them?' and what would you give us for them? It would be vastly different to what they would get now for them. Because Danny Simpson has been all over the place; Wes Morgan was at Nottingham Forest; Robert Huth has been all over the place. No one knew the free transfer player Christian Fuchs. Riyad Mahrez was in the French second division two years ago. Maybe one or two knew about N'Golo Kanté, because he was £6m, so he wasn't a gift. And with Danny Drinkwater, there was that wonderful picture we saw with him, Harry Kane and Jamie Vardy on the Leicester bench in the Championship play-off. If you are lucky, you can put a good team together without spending £100 million and without having to keep the Dutch league going for another few years."

Mauricio Pochettino planned to watch the game against the Hammers but won't going "crazy" hoping they will lose. Despite himself and his players becoming Hammers supporters on Sunday afternoon, he will not be tearing his hair out. "It is important to be calm and have a clear idea what you need to do. We cannot affect what is going to happen on Sunday. I will watch. It is not difficult. I am not a crazy man. It is a healthy competition between teams that want to win and achieve big things and it is good in football. It is true the opponent who plays Leicester, I push a little bit more for the opponent."

Spurs players trained in the morning and were free to watch the Leicester game together, but Pochettino said there was no plan in place. "Maybe after training we are on lunchtime yes, but it is not a rule," Pochettino said. "We are not preparing to watch all together the game. They are free to go home after training, after lunch."

THE LEICESTER WAY

Leicester had brought 4-4-2 back into fashion with Ranieri using Vardy alongside Okazaki or Ulloa. Ironic that it took an Italian to return to the once most popular shape in England.

Leicester used 4-4-2 and, according to Opta, had done so in 30 of the 33 games they played in the Premier League. No team used the formation more. The only other two clubs who use 4-4-2 are Watford and West Bromwich Albion, showing how rare the old-fashioned formation has become. As for the other 17 sides in the Premier League, 12 use 4-2-3-1, such as Spurs and Arsenal. Then the five left over use 4-3-3, 4-1-4-1 and 4-4-1-1. The stats show the Leicester Way; The Ranieri Way.

For so long, passing was the perfect way. Tiki-taka, Barca, Arsenal and they all want to follow that example. That's not for Leicester. Only two teams completed fewer total passes, West Brom 10,431 and Sunderland 11,000. Leicester just 11,614. The top five passing teams are: Arsenal made the most with 17,441, followed by Manchester City (17,379), Chelsea (16,586), Manchester United (16,535) and Tottenham (16,171).

Leicester were also joint last in the Premier League for accuracy, with only West Brom as poor at passing. They are both on 70 per cent. The reason they make so few passes is because they are willing to give up possession. Leicester average just 42.9 per cent possession per game - the third worst in the Premier League. Only Sunderland (41.2) and West Brom (39.9) averaged less. Eighteen of their 21 wins in the Premier League came when Leicester had a lesser share of possession. Last year, Chelsea were champions averaging 55.8 per cent, the season before that, Manchester City won the title with 57.9. Manchester United in 2012-13 on 56.5.

Morgan and Huth played 5,850 minutes together - more than any pairings at Arsenal, Tottenham and Manchester City. The no frills back-to-basics centre backs are a perfect pairing, more so even than Spurs' Jan Vertonghen and Toby Alderweireld.

Leicester were doing it their way and having a laugh, and the world was laughing with them!

SUNDAY, 17 APRIL

LEICESTER CITY 2-2 WEST HAM UNITED

Leonardo Ulloa's stoppage-time penalty salvaged a point for 10-man Leicester in one of the most dramatic games of an already dramatic season as West Ham threatened to derail the title charge.

Sub Ulloa scored with virtually the last kick when it seemed no way back for a team that had been angered by a sending off and a penalty award against them.

It turned out to be an amazing finish as unexpectedly 10-man Leicester rescued a point while West Ham threw away what looked a nailed-on victory.

Ulloa showed remarkable calmness as he made no mistake, sending Adrian the wrong way and finding the bottom right corner with a penalty that might yet prove decisive in the title race.

The gap at the top was now eight points when it could so easily been seven, with Spurs having a game in hand, at Stoke on Monday evening.

The game swung manically one way then the other. First Leicester surviving an early scare when the ball struck both posts before Vardy's first-half strike gave them the lead before he received a second yellow card in the 56th minute for a dive in the penalty area. Vardy was unlucky to have received his first yellow for a relatively tame tackle that was slightly mistimed. He is only the second Leicester player to score and be sent off in the same league game (David Lowe vs Wimbledon in 1994 is the other). He will be sorely missed through suspension as well as leaving his team vulnerable in this game. Little wonder he was furious with the ref when shown the red card, he didn't think he had dived as there had been contact.

Andy Carroll equalised from the spot before Aaron Creswell smashed home a brilliant second from outside the area against a tiring Leicester who had defended valiantly, virtually pinned in their own half.

There were tears in the stands when Creswell struck. One young fan was crestfallen as he buried his head in his mum's lap, pouring his eyes out.

Having given one penalty for wrestling at a corner, Huth went down with Ogbonna's arm wrapped round his neck, but 'Public Enemy No 1' Jonathan Moss waved away the protests. If the foul on Reid was a penalty, then so was that, surely.

But with seconds left Ulloa converted after Carroll had needlessly fouled sub Schlupp right in the corner of the box. That equalising goal came from the 11th penalty Leicester have been awarded this season, the most in the Premier League. In contrast, West Ham's penalty was their first away in the Premier League since October 2010. Leicester had actually scored with both of their shots on target.

Referee Moss was escorted from the pitch by security as Huth continued to point an accusing finger at him while Ranieri, who was almost motionless when the last second penalty went in, walked back to the dressing room straight away.

TALKING POINTS

One or two post-match talking points that's for sure: with Leicester leading 1-0, Vardy - who had earlier been shown the first yellow card of the day for a foul on Cheikhou Kouyaté - went to ground after tangling with Hammers' defender Angelo Ogbonna inside the area. Referee Moss said no penalty, and showed Vardy a second yellow card for diving. Yet, there was definitely contact between Ogbonna and Vardy inside the box, but the replays showed that Vardy engineered it, and exaggerated his fall. Vardy reacted angrily after being sent off. He was therefore suspended for next weekend's home game against Swansea and missed his first Premier League game of the season.

Not far behind was the way Moss warned Huth and Morgan for pushing and pulling opponents inside their own penalty area, then pointed to the spot moments later when Reid falls to the floor after being held by Morgan from a corner. Hammers striker Carroll stepped up to make it 1-1.

With Leicester trailing 2-1 to Cresswell's superb strike, they threw men forward to try to force an equaliser. Ogbonna grapples with Huth as he tries to get on the end of a long throw, grabs him around the neck as Huth goes to ground, but Moss allows play to continue when, if he was to be consistent having given the first one to the Hammers, it was a clear penalty.

However, Leicester had the last laugh, when, in the final minute of stoppage time, substitute Schlupp picked up the ball and ran down the left-hand side of the West Ham area. Carroll blocked him with a shove, Schlupp went down, and Moss pointed to the spot. Carroll was adamant he had not fouled Schlupp, saying: "He was going down before I got to him - 100% he took a touch, the referee has looked to even it out"

Ranieri commented: "The sending off changed our match. I judge my players not the referee, the referee is not my matter. Our performance was fantastic, this is our soul, we play every match with this, blood, heart and soul, it was magnificent. This point is very important psychologically. It was a very tough match. We were lucky at the beginning when they touched both posts. After that we scored a great goal and we had an opportunity to finish the match at the beginning of the second half. After that the sending off it changed our match. I never spoke about the decision of the referee. Two yellow cards, that's it. Our performance 11 v 11 and 10 v 11 was fantastic."

Ulloa did not let the enormity of the late penalty get to him, indicative of the mentality the entire team were showing. "I didn't think about the pressure of the situation at that moment," said the striker, whose winner against Norwich in February created an earthquake measuring 0.3 on the Richter scale. "I felt after I scored how important the goal was. The feeling was so good. I appreciated the moment and everyone enjoyed it. I know about this earthquake, but I just enjoy it when I can when I score some goals. I also practise my shooting, I was confident, last season I got some penalties I do not think about the pressure. It was a good moment, after the goal I feel how important the goal was."

Ulloa has not started a league game since 2 January and 28 of his 33 league appearances came as a substitute. "We had one player less, so (Ranieri) told me to stay in the middle, keep the ball and put on pressure when we can. It was a difficult moment because we were down to 10 men, but we defended well and then attacked when we could. We showed great character. I love to play with this team because we all fight together. We fight together until the last minute and we got the penalty, and afterwards we are all happy. I love to play with this team because they have this character when we are losing or in a bad situation. We are always fighting together. We are a team and that is more important, not for me but for everyone. When we are on the pitch, we work together and help each other."

Ulloa would start when Leicester return to action against Swansea on Sunday, with top scorer Vardy absent through suspension.

Danny Simpson said: "We have shown today our team spirit and togetherness. We will always fight to the death. We cannot control other things, we can fight and work hard. Jeff Schlupp did well to get a penalty and Leonardo Ulloa slotted it away when there was a lot of pressure on him. I think that will turn out to be a massive point, not many teams go 2-1 down and do what we did, psychologically it will give us a massive boost." He was confident Vardy's absence will not derail Leicester's title bid. "Vardy has been one of the best players in the league, but Leo came on and got a point for us - that was a lot of pressure for anyone. Other players have scored in the team and before last week Vards hadn't scored for five or six games, so we'll deal with it. We've got other players who can come in. Just look at the game - Jeff came on and won us a penalty and Leo came on and scored. Dema (Demarai Gray) has come on in the last few weeks and showed for a young lad his maturity and he's an attacking threat. So I'm sure we'll cope with it well."

Simpson concedes the one-match ban was "unfortunate" for both Vardy and Leicester, but was keen not to join the chorus of criticism aimed at the referee. "Horrible," Simpson described the encounter with the Hammers, "But I think we showed our togetherness and team spirit and fight. We could have got our heads down when we went down to 2-1 and accepted it, but that's not us and that's not our group. I think psychologically that proved to the world how together we are. Psychologically I think it's a massive point. I think we proved we're not easy to beat. We want to win every game, we want to keep clean sheets - that's the team we are. It didn't happen, but to draw in the last second of a game gives you a boost."

Slaven Bilić thought he was going home with all three points: "We are gutted, we did enough to win the game, before last five seconds. The game went that way, hard for referee with the crowd. I feel for him. Although it was not a penalty. On one hand Leicester is right, it is not a penalty, they have been doing this all year. We showed character and quality, even in the first-half. They scored from counter-attack but we didn't lose shape, we coped well in second-half with counterattacks after equaliser we didn't stop searching for a second goal. Cresswell scored a great goal and then that happened. We did enough to win the game and deserved to win it. It was a good game of football. We showed determination, character and quality. We turned the game around. We were dangerous, and after sending off we totally dominated the game. After our second goal I thought we had done enough to win the game, maybe we could have coped with added time better in terms of keeping the ball but they took the risk. It was extremely hard for referee, but I mean that was no penalty at all."

Winston Reid added: "It was a fun match but again it was a game we couldn't hold onto the result, that is the third or fourth time in a row. It is a bit disappointing, there were some dodgy decisions. Take your pick. At the end of the day he (Wes Morgan) has pulled me, some are given, some aren't."

WHO'D BE A REFEREE?

But what did the 'neutral' pundits think:

Former referee, Graham Poll, gave his considered verdict on the *Mail* online and expressed his view that he felt Michael Oliver, Martin Atkinson or Mark Clattenburg should have been appointed to referee this game.

18 minutes - Huth forearm on Reid

The antics inside the penalty area began with Huth blocking Reid with his forearm - a clear foul and a penalty for West Ham which was not given. West Ham were exacerbated by Leicester scoring within seconds of the Reid/Huth clash.

Verdict: Incorrect - penalty for West Ham .

28 minutes - Vardy yellow card

Vardy's foul was a minor one, actually only knocking Kouyaté over as he slid after mistiming his tackle…it came at a point in the game when the tackles were flying in from both teams and it was no surprise that Moss decided that he needed to assert his authority with his cards. Vardy was the first but Reid, Noble and Payet followed before the half time break.

Verdict: Correct - perhaps harsh but the timing of Vardy's challenge was ill advised.

57 minutes - Vardy second yellow card

This was the clearest decision for me and one which Moss saw and didn't hesitate to give. Vardy chasing down another through ball came shoulder to shoulder with Ogbonna. The West Ham defender did raise an arm but it was Vardy who sought contact with Ogbonna's legs and then clearly dived to try and win a penalty.

Verdict: Moss 100% correct.

84 minutes - Penalty for West Ham

The pull back by Morgan on Reid was quite minimal and while technically a penalty it looks harsh. If you watch the whole game and see the way Leicester defenders continually hold and block West Ham players you can see why Moss appeared to tell Huth and Morgan together that any more would result in a penalty kick.

Verdict: Correct decision

90 minutes - Ogbonna foul on Huth for penalty not given. From a long throw-in it was clear Huth was prevented from jumping by Ogbonna.

Verdict: Incorrect decision - penalty for Leicester

90+4 minutes - Penalty for Leicester.

Carroll ran across the penalty area and knocked Schlupp over with no intention of playing the ball; contact occurring just inside the penalty area.

Verdict: Correct penalty for Leicester.

Mark Lawrenson:

"In the end I think Leicester have a penalty that isn't a penalty. The crowd are slaughtering the referee but he might have given them the penalty that helps them win the league. That is a very well taken penalty under enormous pressure, but if we are giving penalties for that then there are 10 a game."

Alan Shearer and Ian Wright on *Match of the Day 2*:

"The game became too much of a pressurised situation for him. He could not handle the pressure and I think that clouded his decisions," said Shearer. "The inconsistencies were mind-boggling."

"I would give Moss a mark of three out of 10, and I think I am being quite generous," added Wright.

Vardy sending off:

Shearer: "This was the decision that changed the whole dynamic of the game. It had looked like we were heading for another 1-0 Leicester win - suddenly they were down to 10 men and there was a very different atmosphere. I did not think the tackle that got Vardy his first booking was worthy of a yellow card at all, but this one was definitely a dive. As much as you can criticise the referee for what happens later, Vardy has to take some criticism because it is blatant. There was no need for him to dive, because he has got the wrong side of the defender anyway. He was expecting contact, contact didn't come and there was even a little pirouette in there just as he was going over."

Wright: "Vardy hardly touched Kouyaté - that one was a very, very harsh booking. The referee could easily have had a word with him for that. For his second yellow card, it looks like a dive to me because of the way he goes into Ogbonna and then gets his legs all tangled up. That is why he got sent off."

84 min: West Ham penalty:

Wright: "Reid had the march on Morgan, who had to try and catch him up. It is soft, but he had grabbed him. If the referee tells the teams in the dressing room before the game that he will not stand for any holding inside the box, then he should not have to tell the players again during the game. He has warned them, so he can give a penalty when it happens."

Shearer: "He warned Huth and Morgan just after half-time but here is no need to give a warning. If it is a penalty, give a penalty. You don't get a warning for a foul outside the box, do you? I am staggered that the referee chose the 34th game of the season for Leicester to make this point about pulling and shoving in the box. Why not make the point at the beginning of the season, and go into all the dressing rooms and say 'we are going to try to stamp this out completely so don't complain and moan when we give penalties for holding'. Do it then, not in the 34th game. This is something that has gone on not only all game, it has gone on all season and it will continue to go on until all referees make the same point. Moss actually gives this penalty for the softest offence. There were far worse incidents in the game than this one. Reid goes down far easier than he should do - he dives as well. Morgan pulls him a little bit, but he actually falls forward so it is not as though he is pulling him back. I don't think that was enough for a penalty - if it was, then there should have been four penalties in the game, at least. Technically, this one is a foul but, if he gives it, he has to give the others too."

89 min: Ogbonna grabs Huth around the neck - nothing given:

Shearer: "This is bizarre. It was five minutes after Moss had given a penalty to West Ham for Morgan holding in the box, so he should be looking out for things like this. It shows why lack of consistency from referees is part of the problem."

Wright: "West Ham know Huth is a danger in the air in the opposition area. Ogbonna has got his hand around his neck so he cannot jump and that is impeding him. I cannot see the difference between this one and the West Ham penalty that was given. I have got no problem with that one, as long as this is given too."

94 min: Leicester penalty:

Wright: "The most you can point your finger at Carroll for is to say he was running back in there recklessly and he made contact. He should have shepherded him away from goal, but a penalty? Really? If I had been playing for West Ham in that game, I would have felt that the referee had tried to even things up, even if he did miss the foul on Huth. It was very soft."

Shearer: "It was never a penalty in a million years. I think the referee realised he has messed up in not awarding a penalty for the foul on Huth, which is why he has given this one, with the last kick of the game."

Jamie Carragher defended under-fire referee Jon Moss, claiming the official had a "fantastic" game and got "almost every decision right". Talking on Sky Sports, he said: "I think the criticism he's taken has been a joke. He's been called weak, and he's been called a poor referee by former referees. He has some big calls in this game and got the majority of them right. Do I think (Vardy's first caution) is a yellow card? No. But can I understand why he's given it? Yes, because there's been two or three fouls where he's let things go, and it sends out a message to the players. Maybe it's harsh, but I can totally understand him getting that yellow card. The problem with the second yellow isn't the referee, it's Jamie Vardy. He's only got himself to blame. Stop looking at the referee and start looking at the players involved in this game and the problems they gave the referee. As soon as I saw the incident I thought "dive" and my opinion's not changed. This is something Jamie Vardy has done over the last few years. We saw it last season against Manchester United and Swansea. I thought the referee was absolutely fantastic on this decision. He reads the game brilliantly well, he can see something is going to happen. The position he is in is fantastic. He's got it 100% right. This is a man who has been called weak today, but it was a brave decision. It's a second yellow card. Off you go."

Moss placed himself in a difficult position by failing to address grappling inside the box earlier, but Carragher understood why Morgan was penalised for holding back Reid. "This is where the referee has given himself a problem," he said. "I think if you're going to make a decision like this, you have to make it early in the game and stamp it out. There was one from Huth, and then there was even an incident before the penalty was given. But I have no sympathy for the players, as he's spoken to them. Wes Morgan should know better. The hands are around the waist…you can't do that. I think Reid's dived. He's made more of it. But look at the referee's angle. All he can see is the arms around the waist. We can look at different angles. The referee can only give what he sees. That's a penalty."

Matt Piper, former Leicester winger, was on BBC Radio5 live talking about Vardy's red card, "As much as it pains me to say it I think the referee got the Vardy one right. Jamie's done that a few times this season. I wouldn't really call it diving but he puts himself in a position to create the contact and then he flings his legs up. After he's made that decision, he's got to give him the yellow card like he did. Moving on, every single decision the referee made after that, I think he got wrong. The emotions are flying with all the players at this stage of the season. I've just got my fingers crossed that Vardy doesn't get any retrospective action. It would be really huge. He's been wonderful this season. His goals are huge for the club. We've got some huge games coming up so he'd be a massive miss."

As for the game:

Shearer on *MOTD 2* was full of praise: "It was a tremendous point for Leicester at the end. Their right-back Danny Simpson came out afterwards and talked about how that showed they would fight to the death. It was a bit like when I won the title with Blackburn in 1995 and our goalkeeper Tim Flowers came out after we had battled to beat Newcastle 1-0 right at the end of the season and said 'we have got bottle'. Nobody remembers we were hopeless in that game, and that we were lucky to win it, people just remember we won 1-0.

It is exactly the same with Leicester here - they were nowhere near their best but picking up points in games like this to get across the line is all that matters, not the way they do it. The impressive thing about Leicester against West Ham was their team spirit, and how they did not give up. They were up against it, a man down, 2-1 down and under the cosh with a couple of minutes left. Some people might have thought this was the blip they have been waiting for, but then Leicester came up with another answer, which is what they have done for the vast majority of the season. You have got to admire how they have kept on going and fought back for what could be a very valuable point in the title race."

Alan Smith posed the question in his *Daily Telegraph* column how much the team will miss their top scorer for the first time in the league. "Everything good about Leicester City in recent times has heavily featured the striker, who got sent off on Sunday for the first time in his senior career. Suspended after two yellow cards against West Ham, Vardy must now sit in the stands, hoping that his team-mates can cope.

Manager Claudio Ranieri, meanwhile, takes to the training ground this week to tweak a playing style that depends so much on their top scorer's searing pace and fine finishing skills. It will not be straightforward. Danny Drinkwater, for instance, knows that, against Swansea, he cannot ping those accurate long balls without even looking, knowing Vardy will instinctively be already on his bike. Marc Albrighton will not be able to float a clever pass over the centre-half's head towards a razor-sharp forward lurking on the last line. Leonardo Ulloa and Shinji Okazaki work in different ways. Their skill sets do not concentrate on such aggressive incision.

As a result, of all the tactical decisions Ranieri has made this season, this one could prove the trickiest of all. For that, Vardy is culpable. He must look at himself honestly. I mean, he knows deep down that he dived in the box after deliberately trying to initiate contact with Angelo Ogbonna by stepping across the big defender's path. Despite the yells of innocence and burning stares of injustice, it was a theatrical piece of simulation that rightly did not cut the mustard with referee Jonathan Moss, who, all things considered, did pretty well in a match that must go down as one of the most difficult to take charge of this season. Granted, Vardy was unlucky to get booked in the first half for an innocuous challenge that, to my mind, simply should have been called a foul. Once on a card, though, he should have known better than to take this risk, especially when he could have stayed on his feet to fire in a shot rather than playing for the penalty. It is not as if he is not capable of using his left foot. A fantastic finish earlier on had superbly showcased the power on his less favoured side. With little of the goal to aim at, Vardy's ruthless strike across West Ham keeper Adrián took the breath away. Watching from the stand, Roy Hodgson could not fail to be thoroughly impressed. With the 29 year-old surely already a shoo-in for a place in England's squad for Euro 2016, this kind of feat can only push his claims for a starting place. What followed, in all honesty, should not harm those claims. Vardy, after all, is far from being on his own when it comes to hitting the deck without much encouragement. It just so happens that he has been punished for doing it this time at a crucial stage of this mesmerising title race."

Gary Lineker provided a running commentary on his Twitter account - @GaryLineker: - This title race will be the death of me. It's too excruciatingly tense for my old heart.

- They may have been given a bit of help but credit where it's due, that's one hell of a volley from Cresswell.

- Good heavens this is a tough watch!

- I don't think that's a penalty, to be honest but sod it! Great point.

- I'm too biased to comment, I know, but the inconsistency of the refereeing is remarkable.

Rather than the game itself, the back pages were more focussed on the reaction of an incandescent Vardy, publishing some disturbing images. In fact, in the *Telegraph's Total Football* supplement there is a suggestion that Vardy may face an extended ban.

Spurs, meanwhile, sensed an opportunity as Harry Kane posted a picture on his Instagram account of a pride of lions shortly after the Foxes draw.

MONDAY, 18 APRIL

Vardy was charged with improper conduct by the FA just before 5pm.

An FA statement read: "Leicester City's Jamie Vardy has been charged with improper conduct for his behaviour following his second-half dismissal against West Ham United on Sunday 17 April 2016. Leicester have also been charged for failing to control their players following the awarding of an 83rd-minute penalty to West Ham. Both the player and the club have until 6pm on Thursday 21 April 2016 to reply to their charge."

Vardy, crucially, could now face a two-game ban.

Ranieri defended Vardy over the red card, saying after the game: "He never dives. Always he goes very fast and at this speed if you touch a little (the player goes down]."

Ranieri was asked if Vardy swore at the referee before leaving the field. The manager did not deny it, or confirm it, replying: "I don't want to speak about referees…Vardy…the situation. I want to stay calm and speak about football."

Mauricio Pochettino declared every single player will deserve to have a "statue" built of them if they manage to overhaul Leicester and win the league for the first time in 55 years. Dropping two points gave Spurs hope that they could still catch Ranieri's side even if the games were running out. If Spurs beat Stoke then Leicester's lead was reduced to five points with four matches to play. "If we won the championship, I think that every player would deserve a statue," Pochettino said. "The challenge is big because it is a big gap. But to keep fighting in the way that we have fought and in the end win the title, all the people would recognise our value. And we would be happy, too."

He acknowledged that an added pressure for his team was that most neutral fans were rooting for Leicester. "I think it's good. They deserve to (win), but I think we cannot fight against all that happens around Leicester. We need to fight against them, and against us and our opponents and it's a very good challenge. We know that all the people want Leicester to be champions but we need to believe that we can change the story. I am a very positive person in my life, I always believe that things can happen, good things for us. I never wish for bad things for them but I want them to drop points in the next few games, and we win, and reduce the distance to them and try to win. In football, anything can happen. One thing can change things. We are in love with football because it is not predictable, and now we need to believe that something can happen for us on Sunday and then we need to do our job. This is important. Only that. We need to do our job."

Just over half an hour to kick off, Pochettino on Sky Sports: "Of course I watched the Leicester v West Ham game, I was with Daniel Levy drinking wine at my house. It was a good result for us, Leicester dropped two points and now we have to do our job. We have to win otherwise it doesn't matter that Leicester dropped points. It is an opportunity, a chance for us. We have five games to play and the gap is big but we can reduce it. If we want to win the league we must win."

STOKE CITY 0-4 TOTTENHAM HOTSPUR

Pochettino 'sends Leicester a message' as Spurs continued to believe in their dream of winning the title after they moved five points behind as Kane and Alli both scored twice taking Stoke apart 4-0 and could easily have been five or six at the Britannia, with the north London club raking up a vastly superior goal difference.

"We showed that we believe, we really believe," the Spurs manager said. "This is our dream, to win the title. Always we try. You must never give up. You can feel every day this season from the beginning was special."

Spurs had won 10 of their past 13 Premier League games to keep pace with Leicester and play on Monday night again in each of the next two weeks. "The most important thing is that the performance we showed was perfect," Pochettino said. "It was a big signal that we are there waiting and fighting."

Kane took his haul to 24 league goals with clear day light ahead of the suspended Vardy. He was asked, in his Sky Sports interview immediately after the game, about his provocative Instagram posting and claimed it was a light hearted dig at Leicester, nothing more.

"We are not going anywhere. We are on their tails," Kane added. "Leicester had a tough game against West Ham and dropped a couple of points and we were ready to put the pressure on. We think we can do it, otherwise there's not much point being involved. Leicester are still in the driving seat being five points ahead but there are four games left and we've reduced the gap. That's all we could have done. If we keep playing like that there are not many teams who will beat us."

Mark Hughes was full of praise for Spurs, and backed them to catch Leicester. "Spurs were very impressive - stronger, faster and they had more power in the team than we were able to put out there. Sometimes you have to give credit to the opposition. They are quick and sharp and have got that edge that chasing major trophies gives you. With their mentality at the moment, you wouldn't bet against them catching Leicester."

"LEICESTER CITY, WE'RE COMING FOR YOU"

Gary Lineker, who played for both teams, responded on Twitter to the chants directed at his hometown club.

@GaryLineker - Spurs fans singing "Leicester City, we're coming for you." Just beautiful to hear Leicester mentioned in such a song.

TUESDAY, 19 APRIL

A much-welcomed quieter day.

Ranieri, in an interview with Barcelona paper *Diario Sport*, tried to put everything into perspective: "This year is an exception and we should know that. We are here because the favourites have all slipped up a lot and that will not happen next season. Our reality should be being in the top ten."

Asked if he thought there would be an exodus of stars he replied: "No, but when I arrived here the objective was to build a project. That was the initial job and if there are departures, because they cannot be avoided, we will have to look at how we rebuild."

Leicester's fairytale has caught the imagination in Spain where Ranieri coached both Valencia and Atletico Madrid. He admits in the interview that there were doubts about him when he took over. "I know there were and I have no problem with that. The first thing I said to the players is for them not to worry too much about tactics. I believed in them because I had seen the great work they had done in the previous two seasons. The idea was just to carry on the same road."

He enjoyed the prize of a post-match pizza and decided not to change. He said: "I have not changed anything! This same team won promotion and then saved themselves (from relegation) and they did it in a certain way. Footballers are people and they know what they need to do."

Leicester's exploits were likened to Atletico Madrid's success in Spain two years ago and Deportivo's championship at the start of the decade. Ranieri added: "We have spoken up for the little club. We have shown what can be done. We are showing that things can be won in various different ways. A team has to fight and it has to believe."

Asked if Leicester winning the league would be the biggest surprise in football history he said: "With football as it is right now yes. But this team is already making history day after day."

WEDNESDAY, 20 APRIL

Leicester will definitely play in the Champions League group stage after Manchester City's 1-1 draw with Newcastle on Tuesday night guaranteed them a top-three spot. Leicester were now 12 points clear of City in third, with four games to play, and 13 clear of Arsenal in fourth, but neither chasing side can take maximum points between now and the end of the season as they face each other in May.

José Mourinho will manage England against Ranieri's Rest of the World for the Soccer Aid match at Old Trafford on 5 June to raise money for UNICEF. Mourinho will be assisted by Sunderland boss Sam Allardyce, with Soccer Aid co-founder Robbie Williams as coach. "I want to be the first one to win the Soccer Aid trophy for both teams," said the Portuguese, who coached Rest of the World to a 4-2 win in 2014. "Sam and I will make a very good partnership and it will be a great feeling for Claudio to finally lose a match." Ranieri added: "It is a great honour that Robbie Williams has asked me to manage the Rest of the World XI and I'm looking forward to helping them defend their title."

Wenger rubbished talk of a summer move for Mahrez, who had also been linked with a big-money move to Barcelona. Wenger, whose side face West Brom on Thursday night, insisted the north London club would not be considering a summer swoop. When asked if he was interested, Wenger said at his routine press conference: "No, even if it was I wouldn't talk about it this stage of the season (out of) respect to Leicester."

Wenger praised Ranieri's side, "It is a fantastic achievement. Nobody expected that. That makes many people happy and it confirms that it is not only down to the amount of money people spend in football. Sometimes, it upsets the natural hierarchy that everyone has in their head in the Premier League."

THURSDAY, 21 APRIL

The England manager, no less, publicly declared that Vardy should not have been sent off for diving. Capped six times by Hodgson, the England boss entered the controversy, "I will go out on a limb. I don't see that as a dive. I think he was unbalanced. I don't think it was a penalty either. I think he was unbalanced, running at that speed. I think there was a very slight contact with the defender, who was trying to cover. But of course all the pundits I hear say he was trying to dive, look how he dived. I don't see it. I wouldn't blame him for that. I sympathise with him. I think he was very, very unlucky."

Hodgson felt the striker's reaction was understandable. "He has reacted like human beings sometimes react. He hasn't just said to the ref, 'that is all right, I understand' and shake hands and have a good game. He has called him a few names. But he is a human being and that can happen."

The views from within the FA itself, made the club think whether an appeal might work, and thought about it right up until the 6pm deadline before officially announcing that Vardy accepted the charge of improper conduct.

"Leicester City Football Club has today (Thursday) accepted a Football Association charge of failing to control its players during the Barclays Premier League fixture against West Ham United on 17 April," the Foxes announced in a club statement via their website, "Furthermore, Jamie Vardy has accepted a charge of improper conduct arising from the same fixture. Jamie has, however, requested a personal hearing. We await the outcome of the FA's disciplinary process."

By admitting the charge, Vardy, who requested a personal hearing, could be given an additional suspension to his current one-match ban. Leicester also accepted a charge of failing to control their players. Vardy misses the game against Swansea on but could also sit out the trip to Manchester United.

Christian Fuchs insisted Leicester could cope without their top-scorer. "It's a new situation for us because Jamie hasn't missed a game yet but I think we can cope," Fuchs told BBC World Service Sport. "We have this confidence, we have the quality. Every time Leonardo Ulloa comes off the bench he has done well and he's a big part of the team. I think we can definitely compete."

Fuchs praised the work by his manager, "He's making us focus on ourselves and the next game. He's telling us every time 'guys, what we can affect is our performance, our game' and he's very right with that. Tottenham can win every game now but we also have the chance to do that and that's what we have to focus on."

Mark Schwarzer gave an interview about a variety of topics.

On Vardy: "We know for sure that we're going to miss him this weekend at home to Swansea, but we have other players that can step in - Ulloa has done very, very well this season whenever given the opportunity. He could reshuffle a little bit, maybe Riyad Mahrez in behind Okazaki up front? But we're more than capable of dealing with Jamie's absence."

On the title race: "Spurs have an opportunity now where they haven't been ever before in the history of the Premier League so they are going to go for it, they have to go for it. We were disappointed at the weekend but we took a lot from the game as well."

On qualifying for the Champions League group stages: "It's a remarkable achievement for a club like Leicester, who were one of the bookies' favourites for relegation this season. It's just been a remarkable season and hopefully it continues."

Title rivals Leicester and Spurs provided eight players between them for the PFA Premier League Team of the Year: Vardy, Morgan, Kanté and Mahrez, plus Alderweireld, Rose, Alli and Kane ensured that the two clubs chasing the title dominated the team selection.

Leicester believed Mahrez had won the PFA Player of the Year award and were making appropriate travel arrangements to get him to the Grosvenor House on Sunday night because Leicester's game against Swansea at the King Power Stadium would only finish at around 6pm.

The PFA insisted on his attendance, leading his club to think the Algerian had, indeed, scooped the top individual prize.

Mahrez was now set to attend, alongside teammates and fellow nominees Vardy and Kanté, with owner Vichai Srivaddhanaprabha providing his personal helicopter, which takes off from the centre circle at Leicester's home ground after each game and takes the Thai businessman home. The London Heliport is based in Battersea and is only a 20 minute drive from Grosvenor House. Leicester booked a table at the event, where captain Wes Morgan was also set to attend after being named in the PFA Team of the Year, alongside his three teammates.

The latest update on the bookies was published. UK's leading bookmakers faced paying out more than £10m if Leicester won the title.

Breakdown of the losses:

Ladbrokes: £3m

Coral: £2m

William Hill: £2m

Paddy Power: £2m

Betfred: £1.1m

At the start of the season, 47 people placed a bet with Ladbrokes for Leicester to win the title at 5000-1 - of which 23 have cashed out, while 24 are still awaiting their fate. "Leicester's win would be the biggest upset in the history of betting," Alex Donohue of Ladbrokes to BBC Sport. "It would be the worst result for us financially and our biggest payout by a distance. If Chelsea, Manchester City or Manchester United would have won, the total payouts would have been in the few hundred thousands. Leicester have been upsetting the odds all season but it is a brilliant Hollywood story that we are a part of. Hats off to anyone who backed them at the start of the season."

FRIDAY, 22 APRIL

The club announced a freeze on season ticket prices at the King Power Stadium for the second year running. The club have chosen to reward their fanbase by keeping the cost of a season ticket the same. The bumper payday from the Champions League and a huge hike in TV revenues helped Leicester's board in their decision but it also represents another PR coup in a season full of good news stories.

Supporters were able to purchase an adult season ticket for as little as £365 for a renewal, with prices topping out at £730 for a new subscriber in the most expensive section of the ground, when they went on sale in a week's time.

On a game-by-game level, that works out at between £19.21 and £38.42 per match. Only three teams in the top flight - Manchester City, Stoke and Aston Villa - offered a cheaper season ticket than the Foxes in 2015-16, according to the BBC's Price of Football survey.

Spurs' least expensive option for this year, at £765, is £35 more expensive than the highest price band at Leicester.

Joining an ever-growing list, Swansea manager Francesco Guidolin publicly declared that he wanted Leicester to win the title just days before facing them. Guidolin hoped his compatriot Ranieri can keep Leicester at the top: "I hope for him that Leicester can win the title because they deserve to win. They have been in first place for many weeks and have played very well. It is a dream for Leicester, the team and for Claudio - I saw the tears in his eyes after the match. Emotion is very important in this period, week by week it is important. He has a lot of experience and tactically, he is very good."

TRY TO WIN THE TITLE!

BBC Leicester Sport, @BBCRLSport - He's finally admitted it...Claudio Ranieri says Leicester City are targeting the Premier League title.

Ranieri, for the first time, conceded that his side were targeting the title. "Now we go straight away to try to win the title. Only this remains. I believe. I wanted 79 points and we have to fight more now. I talk to my players, 'come on, now is the right moment to push'. I always believe, I am a positive man. If Tottenham go above us, congratulations, but I prefer to be five points ahead."

He was ecstatic about being in Europe's premier club competition. When asked about his club's achievements he responded: "It's amazing, amazing. And also, eh man, we're in Champions League. We are in the Champions League, man…dilly ding dilly dong! Come On. You forget, you speak about bla bla bla, but we are in the Champions League, come on man. It's fantastic. Terrific. Well done, well done to everyone. The owners, fans, players, staff, everybody. Everybody's involved - also Anthony (the head of media) here. The music is fantastic. Big teams will arrive. Big challenges. Great achievement. It's a great achievement. Unbelievable. And now we go straight away to try to win the title. Yes, yes man. Only this, only this remain. Only this. I know Pochettino is (saying). But Mauricio keep calm. I believe. Always I believe. I'm positive, man."

Ranieri picked a Premier League starting line up without Vardy for the first time. Who would he select to lead his attack? "You see on Sunday. Not now. We'll have to change something. Without him we make another strategy. I'm sure we'll give a little more to each other to win the match. We know he has one match off and our preparation is without him. He trained very well and he was not happy but he enjoyed the training session. We knew he had a suspension and then we move on."

He welcomed comments from Hodgson on Vardy's situation after the Three Lions chief felt Vardy had a right to feel upset after he received a second yellow card for diving. "It's not only sympathy, it's the truth. He is going very fast and when you touch something you lose balance. Maybe it's not a penalty but sure it's not a yellow card. It's important because Roy is an honest man and said what he watched."

Ranieri had special mentions for Mahrez and Okazaki. "Riyad is our light. When he's switched on. Leicester change colour. That's the truth, and Okazaki finally passed the English test. He can understand when I say something now."

Ranieri managed in four countries but has never won a domestic top-flight title. He was not concerned what a title win will mean for him personally. "I am glad when I see the people happy. Football is a show. I believe if we win a match people go back home happy to their family. They go back to work happy - that is good for me. From the beginning, the fans came with me with their heart and started to sing some songs with me from the beginning. That was good. I know there were some people said 'why Ranieri?' but the fans were always behind me. They were happy."

Ranieri hailed his "Caesars" and promised "fireworks". He once again dismissed concerns over the absence of Vardy. "I think I have 24 stars. I have 24 Caesars, that is our strength. There isn't just one Caesar, there's the other 23. Now is the right moment to say 'OK keep going - it is this season or nevermore'. Well done, we are in the Champions League. Try, believe, if winning the league happens - fireworks. They believe. We have everything in our own hands, I prefer my position to Spurs. It is not important what they do. It is important what we do."

Pochettino was asked whether the suspension of Vardy would have an effect on the title race. "I think it is a big impact for Leicester because Vardy is one of the best players in the Premier League. Sure, it's a big impact for them. Leicester have very good players and are in a position that they deserve to be. But he's one of the best strikers in the Premier League. They will feel that. But I'm sure they have different players that can play the same way."

Pochettino probably didn't mean it, but he said he was delighted that everyone not connected with his club wanted Leicester to win the title. Asked about Cesc Fàbregas's view (Fàbregas spoke on Sky Sports' *Monday Night Football* show that he was hoping Spurs would not win the league, given his Arsenal and Chelsea connections), he said: "I feel proud if other players want Leicester to win the league. Maybe we are worrying them a lot, more than we believe."

Was he concerned that a key part of the Chelsea team that still has to face both title contenders over the coming weeks, might not be suitably motivated when the Blues entertained the current pacesetters on the final weekend of the season? Pochettino added: "I believe that in football the players are professional, the managers are professional. We are too exposed on the media and sometimes we need to say something interesting. Maybe sometimes it's not the case and my press conferences are boring!"

Pochettino understands the nature of television which means, for the second week in a row, Spurs are playing on Monday evening. "I'm happy with the way we take the moment. We need to play after the other teams on Monday. We need to accept that. We know it is football but it is business too. We know the rules and I don't complain - it is no excuse."

Already guaranteed a top-three finish and Champions League football, Ranieri talked to BBC sports editor Dan Roan about his determination to win the title.

"It is this year or never more. We achieved the Champions League - a great achievement for everyone but now we try to win the title with all our strength, all our heart, our soul, everything. We need eight points and we are champions, and we try to do this. I said to my players that now is the right moment to push."

Ranieri had previously deflected questions on the subject of winning the title since Christmas. Sir Clive Woodward, who coached the England rugby team to their only World Cup victory in 2003, tweeted that he felt Ranieri had made a "big error" in talking about the title. "Never speak about anything but your next game, next game is all that you ever talk about, players will be listening."

In the Roan interview, Ranieri insisted he and his players were not feeling the pressure. "When I managed in Italy, you can't believe the kind of pressure you have there. It's not pressure here. I enjoy here."

What Leicester have achieved so far was hailed as a "miracle", a word used in a *Guardian* headline featuring the level of interest created in the owners homeland of Thailand. Ranieri said: "It's not a miracle. It is a strange moment. This is something in special circumstances and that is why I say 'now or never more', because next season will be different. The big teams will be stronger and better but of course we are doing something special this season."

No Vardy? "Without him I don't have another Vardy, but without him I believe we can do something special."

Asked if he was concerned that his star players would be tempted away, "No, I believe they want to follow us. They want to play in the Champions League next season. Here they are the king, if they go to another side they don't know what could happen. If somebody is not happy with us because another good team want them, then I don't worry. I prefer happy people with me."

The bond with his players was key to success. "There's no secret. There are circumstances. This team has had fantastic circumstances throughout all the season. The big teams, no, they had some fantastic matches and then slowed down. When I was a player (at Catanzaro) they were a team and it was unique. We were together for 14 years with eight or nine of my team-mates. We were very friendly and Leicester are the same. The players are friends, they play for each other and help each other - that is one of our keys."

Asked who would play him in the Hollywood movie under development, Ranieri said: "Somebody told me maybe Robert de Niro. Why not? He is a great actor."

SATURDAY, 23 APRIL

Ranieri fiercely denied his reputation as a "nearly man" and told Pochettino to wait for another year to win the title.

Ranieri finished second on four occasions in three different countries since becoming a manager; runners up to Arsenal's 'Invincibles' in 2004, five years later Juventus finished second in Serie A, the following season Ranieri won more points per game than any other Serie A manager but Roma lost their first two matches before his appointment and Mourinho's Internazionale pipped them to the title, and then four years later Monaco finished second to Paris Saint-Germain in Ligue 1 after accumulating 80 points, the most any team have achieved in France without winning the league.

"Every time I was behind," Ranieri said. "I know there are people out there who, if I don't win the title (with Leicester), will say: 'Ah, Ranieri, he always comes second.' Yes, but look at my career. Look at it. I was second at Chelsea. But we had started to build a team during the previous year. I continued to buy people during the first Premier League matches. We came second. At Roma, I was second. I arrived after two matches. We had zero points. We finished with 80 points. Inter had 82. I lost but what more could I do? I arrived at Juventus the first year after (promotion from) Serie B. We were third, then second. What more could I do? I had four or five champions but others were young players. At Monaco we won the second division. Then we finish behind Paris Saint-Germain, second by eight points. Now I try to win this (Premier League title)."

Ranieri was asked whether he had a message for Pochettino. "Mauricio, you can wait. Wait for one more year," he said, smiling, insisting that he was not feeling the heat any more than usual. "The pressure is always at the top. They have been behind all year. I'm not bothered. I would love to stay five points ahead."

Mahrez formed had dipped but he was needed more than ever in Vardy's absence. "I'm very happy with him," Ranieri said. "If you see what Riyad did, it's fantastic. Every time he touches the ball, it's a great ball. He is fouled a lot because everybody knows him and they want to stop him, so it's harder for him. He's very clever and if you remember who makes the right pass to N'Golo Kanté to go on the counter attack last week (for Vardy's opening goal), it was Riyad. Only he has the key to open the defensive line. It's fantastic. Maybe he doesn't look fantastic now but look and you will see what he does with the ball."

Ranieri wanted his two tough central defensive to carry on scrapping at corners. Ranieri knows there is no chance they would go soft. He told Morgan to forget the controversial penalty he gave away. Ranieri said: "I have told them both to keep going. If you watch one thousand or one million matches, there are worst fouls than the one Morgan made. So I say, 'Keep going' because it was a strange penalty against us. It has not been necessary to tell them. I say do your job - don't worry about the penalty last week."

Mark Clattenburg was in charge at the key game at the King Power Stadium. Ranieri added: "Mark Clattenburg is a fantastic referee. I won't change much and hope also that the referee watched what happened last week when we attacked from set-pieces. With Huth and Morgan we would have so many penalties as well. It's okay. It's not my job what the referee decides. I don't have a problem with any of them. They are so experienced and they know every player very well, so it's not a problem."

Leicester attracted worldwide attention. Ulloa told Sky Sports that the mood at the club was "relaxed". "In Argentina and South America, people speak about Leicester, round the world people are speaking about Leicester now," he said. "They have a little feeling about the team, about how we play, this is different. It's a small team fighting with the big teams. But we are relaxed, there are not many people thinking about the game. We know it is important but we are relaxed, it's a normal week for us."

He was sure to replace Vardy. "I don't know if I will play, but I am always ready. I enjoy playing with these team-mates, fighting and giving the option to help the team." Reflecting on his penalty last week, he added: "I didn't think about how important it was, but after the goal I started to feel it. I hope I can make more important contributions for the team."

Liverpool legend, Steven Gerrard, never experienced winning the title and was therefore well-placed to comment on the psychology and pressures of a title run-in. Here are some extracts from his *Daily Telegraph* column:

"The visit of Swansea City will offer the greatest of insights into whether they (Leicester) have the stamina, nerve and depth of resources to hold off the challenge of Tottenham Hotspur.

For two-thirds of this season the Leicester players will have been enjoying the ride, relishing every chance to defy expectations and keep the momentum. Now they're in the midst of a different physical and psychological challenge. The hunters became the hunted and it has become their title to lose, every misstep scrutinised to levels they would never have experienced before. The repercussions become greater the closer you get to the prize and in all likelihood they will never again be subjected to the intensity of pressure they are now. Suddenly, it is not only a case of loving every minute but there is a fear of failure to try to banish, too.

I believe Sunday is so monumental because of what took place against West Ham last week, the first hint of anxiety in what was in danger of becoming a title procession. Everyone pounced on it, suggesting it was the opening Spurs have been waiting for.

Leicester did well to claim a point in the circumstances, but you could see how buoyed Spurs were by what they saw. That was evident in their response at Stoke the following day. Now Leicester must play without Jamie Vardy. If they win without him it will send a message to White Hart Lane that nothing will derail them and it is my belief that victory against Swansea would put Leicester one more win from the ultimate triumph.

I am sure Vardy has been replaying last weekend in his mind every day since, asking himself what he could have done differently to avoid a red card and suspension at such a critical moment. This is how you get affected when the stakes are so much higher. Spurs will have watched that and convinced themselves their time is coming. Mauricio Pochettino will be telling his players there are more twists to come, shifting momentum their way.

In public, managers will always say it is all about their own team, what they can control, and that's the right message. But any player who says he is not obsessing about what the opponent is doing is lying. You watch every game. You will every shot of the team your rival is playing to go in. You want the title contender to make it as straightforward as possible for you, and when the pressure switches because they have played first and won you definitely feel it more. Equally, if your competitor plays earlier in the day and drops points, it feels like there is an extra yard in your game as you see a chance to close that gap.

Leicester's players know if they don't win the title this season, this particular squad will never win it. Sorry to ditch the romance but there is no doubt in my mind this is a freak year for them and they won't get so close next season. It would be great for football if they do win it, proving everything is possible and we don't need to presume the same clubs will share the trophies every year, but let's not ignore the fact there is going to be major backlash from the rich and powerful to stop it happening again."

Eden Hazard stirred things up somewhat when he confirmed he wanted Leicester to win the Premier League, and Chelsea would do everything they can to beat Spurs in their next fixture. The Belgian scored his first two league goals of the season in a 4-1 win at Bournemouth. Speaking on *Match of the Day* afterwards he confessed that no one at the club wanted Spurs to succeed Chelsea as champions. "We don't want - the fans, the club, the players - Tottenham to win the Premier League, but in football you never know. We hope for Leicester because they deserve to be champions this season, but we will see. We have a good game next week against Tottenham, if we can beat them it will be good."

MOTD pundit Martin Keown felt the comment was ill-advised. "The Tottenham players are probably listening to that right now and it's goading them a little bit, but they might say: 'Where has Eden Hazard been all season?'" Former Chelsea manager Ruud Gullit added: "I can understand it, but don't say it."

Leicester's nerves will be jangling but, despite Jamie Vardy's suspension, they will find a way to claim three points against Swansea, was the Jamie Redknapp verdict for Sky Sports. "Leicester are in unchartered territory. Jamie Vardy has been their top scorer and their talisman this season. He's played every league game and fired them to the top of the table with 22 goals. His suspension for this weekend's game with Swansea is a massive blow.

And the truth is, we don't know how Leicester are going to adjust. Their ability to soak up pressure and hit teams on the break is something they've mastered this year. And he's been central to that success, with his pace unsettling the opposition. Boss Claudio Ranieri has options. He could bring in Jeff Schlupp or the pacey Demarai Gray. Or he could play Leonardo Ulloa or even Riyad Mahrez off Shinji Okazaki. But whoever he picks, it may be that Leicester need to play a bit more football on Sunday and move up the pitch in stages, rather than in the direct way they have previously. They might have to be a little bit more patient in their build-up. But it's not the end of the world for them. Vardy's been playing so well but I still think it's something they can cope with for this Swansea game.

They will miss him more for the away game at Manchester United, should his ban be extended, because it's in those games where he's been so effective on the break. After five straight wins, we can't say that result is a blip. But it's a nerve-jangler. It's like in the Grand National when a horse is going well and then it hits a fence. You don't know how the horse is going to react when they get to the next fence.

What will the reaction be from Leicester this weekend? I keep hearing people say: What have they got to be nervous about because they've already achieved so much. But of course they're going to be nervous. This is life-changing. This is history in the making. How can they not be nervous? I'm nervous for them! If they don't win the league from here, they'll regret it forever because a lot of these players will never get the chance to win the Premier League again. Tottenham, on the other hand, look like they could play forever. They look like they could wipe the floor with every team they play at the moment - and that's the scary part of it for Leicester. Spurs are breathing down their necks and Harry Kane, Dele Alli, Mousa Dembélé and Toby Alderweireld are playing like it's August and they're full of energy. They look like they're enjoying the chase. That makes Ranieri's job very important but, like his players, we don't know how he's going to react to this situation, either. He's never won a top-flight title before. It's not like Sir Alex Ferguson when he was playing mind games.

Ranieri deep down must be thinking: 'I've always been a nearly man. This is my chance to ram it down the throat of everyone who said I wasn't a good manager.' This is his opportunity and that brings nerves and pressure. It's not just the whole country focussing on this - sports fans across the world are talking about this. It's unprecedented. And while the Leicester coaching staff will try to keep training fun and fresh this week, when the players go home and turn on Sky Sports News or pick up a paper, they'll start feeling the pressure. They can't hide from the enormity of what they're doing. And they can't hide from the fact they need to bounce back from that West Ham result with a statement against Swansea. Manchester United, Everton and Chelsea follow for Leicester. Tricky tests. If they don't win this one, I'd make Tottenham favourites for the title. That's how much is riding on it. Swansea got beaten 3-0 last week and they can't be as bad as that again, and the Vardy suspension is terrible timing. But I think Leicester will come up with the response they need."

SUNDAY, 24 APRIL

Writing in his *Sunday Times* column, Graeme Souness joined the chorus of pundits who still had their nagging doubts that the fairytale "won't have a happy ending", once again predicting that Claudio's dreamers would falter, blaming the absence of Jamie Vardy.

He wrote: "Jamie Vardy is the last player Leicester would want to be without at this delicate stage of the title race. I've always felt that they would have to come through a nervy moment to win the Premier League and it might have arrived after last week's draw with West Ham and Vardy's controversial sending off during it. Prior to that, they had been getting away with winning 1-0. That was the score in four of their five previous games. Leicester play the simplest form of football: when they win it, their first thought is to turn the opposition back four with a ball in behind them. The real upside of that is that Vardy chases it and takes all the opposition players back towards their own goal, while all Leicester's players remain in their positions...it might not have a happy ending. There's still that seed of doubt for Leicester. Is the loss of Vardy going to compound that? If they drop points today, then on Monday night, all of a sudden, they could be looking in their rear view mirror...they will see Tottenham right on their tail."

The scene was set on the BBC website for a full break down of the day's events starting Mark Lawrenson sharing Souness doubts as he predicted a 1-1 draw, which would be devastating for Leicester: "Without Jamie Vardy's pace, teams can really squeeze Leicester because nobody is going to run in behind them. I think that is a real worry, so I am going to go for another draw here - although Swansea did look like they had just booked their summer holidays in Benidorm against Newcastle last weekend."

Commentator Jonathan Pearce wasn't entirely sure, either: "This is make or break for Leicester City. If they keep their five-point lead they'll withstand the challenge of Spurs, who will yet drop points. Lose, and Tottenham will probably overtake them. Leicester go into battle without Vardy - it's like Richard III fighting at the nearby Battle of Bosworth Field without 'a horse...a horse...a kingdom for his horse!' We know what happened there. But Shakespeare's drama of that Leicester-interred King promised: 'True hope is swift...Kings it makes Gods and meaner creatures Kings'. It's all about belief now. Do Leicester retain enough?"

In the Wat Traimit temple in Bangkok, Thai Buddhist monk Phra Prommangkalachan prayed for the team known in Thailand as 'the Siamese Foxes'. He told Sky Sports News: "Leicester City is a determined club with good intentions to win the league. The coach has good intentions, the players too. My prayers are part of that - I help them prosper and provide encouragement to them. We try to manage the team by using the power of Buddhism, the power of Dhamma and the power of the Sangha."

The monk has been channelling spiritual blessings for Leicester since billionaire Thai owner Vichai Srivaddhanaprabha bought the club in 2010. "Before Mr. Vichai contacted me, I'd never known anything about football. The first time I watched a football game was when I was invited to pray for the Leicester City team." That invitation led Phra Prommangkalachan, along with a retinue of fellow Thai monks, to make the first of a number of visits to the King Power stadium to bless the pitch and offer lucky amulets to the players, handing out special talismans - flags bearing the clubs logo, adorned with ancient Buddhist script, believed to convey protective powers to the lucky owner.

Two such talismans now hang at his shrine in Bangkok, alongside hundreds of Buddha statues, incense, flower offerings and ceremonial elephant tusks. Phra Prommangkalachan also goes by the name of Chao Khun Thongchai – a title that translates to 'honourable bearer of the flag of victory'. The monk was aware of the team's current predicament, "The game is still the game. It's a sport competition. We have to understand the varieties of the system, rules and management. The duty of the Buddhist monk like me is to encourage everyone in the team to do the right things by the rules and encourage good Karma."

Alan Birchenall, now master of ceremonies at the stadium on match day, whipped the crowd into a fervour with a rallying speech. The traditional pre-kick-off playing of Post Horn Gallop was accompanied by a deafening greeting for Leicester's players.

LEICESTER CITY 4-0 SWANSEA CITY

Social media was in a frenzy before, during and after the game:

Gary Lineker – "Here we go again, another afternoon of insufferable tension. It's hard to sit and watch comfortably when your bum is squeaking incessantly."

Phil McNulty, BBC Sport chief football writer – "I have made plenty of visits to Leicester City this season. It is always noisy - but it has never been noisier than this. The pre-match announcer is former Leicester City star Alan Birchenall. It was difficult to understand a word he was bellowing into his microphone but it did the job in working the Foxes fans into a frenzy."

Alan Green, BBC Radio 5 live – "I have to say, hand on heart, at no stage of the season have I genuinely believed that Leicester were going to win the title. (But) they are going to win the title!"

Robbie Savage, ex-Wales midfielder at the King Power Stadium for BBC Radio 5 live - "Brilliant first half from Leicester. Ulloa coming in to the side gets the second after Mahrez pounced on Williams' mistake. Can they get another clean sheet? I can't see Swansea getting back into this game. Leicester are just a complete team. Magnificent spirit, they head everything, throw their bodies at everything. How are Swansea going to score past this side that keeps clean sheet after clean sheet? The Swans are neat and tidy but there's no penetration, no threat."

With two more goals in the second half, the eight-point lead over Spurs was restored with relative comfort in stark contrast to the dramas of a week before. Ranieri made all the right choices, all the right decisions. The stadium rocked so much the TV pictures shook as the Sky Sports cameras shook in the gantry, such was the power and emotion within the stadium.

The pressure had been on but the side responded by equalling their best Premier League win, scoring four for the first time since Sunderland were beaten 4-2 on the opening day.

Robbie Savage summarised for BBC 5 live Sport - "People are talking about how Tottenham could take all points from their last games. But so could Leicester. They've only lost three games! They could go to Old Trafford and blow Manchester United away next week. They are rampant. They're running away with it - eight points clear. Leicester winning the league would have to be the best achievement in domestic sport. Ever! It is that incredible. And I don't think we'll see anything like this ever again. I just can't believe it. Everybody here is the same from when I was around; the kitman, the people holding the doors open. But on the pitch they are transformed. It's one of those moments when you think: I was there."

Darren Anderton, ex-Spurs winger - "Pathetic from Swansea."

Chris Sutton, former Norwich striker on BBC Radio 5 live - "I thought today was massive for Leicester because had they slipped up against Swansea - you'd probably only rather play Aston Villa right now - then the doubt really would have started to creep in. But they will go on and win the league now. If Tottenham fail to beat West Brom on Monday and Leicester win at Manchester United next Sunday then the Foxes were champions."

Gary Lineker - "Sat on my own watching the telly, jumping, cheering and even crying a little. It's what only football can do."

"BARCELONA, WE'RE COMING FOR YOU"

It all began with a touch of fortune and brilliance in the same breath. Ashley Williams' poor clearance struck Mahrez as he closed down and although it struck the point of his elbow he got away with it to score with a composed finish looking to curl into the far corner but sweeping it cheekily into the small gap at the near post.

Leonardo Ulloa stepped into the space left by Vardy to answer all the doubters. He brushed aside the powerful Williams for a close range header form Drinkwater's superbly delivered free-kick before the break, then scrambled in the third from a loose ball on the hour virtually by the far post after the impressive Jeff Schlupp had broken clear. Substitute Albrighton added a fourth to leave Leicester needing a maximum of five points to win the title. In theory, at least, they could clinch it with victory at Manchester United next weekend if Spurs slip at home to West Bromwich Albion on Monday night, although that was an unlikely scenario, but the title was within their grasp and now even closer!

Ulloa fully repaid manager Ranieri's faith to replace the man with 22 Premier League goals. Having earned a vital point with a last-minute penalty against West Ham, the 29-year-old Argentine striker, a record £8m buy from Brighton in July 2014, ran selflessly in attack and defence contributing two goals before limping off near the end with a bad back. The two-goal striker was rewarded with a standing ovation when he was substituted; Vardy watched form his private box with his wife-to-be and friends but he was not missed and that is no greater praise of Ulloa's performance.

The final seconds were played out to roars of "Barcelona, we're coming for you". Hard to believe, but true.

The Tinkerman had hardly tinkered at all, as he relied on a bedrock of the same 11 players, but when he needed to make selection decisions, he got them spot on. Besides the obvious replacement in attack, he backed another winner when he dropped Albrighton down to the bench and brought in Schlupp. The 23-year-old Ghana international is erratic, but his direct, strong running unsettled Swansea and he set up Ulloa for his second goal. He also earned a standing ovation when he was substituted. Albrighton emerged from the bench to score the fourth late on as Ranieri got just about everything right. Leicester registered their 22nd victory, their biggest haul of wins ever in a top-flight season.

Ranieri commented: "It's a fantastic performance. Be hungry, be solid. Without Jamie Vardy everyone gave something more. We knew we had some difficulties but with the fight of everybody we had a good match. I asked for this kind of performance. I was delighted with Ulloa and Schlupp. I am very, very pleased with Leonardo. He jumped, he scored two goals, he attacked, he defended. Well done. I am very pleased with Schlupp. It's important because everyone wants to see our answer without Jamie Vardy and that was a fantastic answer in my opinion. If Jamie takes another day off with suspension it's important to be solid and stronger than today. United is a very good team.

They haven't played a lot but I told them 'now we need you'. Mahrez is the light and when he is switched on the King Power is fantastic. We know it will be tough because Tottenham are a good team but we will fight until the end. We dream and now it is important to make the dream a reality. It is important to fight for that reality. I am optimistic, I am positive. I know it's not easy because in my mind Tottenham will win all their matches and we will need five points. Three matches, two away and one at home."

The King Power Stadium shook like never before - and that's saying something - to the sound of supporters chanting about winning the league. "Our fans maybe wake up from the dream and they say, 'Come on'," added Ranieri. "We only have one match at home and they want to enjoy with us and push with their hearts. We are ready to fight until the end."

He was not out for revenge after being tipped to be one of the first managers to be sacked. "There isn't revenge, I am the same man. If I was stupid at that time, I am stupid now. I never think the fans were negative with me, never. (Only) some of you, some of my sharks (journalists)."

Mahrez said: "Now there are three games to go and we are closer but everyone is working for each other and it is a great team spirit. In this team we don't need just one player. We are really together with our team spirit and we work for each other. Sometimes I score, sometimes Vardy scores and sometimes Leo scores but we are a team. It is always a pleasure to play here. The fans are unbelievable. We are closer now but there are still three games to go and we have eight points more so it is all in our hands now so we have to stay focused. We are getting in the helicopter now with the others and we will see what happens tonight."

Sky Sports pundit Jamie Redknapp praised the Algerian, but believed his selfless team-ethic underpinned Leicester's charge to the top. "Mahrez was again magnificent, some of the things he does with a football are unique. He is so lovely to watch. Always easy on the eye, lovely touches. But what he's also brought to his game is the ability to work for his team, because he's bought into the team ethic here."

Ulloa was overjoyed: "I'm happy because this team is unbelievable. We played so well. We miss Jamie Vardy because he is a good player but we can still play well and I enjoy playing with this team and with these team-mates. I am always ready to play when I can help the team and I always work for this, I am happy because I could score two goals and help the team. We played a really good game and it is a massive three points. It is good for me because I needed confidence and after the last goal I was more confident, but I am more pleased about the three points."

With little time for celebrations Mahrez and his team-mates sped off to the PFA dinner having registered a joint-league-high involvement in 28 top-flight goals (17 goals, 11 assists), level with Vardy. Drinkwater provided his sixth Premier League assist, his first for anyone other than Vardy. Ulloa scored three in his last two PL games, as many as he'd scored in his previous 25 this season.

Mahrez was favourite to be crowned PFA Player of the Year, but Ranieri remarked: "I am the manager and I would like it if everyone could win but that is not possible, but for me they are all winners."

The club paid for a fleet of five helicopters to fly the Foxes from their Belvoir Drive base to Battersea Heliport for a quick hop to west London for the ceremony. They travelled by coach to the club's Belvoir Road training ground and took off shortly after 7pm, landing at Battersea Heliport after a flight of around an hour before being driven 20 minutes to the Park Lane venue. That need for speed almost cost Gray as he bounded off the chopper ahead of the rest of his group. In a tracksuit and cap, the winger made a wrong turn and headed straight towards the spinning blades at the rear of the aircraft. A quick-thinking steward ordered him to stop.

The whole Leicester squad came to London, a 24-strong party including Ranieri and some staff, and finally arrived in the main ballroom to rapturous applause from all in attendance.

Riyad Mahrez won the Professional Footballers' Association Player of the Year award. With 17 goals and 11 assists in 34 league games he has done as much as anyone to take Leicester to the cusp of the title, but with that added magic ingredient - genius.

"All the credit is for them, seriously," Mahrez said. "And for my manager and the staff. Without them I wouldn't receive this award and I wouldn't score. It's the team spirit, and I want to dedicate it to them. It's extra special because if the players vote for me it's because they've seen I've been great this year so I'm happy. Without my team-mates I wouldn't get this award."

The Leicester City Secret? "The secret has been team spirit. We work so hard for each other. We are like brothers, it's everywhere on the pitch. That's our strength. If sometimes we are not good, we know we are going to run and make the effort for our team-mates. That is the secret of our success."

Two years and three months since his first game in English football against Middlesbrough in the Championship, he was proud to be the first African to win the PFA award. "I didn't know that. I am very proud. That's something big. Didier Drogba and everyone was better than me! I didn't know why they didn't get it."

Thierry Henry, Cristiano Ronaldo and Gareth Bale had been previous winner which made him even more proud. "I don't know. I don't want to be compared to them. They are big, big players. Me? I am just starting my football, my career. So we will see. Like I said, it's not a final thing. I still have to work and we will see."

The title beckoned next. "We don't need to be nervous. This is just a bonus for us. Nobody expected us to be where we are so this is a bonus. If we do it, we do it. If not, that's life. Like I said, we are not a big club. We don't have to win the Premier League."

Mahrez is only the second winner of the PFA award from outside Europe. Uruguay striker Luis Suarez won it in 2014 while playing for Liverpool.

Rivals for the Premier League title, Leicester and Spurs, provided eight between them for the Professional Footballers' Association Premier League Team of the Year:

GK - David De Gea (Manchester United)

RB - Hector Bellerin (Arsenal)

CB - Toby Alderweireld (Tottenham Hotspur)

CB - Wes Morgan (Leicester City)

LB - Danny Rose (Tottenham Hotspur)

Mid - Riyad Mahrez (Leicester City)

Mid - N'Golo Kanté (Leicester City)

Mid - Dele Alli (Tottenham Hotspur)

Mid - Dimitri Payet (West Ham)

CF - Jamie Vardy (Leicester City)

CF - Harry Kane (Tottenham Hotspur)

Vardy's consolation for missing out on the main prize was that he was honoured for his phenomenal season by being awarded a commemorative plate for breaking Ruud van Nistelrooy's record of the most goals scored in consecutive games. The shield has the Leicester crest placed at the top along with the club badges of the 11 teams he scored against when he broke the record.

Close to midnight at the Grosvenor House hotel, Mahrez stood in a quiet corner of the lobby surrounded by the media as is the tradition for the winner to give an interview to the press. He recalled a conversation with Kanté in January while his team-mates were celebrating another win; they began to talk about the possibility of winning the title, although they didn't believe that by the end of April they would be five points away from the title. "I speak a lot with N'Golo Kanté and maybe January we started to talk about the league. We just said: 'Imagine if...' We didn't go into much more, we just said that, 'Imagine...' But that was only for about 30 seconds and then we would say: 'No, let's stay focused and let's see.' It was still a long way to go. Maybe 15 games to go. Nowadays we are like: 'It's not done yet because Tottenham are very close to us. We have to keep going and focus on every game because it is difficult. It is not done yet'." He said the belief came when they won 3-1 away at Manchester City on 6 February.

Yaya Touré, @YayaToure - Congratulations to @PFA player of the year @Mahrez22 Great to see my African brother win it!

Gary Lineker, @GaryLineker - Congratulations to @Mahrez22 on winning the PFA player of the year award. He's a magnificent footballer and an absolute joy to watch.

MONDAY, 25 APRIL

"Hey man!" the Italian declared in a press conference. "We are in the Champions League. Dilly-ding, dilly-dong," he added. "Oh, it's fantastic. Fantastic. Terrific."

"Dilly ding, dilly dong"…surely one of the most unusual quotes of the season.

And so, in this 'ding dong' race, the attention turned to White Hart Lane.

Mark Lawrenson got it wrong before the Leicester game going for a draw, and now he's tipped a 3-0 win for Spurs, as he explained: "West Brom have taken only one point from their last five games and it is hard to see their form improving on Monday. Leicester set down a marker by beating Swansea so convincingly, but Spurs will win this and keep the pressure on."

TOTTENHAM HOTSPUR 1-1 WEST BROMWICH ALBION

The Fox Hunt was virtually over.

Spurs were "cruising" in the first half, as Gary Lineker tweeted, but hit the woodwork so many times they should have been out of sight. They weren't, though, and West Brom staged a magnificent fight back when they had nothing riding on it. As Graeme Souness rightly observed on Sky Sports it could only happen in the hugely competitive nature of the Premier League.

So Spurs were dealt a severe and unexpected blow as Albion defender Craig Dawson's second-half equaliser put Leicester City within one win of the Premier League crown.

Spurs looked set to narrow the gap to five points with three games left after Dawson bundled Eriksen's wickedly accurate free-kick into his own net. But he made amends by heading in Gardner's corner from six yards leaving Spurs seven points adrift, meaning The Foxes needed three points to guarantee becoming the English champions for the first time. A victory at Old Trafford on Sunday 1 May would do it!

Pochettino refused to throw in the towel but the look on the faces of the players at the final whistle told the story that they now believed they had blown it. The Spurs manager told Sky Sports: "We were unlucky in the first half and created a lot of chances but this always happens in football. We allowed them to believe and we conceded a goal, but I am very proud because it was a big effort. We still need to believe. Seven points is difficult but we still need to fight in the next three games.

We felt comfortable on the pitch and created chances, but we lost control of game and allowed them to create chances. But I think we deserved the three points. Mathematically it is still possible. I have nothing to complain about and we need to be strong in our mind and prepare for the next game. It is difficult but we need to fight for the points. We are not going to give up. We understand it was a game we must win. I must now lift the players for the game against Chelsea."

Kane commented: "It has not gone. We need to keep fighting. We felt we needed to win this game so we are disappointed. We had enough chances in the first half to put it to bed. But we weren't good enough in the second half. We felt we could easily have won the game if we played in the second half like we did the first. It is football. All we can do is keep fighting. We have Chelsea next. Hopefully Man United can do us a favour."

Tony Pulis insisted before kick-off that his side needed to "hold a flag up" for the competitiveness of the Premier League - which they eventually did. Pulis, also speaking to Sky Sports, remarked: "I thought they came out of the blocks. Tottenham dominated the game and we sat back while they danced around us at times. The best thing was we came in 1-0 down at half-time. It became a more open game in the second half and I am really pleased with the players. We lack quality at times but the work-rate was good. You come to places like this and you can be on the back foot before the game even starts. But we are fit and we can cause people problems. We can make it a game with good organisation and players giving it a go. Tottenham are a very, very good side. Dembélé was outstanding today. They are a young team as well and they will only get better."

As for the title race? "I just want Leicester to win it," declared Pulis. "No disrespect to Tottenham, but it is such a wonderful story. It can't happen anywhere else but in this country. The Premier League is such a tough league and Leicester can dig results out. They have played exceptionally well and won games but when they haven't they have dug them out. I think Tottenham will be an exceptional side. It will be an exciting place to be, this club."

Gary Lineker had spoken to *Match of the Day* chief, it emerged, hoping to back out of a pledge to present the show in his underpants. "You'll have to wait and see. I've kind of said I'll have to do it,' the 55-year-old told the *Radio Times*. "The conversation's been had. I've told them many times, 'Please tell me I can't do it'. When I sent the tweet in December I categorically knew there was zero chance that (Leicester) would win. I'm in good shape. For an old b*****d. I'll probably work out for the two weeks beforehand very, very hard."

TUESDAY, 26 APRIL

Jason Bourne, BBC Radio Leicester Sport: "Last night's result at White Hart Lane has hammered the fairytale home for a lot of Leicester City fans. There was a real outpouring of emotion from my family and friends as West Brom's equaliser - and what it could mean - hit everyone like a sledgehammer. It's happening. It's really happening. For this season's 5000-1 outsiders to actually win the Premier League title at the home of Manchester United would cap off an incredible season and go down as the greatest day in the club's history. This doesn't happen to Leicester City - but it is. It's going to happen. The dream is becoming a reality. The champagne is on ice."

There was a blow ahead of potential title-winning clash at Old Trafford on Sunday when it was announced by the FA that Jamie Vardy would be banned for an additional game for improper conduct. He requested a personal hearing in the hope of avoiding additional punishment, but was also fined £10,000. The three-man panel decided Vardy's angry reaction to being sent off against West Ham was worthy of further punishment and Ranieri had to do without his top scorer for a second match in succession. Diego Costa and Gabriel were given the same sanction for similar offences of improper conduct following red cards earlier this season.

The club were refused permission for their supporters to watch them potentially be crowned champions at Old Trafford on a giant screen on the King Power Stadium pitch, according to a report by Ben Rumsby in *Telegraph Sport*. The article stated that the Premier League turned down an approach by the club to broadcast the game at Old Trafford, and final match of the season at Chelsea. The club were told that Premier League teams are not allowed to do so for matches shown live on Sky Sports or BT Sport due to the potential impact on the numbers of those paying to watch at home or at local bars and pubs, which rely on live football to attract customers.

Leicester's game at United was due to be shown live on Sky Sports and their trip to Chelsea certain to be shown by the broadcaster. The club were allowed to screen matches within the hospitality areas, but the Keith Weller Lounge, Walkers Hall and 1884 Sports Bar are only able to accommodate 1,600 fans per game. Tickets cost £5 for adults, £3 for under-18s and include a free bottle of beer or a bottle of water, with all profits donated to the LCFC Foxes Foundation.

A petition was set up by two supporters, Kris and Donna Robinson, for the club and Leicester City Council to erect screens outside the King Power Stadium or elsewhere in the city to show the team's matches for the rest of the season.

A spokesman for the council said: "LCFC has decided to show the two away fixtures on screens at the King Power stadium. Also, many pubs both in the city centre and other neighbourhood family pubs have paid very high commercial rates to screen the matches. The city council will help facilitate the club to put on other events, but we would not want to take trade away from pubs across the city that rely on matchday income."

The Premier League's substitutes' board's number will be replaced by a new design next season. Ranieri and Peter Schmeichel helped unveil designer watch makers TAG Heuer as its official timekeeper along with a brand new hi-tech board for its fourth officials. Speaking at the launch Ranieri confirmed his feelings after Spurs had dropped two vital points against West Brom, "I was a little more light. A little. I say with my heart, we try to do our best but if the others are better than us, I want to say only 'congratulations'. Of course now we are there, we are so very close. We have to continue to fight."

Ranieri admitted that winning the league "never did come in my mind" when he returned to England, "It is unbelievable what has happened this season. We start with the goal to save the team. But slowly, slowly we are getting better. The players believe in something special and to try to compete with big teams. Now of course we are there. We want to fight until the end. Everybody says it's done. In my opinion, no. I believe only on the mathematics."

Ranieri was again without Vardy and was refusing to take the game for granted. Given the opportunity to possibly win the title at the King Power Stadium during next weekend's visit by Everton, in front of the club's own fans, Ranieri said he would like to do so anywhere. "I don't know. Of course Manchester is a fantastic stadium," he said. "But also Manchester are playing very well. There are some young players. It is important to try to win every match. Every match. I don't know when, but it is important to get this goal. I talk to my players always: It is not important the result, is important the performance. I want them to play as a team. Football is a team game. I said to them, we have to play as XI. Because I don't know how many players there are in front of you. It is not important the name of your opponent, it is important what you do during the match and help each other."

Ranieri praised Mahrez for being named PFA Player of the Year, but insisted all his team deserves credit. "I am very proud because Riyad is very humble man. He asks every time, 'What can I do to improve?' That is fantastic. He is a genius, our light. But I want to say also all the players are doing a fantastic season, with very great professionalism. I am a very lucky man because my players are so fantastic, they play with heart and soul and blood and they enjoy the people. I am very, very proud of them."

Peter Schmeichel, meanwhile, was talking at a twin event in Hong Kong, and revealed he gets more nervous watching his son Kasper play than he did when in goal for United. "It's much, much worse watching Kasper play," he said, adding: "Claudio, fantastic work. I know you're going to get the job done. They are not going to crack under pressure."

Ranieri said that the chemistry he has with his players is the secret. "There are many ways of reading what has happened," Ranieri told Italian broadcaster, Radio 105. "Our secret? Speaking now while everything is in turmoil is difficult, there are endless interpretations of what has happened. We have a good club, good players, a special League because the big clubs haven't had the consistency to go with their strength, we've had that instead. Then there's the feeling, the chemistry which has developed between me and the players. The English have asked me so many times how I deal with the stress, but they don't realise what we Italians put up with! We know very well that the only calm moment is the 90 minutes of the game, from Monday until seconds before kick-off it's all very tense.

Right from the start the President (Vichai Srivaddhanaprabha) asked me to build a team to compete for Europe in the next few years, then the Champions League. This has been a special year, now we're in the Champions League and all we're missing is the big dream (the title). We must keep our feet on the ground and see what we can do."

Ranieri said it came as no surprise to him to see the performances of Schlupp and Ulloa. Speaking to lcfc.com Ranieri explained that he continued to be proud of everyone in the squad as they battled to a four-nil victory. "Unbelievable. Thank you to our fans. The atmosphere is great when we play at home but also when we play away. You listen, our fans push with us and we are together. No pressure. They (Ulloa and Schlupp) wanted to play and deserved to play because not all the time they play but they deserve it. The first XI played so well and for me it`s difficult to change when the team works so well. I changed a little because I wanted the power of Jeff and the heading ability of Leo. Everybody contributes to make Leicester top of the league. Demarai too has a very good future if he stays calm, listens and improves."

WEDNESDAY, 27 APRIL

TO BET OR NOT TO BET

Tom Hanks said he put a £100 on Leicester to win the Premier League at the beginning of the season. When asked about his "beloved football team", Aston Villa, at the premiere for his latest film, Hologram for the King, the Castaway star jokingly replied: "what are you trying to make me do?

Are you trying to make me cry on TV? That's bad but you know what I did at the beginning of the season? Put 100 quid on Leicester so I think I'll do okay." When pushed on whether he was telling the truth, Hanks responded enigmatically, "maybe I did, maybe I didn't." Hanks claimed to be an Aston Villa fan in 2001, saying he "liked the name". He attended a pre-season match between Villa and Portland Timbers in 2012.

Meanwhile, John Micklethwaite forgot to bet on his team to win the title for the first time in 20 years. He put £20 on the Foxes to win the title every season since 1996, but the 53-year-old old moved to New York for work last summer and forgot to make his wager, missing out on a potential £100,000 payout. John, originally from Rutland, said: "As Leicester started to win, I felt happy. Mainly because I wanted them to win, but partly because I pessimistically thought Leicester would never win the league. Also because, and this is embarrassing, I miscalculated the odds and thought I had only given up £10,000, not £100,000." John, who is the editor-in-chief of international news agency Bloomberg, added: "I started betting on them in the 1990s under Martin O'Neil. I lived in New York for 1998-2000, so I may have missed a year then, but I remember doing it at least one year while in the States, because I had to explain it to American friends. It was consistent after that, and I did win a few times - League One and Championship - but it became a ritual end-of-summer expression of hope and loyalty - with a slightly lottery ticket feel."

Another fan was labelled the "world's most calamitous punter" after losing 5p on a bet on the Foxes to win the Premier league. The unnamed gambler put 50p on Ranieri's team to finish top before the season began at odds of 5,000-1, but he cashed out after an opening-day win for 5p less than his stake and misses out on a £2,500 pay day. Ladbrokes spokesman David Williams said: "It is an absolute mystery. He must be feeling pretty sick. He must go down as the most calamitous punter in history. He must have thought the wheels were going to come off after the first win and decided to cut his losses." Ladbrokes were trying to contact the man, who lives in the East Midlands, to offer him a consolation to "soften the blow".

Martin Davies, 59, staked £11 on the Foxes winning the title at 5,000-1 in a "joke bet". He stands to win £72,000. He made the bet along with a friend who staked a fiver at the same time and could win more than £30,000. Mr. Davies is a lifelong fan, who owns a hair salon in Birmingham City centre together with his daughter Sarah Simpson-Davies. He planned to be at Old Trafford. Sarah said: "Dad has been a massive Leicester City fan since he was nine. He put the bet on as a bit of a joke at the start of the season with a friend and he can't believe that he may now actually win it. It will be a great present for his birthday if they do. I don't think I'll be getting any of the winnings, but my sister's getting married next year, so some of it might be spent on that." Sarah, who is a hairdresser and yoga teacher, added: "On Monday night, when Tottenham drew, Dad had no sleep at all because he was so excited. The money is an extra. But the biggest thing for him is that Leicester win the title. He is going to Old Trafford to watch on Sunday and is also going to the last away match against Chelsea. When he made the bet the odds were 5,000/1."

Karoshma Kapoor, 20, a business student from Leicester, placed a £2 bet with Ladbrokes. She stood to win £10,000. She said: "I'm, very, very nervous. I've been tempted to cash out, but I just had to see it through. The winnings will be shared with my aunt – we put £1 on each. I'll try to save a bit but some of it will be used for Champions League tickets next season."

BONUS TIME

Ranieri, though, might have taken out the best bet of anyone.

It was reported that his bonus is in excess of £5million, for Leicester City winning the title. His three-year deal at £1.5m a season included many clauses which would have made a parting of the ways straight-forward and cost effective for Leicester in the event of failure. But to balance out the potential for success Ranieri included heavy incentives, from Europa League qualification, Champions League qualification, to winning the league, plus a clause for £100,000 per each finishing position from 17th and above, a cool £1.7m for coming first. The bonus for winning the title is separate to that, making a total payment of more than £5m. Earlier in the season, he was asked whether his players would receive bonuses for winning the title and replied: "I don't know if there is a clause (for players) and I don't tell you. They made a mistake if they didn't arrange it. I considered if I win the league."

But the club could afford to pay out as they would collect £93m in television money. They earned £72m for finishing 14th last season and the majority of the extra £21m is due to the league position. Each Premier League club receives £54m in TV money regardless of what position they finish in, with extras depending on factors such as final league position and the amount of times a team has been shown live on TV. Each team receives £880,000 for every one of their Premier League matches which is shown live on TV. Leicester had 16 matches broadcast across Sky and BT Sport, leaving them with an income of around £14m, £5.2m more than last season when just 10 of their games were shown live. They received £8.7m for finishing 14th last season, which rises to £25m if they win the league, which they are now expected to do. Leicester receive a huge financial boost for qualifying for the Champions League, merely by appearing in the groups stages they collect £30m in prize money and TV money. Additionally, their status as champions opens new doors for sponsorship and a stronger position renegotiating current deals.

The fans, though, will think he's worth every penny.

Ranieri might have to pay for a bottle of wine, though, following a hint by Albion coach Tony Pulis. After their unexpected draw at Spurs, Pulis said "I hope he buys me a nice bottle of red. I'm delighted for the players and also delighted for the league because it shows never mind where you are in this league you'll play against a team capable of having a go."

Ranieri, speaking on the TRT World News Channel, struggled to hold in his emotion after being shown a video of the fans thanking him. At first, he looked nervous about being shown the clip but was soon smiling as the people of the city expressed their love for him. He said: "No, no, I don't have an idea about that...No! I don't want to know...no, no, no! I do hope it is a good thing."

Then he was happy...

"Hello Claudio, I'm Vicky from Leicester Market and we've met before, we did have a selfie and I just want to say how fabulous you are and what you've done for the city is amazing, we all love you. I would literally hug you if you were here because for this city, what you've created, the family, the essence of the stadium, it's fantastic. Follow your hometown and believe. Leicester is a true testament that if you believe in your dreams, who knows where the fairytale takes you. We'd like to thank you very much for everything you've done for Leicester City Football Club since you came and we're all very proud and rooting for you and hope you manage to do it. Claudio, you've done amazing things for this club and we need you here in Leicester, you have to stay here. We've never seen anything like this before, it's incredible and thank you for everything you've done so far."

A slightly tearful Ranieri was clearly touched. He said: "Thank you, thank you so much, wonderful. I make this job because I am very, very happy when all the other fans are happy. All my sacrifice is this and I love this. I'm pleased you have given me this."

At his next press conference Ranieri added: "The video was amazing. Everybody wants to see me emotional, I know. Wait five more minutes and I will be an actor and cry for you."

Italy legend Alessandro Del Piero played under Ranieri at Juventus. He says their fairytale story proves that "nothing is impossible in sport. Leicester are ever closer to the Premier League title," the 41-year-old told Sky Evening News, "I really hope it ends the way we all hope it will, because this really is something to tell our grandchildren, it shows that nothing is impossible in sport."

Dino Zoff, the 1982 World Cup winner and former Juventus star keeper, was asked why Ranieri was known in his home near Rome as "Il Romano Inglese" - the English Roman. "He is of course very tied to this city - he was born here, grew up here, so it's natural it should be a big part of his identity," Zoff said. "But at the same time he has been able to go about things with a certain steeliness and focus which are perhaps not typically the most Roman characteristics! I used to play against him during our playing careers - he was a footballer, but as a manager one could perhaps say he has had a bit more success! In Italy, there is a tendency to over-analyse and over-complicate. To make football like a game of chess. He makes things clear and plain and that's a great gift. I, of course, don't want to jinx things because it's all still to play for, but they are doing brilliantly."

FIFA President Gianni Infantino hailed Leicester City's "fairytale" as an example of football's ability to delight with "beautiful stories" that proves cash is not always king. Surely no one knows more about cash matters than FIFA! "That's why we all love football, it's the magic of football. And fairytales like the fairytale of Leicester are exactly showing us that football is unpredictable," he told reporters. "Football brings us every year, everywhere in the world, these kind of beautiful stories." He was speaking in the King Power Pullman hotel in Thailand, part of a downtown complex including a mall owned by Vichai Srivaddhanaprabha.

Former owner Milan Mandarić, 77, who sold the then Championship club to Thai businessman Vichai Srivaddhanaprabha in 2010, was convinced the clubs success was sustainable. Well, he is 77! "Know-ing those people, they will go as high as possible - they're very ambitious people. They're not going to give up," he told BBC Radio Leicester. "It's now in their blood. It's not just the money any more - you're part of something you never dreamed of. It's just incredible feelings, that's what gives you rewards, not the money. He's got enough money for after Leicester, so I don't think those people will sell very soon. I don't think Leicester will be one of those one-offs - I think they'll continue and see what's possible. They're not going to let go. We get Man City, Man United, Chelsea, Arsenal - they are big clubs, powerful clubs, but mighty Leicester ignored all that. Everything I did there, I did with enthusiasm and whatever I did, I couldn't have done for better people than Leicester City."

Speaking exclusively to *The Independent*, Lineker denied ever promising to do the entire MOTD of the in his pants. "I certainly never said anywhere in that tweet that I would do the whole show," he said. It was certainly squeaky bum time at the business end of the season.

THURSDAY, 28 APRIL

SAUSAGES

W. Archer & Son Ltd, @Warcherandson - Many have tried but nobody can replace the delicious #Ranieri #sausage Order yours now and get free delivery on 3kg

The surge in demand from Leicester fans desperate to witness what could potentially be the greatest moment in their club's history was having outrageous consequences on ticket prices.

Tickets for the potential title party against Everton were offered online for a shameless and obscene £8,600. If Leicester won at Manchester United, they would be presented with the trophy following their match with Everton at the King Power Stadium.

Both home and away supporters were cashing in on the demand of Foxes fans to see this historic moment by selling their tickets on resale websites such as Ticketbis. An assortment of tickets were available on the website ranging from £321 for a seat in the away section to £8,594.53 for a premium seat on the halfway line. The face value of the tickets when officially on sale through the club was between £30 and £50 for adults.

In addition, a space in one of the executive boxes was offered for £13,220.22. Another website - Livefootballtickets - offered seats in the Everton section for between £299.25 and £617.50. Ticketbis was also acting as a reseller for fans offering up seats in the away end at Old Trafford for a pricey £1,850 each. Supporters who bought tickets for the title-decider through official channels paid between £46 and £55 for an adult ticket.

Tickets in the home section at Old Trafford were being sold for between £255.24 and £466.69, with United fans also willing to cash in given the enormous demand from Leicester fans. Both fixtures sold out through the official channels weeks ago.

The Premier League listed Ticketbis on its list of unauthorised ticket sellers and urged fans to 'exercise extreme caution' when buying through them.

NO VARDY AGAIN. NO WORRIES

Danny Simpson believed they would cope without Vardy once more, "I think we have just sent a message to everyone who has been a bit negative about us," the defender said of the Swansea win. "We have players who can come in and do well. Leo was man of the match and Jeff has come in and was excellent. Demarai Gray came on and what a cameo it was from him and Marc Albrighton as well. It is all about the squad. Yeah, we have had a settled team but we have always known the players who are trying to get in the team can do well. We will work hard this week and kick on and try and go for it. We have got our target now and we want to do it. The manager keeps setting us goals. It was safety - get 40 points. Then it was keep going, can we get into the Europa League? Can we get into the Champions League? Then, can we get into the Champions League group stage without playing a qualifier? Then the next thing was, 'Go on then, go for it now'."

Winning the title at Old Trafford would be particularly special for Simpson and Drinkwater, having both come through the United youth system. "Me and Drinky have spoken about it a little bit and said it is a big game. Whenever we are going to Old Trafford, for us it is a big game. We want to enjoy it and are looking forward to working hard this week and going to Old Trafford to try and perform again and get the three points."

When Tottenham faltered to a 1-1 draw with West Brom, Jeff Schlupp watched at home. "I was talking to some friends and thinking: 'We are literally one win away from a dream that I've had since I was young'. It is surreal at times. It is everyone's dream to grow up to play in the Premier League, never mind win it."

The morning after, Ranieri addressed his team. Schlupp says: "He did mention that it is now a reality and how close we were. It's not a secret any more: we're 90 minutes away."

Schlupp was injured when Leicester dismantled title favourites Manchester City at the Etihad in February but that game was the turning point. "I think that one showed everyone what level we're at. I think the players involved started to believe it - and that was the game for me, personally, that made me believe it. We looked like a proper team. And we just kicked on from then."

"Uninspired" Lineker might have been on Ranieri's appointment, but not the players when they heard the news on a pre-season training camp in Austria, prior to the public announcement, they were given the news. "We were all gathered in a room and he walked through and it was: 'Wow, it's Ranieri, he's a big name!' It was just excitement. For the club to go out and get such a high-calibre manager it showed where the club was going. And he's proved himself."

Ranieri told them he would build on their qualities by making small adjustments that would "transform" them. "It's never been a secret our target was to stay up but he almost just filled us with confidence again," continued Schlupp. "He said that he'd watched a lot of our games, that we were a lot better than where we were last season. And the lads felt good about it, from the first training session onwards it was just good vibes. He said the Italian philosophy is to defend and have a good shape and he just wanted to add a few things that he had used in the past and thought worked well. He said it would transform us as a team and that's what he's done."

Schlupp was dropped by Ranieri despite being players' player of the year last season. He began the Ranieri era at left-back but was moved to midfield when Ranieri introduced new full-backs Fuchs and Simpson in response to October's heavy defeat by Arsenal. Then Schlupp lost his place in midfield. "We lost against Arsenal and conceded five goals so the manager changed it. You take it on the chin. I think Danny Simpson's and Christian Fuchs's performances all season since they've come in have spoken for themselves. They've been fantastic. I look at how Christian plays at left-back and I'm learning off him. He's a top player, captain of his country, and he shows why. Danny is the same: he's had a great career with Premier League experience and he shows it when he plays. I've had a few chats with Ranieri, of course, and he says he wants to see me further up the field at left-midfield. I'm comfortable anywhere on the left-hand side so I'm willing to learn and listen to what he says. I'll go from there. Obviously he's an Italian manager and said the philosophy is to defend and have a good shape. It's obviously worked because we're at the top. On Tuesday we had a short meeting and he said that it's now a reality and how close we were (to winning the title). Everyone knows not to get carried away."

CHAMPIONS LEAGUE

The club are allowing fans to opt-in or out of cup games - a different tactic to Manchester United, who make purchase compulsory.

"I am glad the way they have done it," Foxes Trust chairman Ian Bason told *Sportsmail*. "Even though nobody will untick the box marked Champions League! We don't know what fee those games will carry but in general the club have been good on pricing so I don't think they will take the mickey. Just knowing what the owners have done for us before, it could cost the same as for Premier League games."

UEFA will require up to 30 commentary positions for Champions League games. The ground's gantry will have to be extended which will mean a move for some long-term season ticket holders in the East Stand. "I know four people who are having to leave seats they have had since day one and it is proving difficult getting them all sitting together elsewhere," added Bason. "The supporter liaison officer is sorting it, but it means they will lose neighbours and friendships formed over many years. It is the kind of impact that can happen."

European Cup winner Ronald Koeman forecasts some big surprises in the Champions Leagues if Ranieri can keep his star players. The Saints boss scored the Wembley winner for Barcelona in the 1992 European Cup Final, was a European champion with PSV Eindhoven in 1987 and Holland's national team a year later. He believes individuals like Mahrez, Vardy and Kanté are allied to an incredible tactical and worth ethic put in place by Ranieri. "With the spirit and power they have in the team, Leicester are not going to be shown up in Europe. In fact, they will do well in the Champions League, even though the bigger clubs of England will have a better chance than them. But that will depend on how many star players Leicester will lose in the summer transfer window. Transfers will definitely take place, but that's a massive compliment to the work that has been done by the club. And, for me, it is a big question whether Vardy would actually want to leave if a big club came in for him. Jamie has come from the very bottom part of the English league and I think, deep down in his heart, he would prefer to stay with Leicester for the rest of his career. He strikes me as someone who is grateful for what the club have done for him and he knows that it is not going to be easy in a different environment."

Koeman played behind Marco van Basten and Romário, so recognises the qualities of natural-born goalscorers, "Vardy is the man. The man for whom every chance is a goal. That is how I see him. I have not come across a striker who is as direct as Vardy. He does not make things complicated. He is focused on one way of finishing: everything on target."

Koeman rates Mahrez much better value for money than Sanchez and Hazard. "Mahrez has had a brilliant year. He forgets a bit of defensive work now and again, but who cares when you have an attacking player with so many goals and assists in a team? Mahrez has become footballer of the year, thanks to his massive contributions to the team. In my opinion, Hazard and Sanchez are, technically, the best players in English football. But Mahrez has been of more value to his team than them. In midfield, Kanté has been one of the best players in the Premier League. No other player knows how to put opponents under pressure like he does. Together with the clever Danny Drinkwater, who you can't get off the ball, he has been great."

Ranieri played to Leicester's strengths to hide their weaknesses. Koeman said: "The central defenders, Wes Morgan and Robert Huth, are so strong physically. Ranieri has worked things out in a clever way this season. There is no point making the centre-backs push up to the halfway line because they would be vulnerable, with too much space behind them. So, he has told them to stay compact and just defend. That is what they have done all year. Behind them is Kasper Schmeichel, who has been a great keeper, and also has a fantastic kick. He has supplied so much."

FRIDAY, 29 APRIL
#BACKINGTHEBLUES

The City of Leicester prepared to welcome the team home with Peter Soulsby, the Mayor of Leicester, hanging a 10ft Leicester scarf around the Liberty Statue. Soulsby said: "For too long, Leicester people have been modest about their achievements and the city they live in. Now, thanks to the Foxes' phenomenal season, it's our time to step into the international limelight. We are rightly proud of our football club and our city - and by Backing the Blues, we've got the chance to show it."

Thousands of fans supported the Backing the Blues campaign, led by the *Leicester Mercury* and BBC Radio Leicester. The campaign saw buildings in the city turning blue, people wearing blue for the day, offices and shops being decorated and fans using the hashtag #backingtheblues on social media.

Locals churned out commemorative pies, cakes and even two brand new brews - Vardy's Volley and Crowning Glory. Students and workers at Leicester College released 200 blue balloons, a pub reopened as the 'Blue Lion' for one day only, Dean of Leicester David Monteith was pictured in front of his cathedral as it flew a Foxes flag and the local paper - the *Leicester Mercury* - changed the colour of its masthead.

At Brü Coffee, baristas poured Foxiccinos and Vardyccinos, while businesses throughout the city turned blue. On Twitter the hashtag #backingtheblues showed just how much of an impact the Leicester story has had. Leicester Tigers posted a good luck message to their footballing cousins, while former Leicestershire cricketers Jonathan Agnew and Paul Nixon passed on their best wishes.

Estate agents, ice cream vendors, furniture shops and a branch of Marks & Spencer showed solidarity with their team, while restaurants and bars made a handful of special additions to their menus, including the cocktails 'No Fuchs Given' - a blend of Smirnoff, blue curacao, passionfruit, lime and apple - and 'Chat S**t Get Banged', a mix of vodka, plum wine, blue curacao, lemon juice, WKD syrup, plum bitter and caraway seeds.

World renowned chef, Marco Pierre White, who owns Marco Pierre White's New York Italian in the Mercure Leicester The Grand Hotel, pledged to cook a celebration meal for Ranieri and his team if they won. He was snapped holding a replica shirt.

Teachers and builders, gymnasts and shelf stackers, radio DJs and inpatients have all added their voices to the Foxes' charge towards the Premier League title.

From dusk on Friday, buildings including City Hall, Town Hall, the Clock Tower, John Lewis, the spire of the Cathedral and New Walk Museum will be lit up in blue to support Leicester City. They will remain that way until the end of the season.

Good Morning Britain, the breakfast programme on ITV, showed their support with presenters Ben Shepherd and Kate Garraway donning blue and white wigs. Film star Mads Mikkelsen wore the wig with Leicester's colours during his appearance.

KASABIAN

Kasabian planned a gig inside the King Power Stadium at the end of May to celebrate the club's incredible season, performing in front of 30,000 fans.

Serge Pizzorno, one of the band's guitarists and also a songwriter, and lead singer Tom Meighan, announced their plans. "There's such an energy in the city at the minute," Pizzorno told the *Leicester Mercury*, "In a way it feels like we're almost centre of the universe. Everyone is watching. No matter how it goes, we're going to need a place to all stand together and reflect on what's happened, because it is just unbelievable. In the stadium, with us playing the music. There is no better way. We're so proud."

The Foxes booked their place in the Champions League and that excites Meighan. "It's been a lot to take in. We're just praying. I think we're everyone's second favourite team in the world. It's not Barcelona anymore, or Real Madrid, it's Leicester City. Even Arsenal fans want us to win. Whatever happens, this city has been on one hell of a trip. Back from the brink of relegation...from that point, when we survived, it's just been amazing."

Serge told *Newsbeat* that he isn't necessarily writing a song about the season but it was inspiring their new material. "It's bound to in some way seep into the music you know. In some ways because it has been such a big six months. I'm in the studio at the moment experimenting. It's inevitable that creatively it will rub off on you in some way." He added that they were planning to play a concert at the King Power Stadium in 2017 but, after watching the recent Swansea game, decided they needed to move the gig forward. "It's been a mad couple of days and we've managed, with the club, to make this happen this season. This has been an unbelievable year for the city and it seemed like the perfect thing to do in the summer. We can't wait to throw the city the greatest party they have ever seen."

In the past he watched the Foxes from hotel rooms across the world while on tour. "We've had a clear run and we've been able to watch most games and been down to the ground. We'd have been devastated if we had been away for all of this and not experience what is going on in the city of ours. It's mental. Riyad Mahrez is a player after my own heart. He is so silky. I'd give up playing in the band to play upfront this season. Just not when we were in the first division. You can have that, but this season yes."

Newsbeat asked him if he was worried that the club would struggle to repeat this year's success. "I couldn't care less about any other seasons forever more. This is unbelievable, it will never happen again."

John Bennett, BBC World Service - Visiting my dad, who has watched Leicester City since 1958. "Would Riyad Mahrez get in your all-time team?" I asked. "Probably on the bench," he replied. Tough crowd.

BBC *Leicester Sport* reported on the latest press conference:

He remains calm as always. "(The fans) start to enjoy but you know me - I'm a pragmatic man. We need three points more. I watch the players make the same training session. They're very concentrated."

He describes Vardy as "Leicester's RAF". The top scorer and Matty James were the only players unavailable, so will the manager tinker? "I have a lot of choice. I have 24 players. Maybe I change everything. The Tinkerman never change. It's important to have strength of the mind. Now is the real chance to win the title. Next season you never know what happens. Once in a life. Next season, United, Chelsea, Liverpool, City, Arsenal are at the top. But we are fighting. I have felt a lot of emotion."

Ranieri challenged his players to produce a Hollywood ending, in a once-in-a-life-time chance to be champions but it would require their best away performance of the season to clinch the trophy at The Theatre of Dreams.

There was always plenty of humour in these media gatherings. "I'm waiting for all the stadium to chant 'DILLY DING DILLY DONG!'. Why not?" said Ranieri, who also confirmed that his favourite Kasabian song is *Fire*.

"People are waiting for us on the street and the supermarket and at the training ground. They say, 'Thank you for what you are doing.' I think they have to say thank you to our chairman, he is building a very good team. It is not difficult to understand this. It is easy. For the first time in their lives, the people can win the league. It is unbelievable. History. And we know it. It is good we are doing something special. And of course I am very proud for everybody in Leicester, for our community. Internet, web, media, there is a good feeling about this story."

Ranieri felt Kasper Schmeichel should no longer be compared to his father Peter. Kasper was close to completing only the second set of father-and-son Premier League champions (after Ian Wright and Shaun Wright-Phillips) with victory on the same Old Trafford pitch his old man graced. Ranieri said: "I think it's so the right moment not to speak about his father. Kasper Schmeichel is a fantastic player, a fantastic keeper, with his own personality and he deserves this. For me he was never in this shadow. For this reason I say, 'Finish! Stop' (talking about his dad)!" Asked about reports of a move to Barca, Ranieri quipped: "It's fantastic - how much money?! Or we can change Lionel Messi with Kasper!"

PARTY POSTPONED

Louis van Gaal, meanwhile, planned to 'postpone' Leicester City's party as he reminded everyone that he was the first to suggest they could land the title. "We have to beat them because we are still in the (top four) race. We cannot allow them to be champions this weekend at Old Trafford. They shall be champions a week later. We don't spoil the party, only postpone it a little bit. Now we are fighting for the Champions League and still in the FA Cup. We have to fight for something and we shall do it. Hopefully we can beat Leicester City."

"They showed great character, commitment and passion," added Juan Mata. "They are really close to doing it. But hopefully it doesn't happen at Old Trafford. They can wait another week." He added: "It is good for football in a way because it is a little bit of fresh air. But my wish is that we were winning the league."

SATURDAY, 30 APRIL

DIVINE INTERVENTION

Club chaplain Andrew Hulley was helping the Foxes squad with spiritual guidance for a squad that had a renowned spirit already. He offers the players pre-match prayers "to help keep them focused and more mindful." Rev Hulley told *The Mirror*: "The players are embracing the spirituality, no matter their faith, and it's helping their game. They think they can win the title, so do I. Prayers help settle them before a game. They are so fantastic. They play with soul, with heart, with blood. I'm very proud of them." Vardy enjoys sharing a joke with the Reverend, "Jamie's a joker. Whenever he sees me he comes over and says 'Father forgive me, I have sinned.'"

No doubt he would agree that the team will become 'The Immortals'!

With top scorer Vardy suspended, Mahrez would be the main man again.

In an interview in France, the 25-year-old French-born Algerian international recalled a 10-week trial with St Mirren around 2007 which failed to work out because he could not stand the climate. "An agent paid for my ticket to Scotland and I travelled over with my Sarcelles team-mate Dany Bekele. It went well at first. I played four friendly matches and scored seven goals. But they made me wait - for two-and-a-half months. Scotland drove me crazy. It was cold and physical. One day it was so cold that I feigned an injury to go back into the dressing room. I felt I had progressed enough but I wasn't able to leave - so I left in secret. I even left my boots at the training ground. I borrowed a bike from a guy at the hotel and packed my bags without telling anyone. I didn't even tell the lady at the hotel. I took a secret staircase which avoided the reception and went to the airport to go home!"

Mahrez trained with Saints' development squad, but moved to Quimper in France before switching to Le Havre, then in Ligue 2 where he was spotted by Leicester scout Steve Walsh, who persuaded Pearson to splash out £450,000 to take him to England in 2014. Mahrez did not want to sign for Leicester because he thought they were a rugby club. "At the start, I said to myself: 'I will never go'. My agents said: 'Are you mad or what? It is a crazy club Leicester.' I thought it was a rugby club. I swear to you. I had seen the Leicester scout and I said to my mates: 'Never will I go there'. A week later, my agents tried again. They said to me: 'Oh! Riyad. They really want you. Go and see the stadium on the internet.' They insisted and next day I had a look. And I said, OK, that is alright. And I felt that Le Havre didn't want to keep me. They were top of the Championship in England. I said to myself it was better to be first with them than tenth with Le Havre. I signed for a good salary for a player in Ligue 1."

Ranieri sends out his players with words: "Be smart, you are foxes".

"The manager let's us get on with it," Mahrez said. "Except once at half-time against Newcastle. Then he shouted at us. Otherwise, he likes to laugh. In training, he has fun all the time. Less on match days. Then he is concentrated on the job. I try to joke with him, tell him he is late, laugh at his shoes, but even if he smiles, he says to me: 'Oh, oh, concentrate on the match.' His thing is to tell us: 'Be smart, you are foxes'. In Algeria we have the fennec fox as our national emblem. You have to be cunning."

Mahrez was voted PFA Player of the Year. "It made me really proud," he told L'Equipe Magazine.

"I was expecting it a bit because everyone was saying I was going to get the vote but there is always a bit of doubt inside you. I still haven't won anything. I saw that John Terry voted for me. It is flattering. He has won everything. Last year, at Chelsea, he had killed me. He read all my dribbling. This year, against them, I scored and I made an assist. Here you don't lose your marking. You go and drink some water and they follow you!"

Robbie Savage in his Daily Mirror column: "Part of me hopes Leicester don't win the title at Old Trafford on Sunday, but instead lift the trophy in front of their own fans at the King Power next weekend. Jamie Vardy, who is suspended, deserves to be on the pitch when they clinch the deal because he has been such a catalyst for the most incredible football story of them all.

But if they plant a blue flag at the Premier League summit, and copy Arsenal in 2002 by being crowned champions on Manchester United's turf, it will not just be about Vardy, Riyad Mahrez and N'Golo Kanté. Leicester's triumph will be a tribute to a supporting cast who held firm when the pressure was intense. I'm thinking here about the likes of goalkeeper Kasper Schmeichel, set to follow in the footsteps of his father 17 years after his dad won the last of his five titles with United. Kasper didn't even keep a clean sheet until 24 October - but he has marshalled 15 shut-outs in the 26 games since then. That's a remarkable record. No complaints from me that David De Gea was voted No.1 keeper in the PFA Premier League Team of the Year, but Schmeichel and Tottenham's Hugo Lloris cannot have been far behind in the poll.

Every title-winning side has a solid defensive block, and in front of Schmeichel, no centre-half pairing has been more resolute than Wes Morgan and Robert Huth. When they needed to keep their nerve on the run-in, Leicester kept five consecutive clean sheets, including four 1-0 wins in a row. Morgan has been a fantastic captain, but Leicester's results on their astonishing catapult from bottom of the table to champions in the space of 12 months can be traced back to Huth's arrival from Stoke for just £3million. In the Premier League, the Foxes have won 28 and drawn 13 of their 48 games with Huth - who was there on loan for the second half of last season - in the side, keeping 21 clean sheets. The German has been immense, and that partnership with Morgan will now go down with Tony Adams and Steve Bould at Arsenal, or Chelsea's John Terry and Ricardo Carvalho and United's Rio Ferdinand and Nemanja Vidić as a title-winning double act at the heart of their side. I have also been hugely impressed with Danny Drinkwater in midfield, while Marc Albrighton has been an unsung hero providing width and crosses into the box and Christian Fuchs has been a revelation at left-back.

But, looking back, the moment I sensed Leicester were going to win the title was when Leonardo Ulloa - another unsung member of their back-up cast - popped up with a last-gasp winner against Norwich on 27 February. They had been frustrated all afternoon. Norwich had closed down the supply lines to Mahrez and Vardy like a team fighting for their lives needs to, and it looked like Leicester were going to drop important points at home at a time when Arsenal looked like their nearest challengers. But Ulloa found the way through, and that convinced me Claudio Ranieri had a squad who could keep their nerve all the way to the winning post.

It's going to be absolutely incredible if Leicester finish the job on Sunday afternoon. I thought the Leicester team who won the League Cup twice under Martin O'Neill would go down as legends - but this is something else."

Sportsmail's Carragher, Keown and Redknapp, were asked to describe Leicester in just three words:

KEOWN: The people's champions.

REDKNAPP: Miraculous. Inspirational. Team.

CARRAGHER: Never happen again.

Jamie Vardy was informed he will be allowed to celebrate on the Old Trafford pitch if his team win the title despite being suspended. An FA source told *The Sun*: "If he is banned for the game we don't see any reason why he wouldn't be allowed on the pitch after the final whistle."

Barclays Premier League Table at the end of April 2016:

POS	CLUB	P	W	D	L	GF	GA	GD	PTS
1	Leicester City	35	22	10	3	63	33	30	76
2	Tottenham Hotspur	35	19	12	4	65	26	39	69
3	Arsenal	36	19	10	7	59	34	25	67
4	Manchester City	35	19	7	9	66	34	32	64

MAY 2016

SUNDAY, 1 MAY

MANCHESTER UNITED 1-1 LEICESTER CITY

BBC Sport online, Sky Sports, and social media, follow the action from all angles and the build-up is immense...

Chris Forryan, *Leicester Till I Die* supporters' group: "Kenneth Wolstenholme once said during 'that' game of football - "They think it's all over." Well by later on this afternoon it could be. Leicester City could be Premier League Champions. Never did I think I would write that particular sentence. But the past three seasons have been amazing for Leicester City.

2013-14 – Championship Champions breaking numerous club & league records

2014-15 – The Great Escape.

2015-16 – Possible Premier League Champions.

If it happens I am sure there will be tears of joy and I am sure my mates will remind me of it often - but I don't care. It has been a long wait."

Danny Murphy, ex-Liverpool midfielder on *Football Focus*: "For me it is most incredible story. In my life time it is the biggest and best, and probably will be for years and years to come."

Gary Neville, ex-Manchester United: "Imagine going to OT in May and knowing the title can be won in a United v Leicester game yet not by United. The most Incredible story!"

Simon Hare, @SimonHareBBC – "Excitement building inside the KP Stadium as well as at Old Trafford as #LCFC fans gather to watch #LCFCvMUFC on TVs."

Claudio Ranieri, speaking to Sky Sports: "I feel good but we know this will be a tough match. Manchester United are fighting for the Champions League. I ask my players for the same performance, we do not want to change our mind set. I am curious to see if my players feel something different, I hope not but it is important to check. My message to them will be to play the same, I am very excited. The story is fantastic."

Gary Lineker, @GaryLineker - "It's supposed to be enjoyable isn't it? Excruciating watch, but a massive point!"

So, it was two points from the title after holding Manchester United to a draw at Old Trafford, meaning it could be all over on Monday if Spurs fail to beat Chelsea at Stamford Bridge.

After going behind only eight minutes into the game, when the unmarked Martial at the far post drilled home a shot through the keeper's legs from Valencia's cross, the team again showed their resilience to stage a fighting comeback, a hallmark of their entire season, to emerge from adversity.

A measure of that mentality, to never give up, is illustrated in the impressive stat that they lost only one of the last 10 Premier League games in which they have conceded first and that was back in December against Liverpool.

Martial's goal was the first Leicester had conceded in the opening 10 minutes of their top-flight fixtures this season, and with United dominating in those early exchanges you feared for them, but they came back so strongly by the second half they were the superior team until once again reduced to 10-men. The Foxes lost just one of the last five top-flight games in which they have had a player sent off.

Captain Wes Morgan outmuscled Marcos Rojo to head the equaliser just nine minutes after United took the lead. Drinkwater notched his seventh Premier League assist - only Milner (11), Alli (9) and Barkley (8) had more among English players in 2015-16.

Rojo blocked off Mahrez and kicked out at him which should have been a penalty, while Drinkwater was sent off late on after receiving a second yellow card for dragging back substitute Memphis Depay, with referee Michael Oliver ruling it was right on the edge of the area, when the replay showed it was on the line and should have been a penalty.

WE'RE WAITING FOR YOU

Leicester's army of travelling fans celebrated long and loud after the final whistle after their team hung on grimly with 10-men, inflicting a blow to United's hopes of qualifying for the Champions League.

Van Gaal gave Ranieri a warm hug and a smile at the final whistle, with the Sky Sports microphones picking up their conversation, the sporting Dutch coach telling the Italian "to enjoy", with Ranieri responding, "I hope I enjoy!"

The fans applauded Leicester's players as they made their way to the dressing room as the final drama moved onto the next stage at the Bridge. "Tottenham Hotspur, we're waiting for you!" was the chant. There was also a rendition of "We're gonna win the league! And now you're gonna believe us!" Owner Vichai Srivaddhanaprabha was down on the pitch in front of his own fans, to give a thumbs up to the travelling supporters.

Vardy greeted every player as they come off the pitch, a handslap and shake per man as they trooped past him.

RANIERI TO MISS SPURS GAME

Ranieri when pressed insisted he was on a flight back from Italy so was unlikely to be able to watch Tottenham game. Later it emerged he was visiting his mother to take her for lunch. "I'd like to watch the Tottenham match but I'm on a flight back from Italy. My mother is 96 years old and I would like to have a lunch with her. I will be the last man in England to know."

Simpson said the players would be watching to see if Tottenham slip up. "We'll try to get together tomorrow and watch the game. We'll see what happens."

Ranieri expected Spurs to prolong Leicester's wait. If Spurs won at Stamford Bridge for the first time since February 1990, then Leicester could secure the title by beating Everton next Saturday. "In my mind, Tottenham will win all three matches. I am now focused on the Everton match. We must continue to concentrate."

Of the match he said: "The performance was good after the first 15 minutes, when we were a little scared. United started very well and it was difficult for us to restart. After the goal we played better and I think the draw is the right result. I wasn't worried because we have very good heart and I knew we would react. The goal maybe gave us more confidence slowly - without Jamie Vardy, it's difficult for us. Marouane Fellaini kicked Robert Huth and it wasn't a good show from him. For us it was important to show our mentality - the beginning wasn't good but after that I appreciated our performance. For us it's important to continue to work. I met Louis van Gaal in 1994 - he said to me good luck."

Chris Forryan, *Leicester Till I Die* supporters' group: "I am physically drained, But would I have taken that result at kick-off? Too true. 1-1 with 10 men away to Man Utd. It's over to Chelsea now. But I have this nagging feeling it may go down to the last game. It's still ours to lose though and Spurs will have watched that today and feel gutted we didn't lose. Overall United were the better team and when we went behind so early I feared the worst. But we stood tall and the Manchester United fans in the pub said go and win it against Everton."

Gary Lineker, @GaryLineker - One more win. Make it happen. #fearless

Andy King, @10_kingy - Another point in the right direction. Big thanks for the support again!!

Sky Sports, straight-talking, pundit Graeme Souness was "in awe" of the team and felt their performance typified the Foxes' season. "It's incredibly hard to be anything other than utterly complimentary about this team. How many Leicester players at the end of last season were negotiating clauses in their contracts in case they qualified for the Champions League, or won the Premier League? None of them! Their bonus would have been for avoiding relegation. It's really hard not to be totally in awe of this team. It was a typical Leicester performance today. They've ended up with 30 percent possession yet, watching the game, it didn't feel like that. They've come to one of the world's greatest football stadiums today and were not intimidated. They went a goal behind and showed real character and togetherness to get back into it. Somehow they come up with a way of getting a result. United were fabulous for a good half an hour but after that Leicester came back. The so-called smaller team fell behind to the bigger team but, to a man, none of them threw the towel in. You could see them grinding themselves back into the game and in the second half, they were the better team. That 90 minutes typifies what Leicester's season has been all about. When adversity comes, they deal with it. Somehow they come up with a way of getting a result."

Spurs now needed to win at the Bridge but Chelsea 'interim manager', Guus Hiddink, doubted that they had what it takes to land the title. "They experience now being at the top. I'm not too much in statistics, but it's the first time in their history they're now in the end competing for the title. In some players it might cause nerves, they might underperform a bit. Leicester are fearless but some (Tottenham) players might be affected by being on top and think: 'What now?'"

Fàbregas and Hazard had previously stated they don't want Spurs to succeed them as champions. Hiddink said: "We have not to over-evaluate it in the sense it is just Tottenham. We desperately like to win then next game and then we have massive games against Sunderland and Leicester. The players don't need to be told, whether playing Spurs now or another team in the future. If we lose to Tottenham, we might come under some scrutiny. It says Chelsea were very strong in the past playing Tottenham at Stamford Bridge and hope we can do similar. I cannot give a guarantee of the result but I can guarantee effort will be there. They must finish it (the season) in an honourable way."

Gary Lineker, @GaryLineker - Met Claudio Ranieri after the game. He said "Gary, I don't want to see you do MOTD in your pants." Yes you do, Claudio.

MONDAY, 2 MAY

Jamie Vardy was chosen as the Football Writers' Association (FWA) Footballer of the Year. The vote was split between three Leicester heroes with Vardy edging it with 36% of the vote from 290 journalists, ahead of Mahrez and Kanté. Vardy's new record of scoring 11 games in a row clinched it. The last time two different players from the same club won both the main awards of the season was 2004-05 when John Terry (PFA) and Frank Lampard (FWA) were the winners.

The FA were taking no further action against Danny Drinkwater despite some reports that he appeared to swear at referee Michael Oliver as he left the pitch.

Alan Smith in his *Daily Telegraph* column: "When it comes to comparisons with his father, Kasper Schmeichel can sometimes get a bit touchy. He wants to stand on his own two feet, be judged on his merits rather than always be referred to as the son of Peter, one of the greatest goalkeepers to ever grace this game.

But Kasper is also intelligent. He knows that a childhood largely spent watching his dad winning league titles forms a significant part of his character now. Not surprisingly, then, that make-up is solid. Just like his dad, Kasper has turned into a leader of men, even if he doesn't tend to rip into his own defenders with quite the same force.

Nevertheless, Schmeichel junior has developed into a dominant personality within the Leicester City squad. More importantly, he has also turned into a very fine keeper, more than worthy of a title medal to emulate his dad. Fifteen clean sheets in the league have included some excellent saves requiring sharp reflexes and good agility. Trailing 1-0 with United looking sharper and hungrier than they have for most of this season, Schmeichel dropped down to his left to deny Jesse Lingard. The keeper probably saw it quite late, too, seeing as the cleanly struck shot fizzed through Robert Huth's legs. A big moment that, as was the incident when Danny Simpson tangled with Lingard, and the Stretford End howled for Simpson to be sent off. Under the circumstances, it was easy to overlook Schmeichel's part in this. Reacting quickly, he charged out of his penalty area to bail out his right-back with a decisive swipe of the boot.

Once over the line as a celebrated winner, people might stop wittering on about the connection... whilst the United legend was famous for those bowls of the arm to launch attacks with a huge throw, Kasper's neat footwork is capable of achieving the same. Against Swansea, he clipped one out to Jeffrey Schlupp that led to Leicester's third goal. At Old Trafford, he cut across a volley from his hands to confidently find Riyad Mahrez. Jamie Vardy has also benefitted from such accurate service. More generally, Leicester have profited from a commanding presence that forms the base of a no-nonsense defence. On such foundations, titles are built."

Harry Redknapp in his *Daily Telegraph* column: "If this season threatens to prove anything, it's that teams can be successful without always trying to dominate the ball. Leicester City have the lowest passing accuracy in the Premier League and are third bottom when it comes to possession. Atletico Madrid's possession rates are relatively low, and in the Championship, Burnley could get promoted back to the top flight on Monday and you won't see them hogging the ball...at odds with the possession based model that I think we've got carried away with at times simply because of what Barcelona have achieved.

Leicester and the others have helped to remind people that there's another very effective way of winning. There's a danger that we've got hung-up on pass, pass, pass but you've got to go somewhere, there's got to be an end product to that passing. Leicester only had 30 per cent possession against United. But no team has made more tackles in the Premier League this season and no side has committed fewer errors in the lead up to the opposition scoring.

It also shows you that you don't have to be a certain type of manager to be successful. You can do things your way that may be different from others. It's incredible what Claudio Ranieri has done although you do go back to last year when they were the best team in the league for the last 10 games under Nigel Pearson and they've carried on this season. There's a touch of the 'Crazy Gang' spirit about them. I know last season when they stayed up they had a party in the West End and I heard they celebrated a bit like the Wimbledon of old. They've become the team no one wants to play. Opponents know they are going to be worked and worked, that it's going to be a long, tough day against them. It's nice to see that they're not the only ones having success playing that way."

OVER TO YOU TOTTENHAM

Sinead O'Connor was at No. 1 with 'Nothing Compares 2 U', Nelson Mandela was still waiting to be released from jail and Sir Alex Ferguson hadn't won anything yet at Manchester United, the last time Spurs won at Chelsea. And oh yes, guess who got the winner? Yep, Gary Lineker. A 2-1 win in 1990 adding to David Howells' earlier effort. Nayim crossed from the left, Lineker rose inside the six-yard box and nodded past Dave Beasant.   The run of 25 consecutive league games without a victory at Chelsea is the longest non-winning away run of consecutive games by one team at another team in the English top division. Chelsea fans planned a banner at the Bridge, reading: "26 years - don't let it be you".

Eden Hazard's remark that Spurs wanted Ranieri's men to finish top, didn't go down too well with his Belgium team-mate Mousa Dembélé, who believed the 25-year-old made his comments after seeing Chelsea throw away any chance of retaining the title. "He is not the type of person to normally make those types of comments or to envy other people's success," Dembélé told *The Sun*. "I'm wondering whether he said that stuff because it is what he really thinks, or whether he was just talking for the sake of it. But I won't pay too much heed to his comments and those from Cesc Fàbregas, who has said similar things. People come up to me in the street and say 'Did you hear what Hazard said? What's his problem?' I will have a word with Eden before the game, although I will make a joke of it. I won't conduct a half-hour interview with him."

Gary Lineker, @GaryLineker - I'm so excited tonight I could pull Fellaini's hair.

Pochettino, speaking to Sky Sports: "It's a game we must win, this is true, we want to be alive in the title race. There is no other option. We need to play our game. We know it's very important."

Should Spurs fail to win, then Leicester would be the 12th team to win the title without playing since the war.

WHO'S WATCHING THE GAME?

According to reports, Leicester's players will gather at the home of newly-crowned FWA Footballer of the Year Jamie Vardy, who has a £1million eight-bedroom mansion in Melton Mowbray, 15 miles from the city. A 'Vardy Party' in fact.

"I think we have got to watch it," said midfielder Marc Albrighton. "I don't think we can ignore this one. I didn't watch last week (when Spurs drew at home to West Bromwich Albion), but I think when there is a chance to win the league, like this week, we have all got to watch it. I think we will probably spend the night all together."

WHERE'S CLAUDIO?

Claudio Ranieri had claimed that he will miss the momentous fixture because he is returning from a brief trip to Rome to have lunch with his 96-year-old mother, Renata. However, not long before kick-off Pat Murphy, BBC Radio 5 live Midlands football reporter, stated: "The latest news we have got is that Claudio Ranieri touched down a couple of minutes ago at East Midlands Airport. That's a long way from Stamford Bridge. Even though Ranieri has a home in Knightsbridge, maybe he is going to his flat in Leicester to watch the game."

Gary Lineker, @GaryLineker - Never thought I'd not want Spurs to beat Chelsea. Feel like I'm being unfaithful in a way, but this will never, ever happen again.

The streets were deserted, but living rooms, pubs and clubs, and Vardy's house were packed…

THE GAME

Spurs raced into a 2-0 half time lead as first, Harry Kane rounded the keeper to put Tottenham ahead, and then Son Heung-min's low strike doubled their advantage. In pubs and clubs around Leicester, including the 'Vardy Party', the mood was sombre.

However, it was the introduction of Eden Hazard after the break which changed Chelsea's fortunes and provided reason for optimism amongst Leicester fans. The Belgian created the spark and gave Chelsea an incisiveness which had previously been missing. Then, on 58 minutes, a corner was not cleared by Tottenham and Cahill tucked it away.

Chelsea now appeared 'fearless' and Leicester had hope…

The game was becoming extremely open, tempers were fraying, and the minutes were ticking away for Chelsea, as well as for Leicester fans around the globe. And then it happened…a Chelsea break away in the 83rd minute was beautifully finished by Hazard's brilliant, curling first-time shot into the top-right corner. We were only minutes away from sporting history…added time, agonisingly punctuated with yellow cards, dragged on and on, until after 7 minutes Mark Clattenburg blew the final whistle - cue pandemonium and unbridled joy amongst followers of Leicester City!

'Vardy's Party' erupted, champagne corks popped, fans danced in jubilation, car horns echoed around the streets, and disbelief turned to tears of realisation. Leicester City were now **the Champions of England!**

Barclays Premier League Table at the end of April 2016:

POS	CLUB	P	W	D	L	GF	GA	GD	PTS
C	Leicester City	36	22	11	3	64	34	30	77
2	Tottenham Hotspur	36	19	13	4	67	28	39	70
3	Arsenal	36	19	10	7	59	34	25	67
4	Manchester City	36	19	7	10	68	38	30	64

SOMETHING SPECIAL WAS TRENDING

Leicester City, @LCFC - Leicester City. Champions of England.

Gary Lineker, @GaryLineker - Leicester City have won the Premier League. The biggest sporting shock of my lifetime, and it's only my team.

Christian Fuchs, @FuchsOfficial - CHAMPIONS!!!!

Riyad Mahrez, @Mahrez22 - CHAMPIONS !!!!! thank u everyone !!!

Andy King, @10_kingy - From League 1 to Premier League Champions!! Unbelievable feeling.

Premier League, @premierleague - "It's an extraordinary achievement - the most incredible story of the century" - former @LCFC boss Martin O'Neill

Premier League, @premierleague - John Terry: "I'm 100% pleased for Claudio. He's different class and a great person - credit to him and the players"

Premier League, @premierleague - "It's the greatest achievement in the history of our game, it's unprecedented" - Jamie Carragher on @LCFC

Premier League, @premierleague - Has there ever been a sporting story to match Leicester's journey?

Leicester City, @LCFC - Jamie Vardy is #havingaparty!

Leicester City, @LCFC - So, anyone else #havingaparty tonight?

Sergio Kun Agüero, @aguerosergiokun - Congratulations are due for Leicester City, deserving champions of the Premier League!

Mario Balotelli, @FinallyMario - Leicester city.. champion. Congratulations to the players and to an amazing manager as RANIERI!

Vincent Kompany, @VincentKompany - Congratulations to the new Champions of England, Leicester City. Respect.

Gary Lineker, @GaryLineker - Yes! Just Yes! Leicester City are champions!

Mark Austin, @markaustinitv - Things you don't want to hear from your wife." When is @GaryLineker doing that programme in his underwear"?

Kasper Schmeichel, an ever-present in the Premier League, also took to Twitter: "Words cannot describe the love I have for my team-mates. I dreamt of this since I was a boy and I will be forever grateful to you all."

Leicester captain Wes Morgan: "It's the best feeling of my career and I couldn't be prouder that it's as part of this team. Everyone's worked so hard for this, nobody believed we could do it, but here we are, Premier League champions and deservedly so. I've never known a spirit like the one between these boys, we're like brothers. People saw it last season when everyone expected us to be relegated, but we fought back to prove people wrong. This season's been a continuation of that. We've built on the momentum, but I don't think anyone believed it would come to this. Saturday can't come quickly enough. I can't wait to get my hands on the trophy."

Match of the Day pundit Alan Shearer said Leicester's achievement was "the biggest thing ever in football". Shearer, who won the Premier League in 1995 with underdogs Blackburn, told BBC Sport: "For a team like Leicester to come and take the giants on with their wealth and experience - not only take them on but to beat them - I think it's the biggest thing to happen in football."

Mauricio Pochettino began his first TV interview: "First of all I congratulate Leicester and Claudio Ranieri and his players and supporters."

He went on: "Disappointed because I thought we fought to be in the race. At 2-0 up in the first half, in the second half we have to counter and score the third but this happens. When we conceded the first goal anything can happen. Very disappointed but at the same time very proud of my players. It was a derby and we were fighting for the title and Chelsea were fighting. It makes us feel proud how Chelsea show big respect to us and this is the way we want to carry on next season. We respect them, we have full respect for them. It's football, we are men, they are men we need to show we are strong. It was a good lesson for us, we are the youngest squad in the league, we feel very proud and our supporters need to feel proud too, we have massive potential for the future. We are disappointed because of the title but we need to be realistic and congratulate our players. Next season we need to be more stronger than this season and try to be in the race."

Eden Hazard, speaking to Sky Sports: "It's always good to score in front of our fans. This game was very important for Chelsea. We deserved the draw. I don't care who is champions. Leicester deserve to be champions. It's good for the Premier League."

Chelsea captain John Terry: "Players are fighting for league titles, it's emotions. Congratulations to Leicester because they have been superb this year. It still hurts us tonight losing the league after winning it last year. We weren't here to beat Tottenham and stop them doing it, it hurts us conceding it to Leicester but we will be back next year. It boiled over let's not get silly and start banning people, it's a London derby and the fans want to see it. (Ranieri) has been different class, to do what they have done has been unbelievable and given hope to the smaller sides. He's a great manager and a great person. All season long they have kept churning out results."

Leicester City won the Premier League title described on the BBC as "one of the greatest sporting stories of all time".

Robert Huth has now won three Premier League titles. Some of the players who have also won three Premier League titles include Dennis Bergkamp, Cristiano Ronaldo, Patrick Vieira, Ashley Cole, Carlos Tevez and Jonny Evans.

Tinkerman! What Tinkerman? Leicester used the same team on 13 occasions: Albrighton, Drinkwater, Fuchs, Huth, Kanté, Mahrez, Morgan, Okazaki, Schmeichel, Simpson and Vardy. No title winners used as settled a side since 1993, when Manchester United named the same team on 17 occasions.

Fuchs posted a video showing the moment his uncontrollable team-mates became champions. The footage, uploaded to his Twitter account, was recorded as the players watched the match live in Vardy's kitchen, and fans gathered outside to celebrate. Sky Sports cameras were also inside Vardy's home to film the jubilation as the Leicester players embraced each other and jumped up and down cheering. Prior to kick-off all the players arrived two-by-two to Vardy's home in Melton Mowbray, met by fans who stood in the rain cheering outside.

Jamie Vardy was having a party: "It's an unbelievable feeling, I've never known anything like it. We were scrapping to stay in the league last season and on Saturday we'll be lifting the trophy. That gives you an idea of how much hard work has gone into this season from every single player and member of staff. It's the biggest achievement in the history of a great club and we all feel privileged to be part of it. It's even more special to have done it with these lads. Every minute of hard work we've put in on the training pitch has been worth it for this moment."

Andy King: "I thought I'd seen everything with this club, but I never thought I'd see this. It's difficult to put into words. The players deserve it, the gaffer and the staff deserve it, and the fans deserve it. It's been an unbelievable season.

The story of where this team has come from to get to this point has been all over the world recently and I think the lads deserve great credit for the way they've taken it in their stride, stayed focused and kept delivering results - especially with a great side like Spurs chasing us so hard. We've been so consistent and just determined not to let the opportunity pass us by. We deserve this."

Leicester East MP Keith Vaz said: "This is a miracle which has captured the imagination of the sporting world and beyond. People in every corner of the globe now know where Leicester is."

Former Foxes manager Martin O'Neill, who led the club to their previous highest Premier League finish of eighth in 2000, said: "Not only is it a brilliant story, but it gives everyone that little bit of hope again. That romance has not left football. It's been the talk of Europe, there's no question about that. Everything about this season has been remarkable."

Guus Hiddink could have been in charge of Leicester as the club wanted him before they appointed Ranieri, but he needed a break from management after being dismissed as Holland boss. "It is true Leicester asked me for this season," the Dutchman told Telesport. "But I had decided it was time for a rest, and I wanted to just do nothing."

Ranieri contacted Hiddink after the conclusion of the match at Stamford Bridge to thank the Dutchman for ending Tottenham's title bid. Hiddink said of the phone call: "Just after the final whistle, a few minutes after the 'judo', I got a call from Ranieri. He thanked us especially for what we did in the second half and I congratulated him for being champions. They deserved it. It may be a bit of a shock for the established clubs that they did so well. They didn't implode, there was no tension when they started smelling the title. I didn't see any tears because it was not a FaceTime conversation but his voice was trembling a bit. He said five times 'thanks'. His emotion was going up."

Gary Lineker posted: "Extraordinary. I am so emotional, it looked like it was going to next Saturday but I can't get my head around it. I can't think of anything that surpasses it in sporting history. It is difficult to put over in words. I got emotional. It was hard to breathe. I was a season ticket holder from the age of seven. This is actually impossible."

West Ham chairman David Gold: "Congratulations to Leicester City for winning the Premier League against all the odds, magnificent well done. West Ham next year. Here's the thing. West Ham, Stoke, Southampton, Swansea - it could be you next year. That's what this means. All bets are off…"

Phil McNulty, BBC Sport chief football writer: "As someone who predicted Leicester City to be relegated before the start of the season and questioned the appointment of manager Claudio Ranieri, there is probably not enough humble pie to go around. What a story and what a way to be proved wonderfully, ridiculously wrong. There may never be a Premier League story - or arguably a British sporting story - to top the tale of the team that went from relegation strugglers to title winners in 12 months. And there has not been a hint of good fortune about it. Leicester City have been the best team in the country this season, a team full of resilience and character but also great ability. As for Ranieri, the Italian many thought would always remain a nearly man, he has made history. What a triumph for this popular and engaging personality, an absolute gentleman whose victory will be celebrated by everyone with the good of sport and football at heart."

Leicester City supporter Mark Selby won the world snooker just ten minutes afterwards to make it the best sporting half-hour in the history of Leicester. "To be Premier League champions is a fantastic achievement and I want to say well done to Claudio and the boys," remarked Selby.

Robbie Savage, ex-Leicester midfielder on BBC Radio 5 live: "An unbelievable night for Leicester City. This is the greatest achievement in British sport. I was a massive sceptic of Claudio Ranieri but he proved me so wrong. We will never see this again. There is not one better sporting achievement and Leicester thoroughly deserve it. At the start of the season they were 5,000-1. Manchester United have spent more in two years than Leicester have in their entire history. These are free transfers and players plucked from other clubs who were unwanted. This is the biggest story in British sport."

"In terms of domestic football, Leicester City winning the Premier League is the greatest achievement ever and I think it will never be surpassed," Savage added on BBC Sport. "It is incredible. This is a turning point in Premier League history."

Jermaine Jenas, ex-Spurs & England midfielder on BBC Radio 5 live: "To win the Premier League title you have to turn up for the big moments. Leicester City have done that. Tottenham have just not been able to get the job done at the right time. Congratulations to Leicester City."

In response to Harry Kane's recent post of lions hunting down The Foxes, Vardy responded with an image of Mufasa from the animated film *The Lion King* plunging to his death. He who laughs last...

Harry Kane was gracious in defeat though: "I'm so proud of this team and club. We put it all on the line but unfortunately it just wasn't enough. We learn and come back stronger! Congratulations to Leicester on what they achieved. Finally thanks to all the fans! Let's finish the season strong now! #COYS."

TUESDAY, 3 MAY

Premier League, @premierleague - Leicester fans waking up on Tuesday morning, this is not a dream. Repeat, this is not a dream...

On the door to the treatment room at the Belvoir Road training ground, Dave Rennie, the physio, posted a handmade sign. "Closed due to unforeseen circumstances," it read. Beneath was a picture of the trophy and the message "Champions". A corridor away, in a room usually occupied by the parents of academy trainees, Ranieri gave a press conference.

There was sincere applause.

He said he did not bear grudges over some of the unkind statements that greeted his return to English football. "I was busy with the team," he said. "I did not know what was spoken about. But if they ask, 'Why Ranieri?' if they say, 'Others are much better', I say, 'OK Claudio - show. Show what you can do. Always show me everything you've got, and every now and again I will explain a little football to you,' (he told one players' meeting). You maintain this spirit, and on it I will put my Italian tactics. When I was in Austria, pre-season, I watched the group. I was sensitive to the feeling in the dressing room and I said to them, 'It is not important that you understand 25 people here - it is important that you understand me, only me. If you understand me, we could do something good.' I decided to play 4-4-2 then. I told the players they ended the season fantastic with three at the back, and I started like that, but I didn't feel the football. Look, I played it, I played it at Valencia, we won the Copa del Rey, we qualified for the Champions League, and in my first Leicester game we had three, but I didn't like it and I changed. In England a lot of teams play 4-3-3 and then you have three defenders against one. Then I watched Mahrez and every time he made a difference it was coming in from the right side. But Albrighton can make a lot of crosses from the right side, too. So I changed, with Albrighton playing on the left to come inside. Then I realised we were so fast on the counter-attack, so good. I told them, 'We are like the RAF, come on.' They believed in this and we started winning our first matches, so there was confidence and enthusiasm. Then I changed the full-backs. I put Danny Simpson on the right, Christian Fuchs on the left and we were more solid."

'When I arrived, they all thought, 'Oh, new manager, different philosophy, maybe I will go here instead, maybe I go there.' Robert Huth said there would be two training sessions every day but I told them, 'Don't worry, I want to continue with your style, but with my ideas.' And I changed things slowly. It was important for me to show them Italian tactics. I told them not to worry about mistakes. We'll watch the video together, it will get better."

So there's the science bit.

What remains is the unquantifiable, the X-factor that has separated Leicester from the rest.

"There are so many keys to this. Humility, the strength of the dressing room, they help each other at important moments, they play with the heart, the soul, they play 11. There was a good blend. I told them, 'I love the English spirit', because when I was a player I was an Englishman."

He illustrated his point as he smashed a fist into a palm. "Every time, to fight - you have to kill me if you want to win. I love this kind of spirit. There are two games: with the ball and not with the ball, and in modern football everyone must work, and work hard. So I told them, 'Play like this against the others and look what happens.'"

Ranieri knew when his team looked potential champions. It was at the Etihad that the title might be possible; he did not tell his players though. "I was so satisfied. It was an unbelievable performance. Maybe then they started to believe in something. We can win, we can fight until the end. I never spoke about it after. If I get crazy I transmit the nerves. We were like climbers, if you look down: 'Oh God. No, come on, look up.' But that was the day I believed something fantastic could happen, yes."

Asked where he watched the final moments from, Ranieri said "first the armchair, then the ceiling!"

His phone never stopped then, and hasn't since. "This club attracts a lot of people. In Italy, everybody's second team is Leicester. In Thailand, the first team is Leicester. I am getting letters from Uruguay, Paraguay, Brazil.

"Everybody knows the Premier League is big money and big teams and they win the League. But now they can say maybe 99 per cent of the time those teams win. I love it when I see everybody so happy. We have been in the city centre very close to the stadium and the fans are crazy. Crazy with happiness. I'm so glad when I see this happiness and I understand it now because all the people in the world are asking about Leicester, and all of your colleagues come here to find out what happened. This is a moment to live longer, to taste like a good wine, to savour. Now is not the time to think, 'Look what we have done.' Maybe in one or two years we will know.

When you start as a manager, you hope you can win a league. So, yes, this is one of the best moments. But I don't forget where I started, in which division I started. I came from the non-league, and when I arrived in Cagliari in the third division, that was my first fairytale. And I still have love for this fairytale. It is still in my heart. Now I have won the most important league in Europe, maybe the world. I won the Premier League. My career is fantastic. But I want to achieve a little more. At the moment I don't cry but I'm a very strange man. On Saturday, maybe. Inside me there are two people: One, I want to win. I want to win on Saturday (against Everton), I want to win the Premier League, I want to win again, I am never satisfied. The other says, 'Claudio, how many managers are there in the world? Too many. And not everybody is Sir Alex Ferguson or Fabio Capello or Carlo Ancelotti.' So this is a good career. We have done something impossible - so maybe the bookmakers will not try to sack me first. Maybe second."

The nation took to social media to congratulate the new champions, including Prime Minister David Cameron and Labour leader Jeremy Corbyn. Cameron posted on Twitter:

David Cameron, @David_Cameron - "Many congratulations to Leicester. An extraordinary, thoroughly deserved, Premier League title."

THE STORY GOES GLOBAL

The final whistle was blown at 21:55 in west London, 13:55 in Los Angeles, and 03:55 on Tuesday in Bangkok.

Five minutes after the result was confirmed, more than 493,000 tweets using the word "Leicester" were sent worldwide, hitting a peak of 140,000 tweets in the minute right after the final whistle.

The global appeal of this underdog story, was keenly shown in Sydney, Mumbai, Istanbul and Rio de Janeiro and also Thailand even though it was the middle of the night.

The 596,000 people who 'like' the club's official page in Thailand were in celebratory mood. One such fan, Anantawat Jhansubin, asked: "Don't forget to bring the trophy to Thailand!" On Facebook many gave credit to Buddhist monk Phra Prommangkalachan.

The Bangkok newspaper The Nation reported comments by Aiyawatt Srivaddhanaprabha, the chairman's son, that the players would visit Thailand soon, "Thai people should be given a lot of credit as all players acknowledge how much support they have been given," he said. "All players believe, so do all the Thai fans." He hoped to tie blue and yellow flags on the Premier League trophy when it is handed over - blue, as it is the club's traditional colour, and yellow as that is the colour associated with the Thai king.

When the result came in, the convoluted hashtag #lahazanadeportivamasepicadelahistoria ("The most epic athletic feat in history") became a trending topic in Mexico, as did #elsuenosecumplio ("The dream is fulfilled").

Christian Parkinson, a BBC cameraman based in Johannesburg, is Leicester-born and a life-long fan of the club. He learned the result in mid-air on the way to South Africa: "So I'm late to the party - the family and I were on a plane when the Spurs game was happening. A friendly air stewardess whispered the result in my ear and handed me a glass of something fizzy to celebrate. It was a slightly bizarre anticlimax to what has been an amazing, electrifying season - but hey we are champions and that's all that matters. To me this isn't just about football, this is more than that - it's a victory not just for Leicester but for every unfashionable town and city in the country. I've always been proud of my home town but finally people know where it is and how to pronounce it. No more will I have to say 'Leicester, yes it's a small city close to Nottingham.'" #Wearechampions #iloveleicester #proudofmytown #lcfc

France's sports newspaper *L'Equipe* published a detailed online segment dedicated to paying tribute to the success of "the surprise package, this well-oiled machine that has transfixed people way beyond England's shores".

Italy's *La Gazzetto dello Sport* wrote that "there is no football fan in England or outside that does not recognise the achievement of this great little club, and its Italian leader", referring to manager Claudio Ranieri. Their headline was "storico titolo per il Leicester" - translated as "Historic title for Leicester" - underneath which, was "King Claudio" - possibly no need to translate that part.

Italian RAI News - La favola del ##Leicester e di #Ranieri. Cronaca di un successo che nessuno avrebbe previsto - which translates as "The fairytale of Leicester and of Ranieri. A success story that no one would have predicted"

The Times of India's Hijam Raju Singh wrote: "The wait for the 'fairytale ending' of the 'beautiful story' is over. The biggest underdog story in recent times has met the ending everyone was hoping for."

Japan's NTV had it as their main sports story of the day, focusing on Shinji Okazaki and his part in Leicester's "long-cherished wish" to win the league.

Italian PM Matteo Renzi wrote: "The greatest feat in English football history was led by an Italian...Well done, Claudio Ranieri. #crazy"

French, TF1, failed miserably in their ability to pronounce 'Leicester': it became 'Lie-stair', Wes Morgan named 'Vess'.

Spanish, RTVE pronounced it the right way, albeit with a Spanish flourish on the R of Leicester.

Italian, *La Repubblica* newspaper took to the streets. Some people managed to pronounce it perfectly, but in Rome it was mainly 'Lie-Chester'.

Juventus and Italy goalkeeper Gigi Buffon praises Ranieri..."Thanks Mister, because you've shown that one must not stop dreaming."

TAG Heuer, @TAGHeuer - Congratulations to new TAG Heuer Ambassador Claudio Ranieri & his team! It was a real #DontCrackUnderPressure season

CLOSER TO HOME

Wes Morgan the morning after the night before: "You saw some of the scenes and that continued on," he said sheepishly. "A lot of people were down on their knees and there were a few tears as well. I'm a bit emotional myself. I hope Vards' house is alright this morning."

Danny Drinkwater tells Sky Sports News about the party at Vardy's house last night. "When Chelsea's second goal went in it was 10 minutes of madness. Then the final whistle went and it was four hours of madness!" He added: "It'll be something I'll be able to tell my kids about. It's so hard to put into words what it will do for people at this club."

Mark Schwarzer recognised the Ranieri Factor. "He's been incredibly calm throughout the course of the whole season," Schwarzer says. "He's changed very little from when you look at the make-up of the team. He's made little tweaks, he's definitely changed the way we trained a little bit. He's added his own technical nous to our side and he's really continued to play to our strengths and if anything he's enhanced players, encouraged players and probably given players more confidence." Schwarzer was "99.9 per cent sure" he will be leaving but the 43-year-old reserve goalkeeper hoped the club keep their key players, including Vardy. "I think he genuinely loves playing at Leicester, loves the club and he's just recently signed a new deal," said the Australian, who was bought a medal by Chelsea last year after not playing a single league match - and has not appeared in a league game for the Foxes.

Peter Schmeichel tweeted - May 2nd 1993 I am 29 yrs old, we didn't play but won @premierleague because our rivals didn't win. (1/2) May 2nd 2016 @kschmeichel1 29 yrs of age, and @LCFC didn't play but they also won @premierleague because @SpursOfficial didn't win! (2/2)

"Incredible and romantic" is how the club's former manager Martin O'Neill described it; the clubs first title in their 132-year history that "will live long in the memory". He added, "Personally, I don't think we'll see it in our lifetime again."

O'Neill was full of praise for the manager, "Ranieri deserves all the credit in the world, the players have been simply sensational, the owners have been terrific as well. It's been a great story. Everything about it - from away back last year when they just avoided relegation, to this magnificent rise - it has been incredible and so romantic."

Gerry Taggart, the former Northern Ireland centre-half who played almost 150 games for Leicester, hoped the club's triumph would change English football "for good, for the better".

"I've been saying for the last six or seven weeks that I believed Leicester would go on and win the title," he said. "I've watched a lot of this team this season and it's just mind-blowing the way they've got to where they are. The way they play football is good for the game. The backroom staff at Leicester City are first class, they've spent a lot of years trying to perfect what goes on behind the scenes. This is as much about them as it is about the players or the manager, to be honest."

Taggart gave credit to Ranieri as the manager "simplified the game for them, let them go out, express themselves when they've got the ball". Taggart added: "But it's been especially good to see when they haven't got the ball everybody is contributing to the side. That's what has got them over the line - pure and simple teamwork."

Ranieri now wants to follow up the triumph with a top-10 finish next season. He knows 'The Immortals' season is 'unrepeatable.'

Ranieri had followed proceedings in west London. "When something happens to you like this, you can't fully realise it. Tottenham were winning at half-time, so I was a bit downhearted." Ranieri told RAI Sport in Italy. "Then when Cahill scored, I thought something could happen. I did celebrate at Hazard's equaliser. This is a year that cannot be repeated, next year we'll try to fight for a top 10 place, hopefully. We must continue to grow and to do well."

Ranieri had won his first ever league title in a lengthy career. "I am 64 years old, I've been fighting for a long time, but I was always positive and had positivity on my side. I always thought that I'd end up winning a league title somewhere eventually. I am the same man who was fired by Greece, perhaps someone there had forgotten about my career. It's not as if anyone will forget, but I like to point out I am the same man who was on the Greece bench. I haven't changed."

Speaking to Leicester City's official website, Ranieri admitted that winning the Premier League or even a place the Champions League was totally unrealistic. "I never expected this when I arrived. I'm a pragmatic man, I just wanted to win match after match and help my players to improve week after week. Never did I think too much about where it would take us. The players have been fantastic. Their focus, their determination, their spirit has made this possible. Every game they fight for each other and I love to see this in my players. They deserve to be champions. I'm happy for my players, for the chairman, for the staff at Leicester City, all our fans and the Leicester community."

War Horse author Michael Morpurgo wrote a new fairytale to celebrate Leicester City winning the Premier League title against the odds. The story is called *Fox and the Ghost King* (or Uneasy Lies The Head That Dreams The Impossible Dream). He read the short story on BBC Radio 4's Today.

Yours truly was invited to the BBC studios to discuss 'The Immortals' and to put Leicester's triumph into perspective for a global audience of 400m.

After the party at Vardy's house, the players headed into Leicester to Club Republic, driving 2,000 revellers who were already inside toasting their victory into even greater raptures. One onlooker said: "The whole place was going mad, I've never seen anything like it." It lasted until 4am time for a few hours' sleep before 'light' training. Among the first spotted was Vardy, carrying a bottle of Lucozade and looking rather bleary.

Leicester City, @LCFC - The party is so good, we're seeing double! #havingaparty

Jamie Vardy lookalike, Lee Chapman, shot to fame following Leicester City's Premier League win. While doing an interview outside the King Power stadium, he was hauled on board the team's bus by some of the players.

When ITV News caught up with him, he revealed what it was like on the bus with the new stars of the Premier League. "They obviously knew about me; they were all giving me the banter," he said. "I finally got to sit down next to Jamie Vardy, and he's just like, 'I am better looking than you'."

Chapman, who was among hundreds who gathered outside the stadium, said: "They were all laughing and taking the mickey out of Vardy saying that I was better looking than him."

A postman by day, Chapman had sprinted his rounds this morning in order to get to the King Power stadium. When he arrived, dressed in full Leicester kit, he was mobbed by fans. Then the team's bus pulled up, on the way to the San Carlo Italian restaurant in the city centre where they were due to enjoy a celebratory lunch, and he was invited on board.

Around 500 fans lined the streets outside the restaurant as the players got off the coach shortly before 2pm, led by Ranieri and the club's Thai billionaire owner, Vichai Srivaddhanaprabha. By the time they left at around 4pm, it was no surprise players and staff looked worn out.

WEDNESDAY, 4 MAY

The headlines continued...

The Guardian Sport – "Floating on Claudio Nine"

The Sun Sport - "Please Don't N'GOlo"

The *Daily Express* – "Hands off my champs"

In the bowels of BBC Broadcasting House, leading the 5.00 o'clock news live on BBC Global, the big debate was whether this was indeed the greatest sporting achievement and whether the "Fearless" of Leicester City had in fact changed the football landscape.

I told the global audience of 400m, "The real beauty of the story is the way Leicester, epitomised by Ranieri, have handled it with such good grace. Leicester are an exceptionally good team, but are they the best? They are in terms of consistency of results this season. It is a fluke; a one-off and something that will never be repeated. But we applaud them. It is overwhelming to see Prime Ministers from countries all around the world tweeting their joy at Leicester winning this trophy."

Let me now elaborate with time to reflect, but first, Ranieri, the man of the moment, was giving his opinion elsewhere at the same time, and he felt that the rich clubs will dominate the Premier League for the next two decades.

Ranieri's collection of 'Odd Job Men' cost £57m, the cheapest of any currently in the top half of the Premier League. "Big money makes big teams and usually big teams win. Now we can say only 99% of the time," said Ranieri. "Next season will be the same and for the next 10 or 20 years, it will be the same."

He suggested a surprise title winner only comes along every 20 years, Nottingham Forest 1978, Blackburn Rovers 1995, now 'The Immortals'. "How many years after Nottingham Forest and Blackburn have another team won?" observed Ranieri. "The richest, or the team who can pick up the best players to make a team, will win."

Leicester receive between £99m and £150m in prize money from the new three-year cycle TV deal, which is worth £5.136bn but with an extra £3 billion plus for overseas sales. Other clubs still have more money to spend on players than he does. "Maybe now is too early to think what we have done. Maybe in one or two years it will be easier to understand, but now it is important to stay high in the world."

Ranieri's biggest task to prepare for the next season was to keep what he has and to make one or two significant signings as the Champions League requires a much stronger and bigger squad, which provides much more of a chance for tinkering. "My phone will ring this summer but I will say: 'Do you have enough money to buy my players?' I would like to maintain all of them, but if one of my players says to me, 'I want to go there', I try to keep him. If you go away you don't know what happens, here you are the king."

He will not rush into spending big money, "We don't need superstars, we need our players. I want to improve the squad without big stars but the right players."

Let's rewind to Ranieri's most crucial point about the immediate future, and whether the next big surprise will keep us all waiting for 20 years or more. Well, this is the very crux of the point I was making on BBC Global. This was a "fluke" but without taking anything away from Ranieri and his 'Fearless Immortals', it is a one-off that will never be repeated, let alone in 20 years' time. As for changing the landscape of the 'powerful' game, that is simply not going to happen. It's a non-starter.

For all the romantics thinking this is a fresh beginning, whether the ultimate underdog has had his day, and it means there will be more to follow, the big boys have been plotting for months to under pin the strength of the strongest.

I was in on the first ever breakaway of the so-called 'Big Five' clubs which, ironically included Everton and Spurs, when having an inside track with club owners such as Irving Scholar and David Dein. It was considered impossible then that an elitist group would cut itself off from the Football League, driven by sheer avarice. It happened. The next major change in the game will be ignited by Leicester City but, so far from changing the landscape for the good as the fans might perceive it, it will tempt the power brokers to plot towards a more closed shop elitist approach.

It is the same mentality that has blackballed the FA Cup winners qualifying for the Champions League. After all, they are champions compared to the team that finishes fourth. The argument has always been, by an organisation that requires two-thirds to vote anything through, that England's coefficient would be eroded if they allowed the possibility of a minnow to win the FA Cup and represent the country in the Champions league.

Two things: Firstly the so called rich and powerful have eroded the coefficient all by themselves, and secondly, the emergence of Leicester into their patch isn't something they like one little bit. They will plot to find a way it won't happen again. The signs are already there with 'breakaway' factions in clandestine London hotels meeting high powered American executives to discuss, one suspects, these very issues.

Football long ago stopped being the "beautiful game" and as the esteemed football journalist Brian Glanville coined it many years ago: "The Greed is Good League".

While even I as a Spurs fan can rejoice in Leicester's success, and my wife Linda as a Chelsea fan loves Claudio and we all know how appallingly he was treated at Chelsea, as it can be followed in my series of books on the inner workings of Stamford Bridge, their exploits are not liked within the corridors of power.

Let's be frank, the top clubs were a pathetic bunch this season. Chelsea were lazy and complacent in their preparations for their defence and in their ability to get their best ever manager José Mourinho the sack, while Louis Van Gaal's reign of confusion was more comic relief than anything else, and Manchester City were taking on Real Madrid for a place in the Champions League final making a complete hash of their title challenge. As for Arsenal, it was business as usual going for fourth place, the only top club in all of the big five European leagues not to buy a single outfield player last summer.

But none of this will happen again. The big boys will flash the cash in the most spectacular fashion ever. It will be very tempting for one or two of Leicester's biggest stars, and there will some major signings to ensure they make a much better fist of things not just next season but in the foreseeable future. Together with the means and the muscle to facilitate change to their own advantage, the romantics can forget it.

If anything Leicester will change the landscape, but it might not necessarily be for the good of the majority, or the aspirations of the many to emulate Leicester.

As the media frenzy continued unabated, much of it with appearances from fans, pundits, or those inside the game running out of superlatives, inevitably there would come the more pragmatic approach, and on Sky Sports the West Ham co-owner David Sullivan was not dreaming like Claudio. Instead he refused to put his head in the clouds and came out with some fierce realism as only such an abrasive chairman could, describing it as one of the greatest frauds in Premier League history.

"I know how they've done it," Sullivan began, during his appearance on the channel, before going on to explain exactly how he thought they had "done it."

"They've got 11 penalties, lady luck shined on them. They've had virtually no injuries. They've only used 18 players all season. They've had two players who've played out of their skin, scored more goals than they've ever scored in their entire lives. They signed a fantastic midfielder. One of their big signings came good, and that's how they've done it. You don't see them being massively better than you (West Ham) are..."

OK, well at 18 points ahead of the Hammers, taking four points off the London club, there was a massive gap, but you can tell from his tone they plan to bridge that gap and with the additional muscle form their move to the Olympic Stadium they crave Champions League football, to illustrate the intensity of the competition next season.

Sullivan's comments about injuries and good luck ring true, but he also felt the title should have gone to one of the top teams. But Manchester City might have reached the Champions League semi-finals but sat 13 points behind Leicester and lost 3-1 to the Foxes when the teams met at the Etihad. "In contrast, Man City and Tottenham on a good day are real good teams, better than Leicester," before conceding, "The table doesn't lie and Leicester are the champions."

Sir Peter Soulsby, the Mayor of Leicester, said the city would pay tribute to Ranieri. "Street names after him, freedom of the city, statues...I don't know what it will be. I do know we've got quite a lot of partying ahead of us as a city to the end of the season. And then a big celebration. We've been amazed by the performance of the team on the pitch and the inspiration given by two managers, Nigel Pearson first and now Ranieri. They really are something that the city has got behind, and are very, very proud of."

José Mourinho, who won the title with Chelsea last season, offered a curious toast to Leicester and Ranieri. Mourinho was sacked following a 2-1 defeat at the King Power Stadium in December, having taken over from Ranieri in 2004. "I want to congratulate everyone connected to @LCFC; players, staff, owners and fans," he tweeted. "I lost my title to Claudio Ranieri and it is with incredible emotion that I live this magic moment in his career."

A group of MPs have called for Ranieri to receive an honorary knighthood, but the Italian is content with a guard of honour at Stamford Bridge on the final day. "It is good because last time I left the Premier League I went through my players and they made the guard of honour," Ranieri said. "It was amazing. Now I will come back in the same way. It is unbelievable."

Richard Scudamore, Premier League executive chairman, hailed Leicester's success as the greatest sporting story of all time and admitted it has "made mugs of us all". He added: "Nobody saw it coming and even when it was halfway through the season nobody said it could be sustained. It's probably the biggest sporting story ever and the biggest sporting achievement ever. In terms of an overall story, as an overall achievement, it is absolutely the best."

Christian Fuchs could kiss Eden Hazard after his late Chelsea goal. The players watching the game at Vardy's house were on tenterhooks, with Fuchs right in the centre of the celebrations after the final whistle. "The goal from Hazard, he played great. I could kiss him after that goal," he told talkSport, "The spirit is so important. You saw so many videos of us celebrating together at Jamie Vardy's house - it's not normal that all the players, with no exceptions, are coming together to watch the game and then celebrate together. It was an outstanding moment when the final whistle blew and - oh my god, it was insane. We were watching it as a team at Jamie Vardy's house and I must admit I couldn't sit still, I didn't know whether to sit or stand. It was an exciting game and even with Tottenham 2-0 up I still believed something was possible."

When Danny Drinkwater left Manchester United four years ago, gone were thoughts of a title, so he cannot fathom a "bonkers" success with Leicester and becoming an England international. "This wasn't in my thoughts," he said. "You are leaving a big club which is used to winning trophies and probably coming to a club which hasn't got the history and has not got the size. Look how it has turned around. Within three years we have won the Championship, we have won the Prem, it is bonkers, it is hard to put into words."

Drinkwater is suspended for Saturday's game against Everton at the King Power Stadium but will be on the pitch for the trophy presentation. "It will be a special moment for the fans," he said. "It is a huge day and let's just enjoy it. I will be looking back at this for years."

FOREST OR THE FOXES?

The ex-England and Nottingham Forest defender Viv Anderson was asked, which is the greater achievement: Leicester 2015-16 or Nottingham Forest 1977-78? "I am biased," he concedes, "but I would say Forest winning the title is better. It was all new to us. We were used to playing Second Division players, and then went up to the First Division, and played against sides we had only seen on television.

For Leicester to have come along and done what they've done is an absolute breath of fresh air. It is amazing with all the money involved, easily the most fantastic achievement of the Premier League era. But at least they had a season of playing against these top opponents week in, week out. We never had that opportunity. We had to come up and hit the ground running."

Forest "snuck in the back door", in Anderson's words, reaching the top flight after finishing third in the 1976-77 Second Division in Brian Clough's second full season in charge, and the first with Peter Taylor alongside. They went up behind Wolves and Chelsea and were expected to be also-rans in the division above. Instead, with largely the same group of players, they finished above reigning champions Liverpool by seven points. "It was more of an even playing field for us than it is for Leicester with all the millions. Each year there is nothing worse than getting to the start of August and being able to write down the top four on a piece of paper. It is great for football. It shows everybody that if you can put a group of players together, who want to play for each other and the manager, you can achieve all sorts. But it was still a massive jump for us. If you ended up halfway it was a big achievement.

Leicester have had time to adjust. Although they did struggle last year, they ended with seven wins from nine. It does help if you've been in the league before - you've been to Old Trafford, to Anfield. You know the nuances. We never had that opportunity. There wasn't television to study opposition as there is now. We would discuss who the best players were between us before games. We didn't have match reports. We just had to go from game to game, then at Easter thought, 'Bloody hell, we have a chance of winning this.' You have to say their title is a close second! If you speak to a 21-year-old and a 51-year-old, the 21-year-old will say Leicester and the 51-year-old Forest. I can understand the different viewpoint. But I don't have to agree!"

Forest won the League Cup that season, going on to win two European Cups back-to-back, winning another League Cup and went on a 42-game unbeaten league run. He predicts a challenging European campaign for Leicester, and has a bet with a friend that they do not escape the group stage. "If they get out of the group stages of the Champions League it will be an unbelievable achievement. I would tell them to enjoy every minute. You are going in as English champions, a prestige competition, give it your best shot. This doesn't come along so often. I hope it's not another 86-odd years before they're in it again."

MAMA'S BOY

Leicester's official victory parade was to be on Monday, 16 May, from the King Power Stadium to the city centre before ending at a park when there would be no more need to go so easy on the pasta. One of the secrets of Ranieri's success, his 96-year-old mother, Renata, has told an eager world was to take care of her son's dietary needs. "My son needs to stay fit, so he almost never opts for a 'primo'," she told *La Repubblica* newspaper. "Instead he has green beans or a salad."

When he nipped back for lunch to Rome, he ate "a steak and a bit of cicoria ripassata" – a spinach-like vegetable tossed in olive oil and peperoncino - followed by strawberries with lemon juice with a dusting of sugar.

She was moved to tears when her son phoned her to say that Leicester had secured the title after Spurs failed to beat Chelsea, "All the newspapers (in Italy) are calling him the King of England, just imagine that. Claudio was so happy when I spoke to him on the phone. Now we can all relax a bit."

She had never expected her son to take Leicester so far. "He told me he had found a good bunch of players...but that he certainly wasn't training a great team."

Claudio had been undervalued in Italy, she said, but appreciated much more in England. "I know that he settled in well (at Leicester), and that they have always treated him well. In Rome, he was not treated with respect. I was sorry about how it ended. I think he could have won the championship in Italy too. He came very close."

She hoped to be able to see her son soon. "We are so happy. The whole world is paying him compliments, and I thank everyone."

The manager's son-in-law said Claudio was ecstatic that Leicester had won. "Claudio was so happy, not so much for himself, but for the players and the fans," said Alessandro Roja, an actor who is married to Claudio's daughter, Claudia. "He's a calm and serious person but he also knows how to joke around. He is able to gain people's confidence," he told *Corriere dello Sport*.

THURSDAY, 5 MAY

Arriving at training, N'Golo Kanté drove a Mini Cooper S worth £18,840 and the players looked extremely relaxed looked relaxed greeting fans still gathered around the Belvoir Drive gates.

Marc Albrighton described it as a "surreal" week, the players mobbed wherever they go. It hadn't sunk in, the magnitude of their achievement, "I don't think it will for a while, it might sink in later on in the summer," the former Aston Villa winger told the *Leicester Mercury*. "It has been such an unbelievable campaign. It has all felt so surreal. It will take time for us to realise what an incredible time it has been."

He felt that the "never give up" attitude was a major factor, "I think that has won us a lot of points this season," said Albrighton. "Early on this season you've got the draws at Stoke and Southampton, we were 2-0 down in both of them, and 2-0 down in the home game against Villa. That showed our character early in the season and we've continued to do that, we've gone behind at Old Trafford, which is a daunting place. We carried on going, got the equaliser and held on."

Speaking to Foxes Player HD, Wes Morgan said: "It's an unbelievable feeling for everyone involved in Leicester including me and my family. Everyone. The staff too. For everyone who is involved in supporting us in doing the best on the pitch. It's unbelievable and it's still sinking in. There's such a togetherness in the team. The boys, we support each other, back each other and we'd die for each other on the pitch. I think that's why we're in the position we are and we're champions of the Premier League."

Jamie Vardy said: "It's the biggest achievement in the history of a great club and we all feel privileged to be part of it. It's even more special to have done it with these lads. Every minute of hard work we've put in on the training pitch has been worth it for this moment."

Striker Andrej Kramarić went out on loan to Hoffenheim in January, making two league appearances, and three in the Capital One Cup. He was on the phone to his team-mates as they watched Chelsea draw with Tottenham. "Danny Simpson is the biggest playboy, the girls adore him, N'Golo Kanté could run a marathon, 42kms are a piece of cake to him and Huth is the biggest prankster." Kramarić told 24 Sata. "Huth looks dangerous, strong as a bull but he is quite the opposite, great character. Wes Morgan is the captain that never raises his voice, a great example of how to behave, Christian Fuchs is very intelligent and I've never played with a more powerful player than Jeffrey Schlupp, such power and speed like I've never seen before. He injures me once a year then says 'sorry about that'. Riyad Mahrez I have often compared to Vahid Halilhodzic (a former Bosnian footballer and manager, currently head coach of the Japanese national football team, and regarded as one of the best Yugoslav players in the 1970s and 1980s), and Vardy is the guy to raise the atmosphere. When we lose, he comes into the dressing room and tells a joke to cheer us up. He's a fun character. I was watching the Chelsea game and was on the group chat with the rest of the team. We were all convinced that Chelsea would certainly equalise. They played as if their life depended on that game. So it was such fate. We had the feeling that the whole world was with us. I feel proud as a winner of the Premier League."

Gordon Taylor wanted all of the players knighted. "It goes beyond football what they've done," Taylor, 71, reportedly told *Sportsmail*. "It remains to be seen if the choice to add them to the honours list comes from The Cabinet, but I would hope so. As football goes it's probably, in my lifetime, one of the finest achievements I've seen.   Special success stories come from different areas of life. Leicester have shown that sport and football are a very important part of the fabric of this country. They give hope to any team who think they can never make it to top."

To be fair to Gordon Taylor he later made it quite clear to me that he'd actually said, in answer to the question 'in what way should they be honoured?': "the game will honour them (e.g. PFA Awards, PL Team of the Year, FWA Awards etc.) and the City of Leicester and no doubt strong contenders for BBC Team Award and Coach of the Year."

And in response to 'Should they be in the Honours List?', he replied "that would be nice, in some form, as they have set an example to the whole nation not just sport but that would be a matter for Downing Street and Buckingham Palace."

Taylor feels the inspirational nature of their triumph is worth such lofty recognition, which he believes has had a wider effect on society. Speaking at the *On The Board Graduation*, a programme which helps footballers extend their careers into the boardroom, The PFA chief executive added: "For the PFA Player of the Year Riyad Mahrez to have gone from the French Ligue 2, to failing in a trial at St Mirren, to show the resilience and belief to become the Premier League's best player. For Vardy to get released by Sheffield Wednesday, go to Stocksbridge Park Steels to Halifax Town and Fleetwood, to go on trial at Crewe and not be taken on, then suddenly he achieves the record of consecutive Premier League goals and is one of the country's leading scorers. For Kasper Schmeichel to live and play under the shadow of his father, Peter - it's never easy to be a famous footballer's son. There are inspirational stories from every team member, I could name them all. They deserve all the credit they can get. The sum of their whole is so much greater than the individuals. That's what football and life is all about - being a team."

Leicester's title provided "inspiration for the whole world", says the club's vice-chairman in an interview with BBC Sports Editor Dan Roan. Aiyawatt Srivaddhanaprabha, son of owner and chairman Vi-chai, talked about his family's future plans.

He spoke of his relationship with a "special" manager Claudio and striker.

"Claudio is a brilliant manager. The way he managed the media with the pressure of the team, he has so much experience with football. The way he managed the players and put them out on the field was something special. We saw that when we interviewed him. He has something special inside and has all the plans in his head. We interviewed quite a number of managers and he was the one I chose the first time. When I met him, he was the first choice for me."

Interestingly, *Sportsmail* revealed that so low was his stock within football, at that time, that two Championship clubs rejected the opportunity to hire him. It was even suggested that his seemingly, disastrous time as coach of the Greece national team was not included on his CV. Leicester thought differently and credit must be given to Jon Rudkin, the club's director of football, who was tasked with vetting prospective replacements for Nigel Pearson to owner Vichai Srivaddhanaprabha.

A meeting in London was arranged between Ranieri, Rudkin, Chief Executive Susan Whelan, football operations director Andrew Neville and Aiyawatt Srivaddhanaprabha, the owner's son and Leicester vice- chairman. Ranieri's humour, geniality and knowledge impressed according to the *Sportsmail* report which also said there was a second meeting so Vichai could see the same and the deal was sealed.

Ranieri had offers from France and Italy but confided to his agent Steve Kutner during lunch in a Monte Carlo restaurant that he wanted to return to England. Steve Bould, Arsenal's assistant manager, knows Rudkin as they were opposition managers in an Under 18 match in September 2009; when Kutner needed a number for Rudkin, Bould provided it.

Back to the BBC interview: Vardy is now one of the most sought after strikers but was signed for £1m.

"Steve Walsh asked me to buy non-league players and I thought it was funny. Then when he showed me all the information about him, it was amazing. He scores 29 or 30 goals a year so we can see he can score and has a record. When I met him, he was quite a special character. He wanted success, he had the hunger to be the best striker in the team, even though he came from non-league. He talked to me openly about wanting to be in the Premier League and he said he will try anything to take the club to the Premier League. He said to me on the first day he wants to play for England, I said to him, 'I will help you. Anything you want, I will do it'."

But in another interview, it was suggested that Vardy used to drink every day, and even turned up to training drunk, as he struggled to adjust to The Championship. According to Aiyawatt Srivaddhanaprabha, "He went straight from the bottom to The Championship, which eventually led him to start drinking booze every single day. We had no idea what to do," Srivaddhanaprabha told a magazine in Thailand. "I didn't even know about this until someone told me that he came to train while he was still drunk."

Srivaddhanaprabha helped the striker turn things around, threatening to run his contract down if he did not change. "I went to talk to him myself. I asked 'do you wish to end your career like this? Do you want to stay here like this? We'll let your contract run out then release you. Don't expect a better career path.' He said he didn't know what to do with his life. He'd never earned such a large amount of money. So I asked him 'What's your dream? How do you think your life should be? Just think carefully about what would you do for the club. I invested in you, do you have something in return?' Vardy became a 'new person'. After (the conversation) he simply quit drinking and started working hard in training. His physicality wasn't as good as it is now. We know he had explosive acceleration, but we simply had no idea he could be this good. He's adapting, working on fitness training, he's turned into a new person. And that's better."

Back to the BBC interview once more, and the more sedate question about how the story made headlines around the world.

"Is it a miracle? It is. It is inspirational and people talk about it. We set the standard of the sport and inspiration for the whole world. It is not just for the sport, it is life. If people use Leicester as the standard now, if they fight, they try - then they can achieve one day. Everything has to be right as well. It is a miracle for the city, it is a miracle for the players but we have a job to do. They worked hard to be in this position. It is not just lucky. All the middle clubs in the league will try now as they are inspired by Leicester. They will believe so it will be more difficult for the big clubs and for Leicester to try again."

The agent of Mahrez said it was "50/50" whether the Algeria forward would stay. "We will play in the Champions League next season, why would they want to move? I don't see the reason. We will try to keep them but it depends on the players as well. If they want to move, we will talk to them and ask why they have to move. Everything has turned to Leicester over the past seven months of the season. Every team is doing well which is why the league has been so strange. All the teams try so hard to win every match so the big teams slip sometimes and we kept the momentum from last season. We tried to survive in the first half of the season and we achieved it earlier than we thought. It was so nice to see the players try and the fans trying to support them and we have had the success now and it makes us so happy. It is difficult to say how we are feeling now to be the champions of the Premier League. We have been in the first position from Christmas and New Year's Day and people were doubting, they thought we would slip to the middle of the table. We kept belief and dreaming. There is no special secret but the team spirit is so great. They fight for each other and try to cover the mistakes for each other. They never stop and they kept believing. They are a special group of players and love each other. When we bought the club, we said we love football and we will try everything to make the club successful. If you asked too if I believe can we win the league? Maybe not realistically. My father said he wanted the team to be in the Champions League one day, and we set the plan with all the staff.

We will build the team to compete in the Premier League. We will compete in the Champions League next season and I am not saying we will win the big cup, but we will try. We want to keep our best players and we will add some quality players with the right people. I am not sure where we will finish next season. We will try to win the league again. The target is the same, we want to build the squad and we try to stay in the Premier League as long as we can. To win the title again is so difficult. It will be super difficult from now. If we win, we win. We are scouting for players now, we will see when we finish the season. We will talk with Claudio about how many players we want and in which position. I support everything they say. If the scouting team ask me to spend, they need to have some reason. Claudio needs to support it as well. I can't as an owner say, 'you can go out and spend whatever you want. We are going to buy Ronaldo and Messi'. As a club, we have to manage for the long term. Not just next season, but we need to build. The players have to be for the right position. We have to buy quality to add more for next season. Then we already have young players that we have bought like Demarai Gray and many others."

Twelve of the Premier League clubs are in the hands of foreign owners. Srivaddhanaprabha believes his family are doing "the right thing" - and the club's Thai fan base will grow. "Thai people love football and the Premier League interests them the most. To be part of the owners, the Thai people are proud. They are waiting for the players to go to see them because they want to welcome and thank them. If Manchester United and Leicester play at the same time now, they will be switching the television. They want to see the team owned by Thais playing and they love it. If you do the right thing, something good will come. We did last season and the season we got promoted. We supported the players, the staff, the fans. We do everything on and off the pitch. If you have the foundation right, you can be good. Every owner tries to be successful in everything they do. They are devoted people and love sport. We love football, we love sport and we know how important the fans are. I just need them to support the team. If they (the players) play at home, they feel safe - the support is there. Now even away, they feel the same. It is important for the performance. Now they play for the fans, for the support."

Vichai Srivaddhanaprabha was reported in the *Daily Mail* that he would give every player a Mercedes B-Class Electric Drive, worth £32,000 at a cost of £1m, and take them to Las Vegas to celebrate even though that might infringe Premier League rules to pay any bonuses outside of existing contacts; which was £6.5m to be split between the squad.

Leicester City news conference:

Dan Roan - "Standing ovation for Claudio Ranieri as he arrives for press conference & as usual a handshake for every journalist"

BBC Leicester Sport - "Claudio Ranieri toasts their Premier League title. Everyone joins in! Cheers!"

BBC Leicester Sport - "Claudio Ranieri is applauded into the room at the press conference. Everyone is on their feet clapping."

Rory Smith, Football writer for @thetimes - "Champagne for Claudio's sharks. Well done Leicester. I do feel we've all played a part in this."

Dan Roan - "Thought @lcfc couldn't get any more popular? Look what they're giving journalists before Ranieri press conference"

Ranieri sipped a glass of champagne with reporters in his first full press conference as a Premier League champion as the club bought 20 bottles of Moët & Chandon for almost 100 journalists. He usually referred to them as his "sharks" but now suggested those waiting to ask questions were just "piranhas".

After being applauded into the room, he began, "Thank you so much. I didn't see today sharks. Only piranha!"

In attendance were reporters from all over the world. He started by saying he enjoyed the whole season "because from the beginning I felt something special". The Special One perhaps? Maybe that belongs elsewhere. But he adds: "Never I could imagine this, but it's good. We work so hard. I want to say thank you to the players, the chairman, the staff and the fans. They were amazing."

He confirmed that Italian opera singer Andrea Bocelli will be singing at the King Power Stadium as he reflects on what "could be" the greatest moment of his life. "It's my karma. I've fought so hard to achieve so this is special." Ranieri elaborated "He will sing here. He called me, I don't remember one month and half ago, two month ago. He was so happy, what we are doing in Leicester. He said, 'I would like to come and sing something. I said, Great, why not.' I gave all the information to the club and they make all the arrangements. It is great for all the community. He's not friend, I met him a long time ago, I had been to his concert at Wembley. I don't know if he remembers. Now, yes maybe!"

(Bocelli later said "I've followed the story of Leicester for months, I love this beautiful story". He explained he called Ranieri and offered to sing in the "big fiesta".)

Also on the King Power pitch at half time to add to the festivities would be members of Leicester's famous 'Ice Kings' team, including legends Gordon Banks and Frank McLintock. The 1962-63 side were the last to challenge for a title after building a lead through the coldest winter in 200 years but lost their last four games.

On the match that ensured the title would be heading to Leicester: "I watched the match. Half-time I made dinner. Relaxed until second goal. After, I jump! It was a little more quiet than (Jamie's) house."

Imitating the sound of a mobile phone buzzing and ringing constantly was the way he described the reaction to Leicester's title win.

"I'd like to go around the city with black glasses to watch what is happening - it's amazing."

Bizarrely, he was asked whether this was the perfect time to step down - he laughed. "Resign?" he said. "I love to joke but I am not crazy!"

Had the Pope called? Just about everyone else had, so why not? Turns out, he hadn't.

He had given himself a new nickname: "I am the Thinkerman, not Tinkerman."

Ranieri paid further tribute to his players by singling out those who had to spend significant parts of the season out of the team. He adds: "Their professionalism was fantastic because some players don't play but when I did call on them the players did a fantastic performance."

Classic Claudio. "If Riyad is our light, then Jamie is our airplane. He's our RAF."

On the 40-1 odds that they will repeat this feat next season: "I don't believe the bookmakers! They make big mistakes from the team and manager"

On lifting the trophy: "Could be (the greatest moment of my life). My fairytale start in Cagliari. That was my first. This is another"

On his mother: "She's very, very proud, but she's proud because she knows me as an honest man. For that, that was most important".

He said he did not know where he would keep his winners' medal but pondered: "Maybe I give for one moment to my grandchild."

On the fans: "They were dreaming. I say DILLY DING DILLY DONG! They wake up and the dream is a reality."

Ranieri was "very confident" that none of his key players will leave. "I'm very, very confident. I suggest to all my players stay one year more. Don't go. If you go another team, you might not get on the pitch."

The words had hardly left his lips when the internet was buzzing with the story that Mahrez would consider a move to a "big team" and was only 50/50 to stay, according to his agent, who has already attracted interest from a host of top clubs, with Manchester United among them. He would be offered a new contract despite signing a four-year deal worth £35,000-a-week shortly before the start of the season. Mahrez's agent, Kamel Bengougam, said his client was happy at the King Power Stadium, but would consider a move to one of Europe's elite clubs. Asked whether Mahrez could leave, Bengougam told *The Guardian*: "Yes of course there is a possibility. When you have been playing the way Riyad has this season it is bound to attract attention. He is very happy with Leicester and of course it has been a fantastic season. They will play in the Champions League next year as well so he would be happy to stay. But at his age if the opportunity comes to play for a big team then we would have to think about it. I'd say it's 50/50 at the moment whether he stays or goes. We have interest from the UK and overseas. We will have to see what develops over the next few weeks."

Is he looking forward to a rest? "I'm refreshed when I'm involved in the football. Now I am happy to plan my next football and think about 1 July to come back here and prepare for the new season."

In a statement of faith in his current team entering the Champions League, he added: "I don't want big names here. My lads are special. We have to bring some good players but who arrives must have the same spirit. The Manchester City victory can give to my players the feeling to understand they are able to fight with everyone and they can achieve everything. Of course I told you we were going step by step, but to them I said try we can win."

Ranieri stated. "We need our players. I want to improve the squad without big stars but the right players. It is too early to say we need five, six, seven or eight players. We know very well the project was to build the team, make a good foundation the first two years to be safe was our goal. Now of course we made a fantastic season but we have to bring this season and put outside and restart. If one of my players says to me, 'I want to go', I try to keep him. I suggest to everybody this is a fantastic club, we won the title, we can do something good in a few years. If you go away you don't know what happens, here you are the king. You maybe go in the big teams, maybe you don't start very well and stay outside the first 11, you slow down. The lads are my sons. If they come to me I say this: 'Be careful'. Leicester in the long term will go in a very high position."

Robert Huth was suspended for the final two games and the first fixture of next season. Fellaini misses United's remaining three league games but was available for the FA Cup final.

Crystal Palace manager, Alan Pardew, spoke about the title victory: "Leicester won it after 36 games. Last year for 10 games they were in the best form. For near 50 games they've been best in the country. It's proof the underdog can do it. And it will give us a boost for the cup final. Leicester have shattered the glass ceiling, and I thought it was impossible to break. They've gone and done it. Amazing. Football isn't all logic. It's almost like some stardust has fallen on Leicester City Football Club - great for them. Let's hope it falls on us for the final."

Hannah Gill - This is my brother (Tom) he has 36hrs to get a ticket for the LCFC game. He is flying home from Uganda! #ticketfortom

Jamie Vardy might be able to afford to buy him a ticket as he is estimated to cash in to the tune of £5m, starting with a massive advance payment to sign up for the book about his remarkable rise from non-League footballer to Premier League winner. Vardy said: "While my rise from non-league football has attracted plenty of attention, there is so much that people don't know, so I'm really excited that I've now been given the opportunity to tell the whole story, both on and off the pitch. Even now there are moments when I shake my head at the madness of it all - going from the factory floor and playing Sunday morning pub football with my mates, to scoring for my country against the World Cup winners in Berlin. It's the stuff of dreams. It hasn't always been an easy journey, some doubted that I was capable, and at times I was probably guilty of not helping myself, but nobody can question my passion for football or my commitment once I set foot on the pitch. I look forward to sharing all of that and more in what I hope will be an entertaining and inspiring story."

Ebury Press is publishing Leicester City striker Jamie Vardy's autobiography, My Story, on 20 October. The deal for world rights was made between John Morris of Key Sports Management and Ebury deputy publisher Andrew Goodfellow and editor Laura Horsley. The book will tell the story of Vardy's "incredible rise" from non-league football to the pinnacle of the game. Vardy was first rejected in his teens by his "boyhood club" Sheffield Wednesday, and earned just £30 a week while playing for Stocksbridge Park Steels and working in a factory.

Deputy publisher Andrew Goodfellow said: "The story of Jamie's against-the-odds rise to the top goes beyond football, and is an inspiration no matter who you support. His is the biggest sporting story of the year without question." Editor Laura Horsley added: "Having been brought up in a family of devoted Leicester supporters, I'm ecstatic to be working with Jamie to help him make this the most exciting and widely read sports book of the year."

It was reported in the *Sunday Times* that an advance of £250,000 was being negotiated for his memoir. Ebury, naturally, has made no comment on the finances of the deal.

As for the Hollywood blockbuster, producer Adrian Butchart told *Sportsmail*: "We are keen to shoot the movie as soon as possible, but we are now going to have to wait until after the Euros to know where the story ends as these unbelievable events continue to unfold. There are two things that seemed impossible a few weeks ago, Leicester to win the Premier League, and England to win the Euros. But with every match, fiction and reality seem to be coming together, the story keeps writing itself."

All this and a £20,000-a-week pay rise. Not bad when you started on £30. He had a clause written into his contract that if Leicester won the League, his salary would rise from £80,000 to £100,000, £5.2m a year.

Jamie Vardy and his fiancée, Becky Nicholson, are due to marry later this month after bringing forward the wedding due to Vardy featuring in the England squad for Euro 2016.

Vardy relaxed before the title-clinching match with a seven-hour session at body artist Nik Moss-Glennon's studio, and had a clock showing the time his daughter, Sophia, was born inked on his torso. Moss-Glennon said staff at the Belgrave Gate business returned to work on Tuesday to dozens of calls from supporters wanting bookings. The studio is co-owned by Wes Morgan. Moss-Glennon said the week had been "absolutely crazy."

He said: "In the build-up to it, there were a lot of people coming in and making enquiries but I did not anticipate just how crazy it was going to go when they did win. I was keeping track of what was going on with Tottenham then Twitter exploded, Facebook exploded. I tattooed Jamie Vardy that day and my social media started going crazy and it's just continued. That first day back in work after they had won, there were over 70 messages from people wanting Leicester-related tattoos. Towards the end of June is the first time I have anything free at all, so it's difficult because everyone has got the buzz right now and I'm putting in a lot of hours trying to keep people happy."

He was starting earlier and finishing later to help with the waiting list: "I understand the buzz that's going on and considering the Leicester City captain's involvement in this shop, it's a real shame for people to not get it done here."

He started working at the shop just as Leicester went on a winning run last season, "It's an ongoing joke, but I keep making out that they have done well since I started. If they start going downhill, I hope I don't get the sack."

New snooker world champion Mark Selby wanted to join the club's open-top bus parade after missing the moment they clinched the title because he was winning his second crown.

When Leicester won the Championship in 2014, Selby missed the team's bus parade through the city because he was beating Ronnie O'Sullivan to become world champion for the first time. "They had the open-top bus tour on the day of the Crucible final but I hope they can hold it back for me this time and I can be on there with them." Vardy encouraged him to overcome Marco Fu in the semi-finals. "He was texting me through the semi-final, saying 'good luck' and hopefully I'll get a few more messages from the boys."

FRIDAY, 6 MAY

A tasty way to start the day, as reported on the club's official website:

As Claudio Ranieri will tell you, pizza and football are a match made in heaven, and now thanks to Pizza Hut Restaurants, Leicester City fans attending Saturday's game can get one for free!

- Pizza Hut Restaurants are providing free pizzas for all home ticket holders at Leicester City's final home game against Everton on Saturday
- Supporters will receive a voucher entitling them to a free takeaway pizza from any of four Pizza Hut Restaurants in the city

- Claudio Ranieri famously promised to buy his team pizza earlier this season when they kept their first clean sheet

Inspired by the manager's early-season promise of pizzas for his team if they kept a clean sheet, Pizza Hut Restaurants are going one better by providing 30,000 FREE PIZZAS for home ticket holders on Saturday.

Saturday is without question the greatest day in Leicester City history as Wes Morgan lifts the Barclays Premier League trophy for the first time, and thanks to Pizza Hut Restaurants, the Blue Army can enjoy it a little but more with the prospect of a title-winning pizza to look forward to.

All supporters will receive a voucher that entitles them to either an 11" individual Pepperoni, Margherita, Hawaiian, BBQ Americano or Chicken Supreme on an 'All American Thin' or 'Pan' base.

"Pizza Hut Restaurants are delighted we can celebrate the incredible achievement of Leicester City Football Club and reward their amazing fans following what is arguably the most amazing achievement in sporting history," said a spokesperson.

"We feel a close connection to the city of Leicester having supported the club for the last few months and having just invested heavily in refurbishing our four major restaurants in the city. We hope every fan through the turnstiles enjoys their free pizza and that we can help the party be the biggest Leicester has ever seen! Well done Leicester City, we're celebrating with you!"

Pizza Hut Restaurants, we salute you!

Former Chelsea chairman Ken Bates accepted an invitation from Roman Abramovich to attend Chelsea's final game of the season against champions Leicester. The 84-year-old is to be a guest in the directors' box on what will be his first visit to the Bridge in a formal capacity since leaving his post as chairman a decade ago, within a year of the Abramovich takeover. It marks the triumphant return of former boss Ranieri, who will be assured a warm welcome from the fans and owner alike. Ranieri was a popular appointment during his four years in charge before he was sacked by Abramovich and replaced by Mourinho. Bates wrote into the manager's contract a clause enabling him to spend a week each year on holiday at Ranieri's estate in Tuscany.

The club unveiled the new Puma shirt for next season as the players will proudly display the new Premier League patch, worn by the champions. The new design was modelled by Okazaki, Morgan, Schmeichel and Vardy. King said of the new kit: "Again, PUMA have created a kit which looks fantastic. The piping on the front and back which offers hints of gold looks great and will help us stand out on the pitch. We cannot wait to walk out onto the pitch in the shirt at the start of the 2016-17 Premier League season, as we defend our Premier League title." The new shirt costs £50, cheap compared to Chelsea's kit next season costing £90 without name and number printing.

Matt Elliott captained the club to the League Cup triumph in 2000 and lead them into Europe. He paid tribute to this year's skipper. "Wes Morgan and Robert Huth have been out of this world. When defending deep there is no better pairing. They are the two best in the league at defending balls into the box. Balls come flying in and they get good contact with good distance between each other. They're strong, aggressive and protect their ground. Coming from Nottingham Forest shows what Wes made of. It's not an easy decision - they are big rivals. There were a few disgruntled murmurs because of the club he came from. By his own admission he has been overweight. Sometimes these overnight sensations take quite a long time to materialise. On reflection, he won't mind the wait will he? He could be struggling to keep his eyes dry when that moment comes on Saturday. He prides himself on being rough and aggressive but he may need someone looking after him when that trophy is presented to him."

Earlier in the week Morgan had stated he could be overcome lifting the trophy. "I am going to try and hold back the tears," he said. "It is going to be very emotional, it is the biggest moment of my life."

Elliott will be in the BBC's local radio box alongside commentator Ian Stringer, now renowned for his outpouring of emotion in reacting to Leicester's latest exploits.

"It's going to be party time on Saturday - one hell of an atmosphere," Elliott added. "Seeing people achieve gets to me - I like to see happiness in other people. That sort of thing chokes me up a little bit. Even midway through the season people were chewing through their programmes and there were tears at the magnificence of the atmosphere and performance. Hysteria has been steadily growing and it'll come to a crescendo on Saturday. Ian's an emotional wreck - it's been quite entertaining. He gets tearful if Leicester win away at Watford, never mind in Turin or somewhere else in the Champions League."

BBC Leicester Sport, BBCRLSport - Leicester City confirm victory parade will take place on Monday 16th May, starting at 6pm from Jubilee Square.

Jeff Schlupp and Marcin Wasilewski booked in to get celebratory tattoos done at skipper Wes Morgan's Blue Ink studio in Leicester.

Artist Nik Moss-Glennon had already inked tattoos for many of the squad including Vardy, Fuchs, Morgan and both Schlupp and Wasilewski. Morgan is discussing everyone in the team getting an image of the trophy tattooed on themselves. Expect the ink to be dry on a host of new contracts first, which will help pay the bill!

The champions will try to mark their final home match by beating Everton. Ranieri pledged his team would play with their normal intensity. They only got back into training on Thursday, after being given an extra day off to enjoy their triumph. When Leicester clinched promotion from the Championship two seasons ago they lost their next home match 4-1 to Brighton ending a 21-game unbeaten run. The then-boss Nigel Pearson said players appeared to be the worse for wear and substituted Anthony Knockaert at half-time then Mahrez later on. Ulloa, playing for Brighton at the time, scored twice to help earn a move to the Premier League new boys.

Ranieri joked that if that happened again: "I will kill them with my hands!" Ranieri commented: "They lost, yes, somebody told me. If it happens again, I will kill them with my hands. They enjoy celebrating of course, it is a great achievement for everybody. I am very happy when I see the city and the fans happy too. But the players trained very well on Thursday and I'm expecting a very good match on Saturday against Everton. "I watched how they trained on Thursday. It was good. It is important to clean our minds and keep going with our jobs. This is very sweet, but our job is to play. We are champions, but Everton want to beat us so it is right to put our mind on the job."

Ranieri welcomed back Vardy after his two-match ban; he went straight into the team, despite Ulloa scoring twice in his absence against Swansea and leading the line in the draw at Manchester United. Ranieri added: "Jamie is a fantastic player and a fantastic lad. For us it was difficult, but I want to say thank you to the other players, like Ulloa who played when we were without Jamie."

Leicester will soon be presented with the trophy. Vindication for Ranieri? "I don't say anything about criticism because criticism can help a man improve. Sometimes when it is about the person, it is not so good but I continue to respect everyone. If someone doesn't respect me, it is not my fault - their fault."

In an exclusive interview with the *Sunday Mirror*, Vardy's fiancée, Becky Nicholson, talked publicly for the first time about their rise to the top, their home life, and how they are already planning for their life after football.

Becky, set to tie the knot with Jamie later this month, reveals: "We're a team. I try my best to take all the stress away from Jamie's life, so he literally just has to focus on football. Because if he doesn't focus on football then he isn't doing his job properly. But neither of us are silly enough to think football lasts forever. We're trying to prepare for that. You can never take things for granted. We need to make sure we've got the foundations in place to continue to support our family. I'm constantly thinking about what happens when it ends. We're both trying to plan."

The next Posh and Becks? Come on. Now this is going too far. Becky insists: "Obviously we're not David and Victoria - we're still just Becky and Jamie - but of course they're great role models. I admire Victoria as a businesswoman for what she's achieved, just as much as I admire his achievements. She's become successful in her own right, and she's someone I have total respect for. Just calling me a WAG feels very outdated. We're a team in exactly the same way that the Leicester lads work as a team. As a footballer's partner it's not about being arm candy - but I'm sure Victoria would say herself it hasn't happened without her putting the hours in behind the scenes, and that's what I'm doing."

Champagne will continue to flow, but so too will the rum.

If champagne isn't for you then how about toasting Wes Morgan with a glass of rum?

Captain Morgan, the famous spirit brand, have created a special limited edition bottle in honour of Wes Morgan and Leicester City Football Club. On the label they have cleverly replaced their famous buccaneer with an image of the centre-back dressed in blue.

Morgan, the Leicester captain that is, has played every minute of the title winning season so far (3,285 minutes), becoming only the third ever outfield Premier League champion to do so. *Captain Morgan* are famous for their Caribbean spiced rum and with Wes Morgan becoming the first ever Jamaican to win the Premier League, this was a fitting tribute.

Drink Responsibly, Captain's Orders!

SATURDAY, 7 MAY

LEICESTER CITY 3-1 EVERTON

#HAVINGAPARTY

Gary Lineker, @GaryLineker - Today Leicester City will receive the @premierleague trophy. The most ridiculous, magical, wonderful thing I've ever tweeted about football.

The tension had disappeared. It was a party atmosphere, a day to celebrate.

"We know, what we are ... We know what we are ... Champions of England. We know what we are."

Supporters will be given a free beer on their arrival at the Stadium - while their matchday tickets were valid for a free pizza in the city. Ranieri had famously encouraged his players to keep a clean sheet back in October. At the time, the Italian said: "Football is like pizza. The most important ingredient is team spirit and the second is they enjoy training. That is important. Also to sprinkle a little luck is important, like salt. The fans are the tomato. Without the tomato, it's no pizza."

Thousands of fans queued from the early hours of Friday morning to get their hands on the club's new 'Champions' shirt ahead of the trophy presentation as title fever gripped the city. Long lines of people snaked around the Stadium before the club shop opened at 9am and such was the demand staff had to stop printing names on the back at around 1pm to get through the huge numbers waiting to be served. The queue for shirts was halted at 4.30pm so everybody present could get one before closing, but by then medium sizes had sold out.

A fairground was set up alongside the arena while hundreds gathered close to a big screen flashing up the greatest moments of this seismic season, each goal bringing rousing cheers. The long and winding Aylestone Road leading up to the King Power Stadium was packed with fans more than three hours before kick-off. Even those without tickets wanted to celebrate.

The Telegraph reported on several fans' stories: "In the stands, families born in Leicester but now living on different continents were reunited, as were season ticket holders who began sitting next to each other years ago as strangers and have become friends during the long, long wait for victory.

One man flew from Australia to watch the match with his brother-in-law. Another came from Thailand, home of the club's billionaire owner, with 34 of his friends. 'In Thailand, we normally support Manchester, Liverpool or Chelsea,' said Chadchai Pummanee, 'but they don't have the trophy.'

Inside the ground, Craig Sawbridge, a 35-year-old security guard found it bittersweet to take his seat and watch his team claim the trophy. He has been coming to Foxes matches all his life with his father, Barry, who died suddenly last year at the age of 58. Three days after attending his last Leicester game - sitting, as ever, next to his son - the elder Mr Sawbridge suffered a cardiac arrest. 'We're gonna win the league,' he predicted shortly before he died. A lifelong fan, he died wearing a club jersey and was buried in a blue coffin. On Saturday, both his sons sat together in the family's old seats. 'It would have meant the world to him to be here to see the champions lift the trophy,' said Craig Sawbridge. 'I am so joyous that we did it but also sorry my dad isn't here to share in it.'

Not far away sat Andy Ritchie, who can still remember his first match. He was seven when his father, Graham, took him to see the Foxes play Manchester United: he was dazzled by the atmosphere. Now 40 and the owner of a city centre delicatessen, he has stayed true to the club all these years, celebrating its occasional successes and bemoaning its far more frequent tribulations. 'It was painful,' he said. 'We played some awful football.' On Saturday, the Ritchies - father and son - were sitting next to each other in the stands once more, cheering on the team both men love. Arranging for Nessun Dorma was 'classic Ranieri', the younger Mr Ritchie said. 'For any football fan, it makes the hairs on your neck stand up.' Until then, he explained, the week had seemed surreal, something from a Hollywood storyline. 'We've been in a period of not quite believing it,' he said. 'This is the moment it all sank in.'

They were all here, devotees who have stayed with the club through its fallow years and a few who cheerfully confessed to being glory supporters. Glory supporters! At Leicester!"

Wes Morgan and Claudio Ranieri would be handed the silverware by fan Steve Worthy, who was selected by sponsors Barclays. Steve, 39, of Aylestone Park, Leicester, was selected from thousands of fans to hand over the trophy as part of Barclays' 'I Am One' campaign.

Steve, who was watching Monday night's game between Tottenham and Chelsea at home with his family, was clearly shocked as Leicester City legend, Muzzy Izzet, turned up on his doorstep carrying the trophy, surrounded by a camera crew.

He later confirmed that he is dedicating the incredible experience to his 97-year-old grandmother Gladys Kenny who, until last year, was the club's oldest season ticket holder until she had to retire her ticket due to failing health.

Leicester will have to hand back the trophy to the Premier League in the summer, though, so it can be remodelled following the end of Barclays' sponsorship. The bank's name is engraved but can be rebuffed away, while the Premier League logo also needs to be changed to the current version released in February.

The Premier League will make 40 medals available to Leicester, with players making five appearances and Ranieri guaranteed one. 19 members of the squad featured in the requisite number of games, leaving the club with 20 medals to hand out as they choose, mostly amongst coaches and backroom staff.

Robert Huth and Danny Drinkwater, both currently banned, were given the go-ahead to take part in the celebrations, reminiscent of John Terry at the 2012 Champions League final. Terry donned a full kit to join in the post-match party having worn a suit while sitting out Chelsea's win over Bayern Munich.   Ranieri would give Matty James a first squad place of the season and could send him on as a substitute, nearly a year to the day since he suffered the serious knee injury that has kept him out all season. "I think he deserves this because he fights all season to be ready and now I hope he has finished his bad adventure." said Ranieri.

There was a flurry of pre-match tweets:

Leicester City, @LCFC - Beer, crisps, flags and more. Thank you for all of your amazing support this season. #havingaparty

Danny Drinkwater - All smiles for the big day!! Going to be some experience, this.. #LCFC #Champions

Danny Simpson - Arrived in the dressing room. Unbelievable scenes outside. This is actually real #lcfc #champions

Robert Huth, @robert_huth - Going full John Terry today!! #fullkit #LCFC

Andrea Bocelli - Not long now #fearless #leicester

Martin Keown on *Football Focus*: "It is a breath of fresh air for football. The players are all instant legends because it is so unexpected. Looking to the future, with the Champions League, it just gets better and better. I think they are just enjoying the moment."

Phil McNulty, BBC Sport chief football writer at The King Power Stadium: "I arrived at The King Power Stadium three hours before kick-off and it looked like the party that had started when Leicester City won the Premier League on Monday night had been going all week. Thousands were thronging around the stadium, fairground rides were on the go, and inside the presentation platform was being put in place - not for the title presentation just yet but for a pre-match appearance by world-renowned tenor Andrea Bocelli, who is fulfilling a promise made to Foxes' boss Claudio Ranieri by performing here today.   The atmosphere around this stadium is sensational - and everyone connected with Leicester has every right to revel in the last second of it."

More than 90 minutes before kick-off, Alan Birchenall, club ambassador and former player, began his 36th annual charity run round the pitch, as the heavens opened, joined for a lap by each of the players as they emerged for their warm-up.

The players are serenaded with "Champione, Champione, ole, ole, ole" as they enter the pitch for the warm-up. It was absolutely lashing down in the East Midlands. Nothing, though, would dampen their spirits today though. One banner read "A Trophy Earned Not Bought" which epitomised the whole ethos of this remarkable success story. Another, simply stated "The Godfather - Claudio Ranieri".

Some of the fans' songs included: "We're all going on a European tour, dilly ding dilly dong", "We are staying up", "Are you watching Nottingham?", "Tottenham Hotspur, we're waiting for you" and "Barcelona, we're coming for you".

Phil McNulty continues: "Not sure anything can dampen the celebrations for Premier League champions Leicester City here at The King Power Stadium - but one almighty storm has hit the ground. Gone is the sunshine that greeted thousands of fans in the hours before kick-off when they gathered around the stadium and a fairground was in full flow. Now we have thunder and lightning. Will anything stop this party? Not a chance."

Tenor Andrea Bocelli was led out onto the pitch with Claudio's assistance 30 minutes before kick-off. The noise was deafening.

Ranieri looked close to tears as he had a message for the fans: "I want to say to you, we are the champions because you pushed us. Thank you so much. I love you"

Andrea Bocelli was drowned out until Ranieri held his hand up to tell them to calm down. He sang 'Nessun Dorma' (the one-time football anthem from *Italia '90*) during which he removed his top to reveal a Leicester City shirt underneath much to the delight of those watching. There then followed more chanting before Bocelli ended with a wonderfully emotional rendition of 'Con Te Partiro'...this was some show! Claudio was hard pressed to suppress the tears. (He later revealed he steeled himself not to cry on his greatest day, "It was amazing. I tried to be strong without emotion because I can live the moment better. It was amazing when the maestro Andrea Bocelli sang.")

Leicester City, @LCFC - Wow. Thank you to Andrea Bocelli for one of the most unforgettable moments we'll ever see at King Power Stadium. Incredible. #havingaparty

Andrea Bocelli, @AndreaBocelli - Thank you #Leicester and congratulations #LeiEve @LCFC

A football match soon followed.

A loud roar went around as the stadium announcer called out the "new Premier League champions" before reading out the name of each player.

For the record: Wasilewski and King came in, and Vardy returned in place of Ulloa. The starting XI being: Schmeichel, Simpson, Wasilewski, Morgan, Fuchs, Mahrez, King, Kanté, Albrighton, Vardy, Okazaki.

"Ranieri, oh oh oh oh.

Ranieri, oh oh oh oh.

He comes from Italy,

To manage the City."

This was a day *the game* will never forget and the manager and his players ensured they did it justice with the kind of performance that was a hallmark of their season; high intensity, which blew poor Everton away.

Vardy's glancing header after just five minutes from King's clipped cross, meant he scored the opening goal of the game 12 times in the Premier League, more than any other player. "Jamie Vardy's having a party," sang the fans, tapping their clappers. Andy King was next to score. King is the club's top goalscoring midfielder, the only Leicester player to have won Premier League, Championship and League One medals.

What a start and how hard they worked as if they were repaying the fans for all their tremendous support this season.

Ranieri stood on the touchline, hood up with the rain lashing down. Were there tears mingled with the rain?

There was a parade of greats at half-time, including England's World Cup-winning goalkeeper Gordon Banks, former captain and manager Frank McLintock - a league and FA Cup double-winner with Arsenal in 1971 - as well as Dave Gibson and Mike Stringfellow.

Jamie Vardy made it 3-0 from the penalty spot but then also blazed a spot kick high over the bar, and later tweeted: - Can someone please get my penalty off the helicopter please, #shank

#stillbetterthanhuthsfreekick

Kevin Mirallas scored a late consolation for Everton, but this was most certainly Leicester's party and nothing would spoil it.

The players were all on the pitch at the final whistle, hugging and congratulating each other. The Foxes had attempted 33 shots (including blocks) which was their highest total against any opponent in the Premier League this season. The blue and white flags were waved triumphantly as the players made their way off the pitch and into the changing room. Vardy, worryingly, held his left hamstring as he hobbled off. Motorised carts then hauled the podium onto the pitch, put together like a jigsaw by the well-drilled staff.

The Leicester staff soon made their way onto the pitch, led out by the club's Thai owners, and across a 'blue carpet' – what else! They were closely followed by Alan Birchenall, who "had dedicated his last 40 years to this football club," carrying the trophy and proudly wearing a never-ending smile.

Amidst huge roars, Claudio Ranieri was introduced back into the arena, accompanied by his coaching staff. They were first to receive their winners' medals, closely followed by squad members. It was then the turn of the regular team members against a backdrop of joyful singing and fervent flag waving.

Wes Morgan was the final hero to receive his medal and then, together with Ranieri, he was presented with the Premier League trophy and lifted it victoriously towards the, now, blue sky over Leicester. Ticker tape rained down, and fireworks exploded. The party, which had begun days ago, unashamedly rose to a new level of delirium. Leicester City were crowned as Champions of English Football!

"Champione, Champione, ole, ole, ole" sang the fans again as the trophy was passed lovingly from one to the next, each kissing it adoringly.

Robbie Savage, ex-Leicester midfielder on 606 on BBC Radio 5 live - "I have never seen anything like it, Wes Morgan's face when he lifted the trophy, he just could not believe it. I cannot believe what we are witnessing."

Pat Murphy, BBC Midlands football reporter at the King Power - "The most important moment in Leicester City's 132 years, improbably, gloriously, Leicester City Premier League champions 2016."

On-loan full-back Ritchie De Laet was on the bench for Middlesbrough earlier in the afternoon as they won promotion from the Championship - then he was collecting a Premier League winner's medal with Leicester City. He later posted an image on Twitter wearing the two league medals. And, with a master of understatement, he wrote "Not a bad day."

Claudio Ranieri was later holding court at the post-match press conference, and talking about Andrea Bocelli just as Kasper Schmeichel placed the gleaming Premier League trophy in front of him. The delight at seeing the trophy was quickly transformed to one of shock and horror as Christian Fuchs showered him, and some of the media, with champagne. "Tomorrow, training session!" he warned Fuchs. Eventually regaining his composure, and amidst much laughter, Ranieri exclaimed "bad lads, bad lads." And, wiping the stinging champagne from his eyes, he joked, "Yeah, I cry!" and burst out laughing.

Eventually continuing, Ranieri went on to say, "The emotion was at the top but it was fantastic," Ranieri said. "Andrea when he called me and said 'I want to come there, there is something magic in Leicester'. He chose this day and it was brilliant.

I want to say thank you to all our fans. In the bad moment, like when we were losing 2-0, they helped us so back so many times, at home, away. Without them it was very, very difficult now to get this trophy. And, of course, the more important person: the owner. Without the owner, that wasn't possible, that ambition.

I am a strange man. There are a lot of cameras on me to see if I cry and then I say 'today no'. I stayed there but inside the emotion was at the top. It will be a nice celebration but not a disco. No more than 10 times in my life have I been in a disco. There's a little party with the chairman upstairs then I go home to sleep.

It is fantastic the people have been unbelievable thank you to them, they push behind us all season. I was very, very, concentrated on being calm and of course I am very very happy. I think it was an amazing moment for me I am not youngest.

To lift the trophy is something special you are champion of the Premier League that is something special for me of course because I won some cups in Spain and Italy but to be champion here is fantastic. In my career I always thought sooner or later I will win a title but at the beginning I never though here would be the place but why not? This is crazy season big teams aren't consistent in season are we have consistency I believe at the top it is important to have a very good owner and I met fantastic people.

When I first came I thought this is a very good dressing room, all friends and I tried to build the Italian mentality, solid and strong. At beginning wasn't working so well but then after was fantastic At the beginning it was very important to stay in Premier League for a few seasons and then move up but now we are champions. We know very well this is strange year and have to put it aside and be focussed on next season, the foundations are strong.

I don't know next season what happens because this has been a magic season, but you imagine if Leicester start well again - oof, what happens? I don't know. Now, let me think only of this last match, let me go to the sea, recharge my batteries and we restart next season with the same ambition, with the same humility, with the same feeling."

Ranieri pinpointed March and consecutive games against Manchester City and Arsenal as the defining moments. "I think when we won at Manchester City. But when we lost 2-1 at Arsenal, I said to my assistant 'we can do something' because if Arsenal suffer so much with 11 against 10, we can do so much.

Always in my career I thought sooner or later I'll win a title. At the beginning I could never think here is the place. But slowly, slowly I said 'why not? This is a crazy season and the big teams don't have the consistency'. We had the consistency all season.

(Lifting the trophy) was an amazing moment for me because I'm not the youngest! There is another taste now. Because when you lift something special like the Premier League, it's something special for everybody, especially for me. For me of course, because I won a cup in Spain, but to lift the championship here is fantastic. The people are unbelievable. Thank you to them, because they put the push behind us all season.

(Next season) will be a very different season but the people are dreaming. Keep dreaming."

Leicester were, of course, widely tipped for relegation and keeping their hard-earned status was the board's top priority. Ranieri said: "They told me it is very important to stay in the Premier League for the next two seasons."

Ranieri paid tribute to Vardy and when asked if he could compare him to any strikers he has worked with, offered, "He is totally different. I could maybe compare him to Piojo López in Valencia because he was so fast, but the others? No. Jamie is a one-off. He's amazing."

Under pressure Roberto Martinez was furious with his players. "I think first and foremost it is just a day for Leicester City and to celebrate them. I think they've achieved an incredible feat of winning the Premier League and deservedly so. From our point of view, it was a very, very disappointing day. We never turned up, we never understood what was needed. I think we felt that we were part of a celebration - it was a footballing occasion that you could just concentrate on what you were doing on the ball. I thought off the ball we didn't have any intensity, any concentration and when you do that against any team you're going to get punished, but especially against Leicester."

Wes Morgan speaking to Sky Sports: "I am emotionally drained. It was an unbelievable feeling to finally get my hands on the trophy. I had to hold back the tears, I held them back and lifted it up - it was the best feeling in the world. Everyone has been going on about how I was going to lift the trophy and saying don't drop it and putting some pressure on me. There is no better feeling than lifting the trophy. Hopefully, we can crack on from here. It is a big, big season next season but I want to enjoy the moment. It's like a dream but now it's a reality and you just want to enjoy it. We have always believed. We knew on our day we were as good as all the other teams. It was about consistency. We do everything together. There are no egos in our team."

Jamie Vardy, speaking to Sky Sports, calms worries over a possible hamstring injury: "It was just a bit of cramp - it completely seized up. A bit of TLC needed. It would've been a lot better if I didn't put a ball over (from the penalty). It is an unbelievable feeling for everyone involved. I can't describe it - it is mental.

I think someone must have put a spell on me to make it happen.

Everyone works hard for each other. It if weren't for the lads then I wouldn't be on the goals that I have scored. You don't get nowhere by not having foundations and players having the talent to get results. We are like brothers. We are always going out with each other. After the result (2-2 Tottenham) you looked on streets and the police had to shut the road as there were so many people. It's taken a lot of hard work and I'm proud of what I've achieved personally but without the lads I wouldn't be here so have to thank them."

Riyad Mahrez speaking to Sky Sports: "It is something amazing what we have done. We are enjoying without families and it is fantastic. The fans are unbelievable, everything is for them and the families. It is a dream and today is very special. It is amazing. It's unbelievable. To be champions with our team I'm very happy and proud."

Kasper Schmeichel on Sky Sports: "It was a tough game knowing we would be presented with the trophy but I thought we played fantastic, it was a testament to our character. This is what dreams are made of, it is what you dream of as a kid. It is hard to put into words. You can see everywhere we go we have had a fantastic response. We have received a brilliant reception everywhere and had standing ovations at numerous Premier League grounds which is amazing."

SUNDAY, 8 MAY

Once again, Leicester City were making the headlines on the national newspapers.

The Independent headlined with, "Pitch perfect: superstar tenor Andrea Bocelli helps Leicester lift the trophy:

The BBC summarised the headlines:

In an eight-page pull-out, the *Mail on Sunday's* chief sports writer Oliver Holt says Leicester "have breathed new life and new possibilities into the English game. They have smashed the smug old order with its might-is-right philosophy and they have allowed us to believe that anything is possible again," he writes.

The Observer's Jamie Doward reports from Leicester on the celebrations, saying the presentation of the trophy was "confirmation for those worried that they were still dreaming that their side really was the best in England".

"This is the realisation they have really won the league," fan Lee Chapman tells the *Sunday Express*.

The celebrations in Leicester were more than just emotionally moving, according to the *Sun on Sunday*. The paper reports that students from Leicester University placed a seismometer near the King Power stadium, which recorded a "mini earthquake" as fans "cheered, clapped and stood during goals and presentations".

Thanks to the *Sunday People*, we learn Leicester is not just famous for its football team. According to the paper it has a "rich food heritage". Delicacies associated with the city and county include red Leicester cheese, Stilton cheese, Pukka Pies, Melton Mowbray pork pies, Walker's crisps, and curry.

Whether it be the 'Immortals', 'Fearless', 5,000-1, the greatest ever sporting underdogs, it was front page news here and around the world.

It has been one of my personal greatest book-writing pleasures to have recorded virtually every spit and cough along the way in this wonderful diary of their unique season.

Unique? Yes, unique, as I don't believe it will ever be repeated, not by Leicester City, nor anyone else. This isn't a game-changer. Yes, a breath of fresh air, but don't hold your breath it will be the same old, same old again next season, the grand old order will be re-established.

Having said that, Ranieri is certainly in the mood to defy the odds again. And remember, those who doubt him might be wearing underpants on *MOTD*. For next season, though, he'll need to revert to tinkerman type with the Champions League on top of the defence of the title. This will be a tough ask even for the 'Fearless' miracle workers at the King Power.

There are some incredible statistics around what has happened here. None of them measure the sheer joy, happiness, emotional hike the season has given virtually everyone - barring the majority of Spurs fans.

My own experience is quite interesting in so much the majority of publishers I approached many months ago were sceptical that any book chronicling this season would have any merit unless the team actually won the title, and they didn't think that possible, even relatively close to the finishing line. That is why the crescendo of interest, fascination, is really only relatively new, when it did look like the impossible was possible.

Now I'm heading off to the town for a whole series of signing sessions, including one at the San Carlo Pizzeria where Claudio Ranieri and his players celebrated the day after knowing they had won the title.

Today's Sunday papers were still in a celebratory mood, as well as a more calculating frame of mind. The *Mail on Sunday* estimated that Leicester City were heading towards untold riches as one of the wealthiest 15 football clubs in the world next season, leapfrogging even AC Milan, 18-times champions of Italy, and seven-times European Cup winners.

Leicester were No. 24 on the world's rich list for 2014-15 with an income of £104million. For the current campaign *Mail on Sunday* analysis shows they will climb into the top 20 with income of about £125m. Next season the huge hike in TV deals and the Champions League inevitably take them even higher. So, a top-eight finish and group-stage elimination, income should be £210m. A top-four finish and progress to the Champions League knockout stages could take that to £260m. Of course this is the usual hype. Sadly, it's hardly realistic for *little* Leicester to maintain this sort of momentum when all the big boys will be splashing the cash in spectacular fashion to not just catch up, but to overtake and leave them in their slip stream.

From one of the least-watched Premier League teams last season to the sixth-best watched this season, Leicester have, though, broken through the glass ceiling of this country's powerful elite.

The club's Twitter account can claim to have the 17th most retweeted post of all time. The tweet that read "Leicester City Champions of England" was retweeted over 400,000 times since it was posted on Monday evening. The most shared football tweet, indeed sporting tweet, in history.

Gary Lineker still hasn't presented *Match of the Day* in his pants and after seeing the fully-clothed 55-year-old presenting Saturday night's programme, fans took to Twitter to express how "disappointed" they were, especially as Fuchs said into camera that he can't wait to see what kind and colour he would choose. Gary told the *MOTD* audience to be patient.

Glenn Hoddle, the former Spurs manager, writing in his *Mail on Sunday* column, observed: "It's difficult to comprehend just what Leicester City have done this season. Bitterly disappointed as I was on Monday night as a lifelong Tottenham man, you couldn't help but admire the sheer audacity and spirit of Leicester.

Denmark came off the beach in 1992, when they only qualified because of the late exclusion of Yugoslavia, to win the European Championship. That was extraordinary and they played in a similar style to Leicester. They had fantastic team spirit and real pace and attacking energy. Yet that was an eight-team tournament and they only played five games to win. In a tournament sometimes you can find that run of form. Over 38 games? It's almost unheard of for an underdog to manage that. Nowhere in the major leagues in western Europe in recent times has there been anything quite like this. Atletico Madrid were incredible in getting ahead of Barcelona and Real Madrid to win the La Liga two years ago, as were Valencia in 2002 and 2004. Yet those are both major clubs with their own rich record of previous title wins and pedigree in European competitions. Stuttgart and Wolfsburg have both won the Bundesliga recently but the former are still a bigger club than Leicester and the latter are backed by Volkswagen. The last Italian side outside of Inter, AC Milan, Juventus, Roma and Lazio to win the scudetto was Sampdoria in 1991. And they were a well-funded club at the time.

Certainly there are parallels with Brian Clough's Nottingham Forest and their title win of 1978. There are many similarities in style. Forest played 4-4-2, they wanted to get forward quickly and they had a core of players from one to 11 which they rarely changed and which induced an amazing team spirit. In that way, Leicester are a throwback to the Seventies.

What has been truly impressive is the way in which they have held their nerve. Manchester United, Liverpool and Chelsea never even made it into the race. And even at the end, sadly from my point of view, Tottenham buckled.

But Leicester kept their nerve, even though their players had never had a prize like this in their sights. When they lost, unluckily, in the last minute against Arsenal at the Emirates, they came back with a scrappy 1-0 win against Norwich in their next game.

And then, following the 2-2 draw with West Brom, that run of another four 1-0 wins followed by a 2-0 victory at Sunderland. That looked more like an experienced team who had been there many times before, closing out on yet another title win. It's what you might have imagined from Manchester United 10 years ago, or Chelsea at their best under José Mourinho. It was hard to believe they were rookies.

But for me, the performance of the season came a little earlier, back in February, at Manchester City. If you could bottle up the season and squash it into 90 minutes of football, there it was. Leicester simply took City apart that day. Danny Drinkwater was playing the kind of football I never believed him capable of. And City, who were still very much in the title race, simply couldn't cope with Riyad

Mahrez. Leicester only had 34 per cent of the possession yet, with so little, created so much. They had chance after chance and were worthy 3-1 winners.

Now to the future. They will have to live with the burden of expectation. They have to protect their key players. It's not so much about who they can buy, but can they keep their star men. If one leaves, so be it. If they lose Mahrez, N'Golo Kanté and Kasper Schmeichel, then it will be hard to build on what they have done. This weekend, though, is for celebrating their achievement and enjoying it. It is unique in Premier League history and even a Tottenham man like me can appreciate it."

Mark Schwarzer, Leicester City keeper, on *MOTD2 Extra*, "Claudio Ranieri was written off most of his career. That adds an incentive to prove people wrong. 18 months ago he was written off as rubbish after being sacked by Greece. Now he has won one of the biggest domestic trophies in football. He hasn't come in with his ego. I have only seen Claudio Ranieri lose his cool a couple of times - he hasn't really needed to. We have all clicked, it's gone really well, and of course we have a number of players who want to prove a few people wrong.

This season everything has come together. Now we've got to bring the right players in and it's why our manager has said in recent weeks that he's not going to recruit superstars. It would be the worst thing you could do, recruiting someone that thinks of themselves as above others. It could ruin the dynamic of the squad. I'm sure some of my team-mates are still out celebrating! I have been overwhelmed, excited and happy at what the boys and the club have accomplished this season. We've gone from relegation certainties to winning the Premier League in about 18 months.

After the laps of honour we went back to the changing rooms, chatting and actually it was pretty quiet because pretty much everyone was on their phones! Literally half of them, the kids of today, barely lifted their heads up! All season, nearing the climax, I never sensed nervousness. Everyone has taken everything in their stride, sticking to their jobs, and of course the manager has kept everyone's feet on the ground. As for the party at Jamie Vardy's house? Well, let's just say there are a lot of stories I'm not going to talk about now!"

Amy Lawrence, *Observer* football reporter, on *MOTD2 Extra*, "We've become accustomed to familiar clubs winning the trophy, plus the sense that we know how a season will be. All sorts of people I know, who wouldn't normally watch the football, tuned in yesterday to see Leicester lift the trophy."

Alan Smith's 'Player of the Weekend' in his *Telegraph* column: "With so many choices in Leicester's march to immortality, I have to nominate the captain, a quiet, understated sort who clearly can't believe what has just happened. All the players will tell you. Wes Morgan is held in tremendous respect. It has been one of football's great stories that a centre-half who didn't look particularly special at Nottingham Forest should be transformed into a figure of such solid renown."

His 'Hero of the Weekend': "Obvious, perhaps, but how can you possibly look past Claudio Ranieri, a man who has given so much to our game over the past nine months? Leaving aside the magnificent achievement of leading Leicester to glory, it's the way the Italian has introduced charm, humour and humility to an environment normally dominated by pressure and stress. The compilation of Ranieri's best quips adds up to TV gold. Dilly ding, dilly dong!"

Alan's 'Moment of the Week': "This was quite personal. Because Alan Birchenall, a Leicester City ambassador, a funny, warm-hearted character who has been at the club forever, was given the honour on Saturday of bringing the Premier League trophy on to the pitch. You could see the overwhelming joy and pride, more than a touch of emotion, as he carried it out to the plinth. There are not many around like Birch. A proper Leicester legend."

Jamie Redknapp observed in his *Daily Mail* column: "Winning the title is supposed to happen at Manchester United. It's supposed to happen at Manchester City. Chelsea, Arsenal, even Blackburn when they had Kenny Dalglish and all that investment, were all meant to win the title. It wasn't meant to happen at Leicester. I had the privilege of being at the King Power Stadium and I have never experienced such a positive, happy atmosphere in my life. For Jamie Carragher and I to be pitchside and not cop any kind of abuse is unheard of, though we didn't venture too near the Everton end! When Wes Morgan came to us after the game and you could see the tears in his eyes. He is a colossus of a man but the emotion was obvious. And everybody was feeling it. Football sometimes has a habit of letting us down - from performances on the pitch to behaviour off it - but Leicester's has been the most incredible story in sport. And there is nothing to dislike about them. They have won this title comfortably and in some style. It was a special occasion and to round things off with a win like that was absolutely magnificent. It might have been a beautiful accident, but this has been the ultimate feel-good title win."

Final words to Danny Drinkwater:

Danny Drinkwater, @DannyDrinkwater - Some journey that lads!! 3 years on.. Championship winner 2013/14 & now @premierleague winners 2015/16

Need to drink water.. #Hanging

MONDAY, 9 MAY

In April, Claudio Ranieri won the Enzo Bearzot Award, given by the Italian Football Federation to the Italian coach of the year. The award was founded in 2011 to honour Bearzot, the 1982 World Cup-winning coach who died in 2010. The highly-coveted accolade is voted for by a jury composed of representatives of major Italian sports newspapers.

Claudio flew to Rome to collect the Bearzot award in person. "Honestly, I still haven't realised what we've done," said Ranieri, speaking at the ceremony. "We started off just trying to avoid relegation and you saw what happened. I never met Bearzot but I've been told by people that they see his spirit in me and that fills me with pride."

Italian FA chief Carlo Tavecchio said: "Of all the titles won by Italians, Claudio's achievement is something unparalleled."

He would like to see Ranieri coaching the Italian national team one day. "I'm talking in an abstract manner, not about the next World Cups. Claudio is young and he has time. In his second sports homeland (England) he still has a lot to achieve. And I don't think it would be easy to deprive him of that opportunity. Have we thought about him as a replacement for Conte? It's him who should be thinking about us! We're thinking about a lot of different things right now, but those in his second sporting homeland are wishing him every success."

Ranieri warned Europe that "underdogs can be dangerous". Well, he should know; King of the underdogs.

Equally, Ranieri can keep perspective with Leicester 50-1 to win the Champions League - 100 times shorter price than they were to lift the Premier League last summer.

"I am confident because this team three years ago won the Championship and the Championship is very tough," he said. "They run all the time. I hope we can find good players and make some replacements because next season there will be three cups and the Premier League and it will be important to be able to make good changes and give some rest to the players.

I believe when there will be draw for the Champions League a lot of teams will want to play against us because we are in Europe for the first time and they think we are underdogs. We are underdogs but we are dangerous. Underdogs can be dangerous teams."

Ranieri added: "I will keep my medal in my home and when there is a bad moment I will take it out, look at it and say, 'Hey, come on man, balance.'"

Jamie Vardy, who recently took his goal tally to 24, tried to evaluate the situation. "It is unbelievable. I don't think words can describe it, to be honest with you. You can just see with the celebrations with all the fans and the players, it is unimaginable, frightening."

Vardy put success down to the family spirit within the club. "It's unbelievable - you've seen the team spirit that we've got," he told *Foxes Player*. "It is a scandal how we all are together. We literally are like brothers. When training and matches are finished, we'll all go out and have food together, we're always in touch with each other. That just shows how much as a unit we all are as a team and it shows in our performances week in, week out."

Vardy launched his V9 Academy to unearth the next non-League star, providing mentoring at the Etihad Campus between 14-19 May 2017, with 42 players split into three teams over a five-day residential course, featuring professional coaching. Each player will be assessed technically, tactically, physically, mentally and given a portfolio to help with further progress, while professional clubs will be present to scout those who could compete higher. "We were having a chat over the last few years to think about doing something like this, because of where I come from, and having played against a lot of players who could have played league football," said Vardy. "It's good to have the opportunity to do it now and hopefully find players and give them the chance. It is right to give something back."

Along with backers, Vardy will help finance the Academy, while his fiancée Becky Nicholson, a co-founder, is involved in the marketing and sponsorship.

"I moved to Fleetwood on the last day of the window," said Vardy. "There was a game that night and I was expecting to be on the bench. I turned up looking forward to being in the squad, and then the manager Micky Mellon called me into his office and said I was starting. I managed to put in a man-of-the-match performance and end up with three staples in my head, from a York centre half's teeth going into it."

Vardy was released from Sheffield Wednesday as a teenager because he was only 4foot 11inches but believes clubs should not make decisions until players reach the age of 21. "I was told I was too small," Vardy said. "I was not ready for the physicality of scholarship. I don't think anyone can be told if they're good enough at 15 or 16, when you still have so many years to grow and develop. That was my reason, probably hundreds told the same and had to drop down as well. Hopefully we can find them, get them to the Academy and get them through. I have done it; that is there for people to see it can be done. With the players we get on and if they put the hard work in - and it will be hard, it will not be easy - we will give them Premier League standard-training and coaching, we can give them chance to make the step up. It will be held in the off season when most teams rip up pitches and re-soil so there are not many places that can do it. We have found the right place, with somewhere to stay so players are not driving here, there and everywhere."

Vardy's agent John Morris is a co-founder and will help any transfers that might arise from the Academy. "It is not always the best players who make it," he said. "You have to be tough enough to get through. The amount of times people have said no to me about Jamie, whether it was because of his aggression on the pitch, his lifestyle off it, because he's not great with his back to goal. Every time he has just said: 'Ok, I'll prove them wrong.'"

Vardy confirmed he is happy to stay at Leicester next season and vowed to stick to his high-energy style in the Champions League in the hope it can be effective against Europe's best. "We've just won the league and will be playing in the Champions League next year. I am happy here." Asked whether spirit among players would keep the squad together, Vardy replied: "I think we are hoping it will. There will be names thrown into the hat all summer but the group of lads we have, winning the league, and having Champions League football next season, you hope it keeps everyone together. Nothing has really been spoken about like that between the lads. We're just concentrating on each and every game as they come. One thing we want to do is keep that mentality of winning. We will be back on that training field this week and hopefully putting a performance in on Sunday that gets us another win."

Leicester's counter-attacking, high-energy tempo might surprise Europe's elite. "We are definitely hoping so. We have got ourselves into this situation playing that way, why change it? It has worked for us so we will hopefully make sure it works for us again. I'm not sure we will surprise people. Leicester has been on everyone's radar all season, they will have heard all the stories coming out about how well we are doing. A lot of the European teams will have probably been watching us. They will have to do their homework as well as we'll have to do our homework on them. Once it comes to game time it will be 100 per cent going out and hopefully getting wins."

Retweeted 110,000 times due to their title rivalry, Vardy claimed his decision to post a picture on his Twitter account of the Lion King's Mufasa falling to his death was simply because "that's my favourite kids' film!" Vardy offered this cheeky response to a question about his social media ribbing with Kane, who started the exchange by posting on Instagram an image of a pack of lions after Leicester had drawn with West Ham to open up the title race.

Vardy and Kane would be named in Roy Hodgson's provisional squad for Euro 2016. Vardy, who remained in the contest with Kane over the Golden Boot, said: "When you go away with England you don't really talk about club football. We're away with England to do a job for England and that's all we focus on while we're there. After that when you back to your own clubs, I'm sure a few of us can put a few pictures out and let the media join the dots up themselves."

Vardy responded to claims by Pochettino that Hazard and Fàbregas were unprofessional by airing their 'personal opinion' on wanting Leicester to win the title during the run-in. The comments perhaps hinted that Chelsea might easily be brushed aside. "I can't see any team doing that, to be honest with you. I don't think anyone would like to just turn up and be rolled over to let someone else win, I don't think that is inside anyone. It wouldn't look good on the club if they were doing that and I'm sure the fans wouldn't like it. So I can't see that being true whatsoever."

Facebook, in conjunction with the *Mirror*, held an online football awards poll.

The aim was to celebrate the best of the 2015/16 Premier League season, and it would be the only 'end of season awards' in the footballing calendar to be chosen purely by the fans. In the end, nearly one million votes were cast by fans, from 193 countries.

Voting took place on a dedicated tab on Facebook and through the Facebook pages of *Mirror Football* and ITV Football. Voting opened at 00.01h (BST) 15 April 2015 and closed at 23.59h (BST) on 29 April 2016. Anyone with a Facebook account was eligible to vote.

The 'Player of the Year' award went to Riyad Mahrez. In reply he stated, "It's something special, and something big as well, because it's from all over the world, and I thank them, and thanks to all of my fans. I love all my fans. I am very happy."

Leicester City then completed a hat trick of awards by scooping 'Manager of the Year' for Claudio Ranieri and the prestigious 'Club of the Year' award. The enigmatic Italian's return to the Premier League sparked Leicester's fairytale story, and fans around the world showed their appreciation by voting for him en masse.

Huth, Mahrez and Vardy also featured in the 'Best XI of the Year'.

The winners of these were announced live on ITV Football and the Mirror Football's Facebook pages at 7pm on Monday 9th May 2016. The ceremony was hosted by Sam Matterface and featured Lee Dixon, Robbie Savage and Fernando Morientes providing their insight on the fans' choices.

Leicester's main hospital experienced an influx at its A&E department after their title party. Leicester Royal Infirmary said twice as many people as usual arrived at the unit overnight, with many suffering alcohol-related injuries after tens of thousands of fans poured in to the city to join in the football celebrations. A statement from the University of Leicester Hospitals NHS Trust said: "Last night and this morning we have seen twice as many patients in our emergency department than we would normally on a Saturday night and Sunday morning. We expected it to be incredibly busy this weekend and have the necessary plans in place to safely treat our patients. A plea is for those who do not need to come into A&E to call NHS 111 for healthcare advice."

TUESDAY, 10 MAY

The players asked Steve Walsh not to propose new signings that might unsettle the strong team ethic that has proved such a source of success.

Ranieri's assistant said new contracts have been agreed for himself and fellow No 2 Craig Shakespeare, although the paperwork had yet to be signed but improved terms were sorted out, extending their deals to 2018 to align with Ranieri.

Arsenal had looked at a move for Walsh, while Nigel Pearson wants both at his next job at Aston Villa. Walsh said: "We've not signed but it's all agreed." Vice-chairman Aiyawatt Srivaddhanaprabha said only "small things" delayed it "but both have agreed". He added: "They did a brilliant job here and we are happy to do that."

BERTIE BIG WON'T BE SIGNING

Walsh turned to next season, with squad strengthening for the Champions League a priority. Targeting stellar signings was not on the agenda, with the same scouting methods for unearthing hidden diamonds continuing instead.

"The players have said to me, 'We don't want any Bertie Big'. I think you've got to bring in the people who you think will do the job, people who fit in. Claudio enjoys the blueprint and the way we play, we try and duplicate that, so hence you look for similar type of players who can fulfil the roles in the team that you need. It's not just upon me, because I've got people working for me, bringing information, and we've got to act on it. Obviously then decisions have got to be made with the manager, who can decide."

The club had succeeded on a small budget and with low possession statistics. Walsh revealed the secret to player acquisition was not based on ability alone, he told BBC Radio 5 live. "It's about making sure the players you bring in are strong of character, and can do the tasks we ask them to do when we haven't got the ball. If you just needed to get all the best players, talent scouting would be easy, wouldn't it? You've got to look at the players maybe through different eyes and see what they can achieve. That's the skill. We have a DNA. For me, it's not just about their ability on the ball. It's what they're prepared to give to the team when we haven't got it. Obviously, the character of the person shines through. If you're prepared to put in a shift when we haven't got the ball, that says a lot about you in terms of your work ethic."

Kanté was described as the best midfielder in this season's Premier League by Sir Alex, as ball-winning was key to the fast, counter-attacking style. Walsh persistently urged Ranieri to secure a deal by telling him: "Kanté, Claudio, Kanté."

He added: "We did have that conversation, but obviously he took my advice, brought him in and the rest, as they say, is history. People think we play with two in midfield, and I say: No. We play with Danny Drinkwater in the middle and we play with Kanté either side, giving us essentially 12 players on the pitch."

Walsh, a Lancashire-born former schoolteacher who scouted for Mourinho and who has been with the Foxes in two spells since 2008, knows the real satisfaction is building a title-winning squad from scratch. "Sven-Göran Eriksson brought in Kasper Schmeichel in 2011," Walsh said. "But apart from him, and the kids who have come through the academy, such as Andy King and Jeff Schlupp, we scouted them all. Christian Fuchs, the left-back who we got on a free transfer from Schalke, scored against Real Madrid in the Champions League at the Bernabeu last year. He's captain of Austria. He wanted to come. It was a no brainer."

Walsh admits that he and fellow assistant Craig Shakespeare were "upset" when Pearson was sacked, unsure what to expect from Ranieri. "I had big ties with Nigel, and both Craig and I were very upset when he left," Walsh said. "They chose Claudio, for whatever reason, and it's been a fantastic success. We've all gelled and worked together. Claudio knows what he wants. I think that's the easiest way to put it. He definitely wants to keep a clean sheet and he definitely wants people to defend. It was a while before he kept a clean sheet, hence he put together the idea of going out for a pizza. That tells a tale, doesn't it?"

Players were relatively free of injuries and they played only five cup ties, while compared to Spurs and Arsenal 15 each, and Manchester City 21. Walsh knows they now need a bigger squad to cope with the demands of a minimum of six Champions League fixtures. "I think we're going to need more personnel. We'll go from playing one game a week this year to two games a week. That, in itself, says you need more personnel on the ground. But we're in the Champions League now. It's fantastic for Leicester to actually be in the Champions League. Liverpool haven't won the Premier League. That says it all, doesn't it?"

Nineteen players automatically received a Premier League winners' medal by playing in five or more games, but the club were aware extra personnel and quality was needed. "But with that comes expectations of massive wages and big transfer fees, and that's certainly not the way we're intending to go. That might change, who knows! The problem is you're playing two games a week now. We were fortunate this season that we went out of the cups pretty early, so we only had the league to concentrate on. Clearly we'll need some extra players. There are very few in the squad out of contract, so the ones who did it this season will be given the opportunity to see if they can duplicate that form again."

Danny Simpson and Christian Fuchs believed Champions League football and the prospect of achieving more with Leicester would convince them all to stay. "Whatever the lads decide to do is up to them," said Simpson. "We just hope we can keep this group together because for me it has so much potential to do even more things than what we have." Fuchs added: "We're playing Champions League football next season, isn't that a good enough reason to stay at this club? I think all the lads know what this team is all about. So why not stay? I believe that."

Jamie Vardy felt the manager giving them a week off in February, trusting his players, made a big difference. "It was a great idea. I remember sitting on a sun lounger in Dubai and in the same hotel, Sunderland were there running up and down the beach doing fitness. For me to be relaxing while they're doing the training was quite nice."

Talking of Vardy, *Standard Sport* broke a story that West Ham were "seriously considering" testing the water on a £25m bid for Vardy even though the Thai owners insisted they intend keeping their top stars.

On the back of their move to the Olympic Stadium and an influx of quality players, the Hammers believed they can attract stars of the calibre of Vardy. Liverpool's out-of-favour striker Christian Benteke or Theo Walcott were other possibilities plus Southampton's Sadio Mané, Belgium international Michy Batshuayi and Lyon striker Alexandre Lacazette, all of whom were more realistic than Vardy leaving.

Rennes starlet Ousmane Dembélé rejected a move despite a personal phone call from Claudio Ranieri. European football's most-coveted teenager, chased by Manchester City, Manchester United, Arsenal, Liverpool, Tottenham and a host of clubs on the continent, decided on where his future lies but that will not be with the new English champions after he told Ranieri that he had no interest.

The 18-year-old winger won France's Young Player of the Year award this week after helping Rennes into the top seven of Ligue 1. "I had Claudio Ranieri on the phone," Dembélé told *Ouest-France*. "I was surprised to hear from him, I told him that I will not go to Leicester. I know where I am going."

Scouts from Barcelona and Bayern Munich are among those who checked on Dembélé's first season in Ligue 1 which yielded 12 goals and five assists. Former United and Arsenal defender and now adviser at Rennes, Mikael Silvestre, said earlier this year: "I'm going to be blunt, one day Ousmane Dembélé will feature in the Ballon d'Or shortlist. I saw Cristiano Ronaldo when he arrived at Manchester United at the same age. Ousmane shows similar attributes."

Riyad Mahrez was the Leicester City fans' Player of the Season to add to PFA Player of the Year, collecting the prize at the end of season awards ceremony at King Power Stadium this evening. "It feels good. It's good to be voted for from the fans," Mahrez told the lcfc.com website. "I want to thank them all and I love all the Leicester fans because they are great supporters. I'm very happy. We just know we've done something crazy - something unbelievable. For myself first, the goals I scored for the team, all the wins. The Aston Villa win when we were 2-0 down and we won 3-2, and the Manchester City win away. The stadium is very amazing. The fans are close to us and I feel very good here to play. I just want to say thank you to all the fans - I hope they support us every year." Mahrez follows veteran Argentina midfielder Esteban Cambiasso who won the award at the conclusion of the 2014-15 season. Perhaps not surprisingly, Jamie Vardy's stunning volley against Liverpool in February was voted Leicester's goal of the season. N'Golo Kanté was voted players' player of the season. The 3-1 demolition of Manchester City at the Etihad in February was club performance of the season. Jeff Schlupp won young player of the year. And, Ben Chilwell was voted U21 players of the season with Admiral Muskwe the club's top academy player.

WEDNESDAY, 11 MAY

Ending the campaign on a high was the focus. Speaking to ESPN, Jamie Vardy was eyeing victory at Stamford Bridge and will be putting the team's needs before his own, despite vying for the Golden Boot with Kane and Agüero. He said: "It'd be nice but the main thing is for Leicester to keep trying to have that winning mentality, so we'll go into Chelsea trying to win and if I don't score and we win, that's how it's going to finish."

Vardy remained shocked by his side's incredible success. "It's hard to explain. Obviously no one expected us to be within a shout and we've just kept going all season and made that come to reality. But trying to put that into words is very hard. Seeing Wes and the boss lift the trophy and then it getting passed around to each of the lads to have a little hold themselves before the lap of honour, that's when it did hit home. To try to put it into words is massively hard to do."

Vice-chairman Aiyawatt Srivaddhanaprabha will discuss a new deal with the Claudio Ranieri, whose current contract expires in 2018 having been appointed on a three year at the start of the season.

"We will sit down together. It's not fair to talk now with one game to go," said Srivaddhanaprabha. "At the end of the season we will talk about that with him. When we talk about something, it's long term, not just until September. I like people to work for me when they are happy and enjoy working with the group of people. We are very close as a family and everyone understands the same. The target was to survive this season. We know realistically the club still has to build a lot if you want to fight for the title again, top four, top five, top seven. I don't know. Realistically we have to build the team still because we are in the development process of the club. It is the second year for the club and the owner to be here. We have to build the foundation of the team and if it is like this season again then we are ready, we will go for that. We will try more and more until we are ready to fight for a bigger challenge." Asked whether that meant Ranieri would be rewarded, he said: "Exactly." But the club will want to remove a release clause allowing Ranieri to leave for a minimal fee. Ranieri was enjoying an extended break in Rome with wife Rosanna after receiving his manager of the year award.

Ranieri was named Premier League Manager of the Month for April after guiding Leicester to three wins and a draw. City beat Southampton 1-0 at the King Power Stadium at the start of April followed by a 2-0 victory over Sunderland at the Stadium of Light. The 2-2 draw against an in-form West Ham followed and again prompted questions about Leicester's staying power, but Ranieri's side returned to form with an emphatic 4-0 win against Swansea to end the month on a high. Ranieri was selected ahead of Pellegrini, Klopp and Allardyce as a prelude to being favourite for winning the coveted Manager of the Year award.

THURSDAY, 12 MAY

The meaning behind Ranieri's "dilly ding, dilly dong" catchphrase was unravelled by Gianfranco Zola, who was coached by his compatriot at Napoli. He disclosed that the saying is used when Ranieri believes his players are not concentrating.

Zola told beIN Sport: "Dilly ding, dilly dong... it goes a long way back, to the times of Napoli. Mr. Ranieri has always been very, very colourful when he speaks to the dressing room. I remember sometimes Marcel Desailly would act as his translator for the players. It was funny because Mr. Ranieri didn't realise it, but Marcel used to cut out half of his team-talks to make them quicker and more simple! His communication, though, has always been good and passionate. The 'dilly ding, dilly dong', was always a phrase he used in his speeches. When I first heard it I knew exactly what he meant. 'Dilly ding, dilly dong'... he told me this so many times. Sometimes as a player you just need a wake-up call because concentration is so important in football."

Former Juventus defender Nicola Legrottaglie, who played under Ranieri at Juventus, commented, "He's legendary. I would label him an example of how anyone should spur himself to achieve the impossible if you believe and all work towards the same goal." He told Omnisport, "When there is one and only one mentality, a synergy between the club, the players and the city you can do something amazing. This was Leicester's secret. A lesson that should be taught in schools. Ranieri likes to be up to date, he is meticulous, he always proved to be a decent man first of all. I spent my best years at Juventus with him, two wonderful seasons when I became an international and with (Giorgio) Chiellini I became one of the best central defenders in Italy. Chiellini and I were the best and Ranieri is a gentleman and that makes the difference. Tactics-wise there are better managers, but football is not all about this. The person you are and the principles you give out are very important. That is why I am happy when Ranieri wins, although he won less than he deserved. Some people say that when you stick to the right principles you may win less on the pitch, but according to me you win in life."

Claudio Ranieri had coached Gianluigi Buffon while at Juventus and the two clearly remain in close contact. In fact, Ranieri sent Buffon a Leicester City shirt signed by the players with the message "To Gigi, our legend". Buffon, himself, had just signed a new contract with Juventus until 2018.

In response he tweeted:

Gianluigi Buffon @gianluigibuffon - Una giornata di firme speciali. La mia con la Juve fino al 2018 e poi quelle del #Leicester. Grazie Mister #Ranieri!

Which roughly translates as "A day of special signatures. Mine with Juventus until 2018 and then those of Leicester"

A big Betfred winner, rocker David Cooper, composed a tribute song for the champions.

Pre-season the head-banging bass guitarist of band Smokescreen wagered £6.65 at 1,500/1 on the Foxes winning the league and placed £13.35 on them achieving a top four finish. That won £11,329 from his two bets, which he's had in his bank account since 3 April after Betfred led the way paying out early.

He's already pledged to buy the heavy metal foursome a new van to get around to gigs in Lincolnshire, Cambridgeshire and throughout East Anglia, but after his Betfred windfall was widely reported there has been an upsurge in bookings - and he decided to write the song which has been posted on YouTube.

Thirty-year-old Arsenal fan David said: "So many people have been asking me about the win that I decided to compose a tribute song which can be incorporated into our show. Since the news got out I keep being asked for tips and I have had some more success myself picking up another £10 win from Betfred on the Spurs vs WBA game.

Another thing I have noticed is that I have become a lot more popular at the bar!

It's the most I have ever had in my account. I have paid my dad, Philip, back a thousand (pounds) I owe him for rent and things. The idea of recognising Leicester in music came when I was watching the Leicester vs Swansea game on TV. The crowd were chanting 'were gonna win the league, were gonna win the league'.

My dad said you should turn that into a song and I have done so with the help of Smokescreen singer and drummer Sam Loose. Forget Chas and Dave it's Sam and Dave that will be all the rage!"

FRIDAY, 13 MAY

Leicester City, BREAKING: #lcfc striker @vardy7 named @premierleague Player of the Season. More follows… Well done, Jamie!

The FWA, @theofficialfwa - Special guest @GaryLineker is here to celebrate @LCFC's incredible season. He'll be speaking a little later #FOTY16

Jamie Vardy was presented with the Football Writers' Association Footballer of the Year award at the Landmark Hotel in London.

"It's an absolute honour," said Vardy. "To be on a list with all those other players, some of who I watched when I was younger, it's an unbelievable feeling."

Vardy posed for a picture on Gary Lineker's Instagram account with the former striker's sons and the Premier League trophy ahead of picking up the award.

He was flattered by comparisons to the former Leicester legend. "It's brilliant but it's taken me a lot of hard work and a lot of graft to get me into this situation."

He still pinches himself 'every single day' as he remarked: "I can't lie about that. Like I said it's been a long, hard journey with a lot of hard work and I've managed to carry it on and that's what has got me in this position now. As players we learn to take the rough with the smooth. So much has been written about me and Leicester this season, it is amazing to see my name alongside so many legends (named FWA Footballer of the Year). One thing I would like to say is that my relationship with the media hasn't always been an easy one but it has been made clear to me that I need to make a distinction between football writers and those who don't know anything about the game...although I'm still struggling to make that given most of you thought we would get relegated this season. I'd like to thank my future wife, who has been by my side through so much, we get married in a couple of weeks and it would be the icing on the cake this summer if I get selected and we win the Euros."

Vardy made reference to his Tweet during his time at Fleetwood. "It is hard for me to get my head around this whirlwind, in 2011 I tweeted 'chat s***, get banged' and no one cared whatsoever. This past week or so, I put a picture of my favourite kids' film on Twitter and it turns it into meltdown. I'm the same man, I grew up watching my team Sheffield Wednesday, I was any normal kid who knows what it is like to be rejected for being too small. I have made mistakes, but I have always given 110 per cent. "

Claudio Ranieri praised the team ethic but also had a special commendation for Vardy, "'I was told that Riyad Mahrez was our light, but Jamie was our gun, he was out in front and fought against everyone. We fight behind him, we didn't want to leave him alone to press. Everyone behind him was a family. I was very happy when he scored the 11th successive goal against Manchester United. Very well done. He was unlucky with the last penalty but every champion makes a mistake. In the last match he can fight against Harry Kane (for the golden boot) why not? Believe Jamie."

Gary Lineker took to the stage to praise Vardy, "I still can't really get my head around the fact that Leicester City, the team I have watched and supported since I was the height of N'Golo Kanté have gone on to win the Premier League. If they had written it as fiction they would have torn up the script as impossible. Now we hear Hollywood are captivated. A young man who lands himself in trouble but redeems himself and goes, in four years, from playing non-League football to the team that win the Premier League title and then goes on to score the goals that lead England to Euro 2016 glory - it hasn't happened yet. Jamie's game is not just about goals, this fella is tough. Any player that can run for 90 minutes, even with a bandage on his arm, is good for me. The likes of Bayern. Barca and Benfica won't know what has hit them next season."

Vardy will play through the pain barrier for England before having surgery on his broken wrist, delaying the operation to chase glory in France. *Sportsmail* suggested Vardy required an operation on his right wrist after wearing a blue cast to protect three damaged bones all season. Vardy fractured the bones in a fall against Aston Villa at the start of the domestic campaign and they have not fused naturally as was initially hoped. He now needs surgery to prevent further damage but will not have the operation until after Euro 2016 - good for England but Vardy could miss some of the important pre-season preparation. When asked by photographers to lift the Premier League trophy above his head after last Saturday's win against Everton, he said: "I can't. I have got a broken wrist."

It's easy to see why the Euros means so much to him, as it would take his phenomenal rise even higher. Vardy said winning the Euros would be equivalent to Leicester winning the title, and the honour of playing for his country is as big an achievement as winning the league. "I think you would have to put them on the same level. That would be the pinnacle of this season for me, representing your country, at any time but to be in a tournament and hopefully being a part of something big happening - it can only be one of the best things ever. I haven't spoken to Roy. I saw it like everyone else on Sky Sports News, that the squad had been delayed, so I'll be tuning in on Monday night like everybody else."

Vardy expects the Foxes to be challenging at the top again next season. "I think we'll be doing exactly the same. We've done it this season; the money was already there in those teams. We've turned up and played well - played better than them and got the points so why can't it happen again? Everyone was expecting us to get relegated this season. We'll just keep trying to improve on what we've done. We might have won the league this year but the gaffer will just want us to keep improving as a team. If that's not good enough to win it again then so be it but I'm sure we'll keep progressing because the gaffer wants to keep building. You never know. There's going to be a lot of changes to teams but at the end of the day it's still 11 v 11 when it comes to the game."

Vardy was linked with a move to West Ham, the latest to be interested, but he certainly sounded committed to Leicester, "We've just won the league and we're in the Champions League next year and I think you can see from every one of the lads that we're all happy at Leicester. I'm just concentrating solely on Leicester."

Postman Lee Chapman was inundated with offers of work when a lookalike agency spotted him celebrating the title win with other supporters last Monday. He added: "It's mental. I'm part of it. I'm a hard core Foxes fan and now I've got fans of my own. Royal Mail are taking it in good spirit and have given me a six-month career break. But they want me to do charity work for the Stroke Association while I'm taking time out. I'm happy to do that." He was involved in lookalike stunts including serving Vardy Bomb cocktails to fans after the side's last home game of the season on Saturday. "I've been a Vardy double for less than two weeks and not stopped working. I've even been interviewed by TV host Piers Morgan."

In an interview with Copa90, David Beckham discussed the rise of Jamie Vardy, and how he can have a pivotal role for England at the Euros. For the re-opening of the Adidas store on Oxford Street and the launch of the Man United away kit, Beckham sat down with Poet and Vuj along with grime artist and Manchester United fan Stormzy, and compared Vardy to former Liverpool and England striker Michael Owen. "He's a goalscorer. He's like a Michael Owen. No matter what happens, you know you're going to get a goal from Michael Owen and it's the same with Vardy. He's done it all season long and he'll do it for England because he's not scared to play. He's been down in the lower league and now he's playing for England, it's amazing."

Surely nothing to worry about despite the date! (Friday 13th) The sun is shining, the Chelsea players are preparing their guard of honour, and the parade is all ready to go. What can possibly go wrong…

Well, I've broken a story on my zapsportz.com website suggesting that the Italian Football Federation's desires on Claudio are far stronger than the previous 'they would like him one day' to be their national coach quote. It is even believed that the formal offer to quit Leicester City's Immortals will be made as soon as the season is over and after the team's glorious open bus ride in front of close to 1 million people in the city centre on Monday evening.

Antonio Conte will soon be arriving at the Bridge, once the Euros are over, and the Italians want Ranieri to succeed him, to bring his recently acquired magic dust to transform them back into world beaters again; if he could do it with Leicester City's also-rans, you wonder what he could do with the talented Italians at his disposal.

Ranieri completed his usual round of handshakes before taking his seat for his final media conference of the season, to discuss, among other things, his return to Chelsea, "I've been with Juventus but this time is different. It's emotional. I hope my old fans are happy with me. When I sign the contract, this is my best memory. I was so happy to come back to England."

No one was assuming he might contemplate going, so he was asked how he could improve upon a title-winning side? "We want to build a very good team. It'll be important to find players with the right mentality, intelligent and fighters." It certainly sounded like a manager committed to the cause. However, earlier in the week, he was quoted in an interview with *La Gazzetta dello Sport* as saying "Of course, leading Italy would be something else. I'd never rule that out, and I'd like that very much. And Leicester, after all, have blue shirts just like the Azzurri."

Ranieri understood that Vardy would be fit for the start of the new season, "I think it's a little operation, then I think he'll be ready for the Community Shield. I think now (he will be fine). Afterwards I will speak to the surgery and we will see. He has been amazing. He was playing non-League football four years ago and now he is a champion and playing for his country. It is a story that tells all the other non-league players, 'hey, come on, this is a good sport, good publicity for everyone. If you really want to do something, you must believe and something could happen. Everyone can make mistakes but if you want to do something you must believe and something can happen.'"

Speaking ahead of the Chelsea game, "When I came here I saw the last match was at Chelsea. Now, I come back as a champion. Unbelievable. A good story!" Ranieri took Chelsea to their highest finish in 49 years, as runners-up to Arsenal's Invincibles in 2004, and also their first European Cup semi-final. Abramovich, who had recently bought the club, replaced him with Mourinho. "I don't know if he (Abramovich) comes in the dressing room (on Sunday)," said Ranieri. "When I was there, never at the beginning, always at the end of the match."

Ranieri was asked to reflect on his favourite moment of this season. "When I signed the new contract here - this is my best memory. I was so happy to come back in England. It's difficult to say what I've learned. Of course a lot of things but these things are in my mind and maybe now the computer chips are working and have put everything in the right position to get out next season. To say what I've learned is difficult. Let me relax and think about what happened this season."

SATURDAY, 14 MAY

It transpired in this morning's Charlie Sale column in the *Daily Mail* that, somewhat embarrassingly, Gary Lineker was barred by the club from interviewing Jamie Vardy for his TV documentary. He had expected the interview taking place at the Football Writers' Association's function on Thursday. Gary was there primarily to honour Vardy and was one of the guest speakers.

The proposed interview with Vardy was to be included in his own BBC documentary 'Leicester's Impossible Dream', due to be screened on Tuesday, and produced by Lineker's own independent production company Goalhanger Films Ltd.

Leicester though, were producing their own in-house account of their incredible season and prevented Vardy being interviewed by Lineker, claiming, according to Sale's column, that it had not been organised through the proper channels.

Lineker was spotted in an undignified "heated conversation" with the club's head of media, Anthony Herlihy, during the FWA dinner. Herlihy told the *Mail* on Friday, in clear anticipation of the pending article appearing the next day: "There was a lack of clarity. We didn't know enough details about the BBC programme and we had so many requests for Vardy's time - plus we have our own plans for a documentary."

Lineker was allowed, however, to film links for his programme inside the King Power Stadium on Friday.

But such off-the-field niggles were not going to spoil the party mood.

Claudio Ranieri was planning to take a helicopter from Leicester's victory parade on Monday so that he would be in London in time to, presumably, receive his Manager of the Year accolade from the League Managers' Association. Then, the next day, Leicester were off to Thailand to show off the trophy in their owners' homeland.

First, though, the final game at the Bridge, and Ranieri recalled the guard of honour he received from Chelsea's players on his departure from the club 12 years ago after they had beaten Leeds 1-0 in May 2004.

The players wanted to show their gratitude, with the help from their translator Gary Staker. "My players gave me a guard of honour. Desailly and Terry called all their team-mates together because they knew my job had finished there. It was one of the more important moments of my sporting life. They did it on the pitch. Gary, who is an amazing man, called me to the centre of the pitch and the players made the guard of honour so when I turned around I saw, it was amazing."

Ranieri urged his side to play like the champions on his return to Chelsea to prove they are worthy winners. "(Against Everton) I asked to them to show me what we learned during all the season. Always I've said the result is not important, but it's the importance of the performance, how you play. Now we are champions, we have to play like champions. The answer was fantastic. On Sunday, I don't want the result, I want to see my players show the same attitude and I am happy."

Victory would be Ranieri's 100th in the Premier League and, ahead of his return to west London, he had a message for the home fans. "I want to thank the Chelsea fans. I watched some of them hold up placards with 'Do it for Ranieri' on. It was amazing."

So, sacked by Chelsea, but now back at the Bridge as champions, taking Chelsea's crown. Ironic or what?

Ranieri sang the praises of Okazaki, whose work rate has played a major factor whenever called upon. "I'm very happy with Shinji's performances. He is a hard worker and plays well. The team scored a lot of goals. I understand the strikers want to score always more and that is right but I'm happy. I'm a little sad because I wanted to give to him maybe one full match. I know when arrive one hour, Shinji comes and he's not so happy, but that's normal. He understood we are a team and the manager needs something different during the match. My confidence with him is full. I'm happy if he repeats this season."

Ranieri had arrived last July in the middle of a training camp in Austria and took charge of friendlies against Lincoln, Mansfield and Burton. Now it will be Celtic and Paris Saint-Germain in California, and Barcelona in Stockholm as part of the exclusive International Champions Cup. And, planning for next season already, he said, "The pre-season is more or less the same - just change the name of the opponent. Of course it is important to make some changes to increase the experience of my players. They have never played against these big teams so it is important to feel and understand the difference. I know it's right at the beginning and then maybe when we arrive we will be a little more tired than them - because maybe we will work a little more. It's different because we travel a lot. But just this."

Ranieri's transfer plans hit problems as clubs raised their prices now that Leicester were no longer considered poor relations, having being crowned champions and would be playing in the lucrative Champions League. Cost effective bargains were no longer routine. "Yes, of course (prices are being raised)," said Ranieri. "Now clubs are saying, 'Why sell? Leicester go for players for very little money. But if Leicester want this player then he must be good.' That is normal. But you know the market is always difficult. And now when you ask something - and now it's Leicester - the price is going up and up. That's what we've been encountering."

Ranieri confirmed Pescara striker Gianluca Lapadula was a target. The 26-year-old scored 24 goals in 38 Serie B games this season but his price had escalated. "He is a good striker, he scores goals, he is good in the air, everything. But there are a lot. We are watching all the players in the world!"

Former Inter President Massimo Moratti offered his congratulations to Claudio Ranieri, who was hired and duly fired by Inter in 2011-12. "I am very happy for Ranieri," Moratti told *L'Equipe*. "He has always come close to winning a title but this one with Leicester is a fairytale. It is a wonderful thing from every aspect, both footballing and human. It is a demonstration that in life you have to be patient. It is as if everything was written in advance. Ranieri has acted like a father figure to the Leicester players and the whole world has been supporting them. Even finishing third would have been a miracle. I think their fans are the happiest in the world right now."

The former President, who sold his stake in the club to Indonesian businessman, Erick Thohir, in 2013, reflected on his memories of Ranieri from his time at the Nerazzurri. "In my career as a president I had many coaches. I will always remember him as a great man and a gentleman with whom I had a wonderful relationship." Ranieri lasted six months at the Stadio Giuseppe Meazza before being replaced by Gian Piero Gasperini.

Andy King recalled his time at the Bridge - as a ball boy 12 years ago hoping for a prime spot behind the goal. "If you got stationed there then you knew you might get your head on Match of the Day."

Bit different now. As he recalled in a *Daily Mail* article, "I had my winner's medal on for about 48 hours straight, but I have finally taken it off now," said King. "It has a couple of chips on it already where I've bashed it. I think I whacked it on the table at a party. Getting that medal, getting the trophy, last Saturday was the best day of my life. But this weekend will be special too."

King was on Chelsea's books as a kid. Ranieri was the manager. "It was the start of the Abramovich era and they said it wasn't good enough to be the best lad in London or even England any more. You had to be the best in Europe and they said they would be looking for someone else in my position. I took it on the chin. I could see it. They only kept three or four. I only have good memories from Chelsea but it's nice to go back as a Premier League champion to a club that kicked you out at 16. The manager is probably more keen to rub salt in the wounds than I am. The young players would be ball boys so I was always sitting near to Claudio or across the other side from him. I saw a lot of him. He used to be a lot more animated then. It is strange having watched him give out tactics and now it's turned full circle for him and for me."

Picked up by Leicester after his Chelsea disappointment he was in the team the night a 3-2 defeat at Brighton, in October 2008, dropped them to sixth in League One; Leicester's lowest ever league position,

Now he will play in the Champions League for the first time. "That will be another 'pinch me' moment. I am starting to get sore. We heard all the things people said this season. We knew people didn't think we could do it but, no, we didn't crumble. We are strong and we deserve credit for that."

King started eight league games but appeared as a substitute 16 times. Last week, against Everton, he scored. "The fans wanted me to score because of my story with the club. I had one really good chance and headed it straight to the goalie. I thought that was it. Luckily I got another chance and I wasn't going to miss."

The life of a fringe player can be challenging, but he observed, "There is no culture here of players on the fringes not really bothering. There is no better feeling than playing 90 minutes and winning but the fact that we were up there - after all those horrible experiences I talked about - is what makes you happy and keeps you satisfied and keeps you pushing forwards. It's down to you to take that chance when you get it and now we have a winner's medal round our necks and that's brilliant whether you have played five times or 38 times. Nobody can take that away from you. This isn't just my attitude. I think 80 per cent of players in football have that attitude but I can say here at Leicester that 100 per cent of the players have that attitude. It's fundamental. We are team-mates and good friends here. You saw that at the Vards party. We arrived totally buzzing, thinking, 'Could this be the night that it happens?' Then at half-time, it was like, 'You got any water, Vards? We have training tomorrow.' It was gonna be, 'See you in the morning.' Nobody actually left at half-time but I think we might have. We stayed because there were people outside and it would have looked so bad being photographed going in and then sneaking away at half-time. After the Cahill goal we knew Chelsea would get another chance. It got nasty after that. Chelsea were in their faces and Tottenham lost their cool, understandably. Then Hazard. What a goal. The place just went mad."

In London back in March, King and a small group of Leicester players were refused entry to a Mayfair nightclub after a win at Watford. A group of Tottenham players walked in as the league leaders were asked to stand aside. "I didn't think anything of it. We just got in the taxi and went home. I know loads of people who don't get in nightclubs. It's happened to me before. What do you do? Hang around on the street corner? Course not. We laugh about it and still get some stick for it now. If any of us had said, 'Do you know who I am?' that player would have been bantered for it here for years on end. So I'm glad nobody said it. It's not in our character to say that anyway. But maybe we will go back and try again this weekend after Chelsea." Every chance they will get in this time!

Premier League executive chairman, Richard Scudamore, pledged to fight any plans for the wealthiest clubs to guarantee Champions League qualification regardless of where they finished in the league. Speaking at the Premier League headquarters in London on Friday, Scudamore said that Leicester City's improbable triumph had been a "world story, a human story, bigger than a football story" and was adamant that there would be no change to the top four qualifying for the Champions League despite established clubs wanting to ring-fence their involvement when UEFA agrees a new Champions League format for the next round of television rights.

Jamie Vardy and Riyad Mahrez will wear limited edition VAHREZ boots to celebrate the Foxes' remarkable title. Nike Football presented each with custom VAHREZ Nike iD Hypervenom Phantom II boots. Vardy's right boot is predominantly white, his left is black, while Mahrez's left boot is white and his right boot is black. Additionally, each boot features its respective player's national flag. Mahrez said: "Jamie and I took unusual routes to get to here and this helps our partnership - I'm honoured to wear these boots as symbols of our achievements this season." Vardy continued: "I've worn some special boots this season and these stand out. The last game of this season is going to be an occasion, and I appreciate the understanding I have with Riyad - it's something I'm proud of and the boots reflect that."

Becky Nicholson, meanwhile, was showing her fiancé, Jamie, how to take a penalty even in a red outfit and heels. Home video footage shows her running up and striking a rising shot firmly into the net leaving a family friend, playing goalkeeper, stranded as Jamie looked on smiling. According to the report in the *Mirror*, a friend said: "Becky showed a surprising amount of composure as she struck the ball. Jamie was shouting tips at her as she prepared and took her run-up. But his family were all ribbing him afterwards saying it should have been her giving tips to him after his own miss earlier (against Everton). He took it all in good humour. A hat-trick would have been the icing on the cake but it wasn't to be. He thought the whole thing was quite funny afterwards, saying he'd have to run next door and ask for his ball back. Nothing was going to dampen their spirits on the day."

Labour MP Keith Vaz, a season ticket holder, wrote to David Cameron asking for Ranieri to be honoured. A group of 38 MPs signed a motion. In his letter Mr Vaz writes: "Mr Ranieri's calm and effective management of the club has been instrumental in fostering a team who have become role models, both on and off the pitch, for young people across the country and, indeed, the world. Mr

Ranieri's outstanding leadership of the team has played a major role in Leicester's monumental success, which has undoubtedly made one of the most highly-regarded contributions to English sport in decades."

SUNDAY, 15 MAY

CHELSEA 1-1 LEICESTER CITY

The Golden Glove and The Golden Boot were still to play for. Kasper Schmeichel was in line for the most clean sheets, along with Cech, Hart and de Gea, all on 15 shutouts. If more than one keeper ended up with the same number of clean sheets, then the award was shared. Still in the balance is the race for the Golden Boot; Kane in pole position with 25, Vardy and Agüero on 24.

John Motson, BBC *Match of the Day* commentator at Stamford Bridge - "This is more about the occasion than a football match, with three people in particular guaranteed a rousing reception. One, of course, is Leicester manager Claudio Ranieri, who will get the appreciation and recognition he deserves on his return to Stamford Bridge as last season's league champions salute their successors with a guard of honour. Another is Ranieri's Chelsea counterpart Guus Hiddink, a popular man throughout his two short-term stints at the club who steadied the ship this season after José Mourinho's departure. Thirdly, there's John Terry, Chelsea's captain and a veteran of 703 appearances for the club."

The champions arrived at Stamford Bridge, and outside the dressing rooms Ranieri got a huge hug and handshake from Roman Abramovich, and a very warm welcoming smile. Ranieri said: "It is good to come back, it was my first house in England so it is amazing. This is a very different day. I am very curious because I have asked my players to do the same things. We play against the old champions and they would like to beat us. I hope it is a great match." Ranieri made two changes with Drinkwater returning from a ban and Gray getting a start. Albrighton and Okazaki were on the bench.

Hiddink remarked: "It is important for the whole stadium to end well against the new champions against the old champions. It is a beautiful scenario and hopefully we can end with a win. I don't wish Claudio Ranieri well for the game. He rang me after the Tottenham gave but we want to fight for a win."

Chelsea formed a guard of honour as expected. What wasn't expected was that if there was to be a guard of honour on the final day of the season at the Bridge, the betting suggested it wasn't for the away side. Leicester were given a huge ovation by all sides of Stamford Bridge, with Ranieri handed a ceremonial plate by former goalkeeper Carlo Cudicini. Ranieri looked moved and applauded the supporters, before pointing to them to indicate thank you.

There was a nice surprise for the away fans who were treated to a 'goodie bag', on each seat, with the Foxes badge on the front.

As for the match, Leicester completed the campaign with a creditable 1-1 draw, 10 points clear of second-placed Arsenal, while Chelsea finished 10th, their lowest position in the Premier League for 20 years, their title defence the worst by any team in the Premier League era. Only four Premier League champions won the title by a greater points margin than Leicester (10) - Manchester United in 1999-2000 (18), Chelsea 2004-05 (12), Arsenal 2003-04 and Manchester United 2012-13 (both 11).

Ranieri started with Gray and King but reverted to a more familiar system at half-time, sending on Okazaki and Schlupp.

Kasper Schmeichel was in inspired form early on as he kept out strikes from Fàbregas and Willian. It was Fàbregas who opened the scoring from the penalty spot, before Drinkwater's brilliant 30 yard equaliser, only his second of the season.

Leicester's remarkable season had ended with only three defeats, and the best home and away records in the division.

There was plenty of mutual appreciation amongst the fans: Leicester fans sang Hazard's name, as thanks for the equaliser against Spurs, whilst Chelsea supporters sang Ranieri's name, gave Riyad Mahrez an ovation when he was replaced, 10 minutes from time, and even applauded as Fuchs walked towards them as he prepared to take a corner.

Ranieri told Sky Sports: "The emotion was at the maximum because there was a fantastic welcome back from everybody. I met Roman Abramovich here and when I go out and hear all my fans, and also the Chelsea fans, it was an amazing moment for me. It was a good atmosphere and I want to say thank you to our fans and the Chelsea fans. It was amazing. It was important to finish well and it was a good match. Both teams had great chances and well done to the players. They made a lot of sacrifices in the hot weather to keep pressing."

Ranieri also recalled his time in charge when he gave Terry his break. "He is as my son. I believed in him when he was young and I put him in the team."

On the secret of his team's success Ranieri said: "Our strength is to be a unit and fight for each other. We have to realise what has happened and then look back on our season." And, on his planned celebrations, the Italian - famed for his love of pizza - said: "No pizza tonight - our chairman has invited us for dinner."

Wes Morgan became the third outfield player in Premier League history to play every minute of a title-winning season after Gary Pallister in 1992-93 and John Terry in 2014-15.

I emailed Alan Smith for a comment, and the former Leicester City striker responded for inclusion in this 'Immortals' book: "Like most people, I thought I would never see the day. As a former player, Leicester's magnificent achievement fills me with joy."

Former England manager Glenn Hoddle described "the extraordinary Leicester City story" in his *Mail on Sunday* column adding: "Riyad Mahrez was my player of the year, though Harry Kane, Jamie Vardy, Dimitri Payet and N'Golo Kanté would all have had legitimate claims. And of course, Leicester's Claudio Ranieri was the manager of the season. His achievements will still be spoken about for years to come."

N'Golo Kanté has decided to join the Gunners, according to multiple French press reports, despite options to sign for Manchester City or PSG. Reports persisted that Kanté has a €25m release clause in his contract and the player's representatives informed Arsenal of their client's decision, effectively inviting the Gunners to activate that clause.

The rumour mill was equally bleak about Ranieri staying. Sampdoria coach, Vincenzo Montella, would like to see Ranieri coach Italy. The former Italy and Roma striker guided Sampdoria to Serie A safety following his appointment in November, having impressed during his time in charge of Fiorentina. "If they called me I would think, and I would spend two sleepless nights," Montella told *Corriere dello Sport* over the prospect of the Italian Football Federation making an approach to him. "I think for that role, experience is fundamental. On the Azzurri bench I'd see Claudio Ranieri doing well. He is a balanced man who has experienced so much in football and proved, not just this year, his quality. You know how it is in our job, surprises can come at any moment. For now I see myself at Sampdoria."

Jamie Redknapp's observation in his *Daily Mail* column: "The nearest comparison we can make with Leicester's success is Blackburn in 1994-95, and Claudio Ranieri can learn from their title defence. Blackburn failed to strengthen and lost four of their first six games, our Liverpool side beat them 3-0 at Anfield in September 1995, so it is crucial that Ranieri gets his recruitment spot on as well as keeping hold of the Foxes' stars. He can't afford to bring in any 'big heads' who will upset their team spirit and, with a Champions League campaign on the horizon, he will need to rotate his squad more often and become the Tinkerman once more." 'Bertie Big' to, once again, miss-out.

Ranieri target, Gianluca Lapadula, wanted to form an "explosive" partnership with Vardy and work under "legendary" Claudio Ranieri. In an article in *The Sun*, the Italian striker was quoted as saying: "I have always loved English football, the Premier League. Being approached by Leicester has made me so proud. I used to be a massive fan of Steven Gerrard and Didier Drogba growing up. Drogba was a real top centre forward. But now I love Vardy. He's fantastic - I could really see myself playing alongside him. We both like the same style of football and are physically very similar. Me and him together? The King Power would explode! We would be dynamite together. We would be like two gladiators going into battle."

Nicknamed 'Sir William', he added anyone would love to play under the "legendary" Italian 'Mister'. "For anyone, Ranieri is the maximum. I would be proud to play for him. Ranieri has had a great career in Italy and managed some great clubs. In England, he has made history and become a legend. I think like he does: the team always comes first. I always play every game like it's a final. I would do everything possible to help Leicester win."

Lapadula's rise mirrors Vardy's as he spent several years in the lower tiers of Italian football. He said: "I have sweated a lot and spent many years in the lower leagues - like Vardy. If my dream of going to Leicester were to materialise, I would feel extremely happy and ready for the challenge. I would give it my all to be successful in the Premier League. I am a fighter."

IN FROM THE COLD

Leicester were considering whether to install a cryotherapy chamber in their dressing room at the King Power Stadium, according to a report in the *Sunday Mirror*. They already have a unit at their Belvoir Drive training base. The seven metre-long container is sited next to the gym, and each player must use it as part of their daily routine, suffering the extreme cold for up to five minutes, a treatment dubbed 'an ice-bath on steroids'.

It allows players to train with greater intensity, improves recovery times from soft-tissue injuries and has been credited with aiding sleep. Temperatures can dip as low as -135 degrees Celsius to produce endorphins which give an individual a warm glow.

Now the plan is to give themselves a boost before games. The process is widespread within North American sport where American footballers routinely use the treatment. Boxer Floyd Mayweather and basketball star LeBron James are other converts. Smaller cryo-saunas would easily fit into the squad's changing area.

Back in November, Jamie Vardy had put his record goalscoring streak down to studying every detail of his opponents' weaknesses during the week as well as sessions in a cryotherapy chamber. He said then: "During the week, in training, we look at ways that I can get me into my best positions - especially if I'm up front, and then go through on goal. We concentrate on what their defenders are like, if they're going to come in for the tackle, which side is their strongest and other stuff, then we just have to put it into practice on a Saturday. You can say with the weeks that we've been having, and with scoring the goals, it's obviously working for us." Vardy was troubled with a groin injury back then: "Credit to the physios. They've been working on me constantly. Obviously, the cryo chamber that we've got at the training ground's come in use. It's absolutely freezing, but it helps you in your recovery so fair play to the club for getting that in."

MONDAY, 16 MAY
VICTORY PARADE: Leicester Is #HavingAParty!

The journey around the city centre required four open top buses in order to accommodate all the players and club officials. The buses were decorated in rival east Midland's city Nottingham, by the same firm who carried out the job two years ago when the club clinched promotion by winning the Championship.

Richard Monk, Managing Director of Blueprint Notts, revealed in *The Sun* that four members of staff had been working for 14 hours a day on each bus to ensure they are ready in time for the party. Monk said: "I hadn't even thought about it, but two weeks ago we got the phone call because we had shown we could do the job and be reliable. I know there were other companies begging to do the job and some for next to nothing, so we are proud they came to us. This is the best part of the job. I cannot wait to see them all lined up outside the office and ready to go."

LeicesterCityCouncil, @Leicester_News - What a crowd. What. A. Crowd! #Leicester, you look amazing! #LCFCChampions #VictoriaPark

It was one of the biggest events the council had ever prepared. Maggie Shutt, the city council's Events and Festivals Director, said: "We've done Queen's visits, we've done torch relays, we've done Radio 1 roadshows, the city's hosted a lot of different major events. There's a lot of people involved in this, Leicester City Football Club, all the emergency services, all the different agencies."

Nearly a quarter of a million supporters were in the streets and in the park as the open top bus procession slowly snaked through the streets thronged with people from Jubilee Square to Victoria Park.

LeicesterCityCouncil, @Leicester_News - 240,000 of you lined the route and came to #VictoriaPark. You read that right - 240,000!! #Leicester, you're amazing... #lcfcchampions

Marcin Wasilewski posted a sneak preview from inside the bus at the training ground showing himself behind the wheel, alongside the caption, 'People are you ready to celebrate Championship??? #ontheway'. Danny Drinkwater described Leicester City's season as "madness" in an interview for lcfc.com. "If you'd said that at the start of the season everyone would be saying 'no chance'. But we've proved a hell of a lot of people wrong." Drinkwater added: "We've lost three games this season, which is a reflection on how well we've done as a team. Home and away the fans have been brilliant. They've had a lot to cheer about. Credit to them, they backed us all the way."

Emotions were running high. The manager, players and staff waved and smiled broadly in appreciation as they surveyed the remarkable mass of jubilant fans. Any and every vantage point was filled. Blue shirts, blue scarves, blue banners, blue faces, blue hats, blue flags, and beneath the glorious blue sky were four blue open top buses. The City of Leicester had never experienced anything like this before.

"It is unbelievable, unbelievable. All of the city is here," a clearly emotional Ranieri said from on board the first of the four victory parade buses. "This is something special, a lot of people are happy and I am very glad. The team won but they played with heart, soul and the people understood this. I can say only thank you to all the people."

Several players were interviewed by Sky Sports from the top deck of the bus. Jamie Vardy remarked: 'It's carnage. I heard a little rumour this morning that they're expecting 250,000 people. It's brilliant. Look what it means to the city, it's unbelievable. It's not sunk in but I'm sure it will over time. I'll wait until it does sink in and then I'll have a few days to myself. It's carnage."

Christian Fuchs added: "I can't put it into words. I think people from all over England are here. I'm walking here sometimes," he said pointing to the pavements. "There's not usually this many people."

Marc Albrighton observed: "It's unbelievable, they're out in force. It's crazy. There are kids, granddads, parents, they're all out to support us and say well done. We knew there would be a lot of people but we weren't expecting that. All the lads looked up and saw the long high street packed with people. It just went on for ages, a sea of blue. It is memories that will last a lifetime. We had people swinging on lampposts, people stood on ledges, hanging out of windows. People were standing on seven-storey ledges leaning over. You were scared for their lives but they were only doing it because they are interested in you and what we have done. It's humbling without a doubt. We'll probably never see this again. It's massive for the city...look at the fans here. It shows what it means to this fantastic city."

Leonardo Ulloa said: "There's so many people here to support us. Leicester supporters will enjoy this. There's only 30,000 people in the stadium but everyone is here today. We need to enjoy it. I can't believe it. It's my first time, but two years ago (when Leicester won the Championship) it was the same."

After the 1.5mile parade, the players headed to Victoria Park, where thousands more supporters were waiting as Radio 1 DJ MistaJam kept the fans entertained. One medley led with Ranieri's 'dilly ding dilly dong', while the club's women's team and basketball side also made an appearance on stage.

Chairman Vichai Srivaddhanaprabha saluted the crowd as his son and vice-chairman Aiyawatt, clearly emotional, said: "From the owners we want to say thank you for your support all season, we hope it continues next season." He added with a discernible smile, "I think we need a bigger stadium!"

The stars were triumphantly introduced onto the stage much to everyone's huge delight, and a resounding cheer erupted as Wes Morgan and Claudio Ranieri finally appeared to join the cast of heroes. Claudio looked close to tears - again. In a final interview he was clearly immersed in the magnitude of the day and proclaimed a final thank you to one and all: "Our fans, I want to say thank you, to everybody, because in all the season they push behind us, and they believe in us, every time we was down 2-0 they push, they push, they push! Well done, thank you!"

"Keep dreaming, keep dreaming, don't wake up," he expressed with a glint and a sparkle and maybe a tear.

The trophy was jubilantly lifted once more to a storm of confetti, fireworks and streamers all across the park. What a glorious day!

It wasn't quite over just yet, though...as the stage cleared, and Ranieri embarked on his helicopter flight down to London for the LMA awards dinner, local rock group, Kasabian, brought the house down with a surprise performance much to the huge delight of everyone in the park.

BBC Sport, @BBCSport - "It's like Glastonbury has decamped to Leicester."

LeicesterCityCouncil, @Leicester_News - What an end to the day...@KasabianHQ #LCFCChampions #fire

And even then, the celebrations and accolades continued...

Later that evening Claudio Ranieri arrived safely at the League Managers Association (LMA) annual end of season Awards Dinner together with a 1000-strong audience of fellow managers, football stakeholders and LMA sponsors and friends.

Roy Hodgson, LMA President, had earlier in the day urged England to follow the example of Leicester City as they head towards Euro 2016 with the "dream" of trying to win the championship. "We've seen this year, the example with Leicester City," Hodgson said. "Weeks and weeks turning into months and months of 'how long can this last? Is it all going to crack up? Can you really make the Champions League? Can you finish above this team or that team? Can you win the league?' Each time what they've done is work hard, try hard, tried to make certain going into each game they're capable of winning it. That's all we can do as well." Unlikely winners were Denmark in 1992 and Greece in 2004 and that can be a source of inspiration. "It's happened in the past. Nobody expected Denmark to win it in '92; nobody expected Greece to win the Euros as well; no one expected Leicester to win the league."

And finally, at the end of an emotionally draining day, Ranieri was crowned Manager of the Year by the LMA, with endorsements of the decision coming from all corners of the world. He was also named as the Barclays Premier League Manager of the Year. A measure of this award was the he became only the second non-British manager to win the prestigious accolade, after Arsène Wenger. Ranieri had earlier in the season earned three Manager of the Month awards and was named Italian Manager of the Year in Italy.

LMA Chairman, Howard Wilkinson, said: "We gathered this evening to celebrate the accomplishments of our managers and coaches who have overseen one of the most competitive and entertaining seasons in recent years. Throughout the top four leagues, we have witnessed success against all odds and levels of excitement which have become synonymous with the English game. Tonight's winners are those who have demonstrated the ability to face and overcome the challenges of football management, we applaud those who have exceeded expectations and wish everyone the best of luck next season. My congratulations go to the LMA Manager of the Year sponsored by Barclays, Claudio Ranieri who, in his first year as manager of Leicester City, has achieved the most astonishing of sporting triumphs and thoroughly deserves all the recognition and praise being bestowed upon him tonight."

LMA Chief Executive, Richard Bevan, said: "On behalf of the LMA, many congratulations to the managers who have been recognised by their peers and received LMA Awards this evening. We also congratulate all our members who have achieved their ambitions this season whatever the measure of success, be it promotion, securing their league status or exceeding expectations. We are delighted to honour Claudio with the LMA Manager of the Year award in recognition of his Barclays Premier League title winning season with Leicester City, an inspiring story that has gripped the world. Leicester's achievement has been made possible by the tactical and technical knowledge of Claudio and his coaching staff. His passion for football, humility and charisma has underpinned an incredible ability to manage a team at the very highest level. He is a worthy champion and a true gentleman of the sport."

In addition, Bevan penned a foreword for 'The Immortals', with the manager and the team truly the People's Champions, defying the 5,000-1 odds and in the words of No. 1 fan Gary Lineker becoming The Immortals.

Roy Hodgson presented Claudio Ranieri with the trophy to conclude a most memorable of historic days.

So, that's about it. What a season! It hasn't fully sunk in, has it?

It really was a sporting sensation achieved by a fearless, hard-working team, who were measured at a nominal 5,000-1 to achieve this epic goal. It wasn't even a target, rather survival was. But, the seemingly impossible, guided by a true gentleman, who brought togetherness, spirit and huge self-belief, transpired.

We can regard ourselves as having been very fortunate to have witnessed this unfurling and, let's be honest, ludicrous story; one which has not been chronicled in sport before and one which we may never see again in our lifetime.

And with the parasites plotting, vultures circling, and fat cats licking their wounds the Foxes of Leicester City can, and indeed should, pause and reflect - dream if you like, of the footballing miracle of their 'Immortals'.

Someone once said, not that long ago, "Keep dreaming, keep dreaming, don't wake up."

But do wake up soon, for, on the horizon, there is a European tour...#foreverfearless

2015-16 SEASON RESULTS & STATS

SATURDAY, 8 AUGUST 2015, PREMIER LEAGUE

Leicester City   4-2   Sunderland

Vardy (11'), Mahrez (18', 25' pen),   Defoe (60'), Fletcher (71')
Albrighton (66')

POSSESSION: 44% · SHOTS (ON TARGET): 20 (8) · REFEREE: Lee Mason · ATTENDANCE: 32,242

LINE-UP: 1 Schmeichel, 2 de Laet (substituted for Benalouane, 75'), 6 Huth, 5 Morgan,
15 Schlupp (booked, 90'), 11 Albrighton, 10 King, 4 Drinkwater, 26 Mahrez
(substituted for Fuchs, 77'), 20 Okazaki, 9 Vardy (booked, 49', substituted for Kanté, 82').

SUBSTITUTES: 7 Hammond, 14 Kanté, 19 Kramarić,
23 Ulloa, 28 Fuchs, 29 Benalouane, 32 Schwarzer.

SATURDAY, 15 AUGUST 2015, PREMIER LEAGUE

West Ham United   1-2   Leicester City

Payet (55'), Adrián (dismissed, 90'+2)   Okazaki (27'), Mahrez (38')

POSSESSION: 30% · SHOTS (ON TARGET): 10 (5) · REFEREE: Anthony Taylor · ATTENDANCE: 34,857

LINE-UP: 1 Schmeichel, 2 de Laet (substituted for Benalouane, 66', booked, 88'), 6 Huth,
5 Morgan, 15 Schlupp, 26 Mahrez (substituted for Fuchs, 82'), 10 King, 4 Drinkwater,
11 Albrighton, 9 Vardy (booked, 11'), 20 Okazaki (booked, 54', substituted for Kanté, 62').

SUBSTITUTES: 7 Hammond, 14 Kanté, 19 Kramarić, 23 Ulloa,
28 Fuchs, 29 Benalouane, 41 Maddison.

SATURDAY, 22 AUGUST 2015, PREMIER LEAGUE

Leicester City   1-1   Tottenham Hotspur

Mahrez (82')   Alli (81')

POSSESSION: 35% · SHOTS (ON TARGET): 13 (2) · REFEREE: Martin Atkinson · ATTENDANCE: 31,971

LINE-UP: 1 Schmeichel, 2 de Laet, 6 Huth, 5 Morgan, 15 Schlupp, 26 Mahrez (substituted
for Ulloa, 90+4'), 10 King (booked, 90'), 4 Drinkwater (substituted for Inler, 80'),
11 Albrighton (substituted for Kanté, 78'), 20 Okazaki, 9 Vardy.

SUBSTITUTES: 14 Kanté, 19 Kramarić, 23 Ulloa, 28 Fuchs, 29 Benalouane, 32 Schwarzer, 33 Inler.

TUESDAY, 25 AUGUST 2015, LEAGUE CUP - SECOND ROUND

Bury 1-4 Leicester City

Mayor (49') Dodoo (25', 86', 90'), Kramarić (41')

POSSESSION: 53% · SHOTS (ON TARGET): 12 (8) · REFEREE: Andy Madley · ATTENDANCE: 4,914

LINE-UP: 32 Schwarzer, 29 Benalouane, 18 Moore (substituted for de Laet, 90+1'),
27 Wasilewski, 28 Fuchs, 36 Dodoo, 33 Inler, 7 Hammond, 14 Kanté, 23 Ulloa,
19 Kramarić (substituted for Schlupp, 65')

SUBSTITUTES: 2 de Laet, 15 Schlupp, 17 Simpson, 30 Chilwell,
38 Panayiotou, 39 Olukanmi, 41 Maddison.

SATURDAY, 29 AUGUST 2015, PREMIER LEAGUE

Bournemouth 1-1 Leicester City

Wilson (24') Vardy (86' pen)

POSSESSION: 44% · SHOTS (ON TARGET): 4 (2) · REFEREE: Neil Swarbrick · ATTENDANCE: 11,155

LINE-UP: 1 Schmeichel, 2 de Laet (booked, 13', substituted for Benalouane, 90+1'),
6 Huth (booked, 48'), 5 Morgan, 15 Schlupp (booked, 90'), 10 King (booked, 36'),
26 Mahrez (substituted for Okazaki, 45'), 4 Drinkwater, 14 Kanté,
11 Albrighton (substituted for Dodoo, 71'), 9 Vardy.

SUBSTITUTES: 20 Okazaki, 23 Ulloa, 28 Fuchs, 29 Benalouane, 32 Schwarzer,
33 Inler, 36 Dodoo.

SUNDAY, 13 SEPTEMBER 2015, PREMIER LEAGUE

Leicester City 3-2 Aston Villa

de Laet (72'), Vardy (82'), Dyer (89') Grealish (39'), Gil (63')

POSSESSION: 49% · SHOTS (ON TARGET): 21 (6) · REFEREE: Mike Dean · ATTENDANCE: 31,733

LINE-UP: 1 Schmeichel, 2 de Laet, 6 Huth, 5 Morgan, 15 Schlupp, 26 Mahrez,
33 Inler (substituted for Kanté, 64'), 4 Drinkwater,
11 Albrighton (booked, 45', substituted for Ulloa, 64'),
20 Okazaki (substituted for Dyer, 45', booked, 77'), 9 Vardy.

SUBSTITUTES: 10 King, 14 Kanté, 17 Simpson, 19 Kramarić, 23 Ulloa, 24 Dyer, 32 Schwarzer.

SATURDAY, 19 SEPTEMBER 2015, PREMIER LEAGUE

Stoke City   2-2   Leicester City

Krkic (13'), Walters (20')   Mahrez (51' pen), Vardy (69')

POSSESSION: 46% · SHOTS (ON TARGET): 12 (5) · REFEREE: Andre Marriner · ATTENDANCE: 27,642

LINE-UP: 1 Schmeichel, 2 de Laet, 6 Huth, 5 Morgan, 15 Schlupp (booked, 81'),
26 Mahrez (booked, 58'), 4 Drinkwater (booked, 78'), 33 Inler (substituted for Albrighton, 45'),
14 Kanté (booked, 60', substituted for King, 86'), 20 Okazaki (substituted for Ulloa, 64'), 9 Vardy.

SUBSTITUTES: 10 King, 11 Albrighton, 17 Simpson, 19 Kramarić,
23 Ulloa, 29 Benalouane, 32 Schwarzer.

TUESDAY, 22 SEPTEMBER 2015, LEAGUE CUP - THIRD ROUND

Leicester City   2-1   West Ham United (AET)

Dodoo (6'), King (116')   Zárate (27')

POSSESSION: 39% · SHOTS (ON TARGET): 22 (11) · REFEREE: Peter Bankes · ATTENDANCE: 21,268

LINE-UP: 32 Schwarzer, 17 Simpson (booked, 69'), 29 Benalouane, 27 Wasilewski (booked, 108'),
28 Fuchs (booked, 35'), 11 Albrighton (substituted for Schlupp, 68', booked, 79'),
33 Inler, 10 King, 36 Dodoo (substituted for Kanté, 82'), 23 Ulloa, 19 Kramarić
(substituted for Mahrez, 82').

SUBSTITUTES: 1 Schmeichel, 2 de Laet, 14 Kanté, 15 Schlupp, 26 Mahrez,
30 Chilwell, 35 Blyth.

SATURDAY, 26 SEPTEMBER 2015, PREMIER LEAGUE

Leicester City   2-5   Arsenal

Vardy (13', 89')   Walcott (18'), Sánchez (33', 57', 81'),
Giroud (90'+3)

POSSESSION: 42% · SHOTS (ON TARGET): 16 (7) · REFEREE: Craig Pawson · ATTENDANCE: 32,047

LINE-UP: 1 Schmeichel, 2 de Laet, 6 Huth, 5 Morgan, 15 Schlupp, 26 Mahrez,
14 Kanté, 4 Drinkwater (booked, 72', substituted for Kramarić, 78'),
11 Albrighton (substituted for Ulloa, 64'), 20 Okazaki (substituted for King, 45'), 9 Vardy.

SUBSTITUTES: 10 King, 17 Simpson, 19 Kramarić, 23 Ulloa, 32 Schwarzer, 33 Inler, 36 Dodoo.

SATURDAY, 3 OCTOBER 2015, PREMIER LEAGUE

Norwich City 1-2 Leicester City

Mbokani Bezua (68')   Vardy (28' pen), Schlupp (47')

POSSESSION: 34% · SHOTS (ON TARGET): 16 (5) · REFEREE: Mark Clattenburg · ATTENDANCE: 27,067

LINE-UP: 1 Schmeichel, 17 Simpson (substituted for Benalouane, 65'),
6 Huth (booked, 63'), 5 Morgan, 28 Fuchs, 11 Albrighton, 4 Drinkwater, 14 Kanté,
15 Schlupp (substituted for King, 77'), 9 Vardy, 20 Okazaki (substituted for Ulloa, 70').

SUBSTITUTES: 2 de Laet, 10 King, 23 Ulloa, 26 Mahrez, 29 Benalouane,
32 Schwarzer, 33 Inler.

SATURDAY, 17 OCTOBER 2015, PREMIER LEAGUE

Southampton 2-2 Leicester City

Fonte (21'), van Dijk (37')   Vardy (66', 90'+1)

POSSESSION: 49% · SHOTS (ON TARGET): 27 (7) · REFEREE: Paul Tierney · ATTENDANCE: 30,966

LINE-UP: 1 Schmeichel, 17 Simpson, 5 Morgan, 6 Huth, 28 Fuchs, 11 Albrighton,
4 Drinkwater, 14 Kanté, 15 Schlupp (substituted for Dyer, 45'), 9 Vardy,
20 Okazaki (substituted for Mahrez, 45').

SUBSTITUTES: 2 de Laet, 10 King, 24 Dyer, 26 Mahrez, 29 Benalouane,
32 Schwarzer, 33 Inler.

SATURDAY, 24 OCTOBER 2015, PREMIER LEAGUE

Leicester City 1-0 Crystal Palace

Vardy (59')

POSSESSION: 48% · SHOTS (ON TARGET): 12 (3) · REFEREE: Mike Dean · ATTENDANCE: 31,752

LINE-UP: 1 Schmeichel, 17 Simpson (booked, 65'), 5 Morgan, 6 Huth, 28 Fuchs,
11 Albrighton (substituted for Okazaki, 63'), 4 Drinkwater, 14 Kanté, 15 Schlupp (booked, 67') ,
26 Mahrez (substituted for Dyer, 79'), 9 Vardy (booked, 90').

SUBSTITUTES: 2 de Laet, 10 King, 19 Kramarić, 20 Okazaki, 24 Dyer,
32 Schwarzer, 33 Inler.

TUESDAY, 27 OCTOBER 2015, LEAGUE CUP · FOURTH ROUND

Hull City   1-1   Leicester City

(Hull City win 5-4 on penalties)

Hernández (105'+1)   Mahrez (99')

POSSESSION: 38% · SHOTS (ON TARGET): 12 (2) · REFEREE: Stuart Attwell · ATTENDANCE: 16,818

LINE-UP: 32 Schwarzer, 2 de Laet, 27 Wasilewski, 29 Benalouane (booked, 76'), 30 Chilwell, 36 Dodoo (substituted for Mahrez, 84'), 33 Inler, 10 King, 11 Albrighton (booked, 87'), 20 Okazaki (substituted for Vardy, 65'), 19 Kramarić (substituted for Drinkwater, 65').

SUBSTITUTES: 1 Schmeichel, 4 Drinkwater, 5 Morgan, 9 Vardy, 17 Simpson, 26 Mahrez, 35 Blyth.

SATURDAY, 31 OCTOBER 2015, PREMIER LEAGUE

West Bromwich Albion   2-3   Leicester City

Rondón (30'), Lambert (84' pen)   Mahrez (57', 64'), Vardy (77')

POSSESSION: 52% · SHOTS (ON TARGET): 13 (5) · REFEREE: Anthony Taylor · ATTENDANCE: 24,150

LINE-UP: 1 Schmeichel (booked, 90'), 17 Simpson, 5 Morgan, 6 Huth (booked, 89'), 15 Schlupp, 26 Mahrez, 4 Drinkwater (substituted for Okazaki, 88'), 14 Kanté, 11 Albrighton (substituted for Dyer, 76'), 23 Ulloa (substituted for King, 69'), 9 Vardy.

SUBSTITUTES: 2 de Laet, 10 King, 20 Okazaki, 24 Dyer, 30 Chilwell, 32 Schwarzer, 33 Inler.

SATURDAY, 7 NOVEMBER 2015, PREMIER LEAGUE

Leicester City   2-1   Watford

Kanté (52'), Vardy (65' pen)   Deeney (75' pen)

POSSESSION: 41% · SHOTS (ON TARGET): 12 (6) · REFEREE: Roger East · ATTENDANCE: 32,029

LINE-UP: 1 Schmeichel, 17 Simpson, 5 Morgan, 6 Huth, 28 Fuchs, 11 Albrighton, 14 Kanté, 4 Drinkwater (substituted for King, 90'), 15 Schlupp (substituted for Okazaki, 45'), 26 Mahrez (substituted for Dyer, 84'), 9 Vardy.

SUBSTITUTES: 10 King, 20 Okazaki, 23 Ulloa, 24 Dyer, 29 Benalouane, 32 Schwarzer, 33 Inler.

SATURDAY, 21 NOVEMBER 2015, PREMIER LEAGUE

Newcastle United   0-3   Leicester City

Vardy (45' + 1), Ulloa (62'), Okazaki (83')

POSSESSION: 46% · **SHOTS (ON TARGET):** 18 (7) · **REFEREE:** Mike Jones · **ATTENDANCE:** 50,151

LINE-UP: 1 Schmeichel, 17 Simpson, 5 Morgan, 6 Huth (booked, 31'), 28 Fuchs,
26 Mahrez (substituted for Dyer, 89'), 14 Kanté, 4 Drinkwater, 11 Albrighton,
23 Ulloa (substituted for Okazaki, 73'), 9 Vardy (substituted for King, 77').

SUBSTITUTES: 2 de Laet, 10 King, 15 Schlupp, 20 Okazaki, 24 Dyer,
32 Schwarzer, 33 Inler.

SATURDAY, 28 NOVEMBER 2015, PREMIER LEAGUE

Leicester City   1-1   Manchester United

Vardy (24')   Schweinsteiger (45' + 1)

POSSESSION: 31% · **SHOTS (ON TARGET):** 7 (3) · **REFEREE:** Craig Pawson · **ATTENDANCE:** 32,115

LINE-UP: 1 Schmeichel, 17 Simpson (substituted for de Laet, 80'), 5 Morgan, 6 Huth,
28 Fuchs, 26 Mahrez, 14 Kanté, 4 Drinkwater, 11 Albrighton (substituted for Schlupp, 70'),
20 Okazaki (substituted for Ulloa, 60'), 9 Vardy.

SUBSTITUTES: 2 de Laet, 10 King, 15 Schlupp, 23 Ulloa, 24 Dyer,
32 Schwarzer, 33 Inler.

SATURDAY, 5 DECEMBER 2015, PREMIER LEAGUE

Swansea City   0-3   Leicester City

Mahrez (5', 22', 67')

POSSESSION: 41% · **SHOTS (ON TARGET):** 16 (5) · **REFEREE:** Michael Oliver · **ATTENDANCE:** 20,836

LINE-UP: 1 Schmeichel, 17 Simpson (booked, 70'), 5 Morgan, 6 Huth, 28 Fuchs,
26 Mahrez (substituted for Schlupp, 90'), 4 Drinkwater, 14 Kanté (booked, 23'),
11 Albrighton (booked, 90'), 23 Ulloa (substituted for King, 87'), 9 Vardy.

SUBSTITUTES: 10 King, 15 Schlupp, 20 Okazaki, 27 Wasilewski,
29 Benalouane, 32 Schwarzer, 33 Inler.

MONDAY, 14 DECEMBER 2015, PREMIER LEAGUE

Leicester City   2-1   Chelsea

Vardy (34'), Mahrez (48')   Remy (77')

POSSESSION: 34% · SHOTS (ON TARGET): 9 (5) · REFEREE: Mark Clattenburg · ATTENDANCE: 32,054

LINE-UP: 1 Schmeichel, 17 Simpson, 5 Morgan, 6 Huth (booked, 50'), 28 Fuchs, 26 Mahrez (substituted for Inler, 82'), 4 Drinkwater (substituted for King, 17'), 14 Kanté, 11 Albrighton, 23 Ulloa, 9 Vardy (booked, 46', substituted for Okazaki, 88').

SUBSTITUTES: 10 King, 20 Okazaki, 24 Dyer, 27 Wasilewski, 29 Benalouane, 32 Schwarzer, 33 Inler.

SATURDAY, 19 DECEMBER 2015, PREMIER LEAGUE

Everton   2-3   Leicester City

Lukaku (32'), Mirallas (89')   Mahrez (27' pen, 65' pen), Okazaki (69')

POSSESSION: 33% · SHOTS (ON TARGET): 10 (5) · REFEREE: Jonathan Moss · ATTENDANCE: 39,570

LINE-UP: 1 Schmeichel, 17 Simpson, 27 Wasilewski (booked, 81'), 5 Morgan, 28 Fuchs, 26 Mahrez (substituted for de Laet, 83'), 10 King, 14 Kanté, 11 Albrighton (substituted for Dyer, 71'), 20 Okazaki, 9 Vardy (substituted for Ulloa, 87').

SUBSTITUTES: 2 de Laet, 19 Kramarić, 23 Ulloa, 24 Dyer, 29 Benalouane, 32 Schwarzer, 33 Inler.

SATURDAY, 26 DECEMBER 2015, PREMIER LEAGUE

Liverpool   1-0   Leicester City

Benteke (63')

POSSESSION: 35% · SHOTS (ON TARGET): 7 (3) · REFEREE: Martin Atkinson · ATTENDANCE: 44,123

LINE-UP: 1 Schmeichel, 17 Simpson, 5 Morgan, 6 Huth (booked, 62'), 28 Fuchs, 26 Mahrez (substituted for Kramarić, 80'), 10 King, 14 Kanté, 11 Albrighton, 20 Okazaki (substituted for Dyer, 69'), 9 Vardy (substituted for Ulloa, 69').

SUBSTITUTES: 2 de Laet, 19 Kramarić, 23 Ulloa, 24 Dyer, 27 Wasilewski, 32 Schwarzer, 33 Inler.

TUESDAY, 29 DECEMBER 2015, PREMIER LEAGUE

Leicester City   0-0   Manchester City

POSSESSION: 39% · SHOTS (ON TARGET): 11 (4) · REFEREE: Craig Pawson · ATTENDANCE: 32,072

LINE-UP: 1 Schmeichel, 17 Simpson, 5 Morgan, 6 Huth, 28 Fuchs, 26 Mahrez,
4 Drinkwater (substituted for King, 80'), 33 Inler (substituted for Ulloa, 67'),
14 Kanté, 11 Albrighton (booked, 81', substituted for de Laet, 90'+3), 9 Vardy.

SUBSTITUTES: 2 de Laet, 10 King, 20 Okazaki, 23 Ulloa, 24 Dyer,
27 Wasilewski, 32 Schwarzer.

SATURDAY, 2 JANUARY 2016, PREMIER LEAGUE

Leicester City   0-0   Bournemouth

Francis (dismissed, 57')

POSSESSION: 54% · SHOTS (ON TARGET): 16 (2) · REFEREE: Andre Marriner · ATTENDANCE: 32,006

LINE-UP: 1 Schmeichel, 17 Simpson (substituted for de Laet, 74'),
5 Morgan, 6 Huth, 28 Fuchs, 26 Mahrez, 4 Drinkwater, 14 Kanté,
11 Albrighton (booked, 62', substituted for Okazaki, 65'),
23 Ulloa (substituted for Dyer, 45'), 9 Vardy.

SUBSTITUTES: 2 de Laet, 10 King, 20 Okazaki, 24 Dyer, 27 Wasilewski,
32 Schwarzer, 33 Inler.

SUNDAY, 10 JANUARY 2016, FA CUP - THIRD ROUND

Tottenham Hotspur   2-2   Leicester City

Eriksen (8'), Kane (89' pen)   Wasilewski (19'), Okazaki (48')

POSSESSION: 26% · SHOTS (ON TARGET): 10 (5) · REFEREE: Robert Madley · ATTENDANCE: 35,805

LINE-UP: 1 Schmeichel (booked, 89'), 2 de Laet,
27 Wasilewski (booked, 15'), 29 Benalouane, 30 Chilwell, 24 Dyer, 33 Inler, 10 King,
14 Kanté (substituted for Okazaki, 45'), 22 Gray (substituted for Albrighton, 65'), 23 Ulloa.

SUBSTITUTES: 4 Drinkwater, 5 Morgan, 11 Albrighton, 17 Simpson,
20 Okazaki, 26 Mahrez, 32 Schwarzer.

WEDNESDAY, 13 JANUARY 2016, PREMIER LEAGUE

Tottenham Hotspur   0-1   Leicester City

Huth (83')

POSSESSION: 38% · SHOTS (ON TARGET): 10 (2) · REFEREE: Lee Mason · ATTENDANCE: 35,850

LINE-UP: 1 Schmeichel, 17 Simpson, 5 Morgan, 6 Huth, 28 Fuchs,
26 Mahrez (substituted for Dyer, 90'), 14 Kanté, 4 Drinkwater, 11 Albrighton,
20 Okazaki (substituted for King, 77'), 9 Vardy (substituted for Ulloa, 71').

SUBSTITUTES: 10 King, 22 Gray, 23 Ulloa, 24 Dyer, 27 Wasilewski, 32 Schwarzer, 33 Inler.

SATURDAY, 16 JANUARY 2016, PREMIER LEAGUE

Aston Villa   1-1   Leicester City

Gestede (75')   Okazaki (28')

POSSESSION: 43% · SHOTS (ON TARGET): 12 (5) · REFEREE: Roger East · ATTENDANCE: 32,763

LINE-UP: 1 Schmeichel, 17 Simpson, 5 Morgan, 6 Huth (booked, 76'),
28 Fuchs, 26 Mahrez (substituted for Ulloa, 69'), 4 Drinkwater, 14 Kanté,
11 Albrighton (substituted for Gray, 85'), 20 Okazaki (substituted for de Laet, 59'),
9 Vardy (booked, 85').

SUBSTITUTES: 2 de Laet, 10 King, 22 Gray, 23 Ulloa, 27 Wasilewski,
32 Schwarzer, 33 Inler.

WEDNESDAY, 20 JANUARY 2016, FA CUP - THIRD ROUND - REPLAY

Leicester City   0-2   Tottenham Hotspur

Son Heung-min (39'), Chadli (66')

POSSESSION: 40% · SHOTS (ON TARGET): 11 (4) · REFEREE: Anthony Taylor · ATTENDANCE: 30,006

LINE-UP: 1 Schmeichel, 17 Simpson (substituted for Albrighton, 63', booked, 90'),
27 Wasilewski, 29 Benalouane, 30 Chilwell, 10 King, 33 Inler,
4 Drinkwater (substituted for Okazaki, 45'), 24 Dyer (substituted for Vardy, 74'),
23 Ulloa, 22 Gray.

SUBSTITUTES: 5 Morgan, 9 Vardy, 11 Albrighton, 14 Kanté, 20 Okazaki,
26 Mahrez, 32 Schwarzer.

SATURDAY, 23 JANUARY 2016, PREMIER LEAGUE

Leicester City 3-0 Stoke City

Drinkwater (42'), Vardy (66'), Ulloa (87')

POSSESSION: 45% · **SHOTS (ON TARGET):** 15 (5) · **REFEREE:** Mike Dean · **ATTENDANCE:** 32,018

LINE-UP: 1 Schmeichel, 17 Simpson, 5 Morgan, 6 Huth, 28 Fuchs,
26 Mahrez, 4 Drinkwater, 14 Kanté, 11 Albrighton (substituted for Gray, 88'),
20 Okazaki (substituted for Ulloa, 62'), 9 Vardy.

SUBSTITUTES: 10 King, 22 Gray, 23 Ulloa, 24 Dyer, 27 Wasilewski,
32 Schwarzer, 33 Inler.

TUESDAY, 2 FEBRUARY 2016, PREMIER LEAGUE

Leicester City 2-0 Liverpool

Vardy (60', 71')

POSSESSION: 36% · **SHOTS (ON TARGET):** 13 (6) · **REFEREE:** Andre Marriner · **ATTENDANCE:** 32,121

LINE-UP: 1 Schmeichel, 17 Simpson, 5 Morgan, 6 Huth,
28 Fuchs, 26 Mahrez (substituted for Ulloa, 90'), 14 Kanté, 4 Drinkwater,
11 Albrighton (substituted for Gray, 79'), 20 Okazaki (substituted for King, 87'), 9 Vardy.

SUBSTITUTES: 10 King, 22 Gray, 23 Ulloa, 24 Dyer, 27 Wasilewski,
30 Chilwell, 32 Schwarzer.

SATURDAY, 6 FEBRUARY 2016, PREMIER LEAGUE

Manchester City 1-3 Leicester City

Agüero (87')   Huth (3', 60'), Mahrez (48')

POSSESSION: 34% · **SHOTS (ON TARGET):** 14 (7) · **REFEREE:** Anthony Taylor · **ATTENDANCE:** 54,693

LINE-UP: 1 Schmeichel, 17 Simpson (booked, 46'), 5 Morgan (booked, 36'),
6 Huth, 28 Fuchs, 26 Mahrez (substituted for Gray, 77'), 4 Drinkwater, 14 Kanté,
11 Albrighton (substituted for Dyer, 86'), 20 Okazaki (substituted for Ulloa, 81'), 9 Vardy.

SUBSTITUTES: 10 King, 22 Gray, 23 Ulloa, 24 Dyer, 27 Wasilewski,
30 Chilwell, 32 Schwarzer.

SUNDAY, 14 FEBRUARY 2016, PREMIER LEAGUE

Arsenal 2-1 Leicester City

Walcott (70'), Welbeck (90'+5)   Vardy (45' pen), Simpson (dismissed, 54')

POSSESSION: 28% · SHOTS (ON TARGET): 7 (3) · REFEREE: Martin Atkinson · ATTENDANCE: 60,009

LINE-UP: 1 Schmeichel, 17 Simpson (dismissed, 54'), 5 Morgan, 6 Huth,
28 Fuchs (booked, 52'), 26 Mahrez (substituted for Wasilewski, 58', booked, 90'),
4 Drinkwater, 14 Kanté (booked, 57'), 11 Albrighton (substituted for King, 83'),
20 Okazaki (substituted for Gray, 61'), 9 Vardy.

SUBSTITUTES: 10 King, 22 Gray, 23 Ulloa, 24 Dyer, 27 Wasilewski,
30 Chilwell, 32 Schwarzer.

SATURDAY, 27 FEBRUARY 2016, PREMIER LEAGUE

Leicester City 1-0 Norwich

Ulloa (89')

POSSESSION: 58% · SHOTS (ON TARGET): 13 (3) · REFEREE: Neil Swarbrick · ATTENDANCE: 32,114

LINE-UP: 1 Schmeichel, 13 Amartey (substituted for Ulloa, 78'), 5 Morgan, 6 Huth,
28 Fuchs, 26 Mahrez, 4 Drinkwater, 14 Kanté (substituted for King, 70'),
11 Albrighton, 20 Okazaki (substituted for Schlupp, 69'), 9 Vardy.

SUBSTITUTES: 10 King, 15 Schlupp, 22 Gray, 23 Ulloa, 24 Dyer,
27 Wasilewski, 32 Schwarzer.

TUESDAY, 1 MARCH 2016, PREMIER LEAGUE

Leicester City 2-2 West Bromwich Albion

Olsson (30' og), King (45'+1)   Rondón (11'), Gardner (50')

POSSESSION: 65% · SHOTS (ON TARGET): 22 (4) · REFEREE: Mark Clattenburg · ATTENDANCE: 32,018

LINE-UP: 1 Schmeichel, 17 Simpson, 5 Morgan, 6 Huth,
28 Fuchs (substituted for Gray, 79'), 26 Mahrez, 10 King, 4 Drinkwater,
11 Albrighton (substituted for Schlupp, 63'), 20 Okazaki (substituted for Ulloa, 63'), 9 Vardy.

SUBSTITUTES: 13 Amartey, 15 Schlupp, 22 Gray, 23 Ulloa, 27 Wasilewski,
32 Schwarzer, 33 Inler.

SATURDAY, 5 MARCH 2016, PREMIER LEAGUE

Watford   0-1   Leicester City

Mahrez (56')

POSSESSION: 50% · SHOTS (ON TARGET): 14 (7) · REFEREE: Jonathan Moss · ATTENDANCE: 20,884

LINE-UP: 1 Schmeichel, 17 Simpson, 5 Morgan (booked, 90'), 6 Huth,
28 Fuchs (booked, 74'), 26 Mahrez (substituted for Amartey, 85'), 4 Drinkwater, 14 Kanté,
11 Albrighton (substituted for Schlupp, 45'), 9 Vardy, 20 Okazaki (substituted for King, 45').

SUBSTITUTES: 10 King, 13 Amartey, 15 Schlupp, 22 Gray, 23 Ulloa,
27 Wasilewski, 32 Schwarzer.

MONDAY, 14 MARCH 2016, PREMIER LEAGUE

Leicester City   1-0   Newcastle United

Okazaki (25')

POSSESSION: 50% · SHOTS (ON TARGET): 10 (1) · REFEREE: Craig Pawson · ATTENDANCE: 31,824

LINE-UP: 1 Schmeichel, 17 Simpson, 5 Morgan, 6 Huth, 28 Fuchs,
26 Mahrez, 14 Kanté, 4 Drinkwater, 11 Albrighton (substituted for Ulloa, 75'),
9 Vardy, 20 Okazaki (substituted for Schlupp, 65').

SUBSTITUTES: 13 Amartey, 15 Schlupp, 22 Gray, 23 Ulloa, 27 Wasilewski,
32 Schwarzer, 33 Inler.

SATURDAY, 19 MARCH 2016, PREMIER LEAGUE

Crystal Palace   0-1   Leicester City

Mahrez (34')

POSSESSION: 44% · SHOTS (ON TARGET): 8 (3) · REFEREE: Mike Jones · ATTENDANCE: 25,041

LINE-UP: 1 Schmeichel (booked, 30'), 17 Simpson, 5 Morgan, 6 Huth, 28 Fuchs,
26 Mahrez (substituted for Schlupp, 86'), 14 Kanté, 4 Drinkwater, 11 Albrighton,
9 Vardy (substituted for Amartey, 90'+1), 20 Okazaki (substituted for Ulloa, 76').

SUBSTITUTES: 13 Amartey, 15 Schlupp, 22 Gray, 23 Ulloa, 27 Wasilewski,
32 Schwarzer, 33 Inler.

SUNDAY, 3 APRIL 2016, PREMIER LEAGUE

Leicester City   1-0   Southampton

Morgan (38')

POSSESSION: 46% · SHOTS (ON TARGET): 11 (4) · REFEREE: Michael Oliver · ATTENDANCE: 32,071

LINE-UP: 1 Schmeichel, 17 Simpson, 5 Morgan, 6 Huth, 28 Fuchs (booked, 88'), 26 Mahrez (substituted for Gray, 79'), 4 Drinkwater (booked, 51'), 14 Kanté, 11 Albrighton (substituted for Dyer, 90'), 20 Okazaki (substituted for Ulloa, 64'), 9 Vardy.

SUBSTITUTES: 10 King, 13 Amartey, 22 Gray, 23 Ulloa, 24 Dyer, 27 Wasilewski, 32 Schwarzer.

SUNDAY, 10 APRIL 2016, PREMIER LEAGUE

Sunderland   0-2   Leicester City

Vardy (66', 90'+5)

POSSESSION: 55% · SHOTS (ON TARGET): 16 (7) · REFEREE: Anthony Taylor · ATTENDANCE: 46,531

LINE-UP: 1 Schmeichel, 17 Simpson, 5 Morgan, 6 Huth, 28 Fuchs (booked, 30'), 26 Mahrez (substituted for Gray, 81'), 14 Kanté, 4 Drinkwater, 11 Albrighton (substituted for Amartey, 84'), 20 Okazaki (substituted for Ulloa, 62'), 9 Vardy.

SUBSTITUTES: 10 King, 13 Amartey, 22 Gray, 23 Ulloa, 24 Dyer, 30 Chilwell, 32 Schwarzer.

SUNDAY, 17 APRIL 2016, PREMIER LEAGUE

Leicester City   2-2   West Ham United

Vardy (18', dismissed, 56'),   Carroll (84' pen), Cresswell (86')
Ulloa (90'+5 pen)

POSSESSION: 43% · SHOTS (ON TARGET): 6 (2) · REFEREE: Jonathan Moss · ATTENDANCE: 32,104

LINE-UP: 1 Schmeichel, 17 Simpson, 5 Morgan (booked, 77'), 6 Huth, 28 Fuchs, 26 Mahrez (substituted for Amartey, 78'), 4 Drinkwater, 14 Kanté, 11 Albrighton (substituted for Schlupp, 54'), 20 Okazaki (substituted for Ulloa, 59'), 9 Vardy (dismissed, 56').

SUBSTITUTES: 10 King, 13 Amartey, 15 Schlupp, 22 Gray, 23 Ulloa, 27 Wasilewski, 32 Schwarzer.

SUNDAY, 24 APRIL 2016, PREMIER LEAGUE

Leicester City 4-0 Swansea City

Mahrez (10'), Ulloa (30', 60'),
Albrighton (85')

POSSESSION: 38% · **SHOTS (ON TARGET):** 18 (9) · **REFEREE:** Mark Clattenburg · **ATTENDANCE:** 31,962

LINE-UP: 1 Schmeichel, 17 Simpson, 5 Morgan, 6 Huth (booked, 81'), 28 Fuchs,
26 Mahrez, 14 Kanté, 4 Drinkwater, 15 Schlupp (substituted for Albrighton, 82'),
23 Ulloa (substituted for King, 79'), 20 Okazaki (substituted for Gray, 73').

SUBSTITUTES: 10 King, 11 Albrighton, 13 Amartey, 22 Gray,
27 Wasilewski, 30 Chilwell, 32 Schwarzer.

SUNDAY, 1 MAY 2016, PREMIER LEAGUE

Manchester United 1-1 Leicester City

Martial (8')   Morgan (17'), Drinkwater (dismissed, 86')

POSSESSION: 29% · **SHOTS (ON TARGET):** 14 (3) · **REFEREE:** Michael Oliver · **ATTENDANCE:** 75,275

LINE-UP: 1 Schmeichel, 17 Simpson, 5 Morgan, 6 Huth, 28 Fuchs,
26 Mahrez (substituted for King, 88'), 14 Kanté, 4 Drinkwater (dismissed, 86'),
15 Schlupp (substituted for Albrighton, 77'), 20 Okazaki (substituted for Gray, 67'), 23 Ulloa.

SUBSTITUTES: 10 King, 11 Albrighton, 13 Amartey, 22 Gray,
27 Wasilewski, 30 Chilwell, 32 Schwarzer.

SATURDAY, 7 MAY 2016, PREMIER LEAGUE

Leicester City 3-1 Everton

Vardy (5', 65' pen), King (33')   Mirallas (88')

POSSESSION: 41% · **SHOTS (ON TARGET):** 32 (8) · **REFEREE:** Andre Marriner · **ATTENDANCE:** 32,140

LINE-UP: 1 Schmeichel, 17 Simpson, 27 Wasilewski, 5 Morgan,
28 Fuchs, 26 Mahrez (substituted for Gray, 90'+1), 14 Kanté, 10 King,
11 Albrighton (substituted for Schlupp, 67'), 20 Okazaki (substituted for Ulloa, 62'), 9 Vardy.

SUBSTITUTES: 13 Amartey, 15 Schlupp, 22 Gray, 23 Ulloa, 30 Chilwell, 32 Schwarzer, 33 Inler.

SUNDAY, 15 MAY 2016, PREMIER LEAGUE

Chelsea   1-1   Leicester City

Fàbregas (66' minutes pen)   Drinkwater (82' minutes)

POSSESSION: 46% · **SHOTS (ON TARGET):** 18 (5) · **REFEREE:** Craig Pawson · **ATTENDANCE:** 41,494

LINE-UP: 1 Schmeichel, 17 Simpson, 27 Wasilewski, 5 Morgan, 28 Fuchs, 4 Drinkwater, 14 Kanté, 26 Mahrez (substituted for Albrighton, 80'), 10 King (substituted for Okazaki, 45'), 22 Gray (substituted for Schlupp, 45'), 9 Vardy.

SUBSTITUTES: 11 Albrighton, 13 Amartey, 15 Schlupp, 20 Okazaki, 23 Ulloa, 30 Chilwell, 32 Schwarzer.

SQUAD APPEARANCES (TOTAL, LEAGUE, CUP), GOALS AND ASSISTS

	PLAYER	POSITION	TOTAL	LEAGUE	CUP	GLS	ASSISTS
11	Marc Albrighton	Midfielder	42	38	4	2	6
1	Kasper Schmeichel	Goalkeeper	40	38	2		
14	N'Golo Kanté	Midfielder	40	37	3	1	4
26	Riyad Mahrez	Midfielder	39	37	2	18	11
20	Shinji Okazaki	Striker	39	36	3	6	
5	Wes Morgan	Defender	38	38	0	2	
9	Jamie Vardy	Striker	38	36	2	24	6
4	Danny Drinkwater	Midfielder	37	35	2	2	7
6	Robert Huth	Defender	35	35	0	3	
28	Christian Fuchs	Defender	34	32	2		5
23	Leonardo Ulloa	Striker	33	29	4	6	5
17	Danny Simpson	Defender	32	30	2		
10	Andy King	Midfielder	29	25	4	3	2
15	Jeff Schlupp	Midfielder	26	24	2	1	3
24	Nathan Dyer	Midfielder	14	12	2	1	1
22	Demarai Gray	Midfielder	14	12	2		2
33	Gökhan Inler	Midfielder	10	5	5		
27	Marcin Wasilewski	Defender	9	4	5	1	
13	Daniel Amartey	Midfielder	5	5	0		
32	Mark Schwarzer	Goalkeeper	3	0	3		
30	Ben Chilwell	Defender	3	0	3		
18	Liam Moore	Defender	1	0	1		
8	Matty James	Midfielder	0	0	0		
12	Ben Hamer	Goalkeeper	0	0	0		

BARCLAYS PREMIER LEAGUE TABLE 2015-16

	Team	P	W	D	L	F	A	W	D	L	F	A	W	D	L	F	A	GD	Pts
1	**Leicester City**	**38**	**23**	**12**	**3**	**68**	**36**	**12**	**6**	**1**	**35**	**18**	**11**	**6**	**2**	**33**	**18**	**32**	**81**
2	Arsenal	38	20	11	7	65	36	12	4	3	31	11	8	7	4	34	25	29	71
3	Tottenham Hotspur	38	19	13	6	69	35	10	6	3	35	15	9	7	3	34	20	34	70
4	Manchester City	38	19	9	10	71	41	12	2	5	47	21	7	7	5	24	20	30	66
5	Manchester United	38	19	9	10	49	35	12	5	2	27	9	7	4	8	22	26	14	66
6	Southampton	38	18	9	11	59	41	11	3	5	39	22	7	6	6	20	19	18	63
7	West Ham United	38	16	14	8	65	51	9	7	3	34	26	7	7	5	31	25	14	62
8	Liverpool	38	16	12	10	63	50	8	8	3	33	22	8	4	7	30	28	13	60
9	Stoke City	38	14	9	15	41	55	8	4	7	22	24	6	5	8	19	31	-14	51
10	Chelsea	38	12	14	12	59	53	5	9	5	32	30	7	5	7	27	23	6	50
11	Everton	38	11	14	13	59	55	6	5	8	35	30	5	9	5	24	25	4	47
12	Swansea City	38	12	11	15	42	52	8	6	5	20	20	4	5	10	22	32	-10	47
13	Watford	38	12	9	17	40	50	6	6	7	20	19	6	3	10	20	31	-10	45
14	West Bromwich Albion	38	10	13	15	34	48	6	5	8	20	26	4	8	7	14	22	-14	43
15	Crystal Palace	38	11	9	18	39	51	6	3	10	19	23	5	6	8	20	28	-12	42
16	AFC Bournemouth	38	11	9	18	45	67	5	5	9	23	34	6	4	9	22	33	-22	42
17	Sunderland	38	9	12	17	48	62	6	6	7	23	20	3	6	10	25	42	-14	39
18	Newcastle United	38	9	10	19	44	65	7	7	5	32	24	2	3	14	12	41	-21	37
19	Norwich City	38	9	7	22	39	67	6	5	8	26	30	3	2	14	13	37	-28	34
20	Aston Villa	38	3	8	27	27	76	2	5	12	14	35	1	3	15	13	41	-49	17

Only 24 teams have ever finished as Champions of England,
here's when each achieved their first title:

1888-89	Preston North End	1923-24	Huddersfield Town
1890-91	Everton	1930-31	Arsenal
1891-92	Sunderland	1936-37	Manchester City
1893-94	Aston Villa	1948-49	Portsmouth
1897-98	Sheffield United	1950-51	Tottenham Hotspur
1900-01	Liverpool	1953-54	Wolverhampton Wanderers
1902-03	The Wednesday (Sheffield Wednesday)	1954-55	Chelsea
1904-05	Newcastle United	1961-62	Ipswich Town
1907-08	Manchester United	1968-69	Leeds United
1911-12	Blackburn Rovers	1971-72	Derby County
1919-20	West Bromwich Albion	1977-78	Nottingham Forest
1920-21	Burnley	2015-16	Leicester City

BETFRED

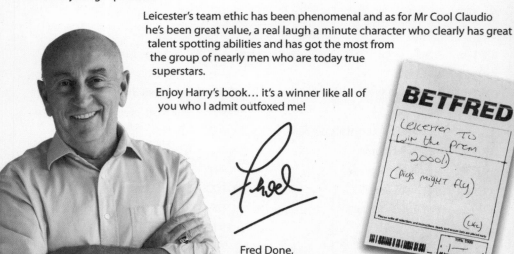

You just couldn't make it up…

Leicester winning the Premier League is a truly astonishing feat and the players (who we all know now don't we?), the manager Claudio Ranieri and all the club's loyal and good humoured fans have my total admiration.

In fact the fantastic Foxes' against huge odds triumph is the biggest sporting shock in living memory.

One supporter John Moss, who I got to speak to recently, has been in the headlines everywhere even America after he won £2,000 from me with his £1 bet at 2,000/1 that Leicester would win the league. He was one of many fans who took us to the cleaners - but what made John's story so different was that during pre-season our Arsenal-supporting Betfred shop manager Neil Samways wrote "Pigs might fly" on his betting slip.

Anyway, have you seen anything fat and pink airborne recently over Leicester or landing at East Midlands Airport?

Like Leicester we led the way and I paid out on April 3, a month before the Foxes were confirmed as champions. That cost me £1.1 million with our biggest winner from Warwickshire picking up £85,000 from two bets totalling £50 on the team he's supported all his life becoming unlikely champions of England.

Along with all football fans I watched fascinated during the season as Leicester kept defying logic giving the big boys a bloody nose. The 3-1 win in February against Manchester City - favourites for much of the season to win the title – finally convinced me that Leicester really could win the world's toughest league for the first time in the club's 132-year history.

Alright I am a Manchester United supporter, but like all fans I have enjoyed the way inspirational Leicester have proved to all clubs and players at all levels everywhere in the world that anything and everything is possible.

Leicester's team ethic has been phenomenal and as for Mr Cool Claudio he's been great value, a real laugh a minute character who clearly has great talent spotting abilities and has got the most from the group of nearly men who are today true superstars.

Enjoy Harry's book… it's a winner like all of you who I admit outfoxed me!

Fred Done,
founder of Betfred

Congratulations to Khun Vichai Srivaddhanaprabha, Claudio Ranieri and his team of Barclays Premier League Champions at Leicester City from all at Footba11legends.

After spending five years living in Bangkok, I know how much this means not only to the Leicester City faithful but to the Thai people who are a nation of football fans.

I have had the honour of spending time with former Thailand national coaches Bryan Robson and Peter Reid and have seen first-hand how the passionate Thai nation adores watching and receiving the Barclay's Premier League Championship.

Footba11legends trades in sports memorabilia, promotes sports Question & Answers with football legends, and is currently working on an online legends fanzine.

Harry Harris is a true legend of sports journalism and it's only fitting that Harry has coined a"new" term to describe the Leicester City players' unique and magnificent achievement this season, "The Immortals".

"The Immortals" should be an inspirational read to the rest of us mortals.

I hope that my team, Middlesbrough, can do a Leicester City next season!

It's also great to see some ex-Boro players picking up some Barclays Premier League winners medals.

Keep dreaming!!!

Good Luck Leicester City on your Champions League adventure next season.

Ant Verrill

@footba11legends

My appreciation goes to the wealth of information from the BBC Sports website and their regional coverage, and to the fans for their contribution both on social media and in the backing of their team.

WITH SPECIAL THANKS TO OUR SPONSORS

Marco's New York Italian, Leicester
www.mpwrestaurants.co.uk

Mercure Leicester, The Grand Hotel
www.mercureleicester.co.uk

PAZZIA
RESTAURANT

W Archer & Son Ltd Butchers, Leicester
www.warcherbutchers.co.uk

G . A . C

PRINT MANAGEMENT
www.gacprint.co.uk

THE POP-UP DELI

GOURMET EXPERIENCE
www.thepopupdeli.co.uk

Laithwaite's
········ WINE ········

GREENE KING
BURY ST EDMUNDS

Planet Hollywood, London
www.planethollywoodlondon.com

Green Brothers removals & storage
www.greenbrothers-removals.co.uk

Author Harry Harris receiving a Variety Club 'Contribution to Sports Journalism' Award from Leicester City manager Claudio Ranieri.

Harry Harris is a Double winner of the British Sports Journalist of the Year award, British Variety Club of Great Britain Silver Heart for 'Contribution to Sports Journalism', Double winner of the Sports Story of the Year award, the only journalist ever to win the Sports Story of the year accolade twice. He has won a total of 14 industry awards.

Harry has appeared regularly as an analyst on football on all major TV news and sports programmes and channels, including Richard & Judy and Newsnight, BBC News and ITV News at Ten, Sky, Setanta, plus Radio 5 Live, Radio 4, and TalkSport. He has been interviewed on Football Focus, appeared on the original Hold The Back Page, and Jimmy Hill's Sunday Supplement on Sky.

Harry is arguably the most prolific writer of best-selling football books of his generation. Among his 75 books are the highly acclaimed best seller Pele - His Life and Times, 'Gullit: The Chelsea Diary', 'All The Way Jose', Chelsea Century, Chelski, 'Wayne Rooney - The Story of Footballs Wonder Kid'. Autobiographies on Ruud Gullit, Paul Merson, Glenn Hoddle, Gary Mabbutt, Steve McMahon, Terry Neill, Bill Nicholson: 'Glory, Glory - My Life With Spurs.' Biographies on Roman Abramovich, Jürgen Klinsmann, Sir Alex Ferguson, Jose Mourinho, Terry Venables, Franco Zola and Luca Vialli. He wrote George Best's last book, and best seller, 'Hard Tackles and Dirty Baths', and 19 - a history of Manchester United's record league titles.

Harry has written one of the most influential football columns in the country for three decades and is regarded as one of the best investigative journalists and perhaps the best news gather of his generation. He worked for the Daily Mail, Daily Mirror, Daily Express, Daily Star, Sunday Express and Star on Sunday, and as ESPNsoccernet Football Correspondent: 35 years as the No1 football writer.

CURRENTLY: Director/ Co-Founder Fleet Street Sport & Media, Co-Founder/director H&H Sports Media

CURRENT BOOKS: Jose Farewell to the King, Kerry Dixon: Up Front, and Down Memory Lane.

DON'T MISS THIS BOOK OFFER OF THE YEAR

Unique cartoon celebration of England's greatest football achievement

1966 AND ALL THAT!
THE 50TH ANNIVERSARY
BY BOB BOND
AND SOME OF FLEET STREET'S FINEST

ENGLAND 4 W GERMANY 2

FOREWORD BY GEORGE COHEN MBE, ENGLAND'S WORLD CUP WINNING RIGHT-BACK

HOW England won The World Cup 50 years ago this summer is told in brilliant full-colour cartoons drawn at the time.

Cartoonist Bob Bond, who worked for Football Monthly, brings the drama and the humour of the tournament alive, match by match.

His superb penmanship is supplemented by stories from some of the biggest names in Fleet Street who were there.

Patrick Collins, five times Sports Writer of the Year, tells how England manager Alf Ramsey made a secret late night call to a highly distinguished football writer just three days before the Final. On the agenda? The dropping of Jimmy Greaves for Geoff Hurst.

James Lawton, another Sports Writer of the Year, magnificently sets the scene for the tournament, culminating in what Bobby Charlton called 'the diamond of my days'.

John Keith, of the Daily Express, recalls the amazing North Koreans who sent Italy home in disgrace and found themselves three goals up in the quarter final against Portugal before Eusebio ended the fairytale with four goals.

Bob Harris, former executive sports editor of the Sunday Mirror, tells of the savage butchering of Pele.

Steve Curry, former chief football writer for the Daily Express, recounts the full emotion and elation of the final itself, revealing how, as a young reporter, he was left in tears as England prevailed in extra time against West Germany.